THE ARAKMBUT

THE ARAKMBUT OF AMAZONIAN PERU
Andrew Gray

The Arakmbut are an indigenous people who live in the Madre de Dios region of the southeastern Peruvian rainforest. Since their first encounters with missionaries in the 1950s, they have shown resilience and a determination to affirm their identity in the face of difficulty. During the last fifteen years, the Arakmbut have been under threat from a gold rush that has attracted hundreds of colonists onto their territories. This trilogy traces the ways in which the Arakmbut overcome the dangers that surround them: their mythology and cultural strength, their social flexibility, and their capacity to incorporate non-indigenous concepts and activities into their defence strategies. Each area is punctuated by the constant presence of the invisible spirit world, which provides a seamless theme connecting the books to each other.

Volume 1

The Arakmbut: Mythology, Spirituality, and History

Volume 2

The Last Shaman: Change in an Amazonian Community

Volume 3

Determining Self Identity and Developing Rights: Development and Self-Determination among the Arakmbut of Amazonian Peru

THE ARAKMBUT

Mythology, Spirituality, and History in an
Amazonian Community

Andrew Gray

Berghahn Books
Providence • Oxford

First published in 1996 by

Berghahn Books

Editorial offices:
165 Taber Avenue, Providence, RI 02906, USA
Bush House, Merewood Avenue, Oxford, OX3 8EF, UK

© Andrew Gray 1996

Library of Congress Cataloging-in-Publication Data

Gray, Andrew, 1955–
    The Arakmbut of Amazonian Peru / Andrew Gray.
        p.   cm.
    Includes bibliographical references and index.
    Contents: v. 1. The Arakmbut--mythology, spirituality, and
history.
    ISBN: 978-1-57181-835-5
        1. Mashco mythology.   2. Mashco Indians--Religion.   I. Title.
    F3430.1.M38G75   1995
    299'.883--dc20   95-37322
                                                                    CIP

British Library Cataloguing in Publication Data

A catalogue record for this book is available from the
British Library.

Printed on acid-free paper.

CONTENTS

Contents

TABLES

FIGURES

MAPS

SERIES PREFACE

The Arakmbut are an indigenous people who live in the Madre de Dios region of the southeastern Peruvian rainforest. They are one of seven Harakmbut peoples all of which belong to the same linguistic family and which number in total about two thousand people. Despite having been known as Mashco and Amarakaeri during their forty years of contact with Peruvian national society, the people of the community of San José del Karene, with whom I have lived periodically since 1980, request that they be known as 'Arakmbut'.

Since their first encounters with missionaries in the 1950s, the Arakmbut have shown resilience and determination to affirm their identity in the face of difficulty. For the last fifteen years, the Arakmbut have been under threat from a gold rush that has attracted hundreds of colonists onto their territories.

This trilogy traces the ways in which the Arakmbut strive to overcome the dangers that surround them: They use their mythology to reinforce cultural strength; they demonstrate social flexibility in the face of alien peoples; and they show a discriminating capacity to incorporate positive non-indigenous concepts and activities into their defence strategies. Each of these factors reflects the constant presence of the invisible spirit world, which provides a theme connecting these books to each other.

The mythology of the Arakmbut is extremely important to them and to the way in which they perceive the world. On my departure from the community of San José del Karene after two years in 1981, I was told by several elders that I should write up my material around the three central myths. The first volume of this trilogy looks at each of these myths in order to introduce different facets of Arakmbut life.

The first myth, 'Wanamey', tells of the origins of the Arakmbut, the visible world and their social and cultural existence. It provides the impetus for a discussion of Arakmbut social organisation, which is based on various overlapping principles such as gender, age, residence, patrilineal descent and marriage exchange.

The second myth, 'Marinke', tells of the relationship between human beings, animal species, and the invisible spirit world. The visible and invisible worlds interconnect in ways that parallel social relations within the community, and this accounts for the constant presence of spirits and soul-matter in Arakmbut daily life.

The third myth, 'Aiwe', describes the abduction of an Arakmbut child by white people (Papa) who threaten his people with destruction, yet provide the means for their survival. It looks at the history of Arakmbut contact with outsiders, and charts the effects of the rubber boom and the period that the Arakmbut spent in the mission of Shintuya. After their dramatic escape in 1969, the Arakmbut founded their present communities.

The book ends with a discussion about the relationship between myth and history, showing how the Arakmbut recreate their myths at dramatic moments in their history. The conclusion reflects on power relations, the significance of the spirit world, and the relevance of the political concept of self-determination. Furthermore, embedded within Arakmbut myths are strategies for defence against colonisation. By looking at Arakmbut social organisation, cultural diversity, and historical experience, the first volume shows how myth provides a bridge linking the visible and the invisible worlds.

The second volume looks at the changes that have taken place in the community of San José del Karene between 1980 and 1992 in order to establish the two main dynamic factors involved in social, political, and cultural change – shamanism and politics. The book begins at the outset of the gold rush, with the death of the last great shamanic dreamer in the community. It continues by investigating the invisible world and the different techniques used by the Arakmbut to make contact with the spirits in order to promote the wellbeing of the people. Food production and curing are used to illustrate the complicated web of communication linking animals, spirit, and human beings to ensure Arakmbut growth and health. In both cases, a profound knowledge of Arakmbut biodiversity is necessary to enable a shaman to influence spirits.

Arakmbut politics is based on an understanding of the relativity of the social world, linking together the contrasting dynamics of desire and generosity. Through numerous daily encounters, the Arakmbut build up opinions, make decisions, solve disputes and acknowledge skilled persons through titles reflecting their prestige. Arakmbut politics is in constant flux, shifting its emphasis from one social principle to another.

The period from 1980 to 1992 witnessed a marked change of social organisation within the Arakmbut community of San José del Karene, from a comparatively hierarchical to a more egalitarian pattern of life. The book offers multiple explanations for the changes, including the influence of the gold rush, the cumulative effect of the domestic cycle within the community, and the presence of the spirit world.

The book demonstrates that Amazonian communities are not fossilised settlements but that they are, and have always been, highly dynamic. The patterns of change over the last fifteen years in San José reflect shifts that have taken place throughout its history. The generating factor for this change comes from the invisible world, which enters both political and shamanic fields of activity. The conclusion explains why the death of the shaman provides a key to understanding the changes that have taken place and continue to take place in the community.

The third volume looks at the Arakmbut's growing awareness of their rights as indigenous peoples to their territories and resources. This awareness has risen concurrently with the growing development of indigenous rights internationally. The book takes the concepts of territory, people, cultural identity, government, development, and self-determination and looks at their emergence in a non-indigenous framework, juxtaposing them with their relevance in an Arakmbut context. The result is a mapping between indigenous and non-indigenous perspectives. Fundamental concepts such as 'territory' and 'peoples' broadly cohere, whereas concepts such as 'development' or 'self-determination' are present in practice but not expressed verbally.

While there is no necessary matching between human-rights concepts and indigenous perspectives, the Arakmbut quickly grasp the meanings of the terms as they become relevant to their practical conditions. With the violation of their rights, the Arakmbut are beginning to use the concepts of human rights as a means for defending their lives. The conclusion is that whereas non-indigenous human rights legislation receives its legitimacy by judicial means, the Arakmbut find their legal system legitimised through the spirit world. Whether through access to resources, expression of cultural identity, potential for development and the assertion of self-determination, the spiritual features of Arakmbut life are a constant presence. For non-indigenous observers, the invisibility of the spirit world makes it appear non-existent; however, overlooking its importance prevents outsiders from understanding and appreciating its significance in the Arakmbut struggle for survival.

The perspective adopted here is one of an outsider who has been invited into the periphery of Arakmbut social and cultural life in order to explain the complexities and depths of their views of the world to others. The discrimination that the Arakmbut suffer is based on ignorance and lack of respect on the part of non-indigenous people, who consider their territories and existence as a people to be fair game for predatory colonial expansion. These books are not meant to explain away the Arakmbut into tidy packages, but to use the non-indigenous imagery of structures and processes to understand the importance of their survival in the future as a people and to express solidarity with their struggle against adversity. The conclusions here are not timeless truths, but the particular views of a person on the margins of their world.

Each of the three main Arakmbut myths is divided into three parts corresponding to the head word, the centre word, and the whole word. Although each section is independent, it also fits into a series. As with the internal structure of the myths, so with the relationship between the myths themselves: each one looks at a different aspect of Arakmbut life from within a similar framework. The theme which links them together is the blending or separation of the human, animal, and spirit worlds in the face of the constant threat of outside forces – harmful spirits and non-indigenous peoples.

A trilogy is thus an appropriate structure for writing about the Arakmbut, and these three volumes fit together within the framework of their mythology. Each book takes a theme that relates to the three Arakmbut myths analysed in the first volume: creation and organisation of social and cultural life; growth and change in the relationship with the animal and spirit world; and the relationship with non-indigenous peoples, the threats they introduce, and the ways in which the Arakmbut can combat or avoid the dangerous consequences of invasion. However the relationship between the volumes like so much of Arakmbut life, involves the superimposition of layers of meaning covering different aspects of the triadic relationship.

The first aspect is the narrative form which starts from one situation and draws the listener through a variety of experiences to a new set of conditions at the end. Both artistically and ceremonially, a triadic narrative structure is common to many cultures. The famous anthropological example consists of rites of transition marked by three phases: separation, liminality, and reincorporation. The directional nature of these triadic rituals makes them as linear as the triadic narrative convention found so frequently in Victorian novels. The meaning comes from the sequence.

A different view of triadic structures comes from a more spatial perspective, which places less importance on the sequence. Arakmbut myths are 'cubist', in that any section or theme can be taken out of the main structure and transformed into a new story, showing the original narrative from another angle, or complementing the theme. This cubist or sculpturesque point of view is illustrated in Lambert's observation about Eric Satie:

> Satie's habit of writing his pieces in groups of three was not just a mannerism. It took the place in his art of dramatic development, and was part of his peculiarly sculpturesque views on music ... . It does not matter which way you walk round a statue and it does not matter in which order you play the three Gymnopedies' (Constant Lambert, *Music Ho!* 1948:92).

Another aspect of the triadic structure of Arakmbut myth is the way in which each part 'eavesdrops' on the others, picking up themes and characters who reappear in different guises, drawing our attention to various facets of the stories. In this way the myth becomes a triptych in which each 'panel' makes sense in term of its similarities to and differences from the other two parts. John Russell points out that the painter Francis Bacon has frequently painted in groups of three (1985:127): 'Bacon in his triptychs plays over and over again with the idea of the eavesdropper – the figure who looks across to the central panel and directs our attention to it.' Arakmbut myths demonstrate this element through thematic cross-currents, which appear as the shifting of meaning within a framework of imagery such as birth/death, growth or cooking.

Each Arakmbut myth combines narrative, multiple perspectives, and thematic cross-currents, all of which take the listener into different domains, looking at the world from a variety of angles. The three volumes here also share the three aspects of Arakmbut triadic relationships within their mythology. From one perspective, the three volumes constitute a narrative moving from the first volume's description of the difference between mythical structure and historical process, to the second volume's account of the process itself and the third volume's demonstration of the struggle as to who controls history.

The three books can be seen as cubist in that there is a common element in each volume that is investigated from three different angles. This is the position of the spirit world, which is a constant articulating presence for the Arakmbut in their everyday life, as guarantor of mythical knowledge, as cause of the generative process of change and as the legitimiser, arbitrator and guardian of acceptable behaviour.

The final triadic aspect of Arakmbut mythology that connects these three volumes is the constant movement from one aspect of the triptych to another. In each of these three volumes there is information that adds, reflects and comments on the material contained in the others. The creation myth of Wanamey reappears regularly through the pages, pointing to the main crises of Arakmbut existence; the constant relativity operating between human beings, animal species, and spirits appears in different guises throughout the visible and invisible worlds according to the contexts such as the myth of Marinke, in curing rituals or when hunting; and the invasions arising from the gold rush have mythological connotations in the story of Aiwe and appear as a trigger for change with the emerging consciousness of indigenous identity.

In this way, these three volumes fit together as a trilogy, providing an interpretation of Arakmbut experience from a peripheral perspective and trying as far as possible to reflect the aims of Arakmbut mythology – to draw attention to the importance of the invisible spirit world in the present struggle for survival.

PREFACE

The Arrival

There are two routes that lead to the village of San José del Karene by way of the river Madre de Dios. They both take you through the traditional homeland of Harakmbut peoples. You might wish to descend by truck from the ridges of the snow-capped Peruvian sierra to the upper Madre de Dios, the territory of the Wachipaeri, then embark at the mission of Shintuya, a settlement of the Dominican fathers, and from there continue downriver to the mouth of the Karene. Alternatively, you could fly to Puerto Maldonado and travel with a commercial dealer upriver to the Karene, through the squalor of gold encampments scattered on the banks where once stood the communal houses of the Toyeri. Like the Pillars of Hercules, the mission and the mines mark the limits of Harakmbut sovereignty.

The two routes converge at the post of Boca Colorado at the mouth of the river Karene, where you meet turbulent waters, gleaming beaches, and dense green rainforest still in sight of the towering Andes. At last you reach the community of San José perched high on the cliffs of red sandstone that once gave the name 'Colorado' to the river. The Arakmbut who greet you are in no way isolated from the outside world. Some will address you in fluent Spanish learned from the missionaries, while others sport watches or shotguns bought with money from working in the gold placers. The members of the community are survivors, both physically and culturally. Their pride, strength, and vigour have taught them to conceal the wealth, depth, and variety of a culture which they do not readily communicate to outsiders for fear of derogatory misinterpretation.

Sheila Aikman and I first reached San José del Karene in February, 1980. The rainy season was late that year, and the Arakmbut were working gold at a placer downriver from the village. We had first arrived in Peru during August 1979 with the intention of visiting a people living in the Madre de Dios whom we had assumed from the literature were 'Mashco'. We soon realised that the Mashco did not exist, but that there were in fact Amarakaeri, who were a Harakmbut people, living in the area. The word 'Mashco' is a misnomer, erroneously applied to the Harakmbut during their period of initial contact with missionaries. The term 'Amarakaeri' has been used regularly since the 1970s, but is currently under discussion in the communities as an unwelcome term. The people themselves prefer Arakmbut and have requested that I use this name.

Apart from a brief trip to the Mission of Shintuya in November 1979, San José was the first Arakmbut community we had visited. We were given a tremendous greeting by the village, whose President explained that anthropologists were welcome. Other communities had been visited by anthropologists, and they wanted some of their own. We were offered a house with a widower and his sons.

This welcome might seem ingenuous from a group of indigenous people, when indigenous peoples throughout the world do not generally have a particularly high view of anthropologists (Deloria 1970; Aurora 1981). However the community had had a priest with them during 1979 who had recently moved to the neighbouring community of Puerto Luz. The presence of a few visitors was a sign of the continuing importance of the village in the area of the Karene river.

We settled into the daily life of the village quickly. Sheila spent most of her days with the women of the household where we ate. Every dawn she carried the water from the river, made the fire, and cooked, then went to the gardens for weeding, planting, and harvesting or visited the men working gold. She would return in time to help in the preparation of the evening meal. Meanwhile I would go with the men to the gold working area. We would clear the topsoil, then pick and shovel stones for washing.

Life followed this pattern for over a year. It was punctuated weekly by days off when the river rose too far or the men wanted to go hunting or fishing. These days were relaxed and provided time for extended discussions and reading or writing. Periodically, however, life would change dramatically in the face of threats. Then the daily round of activities would be severely disrupted or even stop altogether. For example during grave sickness or after a death the whole community would be affected. Similarly, if a group of gold colonists invaded village lands everyone would be on alert to defend the territory. In this way, apart from trips every two or three months to renew visas, our life consisted of periods when one day seemed much like the next, contrasted with sudden bursts of crisis.

As much as I like living in a community with indigenous people, I don't like 'doing fieldwork'. Gathering data by taking out notebooks or tape-recording interviews makes me feel like a 'peeping Tom' prying into other peoples' business. I was attracted to anthropology out of a desire to broaden my understanding of other peoples and to discuss philosophical ideas. Notebooks and tape recorders are intrusive, and the Arakmbut did not like them. I therefore used notes and tapes only for language work and recording myths or songs. Everything else I could jot down on a scrap of paper and transfer to my notebook at the end of the day.

Data did not fly at me from all angles. The Arakmbut and I took some time to work out the sort of ideas that interested us. Sometimes we were inundated with information; other times nothing much happened for several days. Most of the information presented here arose out of casual discussions. I checked up information with men and women, covering different ages and clans, although I have benefited considerably from the insights and information gathered by Sheila Aikman on Arakmbut female perspectives. She has written from a woman's perspective on life in an Arakmbut community (Aikman, nd).

During our return in 1985 with our son Robbie, I took my thesis, which had been completed in 1983, and left a copy in the community. I discussed it with several people of different ages and clans and as a result revised some of its orientations. In 1991 I returned again with a copy of this manuscript, which was translated with a student, Tomás Arique. We discussed the ideas contained in the work and he checked many points with elders of the community to see the changes that had taken place over the ten years and correct misunderstandings. In spite of all this, the book is not a definitive account of 'the Arakmbut'. To explain why, I will discuss some epistemological questions.

Grounds of Knowledge

The epistemological basis of this work depends very much on the context in which the information presented emerged during our period in Peru. The primary issue is one of commensurability: namely, the ways in which we made contact with the Arakmbut.

Some Arakmbut men spoke Spanish fluently, but the majority of men and women were monolingual. We both started to learn Harakmbut from published word lists and some grammatical notions from the Summer Institute of Linguistics. It took me a year to be moderately proficient in Harakmbut, to the point where I could last all day talking Harakmbut. I had a fairly limited vocabulary, but I was more or less understandable.

Arakmbut communities have quite distinct accents, and they were very tolerant at bending their ears to understand my Harakmbut. They were also extremely skilled at pitching the language so that I could understand them. However if they carried on a fast conversation, even after a year, I could grasp only the gist. This meant that I was able to pick up only what they wanted me to know.

The details of the cosmology and social life were initially formed from discussions in Spanish, which were then developed further by Harakmbut speakers. In this way much of what I write here has been lost or distorted in translation. The myths provide an illustration of this. They were recorded by an elderly man who spent several days preparing himself before he told them. After the sessions I tried to transcribe and translate the myths but found the task quite beyond me. The stories were full of puns and strange words. Eventually a young man agreed to translate the myths, and we spent several days translating them into Spanish. For this reason, the myths presented here are a pale reflection of the original Harakmbut.

Language is but one means of communication and it would be an error to reduce all human contact to its domain. Cohabitation was equally important. Working gold, weeding in the gardens, and visiting every house in the village for a chat at dusk brought us together. But shared crises were the most important experiences in this respect. We were deeply upset by the deaths in the community, and when my mother died in March 1980 the Arakmbut provided enormous understanding and comfort.

Our relationship to the Arakmbut became firmly sealed one day when an armed boat of gold prospectors came up the river. They had been spotted approaching San José's lands. The men of the community were extremely tense and armed themselves with shotguns, bows and arrows. We stood on the cliff overlooking the river and then crossed to where they had landed. The Arakmbut probably caused as much trepidation in their opponents as they felt themselves, with their guns and bows at the ready. The colonists left without a murmur. But I had seen and felt something which was beyond language, and the Arakmbut knew it. As that boat came upriver and passed the village, I experienced what the violation of indigenous lands by armed colonists means.

These anecdotes are designed to show our particular position in the community. We were not Arakmbut, our knowledge of the language was passable but not fluent, but we cared about them and they about us. There was an empathy between us. But we were outsiders, different and could never be of them – nor did we want to be. This is crucial to understand when reading this book.

Arakmbut social and cultural life is a complex diversity of perspectives that are neither completely ordered nor totally anarchic. The perspective that appears here is neither correct nor incorrect. It is an interpretation based on encounters which took place between 1980 and 1981, for some weeks in 1985 and in 1991 and 1992 – a total of about thirty months. However my perspective is still peripheral.

The challenge of writing this book is the impossibility of producing a text that is acceptable to all members of the community; some people would agree with certain aspects, some with others. If I were to emphasise the difficulties, such as shortage of time in the community, problems of understanding details of the language, and my peripheral perspective, this book would be open to the charge that it is largely a product of my vivid imagination. Yet this argument disregards and even insults the Arakmbut who, as teachers, have spent many hours and much patience trying to teach me about themselves and explaining how they see the world.

Conversely, if I were to omit to describe the epistemological conditions of producing this work as many ethnographies do, then the book will be open to the charge that what I have written is the 'truth', engraved in print and constituting an official version of 'Harakmbut society and culture'. Even if I have seriously misrepresented the Arakmbut in some way they will be largely powerless to respond. Furthermore, if I were to present this work as a scientifically accurate text, I would also be open to the objection that I was trying to encapsulate the Arakmbut within a system imposed from outside. This would be a form of intellectual colonisation. Yet this argument again diminishes the Arakmbut, who knowingly invited us into their community in order to discuss and to learn about their ways of life.

These two arguments and their consequences constitute a tension that constantly pushes and pulls at anthropology. No practitioner of anthropology can escape either argument because of the ultimate inequality between the anthropologist and the host communities. Although anthropology is not necessarily the 'handmaiden' of colonialism, the two normally travel in the same direction.

The only way to begin overcoming this tension is through a decolonisation process that recognises the limitations of anthropological understanding. Everyone will find their own way of doing this. For me it has meant combining two factors normally eschewed by anthropologists. One is to respect the mystery embedded in the Arakmbut universe; the other is to understand their political vulnerability in the face of outside threats.

I use the term 'mystery' in two senses here. The first sense is self-reflective, in which 'mystery' has the sense of a detective story (Crocker 1985; Campbell 1989). The fieldwork experience is littered with clues that lead towards many solutions. However in this case there is not one solution, and probably not any. All we have are the clues that we relate to each other; there are gaps, inconsistencies, and ephemeral conclusions that leave most questions unanswered.

The second sense of mystery has religious or cosmological connotations. There are many things that we do not understand in the universe, and one of my reasons for visiting the Arakmbut was to enter into a dialogue with them about these questions. Although many aspects of life are perfectly commensurable, understood through language, empathy, and political awareness, others are not.

The most fascinating aspects of Arakmbut life are the realities which we cannot understand. Arakmbut self-controlled dreaming, the reality of the spirit world, and the direct experience of communicating with an animal all seem impossible. I am convinced that in an Arakmbut context these things are possible. I have seen strange things that can be rationalised away but to no avail. My aim is not to encapsulate and destroy the mystery of Arakmbut life but to respect it.

Respect can take place, however, only if we can get a glimpse into that world of mystery. If we find crack in the door enabling a direct experience of their culture, we can break through the opacity of our own. However, to reduce these experiences for the purpose of intellectual explanation is to destroy them and consume them. This image of a cannibalistic consumption of their lives is an Arakmbut view of colonisation (see the myth of Aiwe and the Papas in Part III).

Yet, standing on the border of my own culture and that of the Arakmbut, I occasionally catch flashes of their world. To me, encountering and feeling these moments of awareness in a world beyond the realms of our reductionist culture makes the anthropological enterprise worthwhile. But avoiding the colonisation of these experiences is difficult, because without some framework, whether artificial or not, the Arakmbut will appear unintelligible.

For this reason I argue that an organising framework, partly mine and partly Arakmbut, can be justified provided it acts as a facilitator for mutual understanding and respect, rather than as a way of dehumanising people. This means that most of Arakmbut life will be as deep a mystery at the end of this book as at the beginning.

Apart from respect for mystery, the second factor for decolonising anthropology in an Arakmbut context is an awareness of the many different ways in which indigenous peoples are threatened with loss of land, eradication of culture, and in certain cases genocide. Sometimes they seek support, sometimes they just want outsiders to go away. The Arakmbut want support as they exercise their rights to their territories, culture, and self-organisation. This constitutes their right to determine their lives for themselves without interference – that is their right to self-determination as a people.

The presence of an outsider writing a monograph about the Arakmbut could be seen as a challenge to their right to describe their social and cultural lives for themselves. However, provided the book does not prevent them from writing about themselves as they see fit and does not strive to present a definitive 'Arakmbut worldview', this problem can be avoided. For this reason my work is centred around notions of relativity, potentiality, and creativity. The Arakmbut themselves make up the reality; I talk only of possibilities.

Respect for the incommensurable mysteries of Arakmbut experience and for their right to self-determination seems to me to be the only way to transcend the tension between fictitious subjectivity and encapsulating objectivity, which have made anthropology a colonial enterprise in the eyes of so many of the world's indigenous people.

Why Write At All?

On the basis of the arguments I have just presented, I have to discuss why I have written this book at all. This book is about the Arakmbut, and the work should be for them. Indeed, this book was written with an Arakmbut readership predominantly in focus. There are currently seven students from the Madre de Dios in Peru studying in Lima, one of whom, an Arakmbut, is a student of sociology. This book, in its Spanish translation, will therefore be read and criticised by them.

I discussed with the people of San José the question of publishing my thesis when I returned to the community in 1985. There were several reactions. The young men were eager that the book be published. They wanted information about themselves known throughout the world, as it would place them on the ethnographic map. This would be useful for them when pursuing their cause nationally and internationally. The old men were amused that the words that I knew would be of interest to others. They were also without any doubts about the value of publicity, providing the book was written sensitively. The political leaders, however, raised several queries about the book. They asked whether there would be royalties and whether, if there were distortions of the facts, they would have the means to correct them.

No one will agree with everything I write, and for this reason my name has to be placed as author. Although I consider the Arakmbut to be friends and colleagues, rather than informants, to make them responsible for my own vision of their world would be misleading. This book is a hypothesis about Arakmbut life presented by an outsider. Sometimes outsiders' perspectives can be distorting, but sometimes they provide insights.

One day the Arakmbut will write their own ethnographies which will make this work pale into insignificance. However, if this work has no more effect than to make people realise the importance and value of the lives of indigenous peoples, then it will have achieved its aim.

Acknowledgements and Intellectual Property Questions

To thank the Arakmbut seems somewhat lame, as without them this book could not have been written. Their patience, encouragement, influence, and friendship not only affected me while I was there but has taught me the importance of the indigenous struggle throughout the world. I feel immense gratitude to them, which will always draw us together.

Similarly to thank Sheila Aikman and our son Robbie for their support does not express how much of them is in these pages and how much they have done for me. Whether in the field or in Europe, they have provided the inspiration for this work. I should also thank my father, William Gray, who provided us with a refuge on our return from Peru in 1981, which enabled much of this book to be written.

Dr Peter Rivière helped transfer what was a 'large shapeless object' when I first came back from the field into a thesis. His guidance, technical advice and anthropological insights were not only important when writing my thesis but have remained a major inspiration. I would also like to thank my examiners, Dr Stephen Hugh-Jones and Dr Robert H. Barnes for their crucial suggestions on the text which I followed when writing this book, and also Dr Joanna Overing for her helpful comments and enthusiasm for my work.

In Peru there are countless people who have helped me in my work. Thomas Moore, Lizzie Wahl, Klaus Rummenhöller, Heinrich Helberg and Didier Lacaze, all have extensive knowledge about the Harakmbut and have provided me with essential insights and the benefits of their work, which are particularly clear in the third part of this book. The Universidad Pontificia Católica del Perú provided me with an affiliation in both 1979–81 and again in 1985. I should deeply thank both Juan Ossio and Teófilo Altamirano for their encouragement.

Indigenous organisations such as the Asociación Interetnica de Desarrollo de la Selva Peruana (AIDESEP), the Federación Nativa del Madre de Dios y sus Afluentes (FENAMAD) and the Asociación de Estudiantes Indígenas del Madre de Dios (ADEIMAD) have all had members and officers over the last ten years who have been of great assistance. In 1991 and 1992 I was affiliated with FENAMAD, to which I am very grateful for providing me with credentials enabling me to visit indigenous communities of the area. Furthermore, members of ADEIMAD have taken a great interest in my work and have helped me very much with comments on the text; among them Elias Kentehuari, Hector Sueyo, and Tomás Arique, who also provided the drawings for the text.

Other people whose help has been of great value are: the staff at the Centro Eori, Puerto Maldonado, who have discussed many of the themes in this book with me; Jaime Regan and the Centro de Amazónico de Antropología y Aplicación Práctica (CAAAP) who were a great support when I arrived in Peru in 1979; Padre Adolfo Torralba and Mixtel Fernández, who are Dominican Priests and Robert Tripp, from the Summer Institute of Linguistics, who have all provided me with much stimulating conversation, and with inspiring comments from their experiences with the Arakmbut.

In Europe I should mention the important influence of the staff of the International Work Group for Indigenous Affairs (IWGIA) in Copenhagen, who helped me form the opinions I developed between writing my thesis and this final version of the book. I would like to thank Jorge Monrás from IWGIA who provided all the maps and diagrams. IWGIA is currently working on a programme of support for the Arakmbut and regularly publishes material on their current situation. IWGIA can be contacted at: Fiolstraede 10, 1171 Copenhagen K, Denmark.

I would also like to mention members of the Department of Social Anthropology at the University of Göteborg, and in particular Dan

Rosengren, who gave me many opportunities to try out my ideas. My work in Peru was financed in 1979–81 by the then Social Science Research Council and in 1985 by a grant from the Danish government development agency DANIDA. In 1989, thanks to Georg Henriksen, the Bergen research programme, 'Social Organisation Systems of Knowledge and Resource Management, supported my research from Norwegian Research Council grant 550.88/013. The final sections were written in 1990–91 while I was on an IWGIA research programme supported by DANIDA. To these bodies I am extremely grateful.

The Arakmbut of San José have provided most of the information contained in this book and its perspective predominantly shares their orientation. Nevertheless, members of other Arakmbut communities have checked some of the information, and although there are discrepancies in detail, the main results are broadly similar. For this reason the information here, outside of its interpretation, is part of the Arakmbut cultural heritage.

Because Arakmbut is a collective tradition it would be inappropriate to attribute each piece of evidence personally. The only exception has been the acknowledgement of Ireyo, the myth teller, who is known and respected for his knowledge. On the basis of my discussions with the community, I am aware of no information in this text that has been told to me in confidence. After extensive talks with members of San José, other Arakmbut communities and FENAMAD, I have received broad support for publishing this book. This in no way obliges those groups to agree with my particular interpretation.

* * *

During my first fieldwork period in 1980,
my mother, Diana Gray, died.
This book is dedicated to her memory.

INTRODUCTION

The Harakmbut

No indigenous people is isolated, and so before embarking on any study it is important to provide some general outline of the social, historical, geographical, and cultural context of regional life. This section looks at the Harakmbut peoples as a whole, their history, and their current demographic and settlement patterns within the context of the Madre de Dios.

The Madre de Dios is both culturally and biologically a highly diverse region of southeastern Peru. The indigenous people of the area number about ten thousand, which constitutes about a quarter of the total population. The majority of non-indigenous people live in the capital, Puerto Maldonado, while most indigenous peoples inhabit the rural areas. During the mining periods, the population of Madre de Dios doubles when colonists and workers, predominantly from the highlands, make their way down to the rainforest to seek their fortune working gold.

The Indigenous Peoples of the Madre de Dios

The indigenous peoples of the Madre de Dios belong to nineteen different ethno-linguistic groups comprising about 10,000 persons living in over forty communities. According to d'Ans (1973) there are four different language families in the Department of Madre de Dios in Peru (see Maps 1 and 2). Tacana languages are spoken downriver from the Arakmbut on the frontier with Bolivia by the Ese'eja (at one time known as 'Huarayos') and possibly Iñaparis. Upriver to the north and west there are groups of Matsigenka and Piro who speak Arawak. To the northeast live various Panoan-speaking groups such as the Amahuaca and Yaminahua. A few Shipibo, Asháninka, Santarosinos and Cocama came down the Ucayali with the rubber prospectors *(caucheros)* during the rubber boom.

Map 1 General map of Peru indicating other indigenous groups neighbouring the Harakmbut

- Towns
- ~ Rivers

Map 2 Indigenous communities of the Madre de Dios

The fourth and central linguistic family in the Madre de Dios is Harakmbut. The language spoken by the Arakmbut belongs to this family. Patricia Lyon (1976) calls Harakmbut 'Haté' and, in her closely argued paper, demonstrates its independence from the other languages of the area.[1] She sees Haté as one language consisting of several dialects such as Wachipaeri and Amarakaeri.

---

1. Previous studies placed the Harakmbut with the Pre-Andean group of the Arawak family, with the exception of Arasaeri, which was classified as Pano (c.f. d'Ans 1973 referring to Rivet & Loukotka 1952, McQuown 1955 and Loukotka 1968).

Ribeiro and Wise (1978) prefer, with d'Ans, to regard Harakmbut as a linguistic family. In *Los Grupos Etnicos de la Amazonía Peruana* (ibid.:203) they divide Harakmbut languages (which they call 'Harakmbet') into two branches. The first consists of the languages of the Amarakaeri (Arakmbut) and Kisambaeri, while the second contains those of the Wachipaeri, Arasaeri, Sapiteri and Toyeri. This linguistic classification largely coincides with other factors such as residence and cultural differences.

The Harakmbut Language

All the Harakmbut languages share the same phonetic system. They have certain identifiable characteristics such as the frequent use of glottal stops, semi-nasal *(mb, nd, d, gn)* and the nasaling of vowel sounds *(a, e and o)*. When speaking Harakmbut the stress comes on the penultimate syllable of a word. A comprehensive structural account of Harakmbut has been produced by Helberg (1984).

Within the Arakmbut language there are dialectal differences between the Wandakweri and Kipodneri. These are mainly lexical, but apart from this the former (who live in San José) generally speak with less emphasis on consonants and with a more nasal sound than their Kipodneri neighbours upriver in Puerto Luz.

One of the interesting aspects of Harakmbut grammar is the 'semantic components of shape'. Hart (1963:1) defines these as follows:

> Amarakaeri abounds with morphemes which classify objects and actions according to the particular shape or combinations of shapes inherent in the item or action under focus. These morphemes occur singly or in combination in noun, adjective, and verb constructions and often show concord between construction on higher grammatical levels. Many of the morphemes have a semantic component of basic body part; others are more clearly tied to basic shapes or qualities not represented in the body, such as liquid, powder, cluster, channel or stinger.

These morphemes usually occur in describing familiar objects, but they are extremely apt for devising new words needed to accommodate cultural items that have been introduced from outside.

Verbs are built up from roots and modified by the use of prefixes and suffixes. There are declarative, dubitative and imperative classes of verb prefixes, while the suffix is reserved for the tense (present, recent past, distant past, future and conditional), negatives and possibility. Helberg (1989:237) points out the extensive use of conditionals, probability and possibility in Harakmbut. Passive constructions are bound in with the use of pronouns.

Whereas all adjectives can be recognised by the suffix '*-nda*', nouns appear to be grouped into two classes. Some have the prefix '*wa-*' before the root while others do not. There is some regularity in the way these types of noun are used. Nouns with the '*wa-*' prefix are mainly generic while those without seem to refer directly to individual entities and species. The difference between individual and species is very unclear in Harakmbut languages as there is no substantive distinction between singular and plural. However, a verbal prefix *mae-* refers to a collectivity.

There are a few other features of Harakmbut languages which are distinctive. Several spatial and temporal locatives are used by means of affixes, but the contrast is often weak. Another important factor is the use of the suffix '*-po*' which in both narrational and descriptional verbs signifies the relation between a reason or cause and its conclusion or effect.[2]

Everyone in San José knew some words of Spanish but on the whole this knowledge was rudimentary. Whereas about 15 percent of the men were fluent Spanish speakers, all but three of the women were monolingual. This made the proportion of completely bilingual Arakmbut about 10 percent. On the other hand, about 50 percent of the population could hold their own in a Spanish conversation. Spanish was spoken almost exclusively to outsiders as a mark of education, and sometimes this even included Arakmbut who were visiting from other communities.

The Harakmbut Peoples

All those people who speak one of the Harakmbut languages as their native tongue are 'Harakmbut'. This term is appropriate as a general name because it is their word for 'people'. The Harakmbut are also divided into several groups, most of which have the suffix '*-eri*' added to their names meaning 'people of'. The groups are settled in specific areas and each speaks a different version of Harakmbut. They received their names from neighbouring groups and recognise their own identity by means of certain cultural traits. The divisions of the Harakmbut are essentially named regional groups and can be

---

2. Tripp's notes refer to the causal particle '*-po*' whereas Helberg (1984) considers '*ia*' to be the correct term. The confusion is easily seen in a word such as '*kachi-apo*', which means 'why?'.

regarded as 'ethno-linguistic' groups (Uriate 1976). (See Map 3-i.) The Arakmbut in San José consider that the other Harakmbut groups were formed from ancestral women who one day, when their husbands went on a long hunting expedition, changed sex and moved downriver to form the other peoples.

Map 3 Harakmbut communities in Madre de Dios

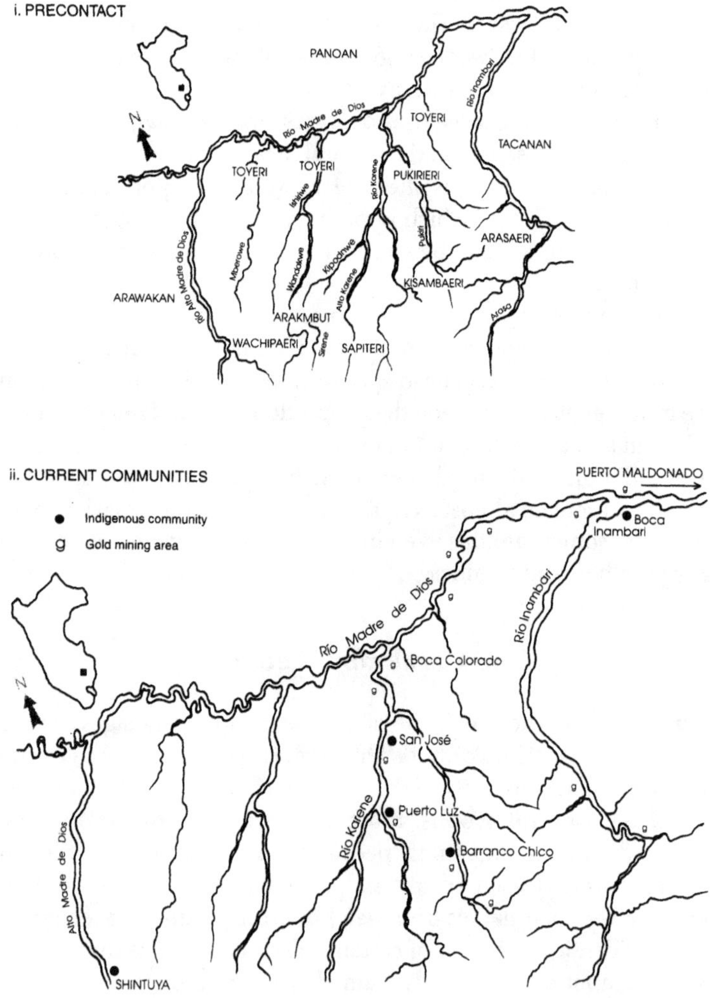

i. PRECONTACT

ii. CURRENT COMMUNITIES

1. Arakmbut (Amarakaeri)

The Arakmbut, the most numerous Harakmbut group, first encountered non-indigenous outsiders in the 1940s. Their homeland was the headwaters of the Karene and Ishiriwe rivers and their distance from the main Madre de Dios river may account for their survival. The Arakmbut use their symmetric relationship terminology in conjunction with a system of seven patrilineal clans and household clusters recruited on a cognatic basis (see chapter four). These are important for their relationship with the visible world of people and animals as well as the invisible world of the spirits.

Since coming into contact with the Dominican missionaries, most of the Arakmbut have spent a period in the Catholic mission system, but have since left and formed their own Native Communities, which are legally recognised by the Peruvian state. The Arakmbut themselves number under one thousand people in total and consist of Wandakweri, who now live in Shintuya (a mission station), Boca Inambari, Barranco Chico, and San José, and the Kipodneri and Kareneri who live in Puerto Luz. With the exception of Shintuya, all the Arakmbut communities work gold. (See Map 3-ii.)

2. Wachipaeri

The Wachipaeri live in the Upper Madre de Dios in the mission of Shintuya and the communities of Qeros and Huacaria, which stretch into the Department of Cusco. There are also a few Wachipaeri in the small community of Diamante downriver from Shintuya. They are the second largest Harakmbut people consisting of about 500 persons although their numbers were decimated by a smallpox epidemic in 1948, which coincided with the opening of the road to Cusco (Lyon 1976:225).

They have had contact for centuries with both the Matsigenka (with whom they intermarry) and highland people (Lyon 1984:252-3). The Wachipaeri have a clan system like the Arakmbut but, in contrast, they place more emphasis on a subterranean underworld, divide their lands into four parts (Califano, 1982:13), and drink manioc beer (*masato*). The areas where the Wachipaeri live do not contain gold and they spend their time working lumber and raising cattle.

3. Arasaeri

Only a few families of Arasaeri have survived the ravages of the rubber and gold booms as well as intensive missionary activity between 1900 and 1940 (Rummenhöller, 1984:7). They live mainly in the community of Villa Santiago on the Maldonado-Cusco road. A sub-group, the Pukirieri, also live near the Cusco road at Kotsimba, where they settled after moving from the headwaters of the Pukiri river. Previously the Arasaeri lived on the Marcapata river, known as the Arasa, which is an affluent of the Inambari. The Arasaeri have had cultural contact with the Wachipaeri (Aza 1927:245) across the headwaters of the Karene. As yet there is little information about their socio-cultural organisation.

4. Sapiteri

The remaining Sapiteri, who number about thirty, now live in scattered gold-mining groups on the river Pukiri and in the communities of San José and Boca Ishiriwe. The major reason for their devastated population has been epidemics of smallpox and influenza that arose after contact with Dominican missionaries and being moved into the mission of Kaichihue in the 1940s. From there they helped the priests make contact with the peoples of the Karene and Upper Madre de Dios.

The Sapiteri were once enemies of the Wachipaeri. They are referred to by the Arasaeri as 'Sirineri', a name that occurs frequently in early encounters with the Harakmbut. The Sapiteri, before contact with the missionaries, lived around the Arakmbut in an area stretching from the headwaters of the Karene to those of the Upper Madre de Dios (Califano 1978a:402). The Sapiteri originally had a clan system and the Arakmbut sometimes say that their Saweron clan is 'Sapiteri'. Califano, in his discussions comparing the different Harakmbut groups, finds similarities in the cultural characteristics of the Wachipaeri and Sapiteri (Califano 1982:69,136).

5. Kisambaeri/ Amaiweri

These people, who number fewer than thirty, once lived on the Wasorokwe, an affluent of the Karene. A few have survived the smallpox and influenza epidemics of the 1950s and live with the Sapiteri on the river Pukiri, at the community of Shiringayoc on the Madre de Dios and at Boca Ishiriwe on the river Madre de Dios. According to Ribeiro and Wise (1978:57), their language is possibly a dialect of Amarakaeri.

6. Toyeri

Toyeri (sometimes written 'Toyoeri' or referred to in the old texts as 'Tuyuneri') means 'those who live downstream'. In this sense, 'toyeri' does not refer to any group in particular, only to those who live downstream from wherever you are. However, Toyeri has become the term used to refer to those Harakmbut people who once lived on the main Eori (Madre de Dios) river, from the upper regions to below the Inambari. The Arasaeri use the name 'Manukiari' for these people. The Toyeri were once the most numerous Harakmbut group but are now the smallest. Most of them were killed during the rubber boom as a result of disease, murder, and slavery. Only a handful of Toyeri have survived the devastations of the rubber boom, and these live at Shiringayoc, near the marine base Lagarto on the Madre de Dios and at the mission of Shintuya.

Little has been written about Toyeri life. Arakmbut told me that much of the information in the book on the Harakmbut by Barriales and Torralba (1970) was about Toyeri. However, the Sapiteri say that most of the ethnographic data in the book refers to themselves.

Each of these Harakmbut peoples consists of clusters of named territorial groups that comprised one or several communal houses (*malocas*) from which they took their names. Many countless maloca names used in the past are no longer applicable because most of these people were destroyed. Among the Arakmbut, however, the original maloca groups are still used in defining interpersonal relationships.

Harakmbut History: From Inca Ritual to Catholic Mass

Several archaeologists and linguists consider the area of the Madre de Dios to be significant in the prehistoric development of language and culture in Peru. Noble (1965) says that the headwaters of the Ucayali were the homeland of a proto-language from which Arawakan, Tupian and Chapacuran sprang 3,500–5,000 years ago. Lathrap (1970) sees a shortage of land forcing peoples from the main rivers to the headwaters and points to the watershed between the Ucayali and the Madre de Dios as a possible refuge for some of the oldest rainforest groups in Peru. D'Ans (1973:43) says that the Harakmbut are the earliest group in the region. However, these authors offer no concrete evidence to back up their theories.

The Incas called the Madre de Dios 'Amarumayu' (serpent river). In the early 'historico-legendary' phase of the Inca period (Kauffmann-Doig 1980:556), the Inca Roca and his son Yahuar Huaca reached the headwaters of the Madre de Dios and the Inambari (Bovo de Revello 1848:8) and built several forts in the area (Göhring, 1877). The later 'historic' phase of the Inca 'Tahuantinsuyu' state saw the first full-scale expeditions into the area in the mid-fourteenth century. Tupac Yupanqui, son of the empire-builder Pachacuti, led an expedition to look for coca. Sarmiento de Gamboa says that the army was divided into three parts, which entered from the head-waters of the Madre de Dios, Inambari and Beni, respectively (Belaúnde, 1911). This reconciles the views of Garcilaso who says that they entered from the Madre de Dios and Cieza de León who says that they entered from the Beni.

There are descriptions in Garcilaso (1945, Tom. I, Lib. IV, Cap. XVI), reported by Bovo de Revello (op.cit.) and Alvarez (1958b), of an expedition by the earlier Inca Roca's son to the Madre de Dios, which, according to Mendoza Marsano (1974:210), not only reached, but entered the river Karene as far as the Pukiri. The problem with this description is that it bears so much resemblance to those of later expeditions that they could be one and the same. However Belaúnde (op.cit.), using evidence of Inca roads into the Upper Madre de Dios, Inambari and Beni, reports that communications between highlands and lowlands were so well developed in Inca times that these reports were likely to be combinations of various trips into the area. On the death of an Inca there were usually ritu-alised journeys taking the blood from the sacrifices at the Corican-cha temple of the Sun in Cusco to the limits of the known world (Duvoils, 1976). It is feasible that the expeditions to the Madre de Dios were a part of this procedure.

The Incas appear in several contexts in Arakmbut culture and, in particular, play a significant role in the mythology. Manco Inca is reputed to have lived in a cave in the upper Ishiriwe, where he was thought to have been responsible for the origin of several cultural features such as maize, chicha and axes.[3] Nordenskjöld (1905) re-ports the finding of an Inca axe in Wachipaeri territory and Mendoza Marsano (op. cit.) does so on the Pukiri. During our stay in San José we came across several axes of stone and one of bronze that may possibly be Incaic (Aikman 1982).

The chronicles refer to the groups living in Harakmbut territory as Opatari, which is the name used by the first *conquistadores* of the colonial area. There seems to have been some large settlement known as Opatari, which took its name from the people of the region, but whether this was an indigenous community or an Inca outpost used by the conquistadores the information fails to make

---

3. Highland influences are common in the lowlands. They are very apparent among the Asháninka (Weiss 1969) and the Shipibo (Morin 1973) where the Incas play a more important role than among the Arakmbut.

clear. In 1535 Pedro de Candía was granted an area of the Upper Madre de Dios by Hernando Pizarro. Subsequently there were several expeditions further downstream by Anzures (1539) and Alvarez Maldonado (1566–8), but only the region bordering the highlands was exploited to grow coca.

There was little interest in the lower Madre de Dios in the seventeenth century but in the following hundred years there were several expeditions into the Harakmbut homeland. In 1768 and 1769, Andino travelled to the Upper Madre de Dios where he contacted a local leader called Mathaguari (*wairi* is the Harakmbut word for 'leader'). He established a few farms but heard of people called 'Apiteris' who intended to attack (Maúrtua 1906: Vol.12, p.166). This is the first reference to a Harakmbut people (the Sapiteri).

A few years later, in 1807, Padres Busquests and Rocamora (Maúrtua ibid.) mention the Guirinieris, who are presumably the Sirineri. They say that these people are members of the 'Mashco' nation. 'Mashcos' is a term first used by Biedma in 1687 in the form 'Maschos' (see Amich 1854:104), probably in reference to a group of Piro in the Mishagua river north of Manu. Throughout the nineteenth century and until quite recently it was used instead of Opatari to refer to the Harakmbut.

The Upper Madre de Dios was still a centre for coca plantations in the nineteenth century, although the number of farms was determined by the demand for the leaf (Bovo de Revello op.cit.). Raimondi (1979: Vol.I, 129) refers to three hundred farms in the area during the 1840s (cf. Lyon nd cited in Wahl 1987). The central years of the nineteenth century heralded a plethora of scientific expeditions to ascertain the resources of the area. Millar (1835), Espinar (1846) and Bovo de Revello (1848) travelled to the Wachipaeri lands of Q'osnipata. Bolognesa (1851) reached the Inambari while Gibbon (1852) and Markham (1853) all reached Pilcopata at the headwaters of the Madre de Dios. In 1861 Grandidier and Saint-Criq entered the area while Faustino Maldonado followed the course of the Madre de Dios as far as present-day Bolivia. Raimondi reached the Inambari in 1864, and in 1868 Nistrom visited the Tono and Piñi Piñi rivers. In 1873 the ill-fated expedition of Baltazar de la Torre provided Göhring with the data on the Wachipaeri, Sirineri and Tuyuneri published in 1877. Indeed, this military expedition was destroyed by a coalition between the Wachipaeri, Sapiteri, and Toyeri, which provides a historical example of a successful inter-group alliance among the Harakmbut.

During the rubber boom the Harakmbut suffered greatly. Fitzcarrald entered the area from Manu and fought the Toyeri, who would not co-operate with him. Thousands of Harakmbut are thought to have died between 1894 and 1904 (Reyna 1942:85). In future years the Arasaeri were decimated by slave raids from Bolivia. Those who escaped fled to the interior of the forest, where warfare with those groups already there escalated.

Reports of expeditions in the first decade of the twentieth century included a reference by Olivera (1907:421) to the 'Maracairis'. He was part of the Junta de Vias Fluviales, which was commissioned by the Peruvian government to seek ways of exploiting the area and securing the boundary with Bolivia. From 1902 the Dominicans worked in the Madre de Dios, first with the Matsigenka and later with the Ese'eja. They gradually moved into the Harakmbut homeland, converting Toyeri and Arasaeri in the 1930s, the Sapiteri and Wachipaeri in the 1940s, and the Arakmbut and Kisambaeri in the 1950s. Their policy was to bring the Harakmbut into a mission and teach them 'civilised behaviour' such as literacy and husbandry. The largest mission station was Shintuya, which during the 1960s held most of the Arakmbut and Wachipaeri. Between 1969 and 1973, several waves of Arakmbut escaped from the mission to establish the Native Communities of Barranco Chico, San José del Karene, and Boca del Inambari. The other community on the Karene, Puerto Alegre (later to become Puerto Luz), was contacted by the Summer Institute of Linguistics in 1957 and spent only a very short time in Shintuya.

Currently the Arakmbut communities are all titled Native Communities. They work primarily with gold, although those Arakmbut still in Shintuya work lumber. Puerto Luz has, since 1980, received more missionary contact with long visits from a Dominican priest in addition to the Summer Institute of Linguistics Bible translator. All the communities have their own schools, run either by State teachers or the Church.

During the last ten years the problems facing the Harakmbut have increased considerably because of the gold rush in the Madre de Dios and the threat to their survival from national and international companies. They have responded by defending their rights through the indigenous organisation Federación Nativa del Madre de Dios y sus Afluentes (FENAMAD).[4]

4.   Particularly important in this context has been the development of FENAMAD over the last ten years, which has brought together indigenous communities from all over the Madre de Dios. FENAMAD is affiliated with the national organisation AIDESEP, which in its turn is a part of the international organisation 'Indigenous Co-ordinadora of the Amazon Basin' (COICA).

Locality, Demography and Settlement

The river Karene is in the Province of Manu, situated twelve degrees latitude south and fifty-two degrees longtitude west of Greenwich. The territory of the Harakmbut comprises approximately thirty thousand square kilometres, currently pending recognition as a communal reserve. Including colonists, the population density was approximately 0.2 pp/km2 in 1980, although that is rising with the influx of settlers since the gold rush, who now number over one thousand miners.

The average temperature is twenty-five degrees C.; however, it ranges from 34 to 40 degrees in the dry season (June until October) and drops as low as eight degrees during the occasional *'friaje'*, or cold spells, that come at the end of the wet season. During the wet season (November until May), the rain can be sufficient to raise the level of the river by six metres. Humidity averages 77 percent in the Madre de Dios as a whole.

San José del Karene is about four hundred metres above sea level, within sight of the high Andes. It is situated in the Madre de Dios river basin, which forms part of the headwaters of the Amazon. The Karene river, on which the village lies, flows northeast into the main Madre de Dios river, parallel with the Upper Madre de Dios, Mberowe, Ishiriwe and Inambari rivers. The settlement stands on alluvial deposits, which are acidic, low in organic material content, and phosphorus, but with an adequate potassium level. On the whole fertility is low but varies according to the area exploited. Geologically the area contains white and red sandstone and recent riverine pebble deposits. These deposits also include fine gold dust, which can be found either on the beaches or in the interior where there are old beds of rivers or streams.

The range of flora and fauna in the area is considerable. Nearby Tambopata is considered to contain one of the highest rates of biodiversity in the world. The Arakmbut cultivate sweet manioc (*yuca*), plantains, papaya, sweet potatoes, pineapple, barbasco, peach palms, sweet bananas, achiote, a little dry rice, and some tobacco and coca. Game caught by the Arakmbut hunter includes tapir, peccaries, monkeys, armadillos, deer, caiman, turtles, and countless species of birds and fish. Availability is determined by season, region, and cultural demand.

Demographic change is difficult to estimate. Von Hassel (1905) gives the following list:

Mashco or Sirineri 6,000–7,000
Huachipaeri 500–800

Tuyuneri 500
Arasaeri 500–800

His total ranges between 7,500 and 9,100. We must remember that
this does not include the Arakmbut, who had not been encountered
at this time, and also that this estimate comes after the initial destruction of the Harakmbut by the caucheros at the end of the last century.
Taking into account at least ten thousand Arakmbut, Sapiteri, Kisambaeri, and Pukirieri from the Karene area, as well as those Toyeri who
were killed in the battles with Fitzcarrald at that time, it would not
seem extravagant to suggest that the Harakmbut at the end of the last
century could have numbered at least thirty thousand.[5]

Ten years after Von Hassel's estimate the numbers decreased. Delboy (1912) and Portillo (1914) both mention six thousand as the number of Harakmbut. By the 1950s Guevara (1953) cites the Mashcos
as totalling only two thousand. Today a generous estimate of the
Harakmbut would still be about two thousand in all (although the
population has declined and grown again since 1953). This would
suggest that in the last hundred years the Harakmbut have been
reduced in population by some 95 percent.

The initial cause of this rapid destruction was the activities of the
caucheros, who not only killed, enslaved, and spread disease, but
forced a movement of population from the main river to the headwaters, which led to bitter feuding between different Harakmbut
peoples. Epidemics of influenza and smallpox wiped out most of the
Sapiteri, the Wachipaeri and Kisambaeri. There are also stories of
the mass extermination of Arasaeri by colonists trading poisoned
food to their communities.

Prior to mission contact, Harakmbut settlements contained
between fifty and one hundred and fifty people. All the present-day
communities are around this size. San José contains between 120 and

5. Denevan, in his article, 'The Aboriginal Populations of Amazonia', says
(1976:221): 'The rate of population decline of the relatively isolated upland forest tribes seems to have been far below that of the more vulnerable tribes of the
flood plains and savannas'. This fits in with the decimation of Harakmbut
groups, such as the Toyeri, who lived by the main rivers, and the comparative
survival of the more isolated Arakmbut. If we follow Denevan's figures for the
Asháninka, who are a people spread over an area not unlike that of the Harakmbut, we find an estimated pre-contact population density of between 1.2 and 1.7
pp/km2. This is perhaps low for the Harakmbut considering how many Toyeri
are supposed to have lived by the main Madre de Dios river on the more pop-
ulated flood plains. However if we take 1.5 pp/km2 and multiply it by the 20,000
km2 of pre-contact Harakmbut territory, we reach the figure of 30,000.

150 people who live in two groups, one about two hundred yards downstream from the other. The annual increase in population is about 10 percent (including newcomers from other communities). The death rate is about 4 percent and the infant mortality rate is 25 percent. Little by little the Harakmbut are beginning to increase in number and now constitute the majority of permanent residents in the Province of Manu.

Another important demographic factor in San José is the proportion of women to men, and this has not changed since 1981. Out of 128 people in the community, eighty-five are men. Of thirty-five adult men, nineteen are married. Five of the sixteen unmarried were unable to find a second wife after losing their first. The result is an acute gender imbalance (see also Rummenhöller 1987 for parallel figures). There is a similar problem in Boca Inambari and Barranco Chico but not in Puerto Luz and Shintuya where the ratio of women to men is more equal. According to Holzmann (1951/6:xxxv:65), when the Dominicans first reached Harakmbut territory in the 1940s, the Sapiteri men complained of a lack of women. It is not easy to ascertain the reason for this phenomenon. Evidence for female infanticide is unclear, although it was almost certainly carried out in the past (Moore personal communication). The practice now seems to have completely disappeared, yet, even without female infanticide, there are still more women than men. There would appear to be no single reason behind this scarcity and it is probably best seen as one of the contingencies of Harakmbut demographic history.

San José Today

During the period we were in San José, the Peruvian gold rush was at its height. At one time, over five hundred workers were illegally mining for patrons within the boundaries of the community. Shootings at Boca Colorado where the Banco Minero was situated were regular events. Arakmbut were threatened and even killed. Gold prospectors would bring young men and children down from the Andes and force them to work at their placers.

The Arakmbut were convinced that the recognition of titles to their territory was fundamental for the survival of the community. The lands were first mapped in 1979 but the government of Belaúnde froze all titling. The Arakmbut fought for their rights, and in 1986 the Arakmbut of San José del Karene received official recognition of their territorial titles. This was a major achievement not only for San José but for several other Arakmbut communities, and was the culmination of over ten years' struggle for land rights.

Since 1985 the community has had its own school run by lay missionaries. The complicated interrelationship between the school and the community is the focus of another study (Aikman 1994). Between 1980 and 1992 there were several changes in the community, all of which took place within the framework outlined in this book. The details of how these changes took place and the reasons behind them are the subject of the second volume in this trilogy.

There have been some cases of Arakmbut bringing highlanders into the village to work for them, and gold work has expanded. However, the economic crisis in the country and the drop in the price of gold mean that the Arakmbut will never become wealthy on the basis of gold.

PART I

We live lives based upon selected fictions. Our view of reality is conditioned by our position in space and time – not by our personalities as we like to think. Thus every interpretation of reality is based upon a unique position. Two paces east or west and the whole picture is changed.

From the writings of Pursewarden, *Balthazar*, Laurence Durrell

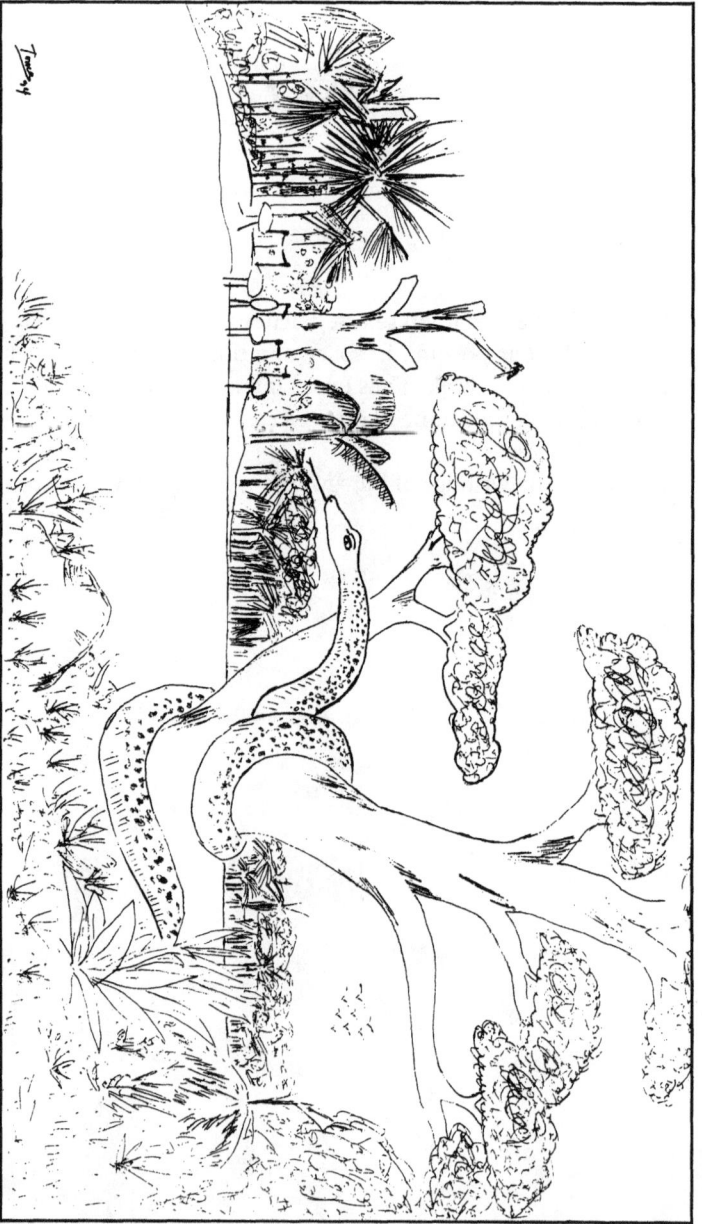

Then the plant of Wanamey began to grow. The tree sprang up.

Drawing: Tomás Arique

PREFACE
Myth and Relativity

When we had been in San José for one year, I began to talk to the Arakmbut about what I should write on my return. I asked them how I should retell the things that they had told me. At various times during our stay, people had referred to the importance of three myths: Wanamey, the Tree of Salvation; Marinke, the Culture Hero; and Aiwe, who escaped from the Papa. Clearly, these three stories had a fundamental significance for the Arakmbut. One day, I stopped and chatted with a young man who said: 'Wanamey, Marinke and Papa: when you understand these stories you understand us'.

Those words have remained with me ever since. Initially I took them literally and analysed the stories. The analytical interpretations of the myths that introduce each part of this book illustrate how the stories relate to fundamental Arakmbut ideas and values. In 1985, I translated my interpretation of Wanamey for a group of Arakmbut. The general opinion was: 'This is not wrong, but it is not how we say it'. This is probably a familiar response of indigenous peoples on reading anthropological analyses. I returned to Europe and pondered the fact that I had understood the myth in my terms but not in theirs. The easiest way out would have been to take an emic/etic or anthropological/native model distinction and resolve our different perspectives that way. But this would remove the significance of the myths for the Arakmbut.

The analysis of a myth, whether in terms of its structure or its imagery, is in itself an exegesis. As outsiders we need to make sense of the myth by unravelling elements which for the Arakmbut make perfect sense as they stand. For me, understanding Arakmbut myths involved breaking down the events in the story onto a 'meta-mythological' level, providing a textual commentary after the myth had been spoken. For the Arakmbut on the other hand, the meaning of a myth lies at the moment of its telling. The moment of the reproduction of the myth's framework and the production of idiosyncratic embellishments is sufficient exegesis for the Arakmbut. The meaning lies in the myth itself.

We are unable to start to understand the connotations of a myth because we know nothing of Arakmbut social and cultural life from the inside. An exegesis is therefore necessary for us first, before we can begin to make sense of the myth in its own terms. We intellectualise the myth, which is a procedure alien to the Arakmbut. They approach the myth in the opposite way. The myth itself is a reflection of their experience, and it makes sense because it fits in with their view of the world. For them a meaningful understanding of the myth does not lie in an exegetical analysis but in a response such as 'ah!' or 'ha!'

The multiple dimensions of Arakmbut myths reflect Kirk's (1974:7) statement that 'there is no one definition of myth ... [they] differ enormously in their morphology and social function'. Not all Arakmbut myths are like the three examples presented in this book. Many are short stories, reflections on events, or detailed explanations of the universe.

Anthropologists have reflected on mythology from many different angles, all of which can be applied to the Arakmbut. Malinowski's myths as social charters, providing models of and models for social and cultural life, are clearly visible in the three main myths. Lévi-Strauss's mythic structures also emerge when we look at the myths. The contrasts and distinctions, while they may not be 'opposites' in a structuralist sense, certainly contribute to the forging of indigenous philosophies of existence, commenting on imponderable notions such as life, death, order, chaos and the purpose of life. My particular interest in this book, however, has not been to adhere to any one approach but to see how Arakmbut myths reflect and influence experience.

Myths are important for the Arakmbut because they reflect a multidimensional view of life. The three myths presented in this book resound throughout Arakmbut social and cultural existence. The images are powerful and the Arakmbut treat them with considerable respect. Arakmbut myths are a commentary on existence shared by the people themselves, distinguishing their views on life clearly from those of others. They are consequently an important element of Arakmbut identity. The variety of versions make distinctions marking the collective experience from those of neighbouring peoples.

Experience is a relationship between people and their socio-cultural worlds, which can take the form of actions, images, and interpretations. We may never be able to encapsulate that experience as an objective reality, yet it can never be so completely subjective that it cannot be shared or interpreted with others. Experience is thus relative to the person or persons who express their perspective on the world. For the Arakmbut, myth places this experience in a context.

As Arakmbut life changes, with more gold work and relationships with the national society, the connection between myth and experience must shift as well. Arakmbut social and cultural life reflects myth telling. People can change and manipulate the existing order, making embellishments, alterations or new philosophies. Furthermore, the myths are also influenced from the outside. These may come from the ethnocidal activities of those who would devalue Arakmbut views of the world, from the physical invasions of colonists onto their lands or even philosophical conversations with outsiders such as anthropologists. As Arakmbut life experiences change, the myths transform. In certain cases they can become irrelevant or boring and will consequently be told less frequently.

The three main Arakmbut myths are frequently described by old men as following a basic triadic structural framework consisting of three parts known as words – *wa'a* (cf. Califano 1978b). The three parts are: *wakuru wa'a, wanopo wa'a* and *aia wa'a* – primary word, central word and whole word. Each part can stand on its own as a story or else fit into the overall framework of the narrative.

However the Arakmbut can take out episodes from their myths and tell them in passing. Particular episodes are frequently embellished and made to relate to other aspects of Arakmbut cultural activity. For example there are songs associated with the myth of Wanamey and in some versions of Marinke there are optional discussions of initiation rituals. Furthermore songs and curing orations occasionally refer to these myths.

Arakmbut myths can be seen not only as a linear narrative telling a long tale, but also as mythical 'cycles' that contain within them a number of different interrelated stories. Whereas the myths can be broken up and expanded, one aspect of myth telling cannot be changed – the sequence of events. Prior to telling the whole myth, a performer will spend up to a day running through the correct order. The effectiveness of this form of preserving the mythical 'text' is very apparent when comparing the version of Marinke (chapter five) that I heard in San José with the version collected in Shintuya over ten years earlier by Mario Califano. Apart from one episode that was removed because it refers to initiation rites that are no longer practised, the sequences and content of the events described are practically identical (Califano op.cit.).

Each section of a myth is thus independent, yet it also fits into a narrative sequence. However, the sequence also provides different ways of looking at the world by the use of imagery. The myth is, therefore, at the same time a narrative structure and a multidimensional way of approaching questions of common concern such as birth, growth and death. The mutual effect of myth and experience parallels the counterpoint between stability and change, creativity and perpetuation, survival and destruction, ideals and actual events, which provides a dialectical tension pervading Arakmbut life.

Perspectival relativity has been reported throughout the Amazon. Transformations between humans, spirits and animals frequently involve looking at the world from completely different angles (Weiss 1969, Crocker 1985). This relativity is encountered not only in the invisible world of the spirits, but throughout Arakmbut life. Wherever you stand in the community the world looks different. This does not imply that the Arakmbut world is one where process determines all and nothing is fixed. This anarchic perspective is too extreme. The effect would reduce all forms of reproduction to production and limit the reflective aspect of history to action. Neither the productive event nor the reproductive structure has a determining role in this world.

Just as with myths, there are relativistic perspectives of social and cultural phenomena within the community, demonstrating the open-ended nature of life among the Arakmbut. People do not have fixed identities but multiple elements, which they use according to the context. Each person constantly shifts and changes his or her position within the Arakmbut social formation and uses cultural means to indicate who and where he or she is. A person is simultaneously identified in relation to others by gender, age, residence, relationship term, clan or cognatic category. Simply by occupying space in a community people change it. Society is constant movement, both physical and social, which means a process of defining and redefining the community through time as perspectives change.

The notion of perspectival relativity is a starting point for breaking away from too sharp an opposition between structure and process. Relativity is an irreducible notion that cannot be used to explain anything; therefore I hope to avoid any reductionist explanations of the Arakmbut in terms of structures, production, language, individual action, or social and cultural processes.

There is a tendency in anthropological writing to overlook the 'excluded middle', reducing phenomena to one of two options. For example, 'society' exists or else it does not; people are either 'authentic' or 'acculturated', the world is either 'static' and 'mythological' or 'dynamic' and 'historical'. My approach in this book is to use these concepts not as parts of an analysis based on mutually exclusive categories but as tools for producing metaphors (Ricoeur 1978:7) in order to illuminate a perspective of the Arakmbut that has emerged out of a dialogue between them and me on the periphery of our respective worlds.

The epistemological status of these metaphors, however, is vague. They neither provide an analysis that can explain the Arakmbut, nor do they deliver a glimpse into a 'reality' that we do not know. Yet they cannot be completely imaginary either, or they would make no sense to the Arakmbut. The presentation here is metaphorical in the sense that it is sceptical of providing any absolute 'truth' or 'reality', while on the other hand it is not completely imaginary either.

Apart from their epistemological aspects, Arakmbut myth takes us into an ontological realm covering areas of existence that recur throughout this volume. Myths take place in a landscape that shares the geographical layout of Arakmbut territory, yet the events described are clearly impossible in the visible world of everyday life. The stories connect the listener with the invisible spirit world where everyday expectations of time and space are suspended, animals and humans change forms, and life-force is malleable. The invisible spirits provide the visible world with life, which constantly needs regeneration, and through recounting myths, the Arakmbut recreate the conditions by which their existence takes on meaning and provides them with a basic understanding of their universe. In the absence of ceremonies and public rituals, the Arakmbut use myth to recreate the mysteries of the invisible world for the entertainment and well-being of their people. Myth is an appropriate starting point for entering the Arakmbut world, because it provides a pillar of spirituality that is available to all people. It is not my intention in these volumes to reveal secrets (the Arakmbut would not have mentioned them to me anyway), but to orient the reader in Arakmbut culture and hopefully arouse respect and admiration for those aspects of Arakmbut social and cultural life that are accessible to those of us at the periphery of their world.

Each section of the book starts by establishing the the mythological background for social and cultural activities among the Arakmbut. The subsequent chapters do not reflect a notion of myth as a detailed charter of dogmatic structural principles, but rather use myth as an opening for discussions of topics embedded within the myth, such as gender, age, residence, clan affiliation, terminological relationships, the person, the life cycle, the invisible world, and history; as a framework in the sense of flexible sets of parameters that people use in their daily lives. The concatenation and individuation of each person in relation to these criteria constitute different elements of personhood and sociality. The Arakmbut world is not a complete flux, but comprises clusters of shared meanings and experiences that shift in significance depending on a person's position.

The first section of the book takes the myth of Wanamey as a starting point. After looking at the myth in its own terms, the section moves onto the areas within Arakmbut life that are connected to its main themes. These are the clusters of shared values such as those mentioned above. The myth thus does not constitute a closed system but has reverberations that are felt throughout Arakmbut social and cultural life. As the myth ends on the foundation of Arakmbut society and the origin of the basic pursuits, these constitute the subject matter of the first part.

After the evening meal the people of San José set out their reed mats on the ground. The old man who is about to tell the story sits near the men while the women and children remain a little way off. The moonlight and the feeling of expectancy create a poignant atmosphere, tempered by the relaxed lounging figures.

The story-teller guides the listeners through the myth. They do not listen in silence but make observations and additions, and join in the jokes and sound effects. The tale follows the basic pattern, but it is up to the teller to vary the rhythm and timbre. The occasional embellishments add to the general effect of a recreational entertainment, which is appreciated above all for its aesthetic appeal and moral reinforcement. He begins.

Chapter 1

DEATH AND SALVATION

The Story of Wanamey

Wakuru Wa'a. The 'first word' – section.[1]

(1) It is said that there was once a flood of fire. Flames of fire came. There were tremendous flames. The fire came from downriver (*toyudn*) to upriver (*kutayon*).

But before this happened, whenever the Arakmbut put food to their mouth it tasted bitter. All food was bitter (*painda*).

At that time, all the animals came to where the Arakmbut people lived. They were tame and entered where all the people were. Then all those men called Wayeri or *Taka* – those who attack people – came too, with the news that they had caught a glimpse of an approaching fire. A mass of fiery flames was burning all stones, trees, and earth. Everything was burning. The warlike people from downriver appeared peaceful to the Arakmbut from upriver. At the time when the fire came to burn everything, all the families and all the Arakmbut received those Taka, who were really bad people, with affection.

Then, when the fire reached nearby, all the large animals tasted bitter. The water too turned bitter. Then came rain. It did not rain as

---

1.   The three sections are divisions that the Arakmbut make. The numbered episodes are my divisions for the convenience of making clearer references. I have separated paragraphs to reflect the narrative breaks that occur in a performance. These are usually punctuated by the word '*kenta*'.

now, but there fell a type of blood. All the time downriver like a horizon they could see the smoke. Smoke rose.

(2) When it appeared far off there came a species of parrot *(ndariyoke-wakewa)*. The bird appeared, bringing in its beak a piece of apple, light red in colour. This was the fruit of Wanamey. The people did not know why this bird had come. It passed over the community. When it saw a young girl *(muneyo)* it would descend and touch her with its wings. But the fruit did not drop.

The people thought that this species of bird must be bringing some means for saving them. It seemed to the people that the bird wanted to leave the fruit in its beak with a girl. 'What can we do?' asked the people. The old men said that they must lay out a girl face up and with her legs apart. Then they tried this with a girl, but she had already had relations with her husband. For this reason the fruit did not drop. In this way, the bird twice more wanted to drop the fruit. But it did not drop, because the girl had had sexual relations. Therefore the piece of apple did not drop from the bird that had brought it.

After various girls came and lay down, one from the Singperi clan came and lay down. The bird descended. The fruit fell. In the same place where it fell it hit the girl in the vagina. Then the plant of Wanamey began to grow. The tree sprang up. Wanamey arose with the girl at the same time as the burning fire was approaching. The people called the tree Wanamey. The name means 'the tree which saved our people; the tree of salvation'.

Wanopo wa'a. The 'central word' – middle section.

(3) The Arakmbut said to the tree, 'Can you lower yourself to our height?' and the tree came down. They said to each other, 'As it is going to grow higher to the sky again, we have to climb this tree.' When it was near, many of the people climbed up, but some were left and had to jump. The men could jump but the women could not.

Then there was a girl and her brother. The girl could not jump. The tree did not reach the ground. The brother was up in the tree. The brother said, 'I am full of grief for my sister. She must come up first.' He grabbed an arm and pulled and saved her. But he wanted to save another so that he could have sex with her. When he was only just above the flames he leant out and held out his hand for her. But the girl was burnt. He only saved her arm. So for this reason he had sexual relations with his sister, which is why we die.

After, when the fire reached right around Wanamey, the tree rose more, higher. From time to time it grew higher, higher. In this way it grew, always growing, growing until it reached a height where the smoke could hardly reach.

(4) And all the things that the people needed, Wanamey provided. For example, because of the smoke, when people could not breathe they cried tears. In the branches there grew something to help the people. This, a mineral, was like a type of plate which they placed on the nose to breathe.

Everyone in Wanamey used it. The people ate all types of provisions. In Wanamey when anyone was hungry they said, 'I am hungry' and the tree gave things such as plantains, manioc, sugar cane and water too. They had everything there. Everything. When the people were tired, they asked Wanamey for a bed. They were shown a place and made a bed in the branches.

All the animals went up into this tree. Miraculously all types of snake, jaguar, peccary, and tapir, all species of animals were in the tree. There was a person who thought that a snake had bitten him. He took the snake and threw it out of the tree into the fire. Then Wanamey threw out the man from the branches but caught the snake and saved it. The people understood and did not do it again. 'To you people, no animal is dangerous. Animals do nothing to you. The snake does not bite.'

(5) Afterwards, they say that the fire did not reach as far as the trunk of Wanamey. There was an anaconda a few paces away from the tree encircling the trunk. Between the snake and the tree was a well that contained water, which was protected from the fire. In the well *boquichicos* (carp-like fish) swam. The snake covered all the area around the trunk and the fire only reached as far as the circle.

They say that the moment when the fire arrived it grew dark. All was dark. They say that there was night for three months. It was the *e'sikon* (sudden nightfall). There were three months of darkness. They could see nothing.

After three months they heard a cricket. They heard a bird singing 'nes nes – day is coming'. The people began to see a bird in the branches singing 'shuchi shuchi'. The people thought, 'Something is happening, after three months without a day. The bird is advising us like one did before.' It was right. It was right. The day was indeed beginning to come. It was, a little.

The leaves of Wanamey, transparent in the light, appeared more clearly. As it began to dawn, the day followed and it was possible to see everything. The leaves of Wanamey were different colours – black, yellow and red. It became clear that all the leaves were birds. The black leaves were black orioles, guans and turkey hens – one white-crested and the other the wood species. The green leaves were the big-headed macaw and the blue and yellow macaw. The red leaves were the red and blue macaws. Then they could see all the animals below them in the tree.

As the light increased, all the parrots began to sing and screech. As the light increased, all the animals began to cry out. They could hear the peccaries at the top of the roots crying out. The roots of Wanamey came out of the sides of the trunk above the ground.

(6) Already it was day. The people asked the tree to go down and it did so. It descended. The people said, 'Let's throw down a stick (*waepa*).' They threw one down and it disappeared into the mud. It did not remain in the ground and the people said that the earth was not yet hard enough. They threw down another stick, and this time a small part of it appeared above the mud. And the people said, 'Little by little it is hardening.' They threw a third stick and it was half visible above the mud. And the people said, 'It is getting harder.' They were pleased.

They waited a while and threw another stick and it was firm. It remained above the earth. The ground was hard. But it was only hard around the tree. Not all the ground was hard. The people told the tree to go down further and it did. All the people went down from Wanamey thinking that the land was firm. But it was not firm and some sank into the mud. Then almost everyone sank into the mud and was destroyed.

Two remained. A brother and sister remained. There were only two of them. They had to have sexual relations. Their sexual relations were the origin of all death. If all the people who had gone up the tree had remained we would not die now. In a while the tree of Wanamey disappeared under the ground. The tree went right below the earth – a long way down. The brother and sister remained with their family above the ground.

They say that at the end of the world Wanamey is going to rise again to save the Harakmbut.

Aiya wa'a. The 'whole word' – the final section.

(7) Then the couple and their family were hungry, and the wood-pecker (*Mbegnko*) arrived. They said to him, 'Do you know where

there is fire?' The bird answered that there was fire in the house of Toto (a harmful spirit) and that he was going to steal the fire.

The woodpecker went to the house of Toto and entered. He said to Toto, 'All the world has burnt.' When Toto was distracted the woodpecker snatched up the *paipi* (stick for making fire) in its beak and left with it still burning as he ran. He returned carrying the fire to where the brother and sister were waiting. First the woodpecker put it on a tall tree, then he landed on a lower tree of achiote (*mantaro*) which ever afterwards has red pods because of the flame. From there, he threw the fire onto the man's shoulder. The man brushed it off onto the ground and there was fire.

Toto cursed the woodpecker. Since then woodpeckers have not flown like other birds but always fly with wings crossed. As the woodpecker flew from Toto's house the spirit grabbed at him, which is why woodpeckers always have a white mark on their bodies. All this is because of the curse of Toto. The woodpecker handed over the fire to the man. The people made fire.

(8) And they wanted water. The water that had been at the foot of Wanamey had disappeared with the tree. Before, when the tree was descending, there was an isula ant in the branches that leapt into the mud. As it ran its sting made furrows in the ground, which made the shape of river beds and channels. Now the man who had survived the descent of Wanamey said, 'Who will put water there?'

A dragonfly arrived and said, 'Around here where I put my tail there is water.' He urinated in the ground and in the places where he put his tail, water appeared and rivers emerged. All the rivers appeared: Ishiriwe, Karene, Inambari, Tambopata, and Madre de Dios. Also there were countless other rivers, lakes, and streams.

(9) They say that there was a tree like the peach palm called *singpa*. Under this tree appeared an egg. The egg turned into a small child. The woodpecker returned again and said: 'I will give the name to him and his people. I will call them Singperi.' In this way he gave the name.

They say that there was another palm tree called *yaro*. Under this tree there also appeared an egg. This egg turned into a child and the woodpecker named him and his people Yaromba.

Then there appeared a large type of oriole called *mbedntoktok*. It carried an egg which produced a person. He and his people the woodpecker named Masenawa.

The leaf from Wanamey which had turned into the white-crested turkey hen (*owing*) now arrived and was itself converted into a person. He and his people the woodpecker named Idnsikambo.

Then there was a swarm of wasps (*wawa*) which became a person. The woodpecker named him and his people Wandigpana.

Then a hanging creeper (*embi*) appeared. This became a person and the woodpecker named him and his people Embieri.

Finally a child went to where Wanamey had disappeared under the ground and reappeared with a collared peccary (*mokas*). The woodpecker named him and his people Saweron.

(10) By this time there were too many people, because the family of the brother and sister had increased. For this reason the woodpecker divided them into different groups. Singperi, Yaromba, Masenawa, Idnsikambo, Wandigpana, Embieri, and Saweron were their names. After giving names to each of these, the woodpecker told them whom they could marry.

Afterwards, the people went down the rivers and each one found a place where they wanted to live. In these places the groups remained on the banks of the rivers.

(11) The woodpecker returned for the last time. The land was flat and level. Because of this the bird made mountains, hills, and high and low ground. With the hills and mountains all was complete. The people said, 'Let us make axes and arrows to make gardens and to hunt.'

At this point the story of Wanamey ends.

–Told by Ireyo in San José, 1980

The myth of Wanamey centres around the notion of *o'chimuyate*, which means 'it was born'. The three sections correspond to different aspects of creation. In the myth, creation is the synthesis or resolution of extremes by means of a go-between or mediator. The first two sections of Wanamey consist of a representation of these extremes while the third tells of the activities of the mediator.

The myth shares several images with some of the origin myths of Judaeo-Christianity. Familiar references to 'apples', 'trees of life', 'salvation' and 'flood' show the influence of missionaries. However, these expressions make no difference to the basic meaning of the Harakmbut myth, which could hardly be more different from its Christian counterparts. When such images appear, they do so more in the form of comparisons or similes than as integral parts of the myth itself.

The content of Wanamey is an account of the origins of Arakmbut society and culture as a prototype of creation and as a 'charter'.

This information is expressed through a set of relationships that reproduces a framework for many aspects of Arakmbut social thought and action.

A fundamental distinction in the myth of Wanamey is between chaos (*menpa nopwewe* – disorder/something incredible) and order (*ndaka e'mae* -everything is fine). The narrative passes from the representation of one to the creation of the other. It begins in an upside-down world in which the events of the story are inversions of what is normal for the Arakmbut. Distinctions that are clear-cut in everyday life become blurred and in some cases cease to exist.

In the first episode a flood comes; but in this case it is a flood of fire. Like the flood of a river, the fire is destructive, but unlike water it comes from downriver to upriver. Usually a flood belongs to the river while a fire belongs to the land. At the time of chaos the distinction between river and land disappears.

As the fire approaches, all the forest animals come to the house. This is an inversion of the normal state of affairs when forest animals keep away from the house and are not at all tame. In the myth, the Taka (called enemies in the story but who are usually all non-Arakmbut) come to the communal houses and are received in friendship. This is a disordered version of the Taka's usual mythological role, which portrays them as warriors who attack houses, kill men, and steal women (see chapter ten).

Furthermore, the story says that it rained blood. Normally blood is inside the body but in this case it appears outside. The fire destroys everything indiscriminately. The flames burn pebbles, earth, and other things that cannot be harmed by an ordinary conflagration.

These examples of chaos in the first episode of Wanamey display a breakdown of the normal categories of organisation in the Arakmbut world. In addition to these inversions there are several events in the account of the fiery flood that are in direct contrast to that of the time spent in the tree Wanamey later in the story. These distinctions are intrinsic to the myth itself.

The first section tells of the burning flood. This is in contrast to the 'long night/sudden night' spent in the tree later in the story. This distinction is most clearly expressed in the description of the food available to the people at these times.

The Arakmbut define food according to taste. There are four tastes:

(1) *painda* means bitter and describes salt, tobacco, ayahuasca, as well as lemon, garlic and chili;

(2) *hotnda* means rich or tasty and describes cooked meat;

(3) *haiya* means tasteless or bland and describes food such as yuca and plantains as well as water;

(4) *setnda* means sweet or rotten, and describes sweets, sugar cane, papayas, and other fruit.

During the flood, both food (specifically the larger animals) and water taste bitter on account of the close proximity of the fire and smoke. In cooking, the Arakmbut either smoke meat or boil it. When it is smoked the meat is placed on a small frame above a fire over the smoke. The meat tastes bitter after smoking unless it is boiled. The bitterness of the food and meat in the first part of Wanamey are related to an excess of smoking by the fire.

In the tree when the people are hungry, they are provided with yuca, plantains, sugar cane, and water. These are either bland-tasting or sweet. Their cooking does not usually involve the close proximity of smoke and fire, as they are either boiled or, in the case of fruit, eaten without preparation. A principal food was *sipikutapa*, which was a plant eaten without cooking. The foods available to the people in Wanamey reflect the absence of fire during the long night. The darkness and the pool of water encircled by the anaconda at the roots of the tree give further emphasis to the lack of fire. Furthermore, Wanamey provides a 'mineral' to prevent smoke from getting too close. Some Arakmbut describe this as a screen that went around the whole tree.

It is possible to see Wanamey, the tree, rather like something which is being boiled. The fire is limited by an encircling object (in this case the anaconda), within which there is water. Wanamey stands in this water in the same way that food is placed in a pot of water for boiling. Thus in the first section of Wanamey, fire is put in direct contact with food, as in smoking, while in the second section fire is separate from the food, as in boiling. In the former case the excess of fire leads to over-cooking when the food tastes bitter, and in the latter the lack of fire leads to under-cooking and bland, sweet or rotten-tasting food.[2] There is more evidence to demonstrate that the time spent in Wanamey is a period when food is undercooked. Some Arakmbut say that in the tree the people had to heat the food up under their armpits as they could not cook it. This stopped it becoming bitter. Parallel with the distinctions between smoking and

2. Lévi-Strauss (1973:416) says: 'The long night described by so many South American myths certainly refers to the rotten world, just as myths about universal fire refer to the burnt world.'

boiling, over- and under-cooking, and bitter and sweet tastes is the division between 'dry' and 'wet', which is of great importance in Arakmbut culture and which will appear frequently in this work.

Cooking, eating, and types of food are important metaphors in the myth because each one is a crucial semantic feature of Arakmbut cultural expression. These images also refer to relations of conjunction in the first section of the myth and disjunction in the second, which are resolved in the complementarity and mediation of the final section, namely in the accounts of the origins of fire and water. What we could say is that the cooking of the tree is the cooking of humanity, which brings us to the second important image in the myth.

The relations between the sexes and their various transformations correspond to the cooking analogies in Wanamey. Sexual activity features several times and is intimately connected with the fate of the Arakmbut. In the second episode the parrot appears from afar with the fruit from which Wanamey will grow. The description of the impregnation of the Singperi girl is clearly sexual. The parrot, who takes the role of the male, comes from outside to inside the community. This is an inversion of usual sexual practices where it is the woman, if either of the partners, who comes from outside. In this account of sexual relations there are aspects of excess and the conjunction of normally disparate categories, which we saw earlier in the description of the fiery flood. The bird is not transformed into a human for the purpose of sexual relations as occurs in other stories, but remains in its original state. In this way the relationship is far more than a usual inter-community alliance because it is an alliance with a non-human.

Although a male Arakmbut normally impregnates a woman from above, the bird actually comes down to earth from the sky, joining two usually distinct categories. We have already seen that the earth and river were indistinguishable in the first episode; now the sky too is no longer truly a separate domain from the world below. The Arakmbut seem to adhere to Tylor's adage 'marry out or die out' because it is through this special example of marrying out that the tree of Wanamey arises, which saves the Arakmbut and provides them with life.

Yet too-close sexual relations can also be dangerous. In the third episode a marriageable woman is separated from her potential partner because she could not reach the branches in time. The couple who remain in the tree are brother and sister, and thus forbidden to marry. The contiguity or conjunction from disparate elements, which we noted in the episode between the parrot and the Singperi girl from which the tree grew, is here contrasted by the close relationship between brother and sister. The conjunction of male and female who are distantly related means life and survival and, as we shall see, the corollary of this holds too: namely that very close relationships between kin threaten the continuance of life.

While the rise of Wanamey signifies growth and life, in the sixth episode of the myth the descent from the tree means death for nearly all the Arakmbut. A man throws down the sticks to test the depth of the boiling mud and the people make the mistake of thinking that all the earth has hardened whereas only a small area around the tree is safe. They disappear into the mud and die.[3]

Death as an inevitability originates with a sexual act performed by the brother and sister who survive the drowning. This is the first example of human sexual relations in the story. The relationship between the brother and sister is too close. It was noted above that very close relationships between kin threaten the continuance of life, so the origin of eventual death for all people is aptly expressed in a prohibited sexual act.

Sexual imagery appears twice in the myth, in the form of parentheses to the 'rise and fall' of Wanamey. In the first case, the tree rises and provides the people with life as a result of the conjunction of disparate male and female elements. Sociologically this union is too distant to be conceived as occurring within the Arakmbut people; rather, it is between someone inside and someone outside. In the second case, the tree descends while men and women who are too

3. In some versions of the myth, the man who throws down the sticks for testing is a toad who is intimately connected with sorcery (see Califano 1978a:411). Other versions of the myth of Wanamey (such as Alvarez, J. 1956/7:210) mention the origin of the Amiko at this point. They are people who are not Arakmbut and who are usually depicted as highlanders or other colonists. They emerge from the foot of the tree, from a place under the ground. These versions relate the destruction of almost all humanity to the beginnings of sorcery and colonisation. The version of Wanamey described here is an Arakmbut version from one village in particular. There are differences in the Arasaeri version (Aza 1936) and what is either a Wachipaeri or Toyeri version (Alvarez J. 1956/7 and also Barriales & Torralba 1970). The Califano references in his 1977 and 1978 papers combine some Wachipaeri, Sapiteri and Kipodneri Arakmbut themes. Tripp's field notes (1963) give another version of Wanamey which comes from Puerto Alegre (now Puerto Luz). There are substantial differences between these versions but there is no space here to set them all out and compare them. The Arasaeri and Wachipaeri make fewer references to the clans in their Wanamey myths. There are differences between the San José and Puerto Luz versions but these are less obvious. The myth alters to a lesser extent between individuals and clans in the same community than between communities, and there is far more variety between the versions of the different Harakmbut peoples.

closely related join together sexually. The result is death. One act is excessively distant whereas the other is excessively close. There two extremes are resolved in the complementarity and mediation of the final section; namely in the account of the origin of Arakmbut society and in particular marriage rules.[4] (A supplementary account of death is sometimes included here where the oriole (mbedntoktok) tries to confer immortality on the Arakmbut but stutters 'pok-pok-pok'. However the rat (*takui*) enters and speaks the word, ruining humankind's chances of immortality.)

In the first section of Wanamey there is a representation of chaos in which phenomena that are usually conceived of as being apart are thrown together. The second part, encapsulated within the parameters of the two examples of sexuality mentioned above, separates these phenomena once again. As the tree rises, the different geographical domains of the world (river, forest, and sky) are distinguished, as are the animals that live in them. This arrangement is apparent in the description of the tree Wanamey itself set out in the fifth episode.

At the base of the tree are the roots (*waiwit*) which buttress the trunk (*wamey*). Between the roots there is a pool of water where fish swim safely in the encircling boundary of the anaconda. Above, in the branches (*wachopi*), there are animals and humans. These creatures usually share the domain of the land. In the tree they live together in peace because no creature is carnivorous. Men hunt no meat and animals never bite humans. This emphasises the bland and sweet diet to which people are restricted while in the branches of Wanamey. Even higher we find that the leaves (*waemba*) of Wanamey are in fact birds. The realm of the sky is the uppermost part of the tree.

The three vertical divisions relate to the three divisions of the cosmos and the animals that live there. This prototype of order can be seen as follows:

leaf: birds: sky
branch: Arakmbut & animals: forest
root: fish: river

The unifying factor of the tree is the trunk, which connects the three domains and the creatures found there. The chaos in the first

---

4. When describing the myth I have used the word society deliberately in relation to the term Arakmbut, which means people. 'Arakmbut' means both human being and social and cultural existence as human beings. It is a word that is more loaded in Arakmbut terms than the word 'people' in English. For those who might comment that Arakmbut society does not exist, I would suggest they consider the possibility that its meaning lies embedded in the word Arakmbut itself.

section has been replaced during the 'long night' by a static tableau representing the three major domains and types of creatures in the world all within the framework of the structure of the tree.[5] The over-dynamism presented in the first section of the myth constitutes the chaos of uncontrolled life, which could be termed 'process', while the static scene in the section is 'structure'. From this interpretation it is possible to see Wanamey as a comment on the importance of balancing the relationship between change and tradition, process and structure, and also history and myth.

Table 1.1 shows several aspects of the first two sections of Wanamey, which can be contrasted in order to understand the resolving and mediating aspects of the third section of the myth.

Table 1.1 Contrasts between the first two sections of the myth

1) **Cooking**	**First Section**	**Second Section**
	Excess cooking	Undercooking
	Fire in direct contact with meat	Fire not in direct contact with meat
	Dry cooking	Wet cooking
	Smoking analogy	Boiling analogy
	Meat tastes bitter	Crops taste sweet/bland
2) **Sexual Relations**	**First Section**	**Second Section**
	Too distant	Too close
	Exogamous	Endogamous
	Approved relationship	Prohibited relationship
	Between inside and outside society	Within society
	Wanamey rises	Wanamey descends
	People are saved – life	People drown – death

5. Roe (1982:136–62) demonstrates the frequency with which the image of the 'world tree' appears throughout Amazonia. In south and southeastern Peru, the image of a tree similar in some respects to Wanamey appears most of the other indigenous peoples.

The Panoan Shipibo (Morin 1973) see the *huito* as the tree of life, which saved a man from a great flood on the advice of the Inca's son. Another Panoan people, the Cashinahua (d'Ans 1975:94–5), tell of a man who saved himself from a flood by climbing a gigantic tree. Aza (1930) says that the Huarayos (Ese'eja) tell of a flood of fire that destroyed all trees except one with spines on its trunk.

The Arawak peoples mention trees that are mythologically significant but that do not play any part in a primeval cataclysm. The Asháninka (Weiss 1969:

3) **General Points**	**First Section**	**Second Section**
	Day/light	Night/dark
	Conjunction of categories: river/forest/sky	Disjunction of categories: river/forest/sky
	Dynamic state of flux	In the tree a static state of suspended animation
	Exaggeration of Process	Exaggeration of Structure

The third section of Wanamey tells first of the origins of fire and water, which relate to the culinary practices we noted in the previous section in the same way that the origins of the clans relate to the sexual episodes earlier in the myth. Although these are origins they do not introduce new elements into the story. There were human beings before the cataclysm, and birds and animals as well. In fact, in the first part a girl is actually called 'Singperi', even though this clan is not named until much later in the story. Origins for the Arakmbut are not beginnings from nothing, but are transformations of the way in which elements relate to each other.

Most of the transformations in the final section of Wanamey are made by the woodpecker, who not only mediates between sky and earth but also between the visible and invisible worlds. An interesting feature of the woodpecker is his name (Mbegnko). The Arakmbut say that Mbegnko has the same name as 'Manko', who is Manco Inca. Manco Inca was reputed to have provided the Arakmbut with maize and chicha and to have taught them the arts of manufacture. Manco and the woodpecker are two aspects of the same phenomenon in that they are both the sources of Arakmbut culture. The Inca does have some similarities to the woodpecker in that he came from the high Andes, which are also half-way between the sky and earth. Other relations between Manco and Mbegnko will be seen in the next chapter.

Chapter VIII) tell of Pachakama, a tree at the world's end identified as an emanation of the all-powerful sun. He is also connected with their culture hero Avieri, who transformed many species of animals and plants into being. The Matsigenka similarly link their culture hero Yabieri with Pachacamue who, after creating natural species and cultural rites ended up staked to the tree at the world's end (Ferrero 1966:389). The Piro tell (Alvarez, R. 1957/8:13–15) of a massive tree inhabited by a race of giants who were overcome by the Piro. When the giants were defeated, all kinds of animals and plants came forth from the tree let out by the woodpecker.

In the seventh episode of Wanamey there is an account of the origin of fire. Fire belongs to Toto, the dangerous spirit or class of spirits, who live in a world different from our own. For human beings, this is an invisible world where souls *(nokiren)* and various types of spirit exist; however, the myth conceptualises the difference between visible and invisible not as different experiential realms but as placed in different geographical locations in the same world. Toto lives far from the cataclysmic fire-flood, but the myth embraces both realms just as in its performance it connects the visible and invisible worlds. The woodpecker tells Toto of the fire-flood as a means of distracting him from his fire. According to the myth, fire is not natural to the world of humans and animals, it is outside their experience. It cannot be made without the knowledge that Toto preserves in his invisible domain.

The woodpecker is the Prometheus of the Arakmbut. He appears as a trickster stealing fire for humans. He does not create fire out of something else, but removes it from the invisible world of the spirits to the visible world of human beings. Mbegnko is the go-between who can transcend the division separating these levels of experience. He is also a spirit but, unlike Toto, is beneficial to the Arakmbut.

The fact that fire is stolen is significant because it shows that there is a tension in the spirit world between those spirits that help humans and those that do not. The episode also tells how communication with spirits is essential for the existence of humanity. Fire is brought from above and dropped onto a man. From this it is possible to see a connection between fire and height as well as dryness. The woodpecker drops the fire on to man's shoulder. This points to the traditional role of man as the fire-maker. In the past, male Arakmbut would rub the *paipi* fire-stick to produce a spark for lighting the fire on which a woman would do her cooking. He must be someone born in the dry season or the fire will not take. The fire that the woodpecker drops is now controlled by man and not of the same uncontrollable nature as the fire-flood. Man asks for fire because he is hungry. Its purpose is to cook and the result of its appearance is culinary activity that avoids the excesses of the earlier metaphors in the myth.

The woodpecker has nothing to do with the origin of water. Without water the Arakmbut could only smoke their food. They do not roast meat and claim that they have never done so. They boil almost everything that is to be consumed immediately, including meat that has been smoked. Fire is useless without water. They relate to each other in that the former is dry and the other wet.

The isula ant (tagnpi) – which literally means 'fire-sting' – forms the courses of the rivers and streams with his sharp sting while the mud is still soft. Water comes later from the dragon-fly (*toku*) who puts its tail into the channels. The transformation of urine to water is no doubt based on the image of this insect flying over water and repeatedly diving down to find food. This is an example of how animal behaviour frequently appears in Arakmbut analogies. The myth also depicts water as being lower than fire – another indication of the parallel between low/high and wet/dry.

Whereas the woodpecker plays no part in the origin of water, he establishes a new state of contiguity between the sky and earth when he drops the fire onto the shoulder of man. In the same way the dragon-fly sets up a separate relationship between the sky, and water when it forms the rivers. There appears to be a division in the sky which relates to the forest and river separately. The triadic structure of sky, earth, and river seen in the tree of Wanamey has now been replaced by a duality contrasting forest and river. The excessive conjunction and disjunction of the first two sections have been replaced by a more moderate picture, which contains elements from both parts. The sky in its turn becomes a distant area outside the realm of normal life (see chapters five and ten).

In the final episode of the myth, the woodpecker returns and names the patrilineal clans (*onyu*). Every Arakmbut belongs to one of these groups. There are two aspects to their origin. The first is the appearance of various natural phenomena, both animal and vegetable, and the second the act of naming (*e'ndikka*) by the woodpecker.

The arrangement of the clans reorganises the triadic structure described in Wanamey itself to fit in with the now more important distinction between forest and river noted above. With the exception of the Saweron, which is a special case,[6] the clan names distinguish aspects of the classification. The Singperi and Yaromba are trees and are tied to the ground, the Idnsikambo and Masenawa are birds and so are from the sky, and the Embieri and Wandigpana come from the realm between the two.

While naming the clans, the woodpecker explains to the Arakmbut who they can marry. The basis of all Arakmbut marriage is clan exogamy, and we see how this relates to the other sexual unions in the myth. The relationship between the girl and parrot in the first section is acceptable as exogamy, but is too distant as it is a union between a male from outside and a female from inside human society. The relationship between the brother and sister, on the other

6. The Saweron are considered to share their name with Sapiteri and had their origin from the roots of a tree. This story is similar to the origins of Amiko mentioned by Alvarez in Note 3.

hand, is between humans, but too close. The woodpecker mediates between these extremes. He parallels each social group with a natural phenomenon so that human and non-human features are linked within each person, rather than any person being categorised as one or other of the duality. Each group relates to the other exogamically. Thus the relationship with the non-human world is preserved but diluted; exogamy, which is the key to life, is maintained and at the same time marriage can take place between humans.

The clans are patrilineal, and by naming them the woodpecker shows an association with male gender that we noted in the origin of fire where he gave the fire-stick to the man. Conversely this may account for his absence at the origin of water, which for the Arakmbut is a domain with mainly female associations.

After the people receive their clan names they begin to travel downriver to look for sites where they can live. There are too many to live in the same place so they disperse. The real contrast here is with the initial movement of the fire-flood pushing and forcing people upriver at the outset of the myth. Now the people spread out over the world in a controlled manner. When they reach an appropriate site they settle there in communal houses, which take their names from natural phenomena in the region. Some Arakmbut say that each communal house reputedly contained the male members of only one clan. In this way the distribution of malocas presented a spatial expression of the clan system.

The woodpecker plays no part in the dispersion of mankind as the major clan distinctions have already been made through his naming. He does, however, return for a final time to form the mountains, hills and high places. This is appropriate when we remember his role as go-between linking the sky and earth, as well as his connection with the Inca Manco who came from the highlands.

The characteristics of the landscape are now complete; it remains for the Arakmbut to do something with it. They start to make axes and arrows. The former represent horticultural work in the gardens and the latter hunting. Production comes after the creation of the rest of Arakmbut society and culture, for it is, according to the implication of the myth, the expression and articulation by the people of all that has gone before.

In general terms the myth of Wanamey is a resolution of extremes. After the chaos of the first section where incompatible elements were thrown together and destruction ruled, the tree heralded a 'long night' when everything stopped and a static separation of the main domain of the world took place. A solution appears in the final part, which reorganises and transforms the incompatible elements of the first section and presents a dynamic articulation and rearrangement of the static system of the second section.

The two principal subjects and analogies in the myth are the production, preparation, and consumption of food and the structure and organisation of society with emphasis on sexual relations and their transformation in a social form, namely exogamous marriage between clans. These two areas are very important to the Arakmbut and we will return to them frequently. For an outsider looking at the interaction between structure and process, the myth of Wanamey provides a useful theoretical orientation. Too much emphasis on process obscures structure, leaving chaos (section one), whereas too much emphasis on structure obscures process (section two). The third section presents a world where both exist in an uneasy balance. The work of these volumes is to look more closely at this unstable relationship.

The remaining chapters of the first part of this work will discuss some of the issues raised by the myth of Wanamey. These are: gender, age, residence, patrilineal descent of the clan line, and marriage exchange. It remains to look at each of these in turn to ascertain the way in which the Arakmbut use them as a basis for meaningful and acceptable activity.

∂ Chapter 2 ॐ

GENDER

Social and Cosmological Exchange

For the Arakmbut, gender is more significant as a dynamic principle of social classification and social organisation than as an aspect
of grammar. The physical appearance of men and women has always
been clearly marked. Hairstyles of the two sexes are completely different; whereas traditionally the men wore their hair long and the
women short, now, with the influence from the missions and the
national society, the styles are reversed. In the past, from the waist
down, women wore a bark-cloth skirt called *asuk*. Above the waist
they were often painted in designs that featured a 'V' motif. Men, on
the other hand, went without clothes but their bodies proclaimed their
age status with complex painted designs. Those of a full-grown man
centred around an inverted 'V' motive (see Califano 1982:102–3).
Now these styles of dress and design have been replaced by the ubiq-
uitous shorts for the men and printed skirts for the women.

Two aspects of Arakmbut gender relations illustrate current discussions on the subject. On the one hand, gender is not a fixed dichot-
omy, but a relative notion that shifts according to context. Although
gender is certainly dynamic and plays in important part in the
process of self-identification (Strathern 1988), the contrast is also a
flexible standard based on pre-existing axioms. Gender is not only
created but reproduced.

A second aspect of gender arises in the contrast between complementarity and inequality (Harris 1978:38; Descola 1989; McCallum
1990). Gender among the Arakmbut is ideologically based on relationships of complementarity, although there are, in certain con-

texts, clear inequalities between male and female. In order to understand these discrepancies, a broader view of Arakmbut social life will be necessary (Collier & Rosaldo, 1981:318). Gender is a fundamental distinction among the Arakmbut, which relates to age, residence, clan affiliation and marriage. This chapter is therefore a general introduction to the notion of gender complementarity, which will be developed in later chapters.

Gender in Production

Gender is a fundamental aspect of the division of labour. Certain activities are clearly differentiated and men and women participate in a complementary way, whereas others are as readily performed by a man as a woman. In the division of labour, gender plays an important part in the production, preparation, and consumption of food, and it is here that the complementarity between the sexes is most apparent.

Throughout Arakmbut mythology, the significance of hunting and cooking is marked. In Wanamey, cooking is an important metaphor in the account of the origins of society and culture, and later in this chapter there are two myths which feature dietary practices and food preparation.

Hunting is exclusively a male activity. A hunter is called *wamachunkeri* which refers to the skill of hunting *(e'machunka)*. It is the ambition of every man to be a good hunter because success in the chase brings prestige in several related areas of social life. A skilled hunter has profitable relations with beneficial spirits. These appear to him in dreams telling him where to go and how many animals he can catch. The spirit takes the form of a beautiful woman. Here are two examples:

> I dreamt that a beautiful girl came to this house. She took off her clothes and was full of love for me. She was very beautiful. Then the next day my family and I caught lots of peccary.

> In the gold camp I was listening to records by the group ABBA. Outside the hut the group itself appeared. The girls in the group heard the music and came in. I was shy that they should see me. They were very beautiful and full of love. This next day I killed many monkeys.

Dreams are extremely important for the Arakmbut as a principal means of contact with the invisible spirit world, and they demonstrate how spirits are the point of access to their resources. On the advice of the spirits the hunter goes to look for prey. Hunters say that the wet season is better than the dry for hunting because footsteps are less noisy on damp undergrowth, and the game animals tend to cluster together. Men hunt singly or in small groups from the same clan or affinal clusters. At one time, they say, men had to hunt in groups to protect themselves against the possibility of meeting a jaguar. Nowadays, most men have a shotgun, which makes hunting easier and safer. The only communal hunt is for the white-lipped peccary, which lives in herds of up to one hundred and is best exploited by an organised trip involving most of the men of the community. (Recently there have been no white-lipped peccary in the area as they have migrated to the headwaters of the Pukiri.)

Men hunt a great variety of animals, birds, and fish. What distinguishes hunting from fishing (*e'ka biign*) is not so much the object of pursuit but the method by which it is pursued. Hunting involves the use of the bow and various different types of arrow. Women should not touch arrows and can handle a bow only when they make the string. There are four types of arrow: for small animals, large animals, birds, and fish. Men 'hunt' fish individually but also use bows and arrows on communal fishing expeditions.

In fact, fishing, as opposed to hunting, refers to the use of barbasco *(kumo)*. This is grown in the chacras on high land away from the river. It is a root that produces a white milky juice when pounded and when mixed with the water from a lake or stream deprives the fish of oxygen and forces them to the surface for air. Whereas hunting is better in the wet season, fishing is better during the dry season, when the rivers are lower, the fish are more concentrated together, and the barbasco works well in the shallow water.

Fishing with barbasco is a communal affair. The groups can be either exclusively female or consist of both men and women. There are always some women present when the poison is used. If the fishing expedition is to be a large one involving the whole community, then it will be arranged by one of the men, otherwise the women arrange it among themselves.

The barbasco is dug up from the chacras and taken to a stream or lake. Usually the correct place has been revealed in a dream as with hunting.[1] A good dreamer can tell if the expedition will be success-

---

1. I have only heard examples of fishing dreams from men. Women are reluctant to reveal their dreams. If a woman has a sexual dream the spirit appearing to her is not beneficial. It is one of the signs of the assertion of male perspectives in Arakmbut social life that beautiful women are considered to be beneficial but attractive men very dangerous. This is probably because of their potential to lure women away.

ful. The men pound the root with stones held in their right hand then place the crushed roots into string bags called *wenpu*. The manufacture of these bags is entirely a female pursuit and it occupies much of their available spare time from dawn until dusk. They are made from twine, which comes from a species of setico (*tonko*).

Usually young men or women are responsible for mixing the barbasco with the water of the stream or lake. The older men and those boys who have bows and arrows stand scattered along the bank waiting for the large fish to appear on the surface, while the women armed with machetes follow the milky white dye and dispatch anything that comes their way. Some women said that, in the past, fishing with barbasco was done entirely by women although now both sexes can take part.

The principal distinction here is between large creatures, which are hunted by men with bows and arrows, and small fish, which are killed by women. After the hunt or fishing trip, the catch is taken back to the village where it is prepared for cooking. A large animal such as a tapir or peccary is cut up into joints by the men while the women take out the innards and wash them in the river. Anatomically the joints are seen as the dry parts of the body and the innards the wet. The innards of smaller creatures are discarded.

The joints are then distributed by the women to other households. Part of the flesh is kept for the use of the household, but most of it is given to neighbours and affines. The innards that have been prepared by the women are not distributed, nor are the small fish they kill on barbasco expeditions.

Meat is not eaten on its own. Every meal includes vegetables such as yuca or plantains, which are grown in chacras (*tamba*). These are either high up on the cliffs (*oteyo*) and have a life of about two or three years, or else on the lower ground *(wendari)* near beaches by the river where the soil is more fertile, allowing the gardens to last for about five years.

All the preparation, clearing, burning and sowing of a chacra takes place in the dry season. The men of the household pick an area outside the village, clear it, and, after a few months, burn it. This occurs around August, and by September, the first sowing takes place. Apart from the initial clearing, men do not spend much time in the chacras. They help out if something needs to be done in a hurry but leave all the routine maintenance to the women. A woman is responsible for the supply of crops for the kitchen and she goes to the chacras most days, carrying back her produce in a string bag. Each household has about five chacras and the produce from them is used specifically for its members. Like the innards of large animals and the small fish, crops are not distributed between households.[2]

The cultivation of 'ritual' foods such as coca and tobacco are done exclusively by men for their own consumption. 'Ritual drink', such as chicha or masato, was made by women from the produce of the chacras prior to contact with the missionaries. The ritual foods are grown just outside the house or in a small area of a chacra. More recently the availability of coca and tobacco in large quantities at the trading post has led to a decline in the amount grown by the community. In the same way that innards and small fish are 'wetter' than joints of meat and large fish, there is a similar distinction between vegetables and fruit, which are 'wetter' than the 'dry' leaves of coca and tobacco. The distinction between wet and dry becomes even more significant when we look at Arakmbut cooking.

Gender and Cooking

Meat and vegetables are almost always cooked by women. Only in a dire emergency, or if there are no women at hand, will a man do anything towards cooking a meal. A woman cooks not only for herself but for her husband. A young woman who accepts and cooks meat given to her by a young man acknowledges the possibility of sexual relations. The meat is called *chindoi*. Cooking is the 'return' for a man providing meat. No man can ever avoid giving meat to his spouse or to the woman who cooks in the kitchen in which he eats.[3] Similarly a woman should not really cook anything which her husband will not be present to eat. When a husband goes on a long journey it is noticeable that the range of food eaten by the rest of the family is curtailed until he returns. For example, tins of fish kept for the time when meat is scarce are rarely eaten during a husband's absence, and the wife and family will eat only yuca and plantains. This is because a man will be hungry when he returns from the hunt and there has to be food for him. This practice has decreased with gold mining because food for workers and the rest of the family has to continue even when the head of the family is away hunting.

2. For detailed figures on the chacras of San José see Rummenhöller (1987: 296ff).
3. Gow (1989) opposes Siskind's (1973a) idea of the exchange of meat for sexual access. Among the Arakmbut the reciprocity fulfils his criteria of a man wanting to provide food, but the complementarity is a reciprocal one between a man bringing in the meat and a woman cooking it.

In the myth of Wanamey, the Arakmbut have two main cooking techniques. One is smoking when the meat comes into direct contact with the fire, the other is boiling when the meat is separated from the flames by a container of water. In the past men were the makers of fire. Nowadays when they do any cooking at all it is almost always of the smoking variety. Occasionally when men go on a hunting expedition, or if there are no women at the gold-washing beach at mealtime, the men have to prepare yuca and plantains. Rather than boil them in a pot they usually prefer to put the vegetables into the ashes of the fire and roast them. This is the only example of roasting in Arakmbut culture as roast meat is considered to be undercooked. The male method of cooking is 'dry' cooking – either smoked or roasted.

Women on the other hand boil food. As women do nearly all the cooking practically all food is boiled but when there is an excess of meat they smoke it to preserve it for future boiling. (Sometimes excess of food or meat is preserved by drying in the sun, but this method is a recent innovation and practised by only one or two families.) Women do not boil small fish but steam them. The fish are placed in bamboo tubes and put over the fire for a long period like smoked meat. In this case the smoking is done within a container and direct contact with the smoke or fire is avoided. Both boiling and steaming are 'wet' methods of cooking, although some steamed food can be left to dry and preserved for longer periods *(e'widnbe)*. Frying was more common in 1991 and was treated as a form of boiling.

There are gradations of dry and wet cooking associated with male and female techniques. The driest method is smoking and the wettest is boiling. Roasting and steaming are less dry and less wet respectively.

The 'ritual' foods tobacco and coca are prepared by Arakmbut men by means of an extreme version of dry cooking. Tobacco is hung over the hearth for weeks until it is dried out and can be smoked. Traditionally the Arakmbut, along with other Harakmbut peoples, used to make the tobacco into powder and inhale it (Califano & Fernandez 1978a). Coca leaves are prepared by drying them in the sun. The lime that accompanies it comes from the bark of the *tayagn* tree. This is burnt and ground until it is a fine powder and then it is moistened and burnt again in a strong fire (Califano & Fernandez 1978b). Coca has become comparatively rare in Arakmbut communities in recent years.

In contrast, drinks such as masato from yuca and chicha from maize are made exclusively by women. The increase in the consumption of beer has meant that the traditional methods of making these drinks are not found so frequently among the Arakmbut. After boiling, the yuca is masticated and put in a large pot or trough. The mixture is then left to ferment for a few days until it becomes slightly intoxicating. This is an extreme version of 'wet' cooking. Arakmbut also make a plantain drink called *koya* (*chapo* in Spanish), which is mashed into a pulp and drunk without any fermentation.

We can now contrast coca, which is cooked in the sun without the intervention of fire, with chicha and masato, which are cooked by fermentation. The lime and tobacco preparations are not as dry as coca as they involve some intervention by fire and even some moisture. Chapo is not so 'wet' in its preparation as masato and chicha, which need to ferment. Sun-drying and fermentation are dry and wet methods of cooking that do not require the intervention of fire. Fermentation is a controlled version of rotting. It is now possible to put together the various methods of Arakmbut cooking and their relative gradations.[4]

Figure 2.1: Relationships between various Arakmbut cooking methods

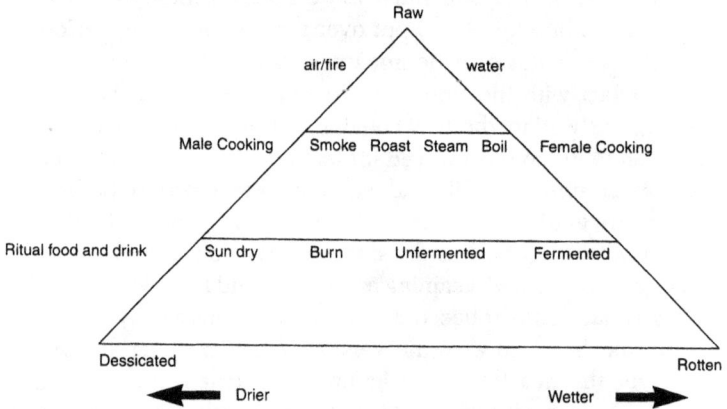

Gender and Substance – Dry and Wet

During the manufacture of arrows and string bags there are techniques which link men with dryness and women with wetness. When men make their arrows they constantly put them into the flames of the fire to strengthen the heads and to make the shafts pliable for straightening. When a woman completes a string bag she takes it

4. This discussion of Arakmbut cooking methods has drawn on the ideas of J.A. Morton (1979, chapter 4).

down to the river where it is washed in barbasco and hung to dry with stones inside. This stretches it and makes it strong.

The evidence points to a strong correlation between maleness and dry-work, as opposed to female and wet work. This connection continues when we look at taste. We saw in the previous chapter that the Arakmbut recognise four tastes: painda (bitter), hotnda (rich, tasty), haiya (bland, tasteless), and setnda (sweet, rotten). Painda foods are comparatively dry – coca, tobacco, salt, chili, and garlic are the main examples, although lemon and alcoholic spirits are also considered bitter. The traditional fire-stick, which could produce a spark for starting fires, was the paipi (literally 'bitter stick'). All bitter foods are hot and taste like fire and so in Arakmbut terms they are dry. It is interesting to note that the main ritual foods dry-cooked by men are all bitter.

In contrast to bitter is setnda which refers to sweet things such as fruits like pineapple or papaya but also to the chapo, chicha, or masato drinks the women make. It would thus appear that bitter tasting foods are classified as comparatively dry, and sweet or rotten foods are classified as wet. Vegetables such as yuca or plantains are called haiya (bland or literally 'tasting of everything'). The Arakmbut describe a bland taste as being the 'taste of water'. This wet taste is contrasted with hotnda which refers to tasty meat and is not as bitter as painda but not as bland as vegetables.

The result of this is that taste broadly coheres with the classification of gender and its relative correspondence with wet and dry. The foods that women mainly produce are sweet or bland and are more connected with wetness than the foods that men produce, which are bitter and tasty and are more connected with dryness. Thus both cooking methods and taste correspond to the relative distinctions male/female and dry/wet.

However it is important not to connect cooking and taste too directly. The taste of food is an attribute of the substance itself and not a part of the cooking. Whereas the ritual foods are clearly distinguished, ordinary foods such as meat are subject to a form of exchange between men and women. Men provide the meat and woman boil or fry it.

Gender and the Physical World

Just as gender distinction is the fundamental social duality, that of forest *(ndumba)* and river *(wawe)* is the basic division within the non-human world outside of the community. A man's hunting activities take him far into the forest. Sometimes he may go on an expedition lasting days at a time. Whenever a chacra is to be cleared the men of a household will transform the virgin forest into an area safe for the women to use by cutting down the trees and burning the vegetation. Women are reluctant to go far into the forest alone. When they go gathering they remain within a reasonable radius of the community, as opposed to the men, who go much further afield.

There are certain activities and ideas that relate women to the river. Barbasco fishing needs a woman's presence and the string bags, which are made exclusively by women, are washed in the poison down by the river after they have been completed. These string bags are also signs of spirits of the river. Where a river spirit passes it leaves the impression of a string bag on the ground. Women also make various types of basket which are used when fishing with barbasco. Women are custodians of the chants used to ensure the growth of barbasco.

The chacras are neither forest nor river but contain aspects of both domains. The upper chacras are higher and on drier ground than the lower areas, which flood annually. When men grow coca or tobacco it is invariably in the higher chacras. The peach palm *(ho)* is an important crop for the Arakmbut, particularly mythologically. It is associated with strength, manhood, and virility. When collecting peach palm, if the tree is high, the men climb it and drop the fruit to the women, or the women use sticks to knock down bunches of the fruit. The trees grow most frequently in disused chacras that have reverted to a semi-forest state and their growth depends on the use of orations known to men. Coca trees, tobacco, and peach palm are not grown in large quantities but are scattered here and there. Peach palm fruit is not classified as sweet or bland but can be used as a substitute for meat with yuca and plantains. It is thus dry and connected with both male and forest.

The crops for which women are responsible grow in the upper and lower chacras and are the bland-tasting vegetables or sweet-tasting fruits. However the most important 'female' crop is barbasco, the fish poison, which is the root used for fishing and cleaning string bags. Planting and tending barbasco is a woman's responsibility and with experience she learns special orations to help its growth. Women's work in the chacras, which takes up most of their time, has several riverine aspects. Plants grow in groups and are sown under the ground, fish swim in groups under the water -particularly the small fish caught by women with barbasco. I have been unable to find an explicit link between crops grown by women and fish in San José, but it is interesting to note that Fernandez (1976:17) says that during the time of planting the crops are treated with songs as if they were aquatic creatures, with the object that they will proliferate in the same way as fish. Women are thus associated with production activities involving groups of plants or creatures below the ground or water, which are conceived as being wet and connected with the river.

In making any correspondence between gender and the forest/ river distinction there are bound to be apparent discrepancies and it is interesting to note how the Arakmbut deal with these. Men do not limit their activities to the forest. They often come back from the hunt with a large fish that they have caught. These fish do not live in shoals but appear singly and as such have the characteristics of a forest animal that is hunted. Another apparent discrepancy is the white-lipped peccary, which goes around in large herds. However these herds are not permanent and a hunter is just as likely to come across a single animal straying from the herd as the whole group itself. The collective characteristics of the white-lipped peccary are not lost on the Arakmbut, though, and it is undoubtedly one of the reasons that the species is regarded as the most river – oriented of the larger animals, as it enjoys swampy areas known as aguajales. The capybara is another animal that the Arakmbut associate with the river. Apart from its webbed 'hoof-like' feet and the fact that it spends much time in the water, it is also an animal that can live in groups of up to twenty or more.

There is a clear parallel among the Arakmbut between the fundamental social distinction of gender and the fundamental non-human distinction between forest and river. What these two pairs have in common is the same relationship to the distinction between dry and wet that pervades the whole visible world. We noted above that gender is not simply a classificatory device or a description of the division of labour but a model or metaphor of complementarity, which manifests itself on the practical basis of a relationship of exchange in which meat is given by a husband to his wife who cooks it for him to eat. In the past, there were similar exchanges of dry and wet elements in marriage. When a marriage had been negotiated a man presented meat to his wife and her family, while the woman would present fish to her husband and his family. The close relations of both the husband and wife would sometimes help in obtaining the meat for exchange.

The exchange of elements from the forest and river was an expression of how not only men and women but also the two domains relied on each other in a complementary manner. In addition to exchanging produce, a man would give his in-laws some arrows while the woman would give some string bags to her husband's kin. There is an account of this type of exchange among the Wachipaeri (Lyon 1967:28–9), where it is possible to see the role of arrows and string bags in marriage exchanges as well as the presence of a communal fishing expedition to seal the union. The Arakmbut would round off the day by eating the food communally. The exchanges between men and women, and their relatives, and between the forest and river domains, provide the basis for a complementarity that pervades both social organisation and the cosmos, enabling the world to reproduce.

A man and woman who are initially separate are united in this way. This joining together is achieved by taking from the woman a female/river element and from the man a male/forest element and swapping them. The word for marriage is *e'toepak,* which means 'to be next to' or 'to join'. Male and female entities become united by the juxtaposition of a male element with a female one and at the same time that of a female element with a male one. Such a straight swap is the principle behind 'sister exchange', which is the conceptual order within which all Arakmbut marriages take place. After the marriage exchanges have been completed the man and woman can unite physically by means of sexual relations. Platt (1980:172) notes a similar operation in the highlands of Bolivia, where he says that with human pairs, reconciliation of duality can be made only by quadripartition. The quadripartition is not the contiguity or conjunction in itself but the pivot through which the alternation from disjunction to conjunction can take place smoothly and regularly.

Dynamic Mythological Expressions of Gender

This chapter has considered gender from the perspectives of the division of labour, food preparation, food products, and taste and also the parallel forest/river distinction. Gender has also been seen as a relative distinction rather than a static binary classification. Dynamically reciprocal exchange is fundamental to the relationship. A pair of myths illustrate the issues raised here. They are concerned with the differences between the forest and river domains mainly from the perspective of men (as is the case with practically all Arakmbut mythology), but directly and indirectly they confirm much of what has been presented in this chapter.

a) The story of Seronwe

There was once a small boy who went bathing very early in the morning. This was dangerous and as he swam he found himself in another world like this one but under the river. He was alone and there was sky, forest, and river. He then saw birds coming. They were the birds of the river such as the heron. They saw him as an enemy and threw stones at him because humans always throw stones at birds. He tried to run away but they surrounded him. He was nearly caught. But the moon *(pugn)* came and saved him. The moon was a giant and got rid of the birds. He took the boy to the house where he lived. They stayed there.

The next day they went fishing. The moon was *pane* and master of the fish. They went to an enormous lake where there were *sikidnmbi* [semi-mythological whale-like giant fish]. The moon waded in. To him the sikidnmbi appeared small like catfish *(tam'et)*. The moon told the boy to go onto higher ground. The sikidnmbi approached and the moon told the boy to keep clear as the river rose. The moon got out his fishing arrow made of peach palm with a vine tied to it. He speared the fish. This was meat for himself.

Then, for the boy, he waded further into the water and made a high wave, which left countless carp-like *boquichico* leaping on the bank. To the moon these were tiddlers. He sent the boy off to get leaves to wrap them, but in the meantime he wrapped them into a leaf packet so small that you would not have thought there were so many fish inside.

Then they went home, smoked the fish and ate the food that lay already roasted by the spirits of the dead who were the moon's servants under the river. A partition separated them from a darkened part of the house where the boy could hear the toto spirits feasting.

In a few days they went out to hunt sikidnmbi again. They took papaya as bait and harpoon arrows. This time the moon put the papaya into the river until the sikidnmbi approached. The moon sent the boy onto higher ground. The moon speared the fish as it came. It made so much noise that the boy ran to see what had happened. The boy was caught in the wave. There was water up to his neck. The moon saved the boy and got the fish onto the bank. He told the boy off for disobeying him.

They went back to the house and the moon told the boy that he would soon have to return to his own village. They waited a few days and in the night they went out to a creek where there were many fish. The moon wove a large fish trap and laid it over the entrance to the inlet. Then he gathered all the fish caught there and threw them onto the beach. Then the moon told the boy to go and find leaves to wrap them so that he would not see what happened next.

While the boy was gone he gathered all the fish and compressed them into a tiny packet of leaves. When the boy came back he could not believe that the moon had put all the fish in one packet. The moon went to find a big leaf to enclose the packet and went off. When the moon had gone the boy opened the packet. It exploded and the fish shot all over the place. When he returned the moon was very angry with the boy and he put all the fish back into the river and then told the boy to return for another leaf.

When the boy returned, the moon led the boy and told him to close his eyes. He pushed him and the boy found himself standing on the riverbank near his own house. All the Arakmbut could not believe that he was standing there. He had grown to be a young man. He told them to prepare a fire for smoking meat. Then he opened the packet and all the fish flew out. There was plenty for everyone. After they had smoked the fish they cooked it as they liked and ate it.

This myth is interesting, not only for what it tells us, but also for its omissions. The setting is the sub-riverine world of Seronwe. The creatures that inhabit this domain are either fish or birds. They are the species of the river spirits (waweri) when appearing in the visible world.

Considering the important relationship between the female gender and the river domain, there are surprisingly few references to female images. There is no mention of string bags and barbasco and all the descriptions of fishing mention only male hunting methods. The master of the domain is male. He is the moon. When he fishes he does not use barbasco but the fishing arrow, which is the weapon of the hunter.

There is a distinction in the story between the giant fish (which are massive to the boy but just large to the moon) and the smaller fish like the boquichicos (which are large to the boy but tiddlers to the moon). The former are hunted with arrows but the smaller ones are washed onto the bank or driven by means of a fish trap. Men sometimes make these to help women with their barbasco fishing, trapping the fish into an area to prevent them from escaping the effect of the drug by swimming away with the current. Even in the capture of small fish no mention appears of female methods of fishing.

The same lacuna is apparent in the techniques of cooking. The moon cooks by smoking, which is the male way, keeping the fish in direct contact with the fire. Furthermore, when the toto ask the boy if he is hungry and he asks for food they give him fish, plantains, and yuca cooked directly in the fire. There is no reference to boiling or steaming, as would be the case if women were involved in the story.

The Arakmbut often say that there are spirits of dead Harakmbut under the river. In the myth they appear as formless servants of the moon who live in his house. They are called toto, which are usually harmful spirits, but not always. The river world is meant to be the origin of the beneficial spirits that wander through the forest and rivers. In Arakmbut dreams and visions these beneficial spirits take the form of beautiful women, such as we saw in the hunting dreams earlier in this chapter. Beautiful women play no part in the myth of Seronwe.

Arakmbut production activities give the river female connotations. In the context of this myth, however, all female elements have been eliminated. One reason for this is that the story tells of the growth to maturity of a boy. He gains from his experience in the underworld two important qualities of a man. Initially his hunting ability is minimal and his contact with the spirits of the river is poor. This is demonstrated at the beginning, when he is attacked by river spirits in the guise of river birds. His developing relationship with the moon illustrates his improving relationship with the invisible world, which is paralleled by his increasing skill in hunting fish.

The lack of female elements in the story makes the point that it is perfectly possible for a man to enter a domain that is in many ways associated with women, and at the same time retain his masculinity. This in no way weakens the connections between women and the river, which are extremely important in other contexts (such as the exchanges we noted which once took place before marriage).

Another significant issue that the myth raises is the presence of male elements in a domain that is in other contexts thought to be female. In examples of exchanges between men and women, we noted that aspects of the river and forest were exchanged. There is a juxtaposition of male and female elements in any conjunction of gender that arises from an initial state of disjunction. In this way, the fact that the master of the female domain is a male and all his activities cohere with male methods and practices is perfectly congruent.

The myth of Seronwe has a parallel tale about the forest.

b) The story of Wainaron

A boy and his father went hunting and, after going a long way, saw a tree with a hole in it. The tree was dry and brittle. The man heard the song of a small parrot. 'I will go up the tree and get the chick, son,' said the father. He climbed the tree, but as soon as he reached the hole, a monster parrot called Wainaron appeared and bit off his head, which fell to the ground. His body fell into the hole.

The boy, crying, wrapped the head up in leaves, picked it up and wandered through the forest. He went by one path and heard the 'taktak' of a woodpecker. He wanted to go another way but then heard the 'taktak' again telling him to go by another path. The third time he tried to avoid the woodpecker but still he was told to go by a particular path.

He followed the path and met an old man (pane). 'What is it?' asked the boy. 'What are you carrying?' asked the old man. The boy told him what had happened. The man said that first they would bury the head and then kill the bird. The man went out with the head and came back picking hair out of his teeth – he had eaten it. The boy realised what had happened but said nothing.

'Where was your father killed?' Still crying, he went back to the tree with the man. 'Ah! My favourite meat is Wainaron. I am going to try and shoot it.' He made a sound 'trontron' to arouse Wainaron. He waited a long time and decided to practise shooting. He fired high and the arrow disappeared. 'Go and bring me the partridge.' The boy went but only saw the arrow pierced through a leaf. 'Bring it,' said the man. As the boy gave the leaf to the man it turned into the partridge. The same thing happened again and the arrow pierced a branch from a bush. This turned into an agouti. They killed many animals for the boy to take as meat to eat.

Then the old grandfather told the boy to take the meat home and to keep far from the tree while he shot Wainaron for himself. 'Keep away from me and the tree, because when Wainaron falls there will be a great wind.' The boy disobeyed and stayed close to the tree. The man climbed the tree and called the parrot. It came out of the hole and the man shot it. The bird flew up wounded and fluttering, then dropped dead, and at the same moment a rushing wind killed the boy.

The old man went and called the boy, looked, and found him dead on the road. He stepped over his body, blew over him and he came back to life.

The boy thought that he had been asleep. 'You have been dead,' said the old man. They went home, the boy with the meat, but they left the Wainaron on the path.

In the house they set up two fires to smoke the meat. One was for the boy's meat and the other for Wainaron. The old man told the child to look after the fires for his meat while he went out. 'I am going to bring the toto to help me bring in the Wainaron meat.' They went and brought the meat and put it to smoke on the fires in the house. When the meat was cooked the old man called the toto to come and eat.

When the old man had gone out to call them, the boy was tempted and took some of the parrot meat. Immediately he dropped down dead. The man returned and again breathed him back to life. Then the man rebuked the boy and said that he must climb onto the platform above the fire where maize and tobacco is dried. If the boy is above the fire the toto will not eat him. The old man gave the boy a fruit in which to urinate as the feast would last a long time. If he were to urinate in the purongo fruit, which has a hollow centre, he would be invisible to them.

The Wainaron meat was ready. The boy went above the fire and was still and quiet. The man shouted again and the toto all came in answering him. The old man invited all the toto to eat the meat. He called them and they came in from the deep forest. The old man told the boy that these toto were man-eating toads so he must protect himself. They were tall and horrible with big noses and long necks. He put out the Wainaron meat and the toto ate.

The boy then urinated in the fruit but he didn't notice that it had holes in the bottom, and all the urine ran out. The toto smelt the urine and realised that there had been a trick. They looked up and saw the boy. They grunted and moved over towards the boy to kill him. They had surrounded him, but at that moment the old man rushed out and sent them all away. He told the boy off again for being stupid and said that the time had come for him to go home.

In order to help, him the old man sat and began to make arrows for the Harakmbut:

The first arrow was the longest. This was for the people named Yaromba. The next longest was for the Singperi. The next longest was for the Wandigpana. The next longest was for the Masenawa. The smallest was for the Idnsikambo. He did not make arrows for the Embieri and the Saweron. They are apart.

The old man then told him the route to return to his people. He said that he would accompany the boy as a spirit. The boy set off with his arrows and saw animals to hunt. His aim was far better than before. Flying above him he saw a woodpecker – mbegnko. He shot at it and slightly hurt it. He shot again and hit its wing. The woodpecker was really the old man who now appeared before him. He was very angry. 'Why did you shoot me twice when you knew that I would be accompanying you to your house. I am Manko the pane of the forest. I am master of the forest. I have no more to do with you.'

Manko then broke the arrows that he had made and left them in pieces before returning to his house in the forest.

The boy was upset and picked up the pieces of the broken arrows. He returned to his people who received him and listened to his story. Then they fitted the arrows together and restored them. From that day each clan has its own type of arrow. The woodpecker, after breaking up the arrows, always breaks up the wood of trees. If woodpecker had not broken the arrows, the Arakmbut would now have perfect shooting ability.

The myth of Wainaron closely parallels that of Seronwe. Both concern a young boy who reaches maturity by gaining experience of the forest or the river. Both regions have a master who teaches the boy how to establish beneficial relations with the spirits of that domain and how to hunt. The boy always disregards the advice of the master and suffers accordingly. The old man (possibly the equivalent of the 'master of the animals' or of fish met elsewhere in South America) hunts monsters while the boy is taught how to catch smaller creatures, which are large by human standards.

Like Seronwe there are many images of manhood in the myth, at the expense of female elements. The killing is done with bows and arrows, and cooking is done by smoking meat. The boy learns from experience the dangers of over-hunting and overeating, and in the toto episode, how to cope with harmful spirits.

The birds mentioned in the story are species of the forest and not of the river as in Seronwe. The woodpecker is especially important and his role is almost a comment on the Wanamey myth. He once again names the patrilineal clans through the making of arrows, which are used exclusively by males. In his appearance in the myth the woodpecker is actually called Manko. Manko and Mbegnko are one and the same.

Manko, the master of the animals, comes into other myths relating to the forest. His sign in these other stories is a golden axe. The Arakmbut never made metal axes, but we have found examples in the soil around San José. They are thought by the Arakmbut to be gold axes from the Incas (in fact they are probably bronze).

Considering that so many aspects of the myths of Seronwe and Wainaron have correspondences, the absence of the sun in the latter is worth consideration. When I asked whether the sun (*miokpo*) had anything to do with the forest, the Arakmbut with whom I spoke replied, 'We only know about the moon, it was the Incas who knew about the sun.' Manko, the master of the forest, represents the Incas in Arakmbut mythology, and only he, the master of the forest, knows about the sun. The Arakmbut explained that all they knew themselves about the sun was contained in a short story.

c) The story of the sun – Miokpo

Long ago there was not just one sun and one moon like today, there were two suns. One was male and the other female. The female sun was as we see it today. The male sun was enormous and was so close to earth that it burned everything and nothing could survive.

For this reason, early one morning a man got up with his bow and arrow and caught the sun just as it was rising. His name was Manko. He shot the male sun in the eye *(wakpo)* and it went out immediately, leaving behind the female sun. The sun we have now is female. Every day it goes over the earth in one direction and at night returns under the earth.

Not only is there now a parallel for the moon in Seronwe in a sun associated with the master of the forest, but we also find that the sun is itself female. Consequently the domain of the river has a male master, the moon, while the master of the forest, even though male (Manko is his name in both Wainaron and Miokpo), is the only means of access to the sun who is female.

The sun and moon represent the presence of a female element in a male domain and the presence of a male element in a female domain.[5] The subdivision of the gender distinction into four parts can be seen mythologically. The sun and moon and the elements exchanged providing a 'cosmic marriage' between forest and river, and in addition their behaviour in relation to each other, parallels that between men and women. This is most clearly illustrated when we compare the role of the celestial bodies with the alternation of day and night. During the day men and women usually carry on their activities separately from each other. At night, although a husband and wife sleep together, their souls leave the hut and wander around separately. The only time when a full contiguous relationship takes place is when they have sexual relations. These should take place at dawn or at dusk. Thus at the point when day becomes night and night day the gender relation becomes contiguous.

5.   The Desana (Reichel-Dolmatoff 1971:17ff.) have an association linking male to forest and female to river. As with the Arakmbut, this can be inverted in certain contexts because, for a hunter, spirits of nature have an aquatic character while, for fishermen, spirits have a forest character.

The celestial bodies have a parallel relationship. The sun is the celestial body of the day. Mythologically, she is a female in a male domain. During the day, the sun is above the earth, and at night she is under the earth. The moon is the celestial body of the night. Mythologically, he is male in a female domain. At night the moon is above the earth, but during the day he is below the river. Changes in the moon are explained by his eating the giant fish mentioned in the myth of Seronwe. If he eats too much he is unable to rise. At dusk and dawn the moon and sun are both either temporarily under the earth or temporarily above the earth. They enter into a relationship of contiguity that parallels that of the sexes. Dawn and dusk are thus boundary points when the sun and moon appear to join, as do men and women and so, by implication, the forest and the river.

In conclusion it is possible to see that the Arakmbut make correlations between male/female, forest/river, dry/wet and above/below. Gender relations among the Arakmbut blend into these distinctions according to the context. Gender in the contexts reviewed in this chapter are complementary in that they shift symmetrically from disjunction to conjunction. This complementarity is most apparent in the dynamic interaction between male and female when aspects from one of the pair are swapped with aspects from the other. The main examples of this reciprocal exchange is the boiling of meat by a wife for her husband, the exchange of certain products at marriage, the notion of symmetric exchange in marriage, and, in the mythological context, the 'sexual displacement' of the sun and moon.

It is important to understand that the structured gender distinction is not rigorously applied by the Arakmbut to a recalcitrant world. The Arakmbut take contrasting concepts for granted and are not overly bothered by the occasional inconsistency. The world is in a constant dynamic flux, and all structural distinctions should be seen flexibly, reflecting an ideological orientation facing the contingencies of daily life ready for interpretation. In this sense, we should think of 'engendering' as a dynamic process rather than as a static structural opposition.

There are other aspects of gender, which have not been discussed in this chapter. One is the complementarity of male and female over time, while the other is the different perspectives of social and cultural life from the point of view of an Arakmbut man or woman. As these differences revolve around the notions of age and residence, it is to these subjects that we must now turn.

◁ Chapter 3 ▷

TIME THROUGH SPACE

House and Community

I: Time and Space

In the previous chapter we saw that relations between units of time (such as day/night or dry/wet season) and space (such as forest/river or sun/moon) correspond with the relationship between male and female. This chapter looks at these aspects of time and space in more detail and gives an account of the related principles of age and residence.

The Arakmbut translate time as *o'poknda* or *o'pogika*. Both of these words signify motion – 'passing' or 'always passing'. The verb *e'pok* from which they come refers also to the flow of a river passing by, or to people taking a walk in front of one's house. The Arakmbut, in this way, liken time to a flowing from past to future where a person is standing in the present. This spatial view of time corresponds to the view of Nilsson (1920:17), who says that it is easier to reckon time from points than from lengths. The concrete aspects of time-indicators provide points to measure change.[1]

---

1. There have been several discussions as to whether there are different types of time. Leach (1961:125) questions the applicability of distinguishing cyclic and linear aspects of time and prefers to picture linear time as passing through repetitive temporal categories, which give rise to oscillations. Bloch (1977) distinguishes a practical experiential notion of time, which is durational, in contrast to ritual time, which is cyclical. Howe (1981) disagrees with this perspective, saying

Time and space are closely related in Arakmbut life. Not only do their major distinctions parallel each other, they also correlate with the complementarity aspect of gender relations and the relationship between the invisible spirit world and the visible world of human beings. There are four main cyclic patterns which illustrate these correspondences clearly.

1) o'sik (night) / o'me (day)

During the day, the sun passes over the earth while the moon is in the river. At night the moon has ascendancy and the sun is below the earth. At night, the wet world of below has predominance over the dry world of above. At this time, invisible spirits roam and a person's soul can leave the body and meet him or her in a dream.

As long as there is light, all people can carry on their activities. However once night has fallen one should not wander off into the forest. Even so, many hunters do because certain animals are easier to hunt at night, but they are aware of the risk they run from encountering a harmful spirit. Women should not make their string bags after dark either, as this is thought to annoy the spirits of the river.

The previous chapter illustrated how the division of labour dictates that men and women spend much of the day apart; the men either hunting or working gold and the women tending or collecting produce from the chacras. At night people are physically closer to each than during the day, because this is the period when people congregate in the house. A husband and wife sleep in the same room as their children. Bachelors usually have a single room, as do newly married couples living with their parents. Even though members of a family are closer at night than they are during the day, when they are asleep their souls wander in their dreams. In such cases men go to meet the beautiful beneficial female spirits and leave their wives or womenfolk. In this way there is a soul separation at night which parallels that during the day.

The sexes come together to eat cooked food and to have sexual relations. Eating usually takes place in the kitchen and sexual relations in the house; both activities take place ideally at the point when day becomes night or night day. Sexual relations occur after dusk and before dawn and are thus nocturnal activities. If a couple want to have a child quickly they must have relations more often, and

---

that duration does not differ, there are only different ways of expressing it, both cyclical and durational. I feel that the evidence that follows fits more with Howe's view although cyclic, lineal, and oscillatory aspects of time are all present among the Arakmbut.

these occur in the middle of the night. (Sexual relations can also occasionally take place outside of the house or during the day if no one else is around.) Eating takes place in daylight just before dusk or just after dawn. When people are working gold and they need to eat more to keep up their strength they will eat an extra meal at midday. Eating takes place in the same room but women sit on the floor by the hearth and men sit on logs further away. It is extremely bad manners to look at anyone who is eating.

The complementarity of male and female as seen over the daily cycle is an oscillation between separation when people work during the day or sleep at night and a contiguity encapsulated by conjunction in house or hearth at dusk or dawn when they eat or have sexual relations. Eating is done when possible at the extreme boundary of the day while sexual relations take place at the extreme boundary of the night. Daily activities involve more separation of the sexes than nightly ones and so eating is marked by men and women being further away from each other than when they indulge in sexual relations. The overall pattern can be seen in Figure 3.1.

Figure 3.1 Separation or contiguity of gender relations in daily cycle

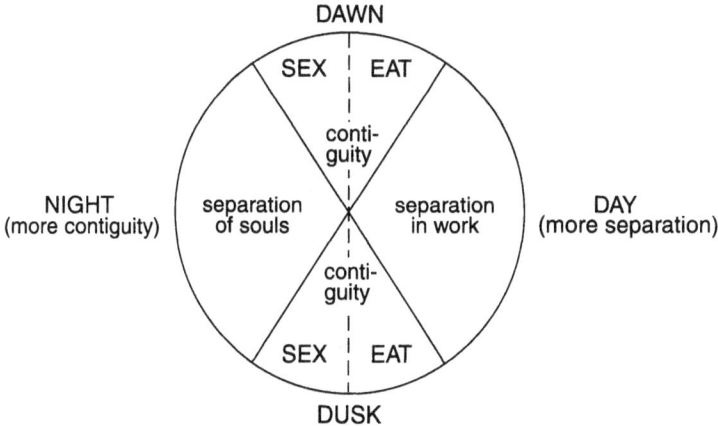

2) wambo pugn (new moon) / pugntone (full moon)

A month is a 'moon' (pugn). It is divided into new and full moon periods. When the moon is new he is still tied to the river where he has gorged himself with fish, but by the time of the full moon he is independent and can leave or return to the river as he pleases. The night is darker when the moon is new and then invisible spirits are encountered more frequently. This is when sessions involving the hallucinogenic drug ayahuasca take place, although they are by no means regular monthly events. Usually at new moon people go to bed early. Providing the weather is good, the full moon is the time when there are fiestas and everyone goes to bed later.

When the moon is full, the Arakmbut lounge outside in the central patio to listen to stories or chat. They sit out in groups with the men and women keeping apart. In fiestas the women always stay together away from the men and, if they drink, get hold of beer or rum for themselves. Men and women are most likely to interact in the evenings between eating and sleeping in the period between the new and full moons when, in the half-light, families cluster around their hearth or outside their houses and talk among themselves. The sexes thus relate to each other more at the points of boundary between the two temporal categories making up the monthly cycle. The complementarity between the sexes follows a similar pattern over the month as with the daily cycle.

3) wawiyok (wet season) / wambayok (dry season)

The year (*wayok*) is divided into two seasons which were described in the prologue. The wambayok not only means dry season but also marks one year from the next. In the dry season the river is low and the forest predominates while in the wet season the river rises and spreads through large areas of the forest. Hunting is more difficult in the dry season because the leaves on the tracks are crisp and make a noise. During the wet season, people are more prone to illness and this is attributed to the increased activities of spirits when the sky is overcast and it is darker during the day. Hunting is also more frequent, not only because of the softer leaves on the trails but because most of the fruits that animals like come out between April and June.

When referring to certain points in the year, the Arakmbut use their 'calendar of flowers' such as the caña brava, which flowers in January, a red flower (*pisnoe*) that comes out in July, and the balsa, which also blossoms in July. Although there is some recognition of the stars, they do not appear to be used to mark the change of the seasons.

During the wet and dry seasons, men and women work at their respective tasks and are more frequently apart than at the end of the wet season and the beginning of the dry, when men and women clear the old chacras of weeds and decide where they are going to make new ones. For a period of about a month the men and women in a household work together in the same area. At the end of the dry season it is the time for burning and planting. Once again men and women work together to get the crops planted and the chacras cleared for the wet season, when less garden work takes place. In this way the points of transition between the seasons are the times of the year when men and women co-operate more.

Another important distinction between the wet and dry season is that the day is shorter and night longer during the wet season while in the dry season the night is shorter and the day longer.

4) wasikon (long night) / wambo o'me (new day)

In the myth of Wanamey we saw how the Harakmbut were saved from the fire-flood by a 'long night' in the tree. This period of disjunction from the world when all was dark occurred after a Singperi girl had 'sexual' relations with a bird. The long night ended at dawn when sexual relations took place between the brother and sister. Wanamey was at its full height for the period of the long night, when the tree emerged from below the ground and was surrounded by a pool of water.

The Arakmbut say that in the future there will be another catastrophe, which they express in terms of a nuclear holocaust when Wanamey will return again to save them. The circumstances will follow the story of the myth, starting with a repetition of the bird bringing the fruit of Wanamey to a Singperi girl who will receive it between her legs. The epochs of Arakmbut history are divided according to the alternating patterns of day and night. At the transition point from one temporal category to the next, male and female interact more contiguously than in the intervening periods.

These four examples of temporal cycles oscillate between a regular set of alternating categories arranged in terms of a contrast between dark or wet (night, new moon, wet season, long night) and light or dry (day, full moon, dry season, new day). In each case the first of the two units is spatially connected with river and below, while the second is related to the forest and above.[2]

The way in which gender relations relate to time and space demonstrates the dynamic and relativistic complementarity between

---

2. The correlations have their limitations. When taking gender relations into consideration, although it is possible to say that 'wet/river' dominant periods contain many female attributes as opposed to 'dry/forest' times, it is impossible to extend this completely to the sociological sphere of the division of labour. The activities of men (hunting) were noted in the previous chapter to be most apparent in the wet season and those of women (fishing) in the dry, which would reject too absolute a division.

male and female, which is apparent with the division of labour. The complementarity between separation and contiguity follows a repetitive pattern when seen through time, which corresponds to the changes of temporal category. Thus men and women interact more at the boundaries between the categories than within the periods of the categories themselves. Gender relations are thus constantly shifting over time within the parameters of complementarity.

There is another temporal context in which the complementarity between male and female repeats itself over time. This is the life cycle. By comparing the gender relationship over a lifetime it is possible to see a pattern similar to those described above.

For children *(isipo)* the gender distinction is completely unimportant and both sexes are treated in the same way. A child remains an isipo until he or she reaches puberty between twelve and fourteen. During this period children go to the village school where they receive a primary education. Both sexes spend most of their time helping their mother in her horticultural tasks in the chacras, looking after younger siblings, doing the kitchen chores, and accompanying the women on gathering and fishing trips. Some of the boys occasionally help their fathers with the gold work, but the majority find it too strenuous to continue for long.

This changes at puberty, when the gender distinction becomes more pronounced and the isipo child names, which are often directly or indirectly a play on the name of some natural phenomenon and are not sex-specific, change to others that are more personal, more secret, and used less frequently. These adult names are different for men and for women.

In pre-contact days, men would pass through two rituals: the *e'ohotokoy* (nose piercing) at about fourteen years when the boy became a *wambo* (new man) and the larger-scale *e'mbogntokoy* (lip piercing), which took place at the age of about eighteen years, when he became a full man *(wambokerek)*. After these two ceremonies, a man was eligible for marriage. In contrast, girls had no ceremonies. After puberty they became young women *(muneyo)* and when they were married and had children, they were recognised as full women *(wetone)*.

Throughout youth and adulthood men and women organise their relationships largely on the lines of the complementarity and repetitive patterns noted earlier in this chapter. An old person is called *watone*. The word refers to both men and women. There is no formal initiation into this age category and the position of its members is of little political influence, although they are respected for their knowledge.

If we compare the passage of life for both sexes in Arakmbut society, it is possible to see an oscillation between contiguity and separation. The extreme points of life, nearer to birth and death, are times when the gender distinction is of minimal importance, whereas the central part of life is the time when the complementarity of the sexes undergoes a disjunction that is only tempered by controlled access to members of the opposite sex. This period coincides with the ability to have sexual relations and produce children.

The complementarity between the sexes fits in with the linear span of the life cycle. The spatial concepts of above/below and forest/river do too. Man plants semen into woman from above and she gives birth in a downward direction. Children are more associated with the domain of the river and, as they grow into adults, they increase in height and have gradually more contact with the forest world. As people grow older the river spirits attract them more and more, calling them to death into the underworld.

Figure 3.2 Comparison of seasonal repetitive aspects of duration and the more oscillatory life cycle.

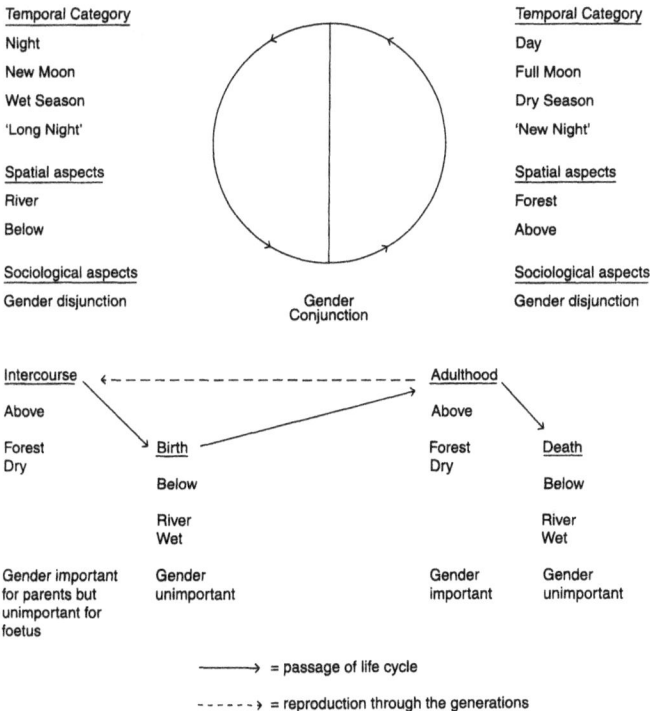

Temporal Category		Temporal Category
Night		Day
New Moon		Full Moon
Wet Season		Dry Season
'Long Night'		'New Night'
Spatial aspects		Spatial aspects
River		Forest
Below		Above
Sociological aspects		Sociological aspects
Gender disjunction	Gender Conjunction	Gender disjunction

Intercourse			Adulthood	
Above			Above	
Forest Dry	Birth		Forest Dry	Death
	Below			Below
	River Wet			River Wet
Gender important for parents but unimportant for foetus	Gender unimportant		Gender important	Gender unimportant

⟶ = passage of life cycle

----→ = reproduction through the generations

II: Age and Residence

Time and space in a social context are age and residence. These notions are important for defining a person's social identity at any moment. The previous chapter demonstrated that the most pervasive distinction for the Arakmbut is that of gender, which is based on a conceptual complementarity between the sexes. However gender differentiates criteria for status distinctions where age and residence play a significant part in marking social position according to male or female perspectives.

Status among men centres around success in hunting, or gold work, obtaining a wife and producing offspring, as well as in knowledge of the invisible world and the ability to cure. Such accomplishments are not always easy to achieve, and competition between men consists of seeking social recognition of their talents. It is possible for a man to gain a reputation only through years of practice, patience, and learning. Experience comes with age and so does status.

Women, in contrast, can perform their daily tasks in the chacras or in the kitchen from an early age. Their problem is that, since there are so few women available as wives, men look beyond the boundaries of the village for spouses, leading to an increase in the number of women from outside. For them status is defined by whether one is an insider or an outsider and is consequently largely dependent on residential factors.

When an isipo boy becomes a wambo he starts to learn the skills of manhood. The age-grade wambo is further distinguished by the difference between *wambosipo* or *wambotone*. There is no official ceremony that distinguishes these younger or older wambo, only a difference in activities and interests. The younger boys hunt birds and small fish and make imitation houses, whereas the older ones help their fathers in large hunts and gold work. The years spent in military service or at university can initially add to a young man's status when he returns, although older men are likely to take him down a peg if he shows signs of thinking too much of his own exploits.

When a young man is recognised as a hunter who can provide for a family he enters the competition for women. We have noted in the Introduction that the gender imbalance in Arakmbut communities is a problem for men, but in San José the scarcity of women is particularly acute as only half the men in the wambokerek age-grade are married. It is a sure mark of status to find a young man married in San José, but bachelors are not without prestige. Single men often become good story-tellers and singers and over time can often build up a considerable amount of ability in curing.

The age-grades are very important for men. The change in status from isipo to wambo to wambokerek is the cause of much impatience among youths who feel they should be treated as members of the grade above. Parallel with the age-grades there are also 'temporal' distinctions between the genealogical levels of the relationship terminology. People of a higher level have some influence and sway over those below. In the case of the watone this influence is apparent only in the relationship between parents and children, otherwise the old members of the community have to adhere to the younger and more prevailing wambokerek and wambokerektone.

When age-grades correlate with the genealogical level of two people the two spheres work in harmony. However there are times when conflicts and frictions can arise. Two of the most frequent examples are as follows.

When there is a large age range between brothers it is quite possible for an elder brother to produce his first child soon after the last of his own younger brothers is born. In this case a man is in the same grade as his own young uncles. They prefer to emphasise the genealogical distance between themselves and their nephew, but he prefers to lessen their higher status (particularly in the marriage stakes) by stressing the age factor (the terms *pagnsipo* or *chignsipo* – little father or little mother's brother are used in this context).

The other common case where generation and genealogical level do not coincide is when brothers of the same genealogical level are in different age-grades. Once again there is conflict over the criteria of status, the older brother stressing age, the younger ones genealogical level.

These conflicts of perception take place mainly among men. In these contexts women do not emphasise age or genealogical level in classifying their position in the community.

Gender relations in Arakmbut society are frequently characterised by male assertion. In marital relationships this takes the form of men making decisions that affect the household, such as when they will work in the chacras, go fishing, or set out on a travelling expedition. Money gained from gold work is spent and distributed by the men. If either party has to leave the community on separation, the woman is usually the one to go. There are occasionally examples of husbands hitting their wives, although this is not considered responsible behaviour by the rest of the community.

Male assertion is reinforced by the fact that men are almost always older than their wives. However there are occasional cases, when a wife is older than her husband (this could occur on a wife's second marriage to a previously unmarried husband). This potential source of conflict is solved by the man trying to treat the woman as if she were younger than he. Age thus provides the first element of asymmetry into the hitherto complementary gender relationship.

There is also the more frequent problem of an elder sister who is on the same genealogical level as a brother. An elder sister, mother or mother-in-law all have the right to chastise and speak their mind to a younger male relative, and they often do, causing embarrassment, particularly if the criticism takes place in public. The reaction of the man is to ignore the woman, but preferably to do his best to avoid any altercation in the first place. The woman with most authority over a man is his wife's mother, particularly when they both live in the same house. The authority is based not only on age and residence but on the marriage tie itself, which is treated in the next chapter.

The most important criterion of status for a woman among her peers is her community of origin or that of her mother if she is unmarried, and the duration of her residence in the community. A man will avoid living outside his community if he can help it and only if he has some close relatives elsewhere will he contemplate leaving his village of origin. There is no prohibition against leaving his village but it does not make good political sense. In another community a man would not have the support of his own clan or family in disputes and runs the risk of being made a scapegoat for all the misfortunes of his new neighbours.

If a man is unable to obtain a wife within his community he will seek one elsewhere. He may be able to contract a union by offering his potential wife's family a sister or else he may simply steal or elope with her. Consequently in an Arakmbut community such as San José there will be few men from outside, but at least fifty per cent of married women are from other communities.

Although there may be advantages in a man marrying a woman from outside and avoiding the customary bride-service owed to a father-in-law, the opposite is the case for a woman. Women from outside are clearly less influential than those who have remained in the same community all of their lives. These latter are usually sisters of the members of the dominant clans who marry endogamously and are influential in the informal women's gatherings that take place as they work on their string bags outside their houses, during visits or when they work in the chacras.

A woman from outside is at a considerable disadvantage when she first arrives in the community, although her position can improve with time. This occurs if she manages to acquire some of the characteristics of an insider. Here are a few of the ways in which she could do this:

(1) She might encourage some of her relations in the other community to follow her.
(2) She could use the prestige of her husband to gain some influence with the other women. This will be of little avail unless she has powerful sisters-in-law with whom she has good relations and who are members of one of the dominant households in the community.
(3) She will have to wait until her daughter is of marriageable age and hope that she manages to make a marriage endogamous to the community.

These alternatives show that it is possible for a woman from outside to gain influence but only if she uses her diplomacy and tact to appear as an insider; otherwise she will have limited influence in the groups of women throughout the community. Acceptance as an insider can take several years.

Women who eat together are responsible for the cooking and bringing in the produce from the chacras. The chacras (gardens) confirm the importance of residence in defining status among the women of a community. Every chacra is associated with someone's name. In practice the land is shared by the household, but the naming of the area is important because it reflects status among the women. A woman who has her name associated with her chacras 'owns' them in the sense that she is responsible for their welfare. Not every woman does own the gardens of her household and naming varies according to the circumstances.

When a chacra is cleared it is initially named after the man who organised the preparation. After the first planting the name can change. The following are the several alternatives:

(1) By far the most common is to call the chacra by the name of the woman who works in it most and is responsible for the food that it contains.
(2) A bachelor who is not a son of a member of the household is expected to clear a chacra for the women of the household where he eats. These women are relatives such as a brother's daughter or a brother's wife and sometimes a sister. In these cases the tie to the woman is either by virtue of their being in the same clan or by virtue of a link through a male member of the bachelor's clan. The chacra cleared by the bachelor will usually be referred to by his name.

(3) A woman who is considered an outsider to the community does not have her chacras named after her; instead, her husband's name is associated with them. This is a sign of lesser status among women. The definition of inside and outside in this context is not absolute as it varies from one woman to another. Any woman who comes from another community will lay claim to the status of an insider by means of the strategies tabulated above. The longer the time she spends in the community, the more of an insider she becomes and the more likelihood there will be of her name being associated with the chacras in which she works.

The naming of a chacra after a woman is a sign that she is recognised as an insider. It is another example of the use made by women of spatial categories to define their status within the community. A woman's prestige can also be enhanced by good use of her chacra crop. If there is a surplus of yuca, for example, the woman of the house will make a non-alcoholic masato drink. Not everyone has enough yuca to spare for making this and its appearance is a sign of a thrifty, hard-working woman. An insider with well-established chacras has a clear advantage in the amount of masato she can make. Women with well-established chacras usually help out their brothers' wives if they come from outside. This aid is an important factor in defining status among women because the new arrivals are to a large extent bound to their sisters-in-law. In this way women who are insiders have clusters of outsiders who are indebted to them.

Status differences among men, achieved through hunting, gold work, marriage alliances, and shamanic skills, are subject to the overriding importance of experience, which only comes with age. In an argument Arakmbut men not only criticise a man's abilities but also criticise his age; he is either too young or too old. Women express their status differences in their political world, which centres around informal discussions on a daily basis, which the men consider to be gossip. The most influential women attract others to where they are sitting and working on their string bags. It is usually possible to tell the insiders from the outsiders because the latter visit the former rather than vice versa.

In this way age and residence play an important part in distinguishing status within the sexes. However we should note how they operate together. For both sexes insiders have advantages over outsiders and the status of all persons increases with age, but this coheres with a gender imbalance in social life because the majority of women are outsiders and husbands are older than their wives. Thus age and residence are not mutually exclusive – women use age between themselves, particularly among insiders, and men who come from outside are usually of a lower status. Furthermore we should not have the impression that the Arakmbut live in a rigid hierarchical society; on the contrary, these distinctions of status do not provide the basis for permanent differences of access to resources.

Residence is an aspect of social organisation that clearly marks different spheres of orientation for men and women, which involves more than status alone. The significance of this is to demonstrate the extent to which men and women in Arakmbut society have different perspectives on their social worlds.

III: Gender, Age and Residence

Throughout the life cycle men and women move their places of residence in line with the passage of age. A man spends several years carrying out bride-service for his in-laws between life in his parents' home and establishing his independent household with his wife and children. For women there is only one change of residence over a lifetime. This is the move from the household of her father to that of her husband.

The basis for community social relations is the house and kitchen, which socially constitutes the household. The household is the unit that brings together male and female while constituting the basis of the domestic division of labour. Whereas in pre-contact times, each household lived in a part of the communal house (maloca) facing a central dancing area, now they are scattered throughout the community, frequently facing a central patio.

The physical manifestation of a household is the house and kitchen, which provides the basic residential unit of the social system within the community. However the house and household are not necessarily the same. Household members eat at the same hearth but may live in several separate houses. This is decided in terms of factors such as available space, a desire to live apart, or independent marital status.[3]

3. In this respect the Arakmbut differ from the Achuar (Descola 1989:153), who see the house as the fundamental social unit. For the Arakmbut the community is also extremely important as an intermediary between the household and the people as a whole. A reason for this could be found in the pre-mission period when the Arakmbut lived in communal houses. Then, as with the Barasana in Colombia now (S.Hugh-Jones 1993), the communal house was the fundamental

Even though men and women both move during their life cycle from natal to marital households, there are some very important distinctions. A woman is always physically and residentially tied to her household in the sense that she sleeps near to where she cooks. This is not the case for a man who can sleep away from the kitchen where he eats, in a different house or even in a different part of the village.

A man will do his utmost to avoid leaving his village. If it does happen the reason is that he is not getting on with his relatives or wishes to woo a woman from another community. Such movements are practically always temporary. Women, in contrast, are not permanently tied to any village. The consequence of this is that, whereas a woman is always tied to the household as a residential base, a man is far more firmly connected to his community.

The association of women with the household and men with the community as a whole is evident in the spatial aspects of production and exchange. The household and the chacras are parallel categories. The changes that occur in family size correlate exactly with the gardens that belong to the family. At first a married couple will share the chacras of the wife's family unless she comes from outside the community, in which case the sharing is, when possible, done with the husband's sister or mother. Gradually as the family increases they will clear chacras of their own and rely less on their in-laws. By the time a married couple has a large family, they become a fully independent unit with well-established chacras of their own.

As a household increases so do the chacras, but equally important is the gradual diversification of crops. At first a couple will grow yuca, plantains, and papaya, while sharing other crops with their in-laws, helping them with the horticultural work. As it becomes more independent, the family begins to cultivate a wider range such as barbasco, pineapple, potatoes, maize, peach palm, and sugar cane. The more independent the household the more independent and diverse are the chacras. The main link between the chacra and the household is the group of women who work there most of the time, which is a feature noted by Descola in his Achuar study (1989).

When women bring the produce from the chacra back to the house it is kept for use by that household alone. It is not distributed to any other family. Occasionally a woman may run out of yuca or

---

unifying factor linking social and cosmological organisation with production. For the Arakmbut, this changed with the breaking up of the maloca into individual houses and the establishment of communities with titled boundaries. Thus the house, community and demarcated lands provide the spatial integrity once embedded within the maloca.

plantains and may ask for a loan from a close relative. This loan is usually repaid as soon as possible or the borrower will get a reputation as a scrounger. There is therefore distribution within the household and balanced reciprocity between households when dealing with the produce from chacras (Sahlins 1974:193-95). The distribution and consumption are the concerns and responsibility of women and have nothing to do with the men.

Men spend most of the time when they are in the village visiting other men, telling stories and arranging hunting trips and drinking parties. Ties outside the household are considerably stronger for men than for women. This can be illustrated by looking at the consequences of any marital strife. If a husband and a wife quarrel seriously and separate for a period, the husband inevitably receives support from people in the community outside his household, whereas the woman has to flee the village and seek refuge with relatives elsewhere. This even happens in cases involving endogamous unions. For all their informal chats and daily discussions as they make their string bags, the level of solidarity among women outside the household is much lower than the clan ties among the men. While women spend most of their time in the chacras, the men are much more concerned with hunting and gold work. In terms of spatial categories both gold work and hunting take place outside the radius of the village where the chacras are found. It is also the task of the men to clear the forest for the planting of gardens, thus transforming the potentially hostile world of the jungle into the safer domesticated areas where the women can tend their crops.

When a man brings meat back to the village a portion of it is kept for his own kitchen but most of it is distributed to other households by the woman responsible for the cooking. The recipients are determined by the political and marriage alliances of the hunter. Although the distribution of meat does not involve an exact or immediate return, some form of reciprocation is expected eventually or the recipient will be considered mean and a poor hunter. In spite of this, there is no real sense in which the distribution of meat can be seen as balanced reciprocity. The prestige for the distribution goes to the hunter, but one should not underestimate the important political decisions of the women, who largely decide the cut, amount and destination of the meat.

Men who go to the bank post at the mouth of the Karene change their gold for money with which they buy various commodities. Some basic commodities such as salt, sugar, rice, or pasta are given to the women in the household for use when cooking for the family but these goods are not distributed to other households, and if anyone does borrow any, as with the produce of the chacras, a balanced return is expected within a short period.[4]

Other commodities that men buy with their gold are beer, rum, and other alcoholic drinks. These are for communal consumption at drinking parties. A man will distribute the drink he has bought to his friends and allies in the community and a generous host is accorded prestige and recognised as a responsible, successful person. The distribution of meat and drink have similar effects on the position of the hunter or gold worker in the community.

An example of asymmetry and inequality between the sexes has emerged since gold washing was introduced. In the past the women would make the beer and distribute it at a fiesta, whereas now beer is bought from the nearest merchants. This has removed an important source of respect and prestige for a woman. Furthermore in the past the fiestas brought together neighbouring malocas whereas nowadays the participants are almost always from the same community. The recent introduction of the kermesse practice to some extent replaces this. At these fiestas neighbouring communities and colonists are invited to a drinking party in order to raise money for community funds.

Whereas generalised reciprocity takes place within the community, exchange relations outside are more exact. When men from San José go to Puerto Luz to get caña brava for their arrows they have either to buy them or to give something in return such as barbasco. From this we can see that the generalised reciprocity practised within the community is in contrast to the balanced reciprocity practised outside.

It is possible to summarise the different perspectives and orientations of men and women in Arakmbut society as shown in Table 3.1.

These perspectives of Arakmbut social life from the point of view of men and women are very different. They are views of the same social organisation but with varying emphases. Even so, they are not totally separate because men and women interact within the household. The exchanges that take place between a husband and wife such as providing meat, eating, and sexual relations are all examples of points of contact between two views of society that at these times come into line with each other like a parallax. The most important merging of the two views comes with marriage, where the two perspectives complement each other to create the basis for a new household.

---

4. This description of the commodities bought with gold money refers to consumables and not to the more expensive items such as shotguns or motor pumps for washing gold. These capital goods are the property of the person or people who buy them and are classified with personal tools or weapons such as bow, arrows, or axes.

Table 3.1 Comparison of the different perspectives of society by men and women

Men	Women
Need not live near hearth	Always live near hearth, which is centre of the household
Avoid leaving community permanently	Can leave community permanently on marriage
Products obtained by men such as meat and also some of the items bought with gold money such as alcohol can be distributed to other households and give prestige to men, even if distributed by women.	Products obtained by women such as vegetables and fruits from the chacras or small fish from barbasco fishing are consumed only within the household. Foodstuffs bought with gold money for women are not distributed to other households. However a woman's prestige stems from a well-run household.
Balanced reciprocity outside community	Balanced reciprocity outside household
Orientation outside chacra and household	Orientation inside chacra and household

This chapter has compared patterns of time and shown how time and space are inextricably linked for the Arakmbut. Sociologically, the principles of age and residence are distinguished because age is an important criterion for marking status differences among men while residence is an important criterion among women. Carrying this further, it is apparent that men and women view their social worlds from perspectives stemming from the community as a whole and from the household respectively. The two positions come together or separate, as the gender relation itself does, in the complementary fashion described in the previous chapter. At the same time, the different emphases on age and residence allow for an asymmetry to enter gender relations since within the marital relationship the man is more likely to be an insider and older than the woman. This potential has been enhanced with the increased colonisation of Arakmbut social life and the availability of bought commodities.

It is now time to look at two other important areas of social life – the clans and marriage exchange. Certain points mentioned in this chapter are worth remembering because the patrilineal *onyu* (clan) constitutes a continuity through time and is centred around relationships between men, whereas the *wambet* alliance units consist of categories of kin who live close to each other and who arrange marital exchange.

cs Chapter 4 so

THE DESCENT OF MAN AND EXCHANGE OF WOMAN

I: The clan (onyu)

One of the distinguishing features of Arakmbut society is the clan which they call *onyu*.[1] Some Harakmbut peoples, such as the Sapiteri and Wachipaeri, have these named groups but others, such as the Arasaeri and Toyeri, do not.[2] They are very important to

1. The Arakmbut do not use the term onyu very much. Some said that they use the word 'onyu', others that they just refer to the clans by their names. Onyu means 'pure group'. It refers to any people who are not mixed. When I asked why some use onyu and some not, I was told that the clan is the purest social grouping among the Arakmbut. I have used the term onyu here as several people have independently mentioned the term. Once thought to have been a rare phenomenon, clans are being reported currently or in the past with more frequency among lowland Peruvian peoples including the Piro, the Ese'eja, the Cocamilla (Stocks, 1981), and the Yagua (Chaumeil, 1983).

2. It might appear strange that the onyu which plays such a significant part in Arakmbut society should be absent from some Harakmbut peoples. However, it is worth noting that among the Yanoma, those groupings which Lizot calls 'lineages' (1977:35–70) and which share several characteristics of the Arakmbut onyu (exogamy, association with animal species, names etc.) are not equally present throughout the subgroups. The subsequent article by Ramos and Albert (1977:71–90) demonstrates that lineages are present among the Saruna Yanomama sub-group but not among the Yanoman. Among the Northwest Amazon peoples, the clans are different from those of the Arakmbut as the clusters of named sibs (which correspond to the onyu) are arranged into a higher exogamic unit. The Northwest Amazon peoples do not have a constant definition of 'sib'. For example, among the Cubeo (Goldman 1963) clans have strong corporate functions and a ritual ancestor ideology, which is different from those of the more flexible Makuna (Århem 1981: chapter ten).

an Arakmbut male who will vigorously defend his own group and fight anyone who insults it. San José consists of a collection of various clans, which relate to each other both sociologically and through the spirit world.[3]

An onyu is a patrilineal group. A person belongs to the same clan as his or her father and father's siblings, while a mother or wife and their respective siblings always belong to a different clan. All members of a clan regard themselves as being descended from common ancestors but are not able to establish an exact genealogical relationship.

Three major factors account for the conceptual cohesion of a clan and are precisely those that constitute the definition of an individual person: the body *waso*, soul *nokiren* and name *wandik*. Members of the same clan share corporeality (Seeger 1981:145). This means that the physical body of each person is an emanation of the body of a common ancestor. The Arakmbut explain this in terms of the nature of semen. Semen (*wandawe*) is a part of the physical and spirit being of a man that is transferred to his wife. The gradual accumulation of semen in her womb results in the formation of a child who is substantially a reformation of the father. Any differences are accounted for by the influence of the shape of the womb or the fact that that several fathers were responsible for the formation of the child. Some women think that several fathers lead to a more versatile child. However the father of the child is the one whose semen is dominant.

The clan is a patriline through which physical substance passes from one generation to the next through the male line. The members of a clan are particles of a whole, yet differentiated from each other to the extent that the womb shapes every individual uniquely. Thus whereas pregnancy involves the continuation of the patriline, it also regulates a clan's dispersion into individual persons.

Even though substance remains constant over time, appearances change. Traditionally certain physical characteristics were, and to some extent still are, thought to be associated with particular clans. In San José the major clan differences in 1980 were between the Yaromba and Idnsikambo. These groups say that they were once physically different. The Yaromba were tall, light-coloured, and hairy; they wore beards and looked like foreigners. In contrast the

3. Other neighbouring peoples have different ways of relating to the spirit world. The Wachipaeri have personal possession by animal spirits (Lyon, 1967:35–6). The Asháninka broadly classify both the spirit and animal worlds with terms taken from their relationship terminology (Weiss, 1969). The Cashinahua have named groups which, according to Kensinger (1984:239) reflect relationships between the spirit, animal, and human worlds.

Idnsikambo were very short, brown in colour, and had no body hair. As time went on the two groups intermarried more frequently and now they are virtually indistinguishable to most people.

The Arakmbut conception of corporeality is that physical substance passes with the patriline from father to child in a continuous chain which links every person to the ancestors of their particular group. However at the same time, continuous marriage and sexual relations have led to a gradual entropic evening out of the differences, because many offspring can take the imprint of their mother's shape.

Clan identity is important in Arakmbut everyday life. People define themselves according to their clans in several contexts. The skills and qualities of a person belonging to a clan often reflect positively on other members, in the same way that criticising faults can be seen as a collective insult. During drinking parties, clan rivalries often come to a head between men who compete for prestige. Men will often identify themselves with phrases such as 'I am Idnsikambo' or 'I am Yaromba' and should someone insult the name of the clan fights can break out.

Women use their clan names to a lesser extent. At the times when women work in the gardens or on their string bags, many of their companions are members of the same onyu, but solidarity is less apparent than among men. Nevertheless when visiting other communities, the Arakmbut pass messages to relatives in the same clan and are the most likely to stay as guests with those of the same onyu.

Each clan has one or more names, some of which refer to mythological events. The main name is fixed but the other names are more flexible. The Arakmbut say that there is no sense in which the clans and the named objects have any direct connection in the sense of identity. For example, the idea that a Singperi is in any way a tapir was received as totally ridiculous. However each name has a position within the Arakmbut universe that relates some phenomenon to the clan according to an association.

There are seven Arakmbut clans in existence, with one (the Sikopo), which possibly made an eighth in the distant past.

The Arakmbut express the differences between the general name and associated names as in the following examples: 'The Yaromba are an onyu. The Yaromba are Yaro Arakmbut, Paron Arakmbut, Wambign Arakmbut, and Toto Arakmbut.' Everyone knows the general names of the clan but not many know the associated names. Clans with more than one associated name can use them interchangeably. No one was able to say whether these referred to sub-units within the clans; old men whom I asked were dubious. Associated names are therefore probably nothing to do with segmentation.

Table 4.1: A list of clan names[4]

Yaromba	Yaro (setico), Paron (turkey hen), Wambign (agouti), Toto;
Masenawa	Mbedntoktok (large oriole);
Singperi	Singpa (wild peach palm), Keme (tapir);
Wandigpana	Wawa (wasp), S'io (small oriole), Akidnet (capybara);
Embieri	Embi (creeper);
Idnsikambo	Owing (turkey buzzard);
Saweron	Mokas (collared peccary).

The names demonstrate two principal features of the Arakmbut clans. On the one hand each clan is a discrete entity providing the basis for a person's physical identity, whereas, on the other, it fits into a scheme of relationships that cover natural species.

Mythologically we have encountered two references to the clans in two important areas of Arakmbut social life – hunting and the organisation of marriage alliances. The myth of Wainaron (chapter two) tells of the manufacture of arrows for hunting and how they are associated with the clans. The myth of Wanamey in chapter one, in contrast, tells of the naming of the clans and how they should inter-marry. There are also specific myths, which tell different origin stories for the clans.

In Wainaron the woodpecker makes and breaks the various arrows which are eventually presented to five of the groups (the Embieri and Saweron do not come into the story). Arrows cannot be touched by women; they are therefore suitable for expressing the ideology of patrilineality which governs the name of the clan from one generation to the next. The different arrows are distinguished in the story by their length, from longest to smallest: Yaromba (for fish), Singperi (forest animals), Wandigpana (fish), Masenawa (birds), Idnsikambo (birds).

The story ends by saying that if the boy had not disobeyed the woodpecker each clan male would be an expert hunter. Unfortunately as a result of his misbehaviour, people miss the mark. The myth explains that in an ideal world each clan would have its expertise related to its arrow related to types of prey.

To some extent it is possible to see some correlations between the arrows and the clans. Fuentes (1982:57) says: 'Each Amarakaeri clan

---

4. This is not an exhaustive list, as there are undoubtedly many names not necessarily known in San José. A possibility is the name 'Great Rocks' for Wandigpana. This has been mentioned by Torralba (1979:92) on information provided by Thomas Moore. The name appears in Puerto Luz but the people of San José do not recognise it. In Shintuya I have also heard the Yaromba referred to as '*wambign Arakmbut*' (form of agouti), but this was not known in San José.

has at least one shaman [*wayorokeri*] who is associated with a particular animal and through this relation involves the rest of his clan companions in a preferential or special relation with the said species.'

This social expectation is emphasised by individual hunters drawing attention to successful catches of their species either when bringing the meat back from an expedition or in telling the story of the chase. There is no evidence to suppose that specific clans actually specialise in hunting certain animals, only that each clan, because of its relationship between dreamers and the spirits, is assumed to have an advantage when hunting certain species connected to those spirits.

In San José during 1980 there were expectations connecting clan with the following species: the Yaromba and Wandigpana were considered to be particularly good at ascertaining the whereabouts of fish. The Wandigpana were also reputedly good at hunting caiman and collared peccary. The Idnsikambo and Singperi were frequently in touch with the spirits of the tapir while the Yaromba were good at hunting the white-lipped peccary. The Idnsikambo were also reputed to be good at catching birds and monkeys.

The importance of the clan in the productive practices of hunting is paralleled by its role in that other accentuated area of Arakmbut social life – marriage. These are intimately connected because it is the prerequisite of every marriage for a man to present some meat, hunted by himself, to his intended wife. Wanamey provides an alternative account of the origin of the clans to Wainaron, which relates not to hunting but to marriage.

The clan is strictly exogamous. Any sexual relations that take place between members of the same clan could lead to deformity of offspring, illness, or even death. Strange family characteristics (such as lack of hair, early deaths etc.) are explained by reference to sexual relations within the clan and bring to mind the example in Wanamey of intercourse between a brother and sister, which resulted in the origin of death. This is not to say that intra-clan sexual relations do not take place. Examples of their occurrence attract great interest, but proof of such a relationship is difficult and rests mainly on gossip. Some say that the multiple names for each clan could have been strategies for people to marry within the clan, but this is speculation.

Although all clans are exogamous, in certain contexts the Yaromba and Masenawa on the one hand, and the Idnsikambo, Embieri, and Saweron on the other, treat each other as kin. The Arakmbut express this in various ways. When talking of the Saweron in Puerto Luz and the Embieri of Boca Inambari (neither of these clans is represented in San José), the Arakmbut say 'the Saweron are really Idnsikambo' or 'the Embieri are really Idnsikambo'. When talking about the Yaromba or Masenawa who live in San José I was told by a Yaromba 'we have the same kinship'. By this he meant that the relationship terminology was applied as if they were in the same clan (i.e. all Masenawa men in the same genealogical level as Yaromba are brothers and those in the first ascending level are fathers).

There is no reason why members of a clan cannot marry into any other, even if the two parties of the alliance 'share the same kinship'. In San José this happened several times between Yaromba and Masenawa. The immediate families of the married couple treat each other as affines but beyond this the two clans continue to regard each other as kin. Two out of three cases of such unions in San José were without offspring. This was explained by the suggestion that the groups were too closely tied for successful conception.

There is an important aspect of the clans that has not yet been discussed in detail. This is the continuation of the line and it is so significant that it could be said to be a defining characteristic. We have already noted that the continuity of the clan is expressed by reference to corporeality shared by members, which is not only physical but includes a certain spirit identity and the essential attribute of the name. The continuation of the clan line centres on the relations between men and women.

The clan is exogamous, and so a woman and her husband are always from different groups. Although a woman retains her clan name and membership after marriage, she passes neither on to her children for they all take the name of their father's clan. A woman is thus a vehicle through which another clan can continue. From the male point of view, all mothers and wives are outsiders in that they belong to different clans from the rest of the family. However, men cannot escape from the fact that without women the clans could not continue at all.

The relationship of females to the patrilineal clans from the perspective of lineality is as follows: a woman breaks the continuity of the clan line by marrying into another, but a woman from a different clan restores the line by marrying and producing children for her husband's clan. The lost sister is replaced by a wife. This transfer of women into and out of the clan patriline is a complementary relationship between one clan and others – between inside and outside consisting of a swapping of elements as described in chapter two.

As will become more apparent later, it is important to balance this 'clan' perspective, in which women appear as outsiders, with the 'residential' perspective, in which most men live for several years with their affines. This shows that, in the short term, the lineal 'cycling' of women is compensated by the husband 'cycling' laterally through the wife's pre-marital residence where he offers his labour and is temporarily the outsider. This does not negate the view that women pass through the clan line, but demonstrates that Arakmbut social life appears different according to one's perspective.

In the last chapter we noted that the difference in perspective of age and residence established a possible asymmetry in the complementary relations of gender. This is very noticeable with regard to the clan. When a woman marries and moves with her husband and children into a new house, the rest of her family are in a different clan. The male line uses the women gained as wives to produce offspring. The female offspring then leave the clan line in the next generation to marry out and produce children for another clan. The cycling of women through the clan is the effect of the combination of patrilineality and exogamy operating through time.

When it comes to reproducing the clan, the woman plays the crucial role of transforming the developing embryo, which is the accumulation of her husband's semen, into a child. We have already noted that semen is the substance of the baby, which is shaped by the mother. Her task is to break up the clan continuity to a certain extent and modify its communal physical and spiritual features into personal characteristics. However, the continuity of the line as a whole is her responsibility.

It is here that male/female inequality becomes apparent. Sterility is not common among Arakmbut women. Young women who do not conceive quickly enough are usually thought to be deliberately exercising their power over reproduction in order to challenge their husband's authority and can even be beaten. When a woman has remained barren for many years it is no longer thought to be her desire but a misfortune that has happened to her as a result of a misdemeanour in her past by herself or one of her family.

Intercourse is prohibited with all parallel relatives, which means not only members of one's own clan but also one's mother's sister's children. There is possibly a particular reason why the Arakmbut prefer to avoid sexual relations with close kin. Semen is the physical and spiritual emanation not only of the father but of all the father's clan. The womb is also physically of the substance of the clan but it has a shape influenced by that of the woman's mother and is common to her sisters too.

If a brother impregnates someone who is related to him as a sister, the brother/husband's seminal embryo is not modified by the womb shape of the sister/wife. As a result, a male child would be too similar to the brother/husband and a female too similar to the sister/wife. The Arakmbut have an aversion to the thought of duplicate people. The result of a brother/sister union would be the possibility of creating similar people across the generations. They say that too-similar people automatically die, which brings a threat to the parents and the rest of the family. The effect of this is that sexual relations between kin infect all connected in the family.

A husband and wife ought not to have intercourse at any time during the pregnancy or for nearly two years after the birth of the child, because there must be time between pregnancies to allow the womb of the mother to lose the shape of its previous occupant. Womb shape alters only within certain parameters. Providing the pregnant woman is of a sufficiently distant relationship to her husband and enough time is left between pregnancies, all should be well.

This issue of prohibited sexual relations is important because it illustrates quite clearly that although women do not contribute anything substantial to their offspring (such as, for example, blood), they do play a crucial role in the actual formation of their children. The effect of legitimate sexual relations is to prevent the continuity of the clan line from causing the creation of too-similar people. To reproduce a person too closely would mean that the substance and spirit of the father would be transferred without modification to the children, and this would lead to a cumulative concentration of clan identity. As we shall see later, in the spirit world especially, concentration of any power is very dangerous and could unleash harmful consequences.

This modificatory control or check on the accumulation of clan power is the prime reason for seeking wives from outside. It is therefore crucial to understand, that even though there is a patrilinearity and strong male ideology within the clan, the women have the ultimate control over its smooth continuation from one generation to another.

The life cycle involves birth, growth, and death and that the patriline line continues through the generations by means of a physical and spiritual transfiguration passed on from father to children. Women are important for determining the way in which the line grows, preventing the cumulative power of the substance from becoming dangerous. What effectively happens is that by marriage and pregnancy women break up the linearity of the life cycle and the clan line into generational units transferring semen from the 'above/forest' world of the father to the 'below/river' world of birth. Thanks to women, the patriline does not disappear at death but divides at adulthood during intercourse with the separation of the father's semen, and this leads to another birth.

Pregnancy is the only time when the clan line is completely in the power of women. They provide the residence for forming the embryo into a person. The observations here parallel with the points in the previous chapter, which stated how women use residence rather than age to make status differentiations and how men were oriented to the world outside of the household. Here the male semen comes from outside and is a foreign, potentially dangerous body that has to be tamed or 'cooked'.

Although it may be tempting to assume that the attitudes and significance of women are of little or no account in discussions of patrilineal units, the Arakmbut case shows this position to be specious. Asymmetry between male and female in the clan's continuation stems from the power of women over procreation, which results in a 'patrilineal problem'. As much as Arakmbut men would like ideologically to limit the position of women in procreation, the contradictions in the system prevent a male-biased ideology from dismissing the position of women in the community.

Men and women have different perspectives of Arakmbut social organisation. With regard to time and the principle of age and patrilineal descent, men see women as the outsider, coming from different clan, who, by cycling through the line, create regular alternations in the life cycle. Women, on the other hand, see the matter more from the principle of residence, where men and semen either come from the outside or are oriented to the world outside the sphere of female relations.

Having seen the relativity in perspectives between men and women it is time to see how they relate to each other when they are a part of marriage exchanges and the repercussions these have throughout Arakmbut social life.

II: Relationship terminology

The relationship terminology of the Arakmbut is a two-lined system articulated by symmetric prescriptive exchange. This is a conceptual model of marriage exchange where categories are organised in such a way as to classify everyone into relationships where parents' opposite sex siblings are classified in the same categories as parents-in-law. The implication is based on a classificatory form of marriage exchange between siblings.

There are three different contexts in which the relationship terminology is used: formal terms, reference terms, and direct address terms. Formal terms are used on ritual occasions such as marriage and death. Examples of these are *apagn* (F), *inang* (M), *apane* (GF), and, *opewadn* (spouse). Reference terms all have the prefix *wa-* and reflect status differences between the speakers and consequently some distance. The relative formality of reference terms can be gauged by the fact that they serve as formal terms for categories other than those above. Direct address terms are comparatively informal, drawing attention to the particular familial relationship between speakers. The relationship terminology as a whole draws attention to the network that relates all Arakmbut to one another.

There are three types of name among the Arakmbut, which parallel the use of the terminology. The personal name is not known by many people and constitutes the essence of a person, binding the body and soul together into one whole. The Arakmbut use informal nicknames to express closeness or to tease someone. Every person also has an ordinary name, which is used most of the time. For old men these are Arakmbut names but those born recently have Spanish names. Surnames come from the parent's Arakmbut names.

The result is a parallel between names and relationship terms as shown in Table 4.2.

Table 4.2 Connection between relationship terminology and names

	Relationship terminology	Names
Rarely used	Formal	Personal
Close persons	Direct address	Nicknames
Distance/Respect	Reference terms	Adult names

There are few differences between direct address and reference terms from a structural perspective. The two most obvious contrasts are the reference distinction between F and FB and the direct address terms for S and D. In spite of these, the basic principle of prescription is equally apparent in both sets of terms, and on the whole both sets share the same general characteristics. In common with other examples of this type of terminology, the Arakmbut make the following equations and distinctions:

$$F = FB \quad FZ = WM/HM \quad MB = WF/HF$$
$$B = FBS = MZS \quad WZ/HZ = BW \quad WB/HB = ZH$$
$$\text{male ego: } ZS = DH \quad ZD = SW \quad BD = ZSW \quad BS = ZDH$$
$$\text{female ego: } BS = DH \quad BD = SW \quad ZD = BSW \quad ZS = BDH$$
$$F \# MB \quad M \# FZ \quad BC \# ZC$$

Key: = means equivalent category # means non-equivalent categoy
F = Father; M = Mother; Z = Sister; B = Brother; W = Wife;
H = Husband; S = Son; D = Daughter; G + letter = Grand-;
combined letters reflect term (FB = Father's Brother;
MBD = Mother's Brother's Daughter).

Two other sets of equivalencies are present but need to be qualified. The equations FB = MZH, FBW = MZ, MB = FZH, MBW =
FZ all hold but in certain contexts a MZH can be the terminological
equivalent of MB (i.e. *chign*). A MZH called chign can never be a person's genealogical MB as this would mean that there had been an
incestuous union between MZ and MB. Instead the genealogical connection would have to be more distant such as FMBS or a MMBS.

The terminology equates all opposite sex members of ego's
genealogical level who are not affines by means of the term *pogn*.
After marriage *chimbui* is used to refer to affines such as a spouse's
same-sex sibling or a same-sex sibling's spouse. The terminology
prescribes marriage with those members of the category pogn who
fulfil the genealogical specification of bi-lateral cross cousin of the
opposite sex for both male and female speakers respectively. As the
category pogn does not distinguish this specification it is through the
equations FZ = WM/HM and MB = WF/HF that the category is
qualified as containing some members with whom marriage is prescribed and some with whom it is not.

The Arakmbut relationship terminology involves classification according to genealogical level, sex and age. There are five
genealogical levels (+2,+1,0,-1,-2). These are clearly distinguished
except in cases of old members of certain categories in +1 who are
classified as if they were in +2. Sex is distinguished except in the
term *wayayo* (grandchild) in -2. In 0 level terms, male and female
speakers use relative sex categories, which also appear in level -1,
when classifying each other's offspring. Relative age is marked by
the suffixes *-sipo* (younger) and *-tone* (older). The word *tong* is a direct
address term for any relative younger than the speaker.

The three medial genealogical levels of the terminology distinguish two classes of relative. The Arakmbut express this in terms of
a contrast between the offspring of same-sex siblings who cannot
marry and offspring of opposite-sex siblings with whom marriage
can take place. For example, marriage is prohibited with the child of
a *pagn* (F), *nang* (M) or *asign* (MZ) who is closely related to the
mother. Conversely, marriage is prescribed with the child of a *mang*
(FZ) married to a *chign* (MB) in the sense that these are the terms

Figure 4.1 Reference Terms in Arakmbut

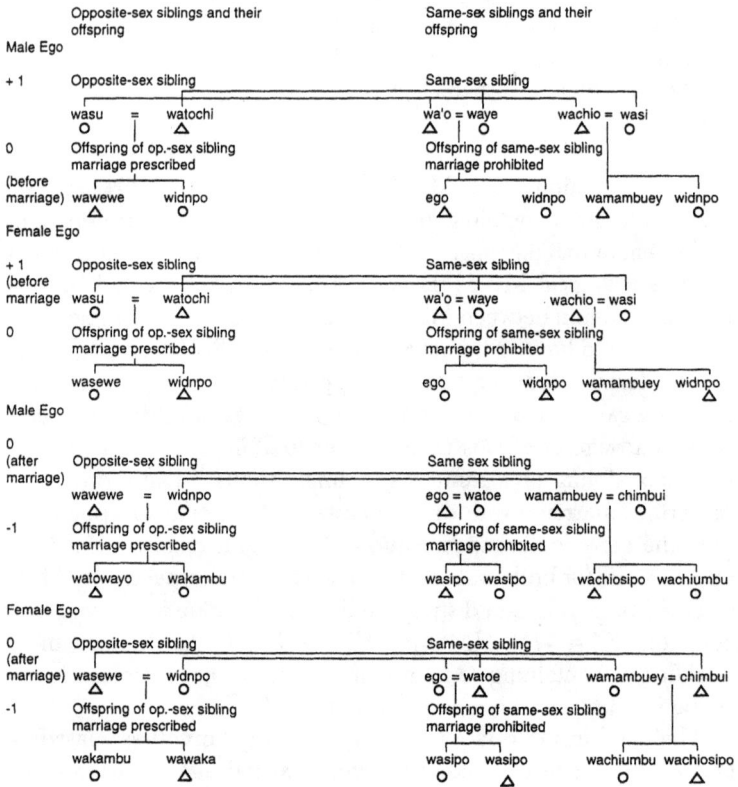

| | Opposite-sex siblings and their offspring | | Same-sex siblings and their offspring | | | |

Male Ego

+1 Opposite-sex sibling

wasu = watochi
O △

Same-sex sibling

wa'o = waye   wachio = wasi
△ | O   △ | O

0 (before marriage) Offspring of op.-sex sibling, marriage prescribed

wawewe   widnpo
△   O

Offspring of same-sex sibling, marriage prohibited

ego   widnpo   wamambuey   widnpo
△   O   △   O

Female Ego

+1 (before marriage) Opposite-sex sibling

wasu = watochi
O   △

Same-sex sibling

wa'o = waye   wachio = wasi
△ | O   △ | O

0 Offspring of op.-sex sibling, marriage prescribed

wasewe   widnpo
O   △

Offspring of same-sex sibling, marriage prohibited

ego   widnpo   wamambuey   widnpo
O   △   O   △

Male Ego

0 (after marriage) Opposite-sex sibling

wawewe = widnpo
△ | O

Same sex sibling

ego = watoe   wamambuey = chimbui
△ | O   △   O

-1 Offspring of op.-sex sibling, marriage prescribed

watowayo   wakambu
△   O

Offspring of same-sex sibling, marriage prohibited

wasipo   wasipo   wachiosipo   wachiumbu
△   O   △   O

Female Ego

0 (after marriage) Opposite-sex sibling

wasewe = widnpo
△ | O

Same-sex sibling

ego = watoe   wamambuey = chimbui
O | △   O   △

-1 Offspring of op.-sex sibling, marriage prescribed

wakambu   wawaka
O   △

Offspring of same-sex sibling, marriage prohibited

wasipo   wasipo   wachiumbu   wachiosipo
O   △   O   △

(In this diagram = means 'married to' and not 'terminological equivalence')

applied to one's parents-in-law. Similarly, in the genealogical level below, one's own children must not marry the offspring of an *egn* (B), *ming* (Z – woman speaking) or *chimbui* (opposite-sex affine of the same genealogical level), but should always marry the child of a *pogn* (Z – man speaking), *en* (B-in-law, man speaking) or *terweng* (Z-in-law -woman speaking). The diagrams above and below illustrate how the contrast between marriageable and non-marriageable categories appear to male and female speakers for both reference and direct address terms.

The Arakmbut make two statements which, as with Figures 4.1 and 4.2, demonstrate the implications of their terminology. They say that whereas a man cannot marry the daughter of a close *asign* (MZ), he must marry the daughter of a *mang* (FZ). In 1992 the possibility

Figure 4.2 Direct Address Terms in Arakmbut

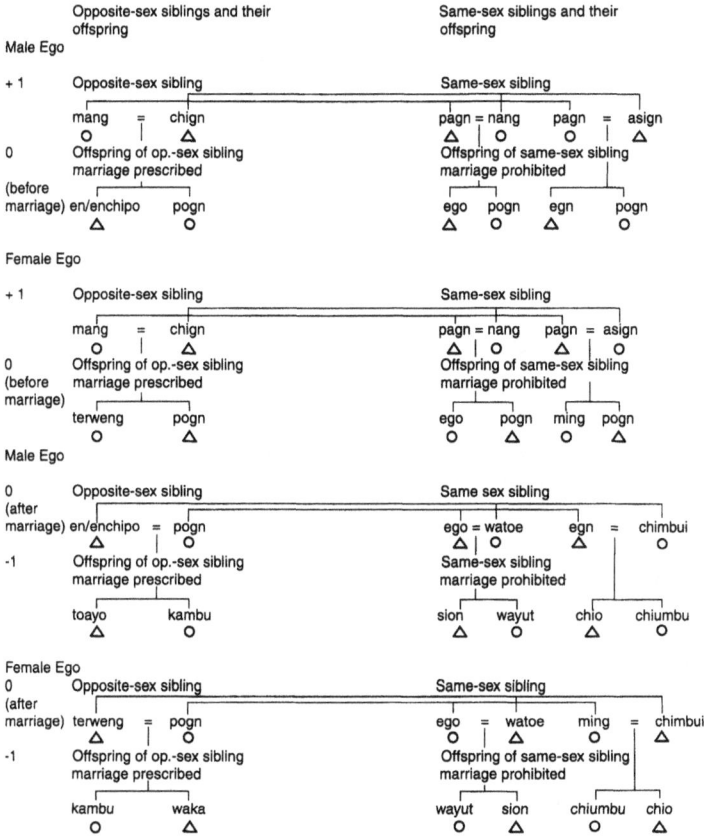

Male Ego

Opposite-sex siblings and their offspring	Same-sex siblings and their offspring

+1   Opposite-sex sibling   Same-sex sibling

```
        mang    =    chign              pagn = nang      pagn   =   asign
         O      |      △                 △  |  O          O     |    △
0      Offspring of op.-sex sibling     Offspring of same-sex sibling
       marriage prescribed              marriage prohibited
(before
marriage) en/enchipo   pogn             ego   pogn    egn    pogn
             △          O                △     O      △      O
```

Female Ego

+1   Opposite-sex sibling   Same-sex sibling

```
        mang    =    chign              pagn = nang      pagn  =  asign
         O      |      △                 △  |  O          △    |   O
0      Offspring of op.-sex sibling     Offspring of same-sex sibling
(before marriage prescribed            marriage prohibited
marriage)
        terweng       pogn              ego   pogn    ming    pogn
          O            △                 O     △      O       △
```

Male Ego

0   Opposite-sex sibling   Same sex sibling
(after

```
marriage) en/enchipo = pogn             ego = watoe    egn   =   chimbui
             △      |   O                △  |  O        △         O
-1     Offspring of op.-sex sibling     Same-sex sibling
       marriage prescribed              marriage prohibited
        toayo       kambu                sion   wayut    chio   chiumbu
         △           O                    △      O        △       O
```

Female Ego

0   Opposite-sex sibling   Same-sex sibling
(after

```
marriage) terweng  =  pogn              ego  =  watoe   ming  =  chimbui
            △      |    O                O   |   △       O        △
-1     Offspring of op.-sex sibling     Offspring of same-sex sibling
       marriage prescribed              marriage prohibited
        kambu       waka                wayut   sion    chiumbu   chio
          O           △                   O      △        O        △
```

(In this diagram = means 'married to' and not 'terminological equivalence')

of marrying the daughter of a distant asign (MZ) was more apparent than in 1980 and is discussed in the next volume, but after the marriage the woman is always referred to as mang (M-in-law). In addition to this, it is said that all marriages imply an exchange of sisters because a wife's chign (MB) is a husband's pagn (HF) and a husband's chign (MB) is his wife's pagn (WF). If marriage practice were to follow this model a person's pagn (F) would exchange sisters with his chign (MB), a male ego with his en (B-in-law) and his chio (BS) with his toayo (ZS). But this view is male and clan biased.

The distinction between the offspring of same-sex siblings and of opposite-sex siblings who exchange siblings is fundamental to the way the Arakmbut conceive of their terminology as a model for marriage alliance. It is the most clear-cut expression of the alliance principle they have. Every person classifies his or her social world according to the rules of the terminological model and so to a certain extent he or she will project its dual distinction onto other areas of the social organisation, but for men, clan is the starting point.

In the previous section, the clans were seen to be defined by patrilineality and an exogamic rule. A member of one clan can marry into any of the others. From an individual's point of view this has the effect of separating *oro onyu* (our clan) from *nogn onyu* (another clan). For a man, all women of his clan are forbidden as marriage partners because they are the offspring of his father and his brothers. The man must therefore seek a wife from another clan providing she is not a parallel cousin (MZD). In this way, from the perspective of an individual, the clan system coheres to some extent with the dual classification of the relationship terminology.

The terminological implications of sister exchange between the offspring of same-sex and opposite-sex siblings, however, can only be very broadly projected onto the clan system. The differences are extremely important because there is neither patrilineality nor a notion of corporeality implied in the ego-centred relationship terminology as these factors are associated exclusively with the clan. In addition to this there are several contexts when the distinction between same-sex and opposite-sex siblings does not fit in with the clan ideology. One example consists of occasions when the clan exogamic rule does not fit in with the terminological prescription. If the clan system were all-embracing within Arakmbut society then a person could marry the daughter of an asign (MZ) as long as she was in a different clan. Among the Cubeo this is indeed the case and clan exogamy overrides the terminological distinction between parallel and cross relatives; however, among the Arakmbut the MZ child prohibition limits clan exogamy and illustrates the overriding influence of the relationship terminology.[5]

A second example relates to the feature noted above that members of certain clans sometimes treat each other as if they were really

5. The Northwest Amazon have two ways of looking at the issue of the children of a mother's sister. The Cubeo (Goldman 1963: chapter four) have exogamic patrilineal phratries and a symmetric prescriptive relationship terminology. MZC can be married. Among the Bara and Barasana there is a category of Mother's Children which cannot be married (Jackson 1972,1983:107 and C.Hugh-Jones 1979:77). I would suggest that the differences are to do with the importance of patrilineality and the extent to which it is independent of the relationship terminology. Thus, among the Cubeo phratric exogamy overrides the terminology, whereas among the Bara and Barasana it does not. The Arakmbut lie in between.

members of only one. The clan as a whole is classified as if all its members sharing the same genealogical level were offspring of same-sex siblings. However in this context the exogamic rule holds even though marriage between clans related in this way is not encouraged. It is evident from this that with so few women available for marriage, unions will occur between clans that ostensibly 'share the same kinship'. When this happens the immediate families of the couple address each other as affines while at the same time preserving the overall conception of the two clans as being one.

These two examples show that there is a discrepancy between the Arakmbut classification of their relationship terminology and that of the exogamic rule of the clan. It is possible for some members of another clan to be classified as offspring of same-sex siblings while other members of the same clan are classified as offspring of opposite-sex siblings. In both cases the prescriptive implications of the terminology override clan exogam and male bias. The Arakmbut iron out this inconsistency by means of an alliance unit called a *wambet.*

III: The wambet and Relations of Affinity

The word wambet has the root *wamba,* which means 'room or area in a maloca where a family live'. A wambet differs from the *onyu* clan because it is not a named group. It is a category of relationships stemming from a particular individual and is relative to his or her position in the social organisation. The boundaries of the wambet are not clearly defined. Certain relations are always included but membership depends on the circumstances of the extended family. In practice a wambet consists of members of certain relationship categories who live in close proximity to each other. The most important relations in a wambet are the following:

(1) Members of a person's wambet include those people in the same clan from grandparents to grandchildren (i.e. grandfather, father and his siblings, ego's own siblings, and brother's children).
(2) A mother is in the same wambet as her children. An asign (MZ) living in close proximity to an individual will be in the same wambet.
(3) Cross cousins are not in a person's wambet. Usually a chign (MB) is in a different wambet. However, there are examples of old bachelors with no parents or married brothers alive who live with their sisters and share the same wambet as her children.

All the people in (1) and (2) who live in proximity to a person, particularly those who eat or ate at the same hearth, are members of the same wambet. In practice this means that one relative is never in a person's wambet – a spouse. All direct affines (i.e. spouse's siblings and sibling's spouses, and parents-in-law) belong to a different wambet. Although it is possible to marry within the wambet it is considered preferable to marry outside because the kin relations do not need to be redefined and balances the male 'clan' perspective.

The information that I received about the wambet came almost exclusively from women. As an alliance-arranging unit, the influence of women within the wambet is significant, particularly that of mothers, who have a detailed knowledge of genealogy, clan membership, and maloca affiliation. Although it is not a 'female' unit of organisation in the same way that the clan is 'male', the wambet reflects the residential criteria which we associated with women in the previous chapter.

A marriage brings together two wambet in an alliance that forms the wambet of the offspring of the union. This means that an offspring's wambet includes members from both the father's and mother's wambet. Each wambet has an actual affinal relationship with the wambet and clan of the spouse (excluding any asign's (MZ) children there may be). Among the Arakmbut affinity is a more distant and potentially violent relationship than that between kin, and much of social life consists of trying to reduce the possible tensions between affinal relatives.

The wambet is a major alliance-arranging unit whose members have an obligation to help one another find a spouse. The wambet constitutes the household of each of the potential marriage partners and neighbours, which, after the marriage and birth of offspring, form the core of a new wambet of the children. The inclusion of the mother and some of her kin shows that the wambet overrides the fixed unilineal boundaries of the clan. From the point of view of the clan both a mother and a wife are to some extent outsiders; however the wambet shows that a mother is less of an outsider than a wife.

From an offspring's point of view, the wambet is a cognatic unit. A person's mother's and father's kin are included among its members and it is an ego-based bilateral category that operates to suppress affinity as a household begins to reproduce. However, the cognatic model does not account for the alliance practices because any cognation in Arakmbut society stems from the amalgamation by marriage of two wambet alliance units. The nature of this amalgamation is a course of development changing the wambet over time.

Like the MZ children mentioned earlier where the relationship terminology overrides clan exogamy, the alliance element in Arakmbut life overrides any cognatic features.[6]

There are two stages in the development of the wambet over a person's lifetime. During childhood a person has no actual affines and so the wambet are all those people who eat at their mother's hearth and who take an interest in his or her life, such as parents, grandparents, and siblings. These people are most involved in organising the future marriage arrangements for the child and are the most frequent recipients of meat distribution from the household.

During their growth to adulthood, children gradually increase their affines as siblings begin to get married and when they themselves marry. As adults, people find that they share food with those who are affines and who are from a different wambet but with whom they join to form the wambet of their children. This shift in the perspective of the wambet is important as it illustrates a change in behavioural patterns over life as some potential affines become actual affines and then become bound together in relation to the future affines of the subsequent generation.

We have noted that the distinction between same-sex siblings and their offspring in contrast to opposite-sex siblings and their offspring is fundamental to Arakmbut social classification. Broadly speaking, parents, their same-sex siblings, and their offspring are all full kin, while the wambet and clan of a spouse or sibling's spouse are actual affines. In between these extremes there are two ways of dealing affinity. One consists of the pool of cross relations who are potential affines prior to marriage and who are treated as kin, while the other consists of affines forged by the marriage, who gradually, through alliance and close relationships, become treated as kin.

The discussion of affinity demonstrates that the Arakmbut interact in a more complicated and subtle manner than the classification system of the relationship terminology allows. The relationship terminology does not make this kin/affinal distinction so clear-cut, and it is only possible to understand how it works by taking behavioural and attitudinal factors into consideration. The following outline of behaviour traces the differences and varieties of relations between kin, affines, and those in between. It is not meant to delimit the way

6. This may account for the Arakmbut's comparatively clear demarcation of affinal relationships after marriage. Unlike other Amazonian peoples such as the Piaroa (Kaplan 1975), the Shiwar (Seymour-Smith, 1988), and the Amuesha (Santos-Granero, 1991), the Arakmbut do not convert affines to kin as a rule but according to the relationship.

in which every individual Arakmbut behaves, but to draw attention to certain considerations that a person will use when relating to his or her relatives.

The most important kin a person has are those who do not produce potential marriage partners – parents and their same-sex siblings. The relationship between a father and son is one of authority and respect and is marked by a formality on which rests a powerful bond. No son would ever criticise his father for any reason whatsoever and should receive criticism from him as sound advice. The other pagn in a person's clan (FB) have similar authority but without the respect owed to a real father. Conflicts between pagn and children in their clan are kept to an absolute minimum. There is not so much interest shown by a father in his daughter except for a certain amount of indulgence in her youth and extreme interest in her marriage partner when she is old enough to marry.

The relationship between a mother and her son is one of strict discipline when the boy is young but becomes more informal when he grows older and is ready to marry. He is likely to treat her as a good-natured old lady whose foibles are amusing but as a person whose will should not be crossed. The mother/daughter bond is very strong. This tie constitutes the strongest affectual bond between women in Arakmbut society. A mother does not have the authority over her daughter that a father has over his son. For this reason, when conflicts do arise between a mother and daughter they can be intense and somewhat disturbing to other members of the community.

An asign (MZ) is basically a surrogate mother. I have noticed that an asign in the same clan as a person's mother is more indulgent to her sister's children than an asign unrelated to the mother. These unrelated asign are potential mothers-in-law (mang). I was drawn to this conclusion by the case of some youths whose mother had died. The role of mother was taken over not by another woman from their mother's clan, but an asign who was married to their father's brother and who treated them strictly. They complained that she was not their real asign as she was not in their mother's clan and for this reason was less indulgent to them.

Whereas the terms pagn (F), nang (M), asign (MZ) and the reciprocal terms chio (same-sex sibling's S) and chiumbu (same-sex sibling's D) refer to people who consider each other to be kin throughout their lives, the terms chign (MB), mang (FZ) and their reciprocals toayo (ZS man speaking), waka (BS woman speaking) and kambu (opposite-sex sibling's D) refer to affines. However, the terms can undergo changes in certain circumstances. Men in the +1 genealogical level who are not in a person's clan are chign, and there are cases when a man will call a categorical chign by the term 'pagn'. This takes place when friendship existed between the father and uncle. The categorical relationship chign takes precedence ultimately, however, because even though ego might refer to a chign by the term pagn as a result of his father's friendship, he can still marry the older man's daughter. After marriage he will call his father-in-law chign as usual.

There is a considerable variety of possible behaviour differences in relating to a chign depending on the relationship and the extent to which friendship is present. Initially a child shares his father's attitude towards someone in this category. If there is a warm relationship between a man and his cross relatives such as brothers-in-law, the children will have a warm relationship with their chign consisting of joking, teasing, and humour. If, on the other hand, there is hostility between a man and his male cross relatives, the children will enter into the conflict, frequently adding fuel to the flames with gossip and exaggeration.

A chign does not have authority over his toayo (ZS) and the men will treat each other as kin, distant allies, or potential affines. However this all changes if a man marries his chign's daughter (MBD). A son-in-law has certain rights and obligations in relation to his father-in-law, which make their relationship more formal than before the marriage. He has rights in relation to a chign's daughter provided his wambet can either offer a woman in return or else he moves in with his new wife's family and works for the chign.

The type of relationship between a chign and a kambu (ZD) depends on whether they are married or not. If they are unmarried they are possible marriage partners. In a marriage the husband can be ten years older than his wife, which facilitates unions across generations and genealogical levels. There are several examples in San José as well as in other communities of a chign marrying a kambu. In the courtship preceding such unions the couple relate to each other as if they were cross cousins where an outer reserve and inner intensity become more blurred as they let their feelings for each other become known.

A kambu who has married the son of a chign is very reserved towards her father-in-law and avoids him as much as possible. This avoidance minimises conflicts and any sexual temptations. On the whole relations between people of the opposite sex are far more reserved and distant when there is any possibility of sexual relations.[7]

---

7. Rivière mentions this aspect of avoidance and sexuality in his discussion of the subject (1969:208).

The relationships that a person has with his or her mang (FZ) do not cover such a range as those with a chign. A mang has neither the authority nor the indulgence of a nang (M) or asign (MZ). Most children do not appear to have much to do with their mang, even those who are their father's sisters. There is no avoidance as such, but a polite formality. In the case where a transition is made from potential to actual affine, the son- or daughter-in-law relates to their mother-in-law with a more distant and frequently very cool formality. In an affinal context all her opinions and criticisms must be accepted passively no matter what they are.

The behavioural and attitudinal traits in levels +1/-1 enable us to make certain refinements to the distinction between kin and affine. At one extreme are parents and their same-sex siblings who are kin throughout life, and at the other are spouses and spouses' parents who are affines. They are treated as kin until such time as some of them become actual affines.

There are two main features in behavioural and attitudinal traits between Arakmbut relatives. We have noticed that the clearest bonds between members of adjacent genealogical levels are between a father and his sons or father's brothers and their brother's sons, whereas among women a mother is closer to her daughter and a mother's sister to her sister's daughters. This is probably because among the Arakmbut men and women tend to spend most of the day apart. For this reason too, men have more dealings with their chign (MB) and women with their mang (FZ), although after marriage more formal relations with parents-in-law mean that interaction is on a strictly 'working' basis.

The other feature of Arakmbut relationships is the difference between those people classified as siblings of a person's father and those classified as siblings of a person's mother. Paternally classified relatives (pagn (F) and mang (FZ)) have a formal and respectful relationship with their reciprocal relatives. A mother and her classified relatives (nang (M), asign (MZ) and chign (MB)) have a less formal and more volatile relationship with their reciprocal relatives. The range is greater than with paternal relations. There can be strict discipline from a mother or asign and possible open hostility with a chign, yet they are capable of indulgent, friendly, and joking relationships.

Although the interaction between same-sex and opposite-sex relatives applies throughout Arakmbut society, the behavioural contrast between 'paternal' and 'maternal' relatives is really only relevant within the confines of a settlement. As people encounter relations outside the wambet and the clan of both parents, the distinction becomes more diluted and not very meaningful because interaction is so scanty. If, on the other hand, a person decided to move to another community to seek a wife, he or she would work out a relationship with the members and use the behavioural and attitudinal expectations as a framework for social interaction. This, added to the chemistry of specific interpersonal affections, constitutes the basis for creating and re-creating relationships.

Within an individual's genealogical level the distinction between parallel and cross relatives is less clear-cut. When I asked the Arakmbut about the classification of relatives in level 0, they said that men distinguish same sex siblings (egn) from cross cousins (en), while women distinguish their same sex siblings (ming) from cross cousins (terweng). However, when I obtained lists of relationship terms as applied to specific individuals I discovered that what was theoretically a distinction between parallel and cross relatives was, in practice, not so apparent. There were several cases of cross cousins being referred to as egn and in conversations I heard a man shift from calling his cross cousin egn to en in a matter of minutes.

The Arakmbut accept that those people whom a man addresses as egn (B) and those a woman addresses as ming (Z) are close and relations are friendly. Similarly, any cross cousins of the same sex with whom a person has close relations will be called egn or ming. En (man speaking B-in-law) or terweng (woman speaking Z-in-law), on the other hand, are more distant. When I addressed men in the village they did not like me calling them en because it did not seem so friendly. In the same way, when cross cousins who call each other egn or ming fall out they revert to the more correct en and terweng terms.

Siblings call each other egn or ming while brothers-in-law should be en and sisters-in-law terweng. People who are potential affines treat each other as kin while, after marriage, if there is a special affection between in-laws they 'suppress their affinity'. However this is an expression of affection as much as a denial of affinity.

The flexible application of 0 level categories is an indication of the presence of a pool of relatives prior to marriage who are not full kin and are not affines. If no clear affinal relation exists, or if there is a special relationship of affection, the flexible system continues across the generations, as we saw with shifts between pagn (FB) and chign (MB).

All members of the opposite sex in a person's genealogical level who are not affines are called pogn (Z). In Puerto Luz, Bob Tripp found that there was a formal term *waenpogn* (literally 'affinal sibling') to fit the category of potential spouse or bi-lateral cross cousin. San

José said that pogn was the only term used and that they had never heard of waenpogn in this context, although it may have existed in the past.

The Arakmbut consider it extremely ill-mannered to refer to someone as a potential spouse. Theories claim that this phenomenon is caused by either excessive embarrassment (Basso: 1970:412) or by the suppression of affinity (Thomas 1978:75–6). These explanations are connected, and both apply to the Arakmbut. We have seen in this section that the Arakmbut often avoid cross cousin terms unless a person is an actual affine, and this can continue through the generations. This functions to cut down social distance, particularly within a community where most youngsters treat each other as kin. With cross cousins of the opposite sex there is a problem because the suppression of affinity makes potential affines closer, yet at the same time a marriage partner must be someone sufficiently distant to make sexual relations successful. The problem is to some extent resolved by using relationship terms for potential affines which would usually be reserved for kin, and at the same time by behaving with reserve and a certain element of formal respect.

The process of affinity formation and suppression takes place throughout life according to the context of each ego-based relationship. A child will recognise the affines of his or her parents and treat them with respect; however, on the same genealogical level, children are called by kin terms and treated as 'potential affines'. As a child grows older, potential affines become actual affines through marriage. For a period, each adult sees the community as separated into affines and kin, particularly through the period of procreation. However as children grow up and their wambet begins to discuss future marriages, affinity can become more suppressed, particularly between in-laws who are close friends. Whereas this process operates on an *ad hoc* basis, it demonstrates that affinity is created, used and suppressed at different moments through life and that the life cycle of the wambet reflects this.

IV: Marriage

There are two occasions when potential marriage partners can meet. Clandestine meetings take place in the forest near the chacras or on the way home from gold work, while parties are excuses for more formal interaction. Traditionally dances were the time when marriage partners would be sought out. Nowadays these do not take place as they used to. Instead, during our stay in San José there arose a custom of 'disco dancing' to records on battery-operated record players or tape recorders. Some of the young men who had been away from the village organised dances outside the houses in the style of Peruvian discos which were attended by most of the community. At these occasions men always tried to dance with potential marriage partners. Sometimes this proved difficult and very young girls (i.e. under ten) were called into the dance to make up the numbers.

While we were in San José a young man got married. I congratulated him, as was the custom, and complimented him on his choice of wife. He replied: 'It is not that she is the nicest woman in the village I can marry but she is the only woman in the village I can marry.' The acute gender imbalance in the village means that there are several men competing for each available young girl. The prime competitors are brothers, for they share the same possible marriage partners. Other rivals in the village are kept at a distance to minimise open conflict.

The time when the unity of the clan is threatened is when brothers compete for the same woman. In San José there were two such instances leading to serious fights, which are usually avoided between members of the same clan. The result of the fights was that one of the brothers had to leave the community for a while until tensions eased. While brothers are inclined to bicker and fight with each other, relations between cross cousins who are not seeking the same women are inclined to be good. This may be the case of a man making friends with potential affines in order to increase his chances in the marriage stakes, or it may simply be that where there is no competition, relations are more relaxed. However, it is noticeable that young men frequently make close friendships with their en (B-in-law). These en they will address as egn (B).

A feature in the seeking of a wife is the extraordinary secrecy surrounding the objects of a person's attraction. For example, several times during my stay in San José I was taken aside by a young man and told in an almost conspiratorial tone that he wanted to marry a particular girl. The objective of this apparent secrecy is to avoid openly admitting a desire to marry a girl but to use the mechanisms of village talk to enable one's name to be linked with that of a certain girl. In this way people try to keep rivalries to a minimum. Furthermore if a suitor is turned down, secrecy prevents humiliation. If marriage is refused, the chindoi meat is returned to the hunter.

The Arakmbut word for marriage is *e'toepak* which means 'to be with' or 'to be tied', sharing the root *toe* with the term *watoe* meaning 'spouse'. Marriages are usually approved by the parents who, when they have checked the relations between the clan of the intended couple, run through all the possible alternatives in the community in case a better union can be found. I was told by a newly-married young man that his parents, deliberating over his choice of wife, went on for months even though the alternatives were few. Indeed, when looking at how prescription and prohibition work in practice, I went through the available young women in San José ticking them off the list because of clan, categorical or other objections. His response was: 'You sound just like my mother.' In fact mothers play a key part in the decision as to the spouse of a child because of their encyclopedic knowledge of relationships – terminological, clan, genealogical, and wambet.

Marriage is sometimes settled by means of a church ceremony in Puerto Maldonado, performed by a priest, but this is comparatively rare. In most cases there is a formal ceremony which is very short and consists of the couple naming their new affines by the appropriate formal term. This is followed by a party at which everyone in the community celebrates.

As watoe (spouse) is a special category of kin rather than an affine, the only term which refers exclusively to opposite sex affines is *chimbui* (spouse's same sex sibling or same sex sibling's spouse). A person and their chimbui try to be friendly. If a spouse dies it is sometimes the case that the widow or widower will marry his or her chimbui. The children of a chimbui can never marry one's own children. I have some evidence which points to the possibility that in certain circumstances a man whose wife died young and is unable to find another wife occasionally has sexual access to a brother's wife (his chimbui). As the notion of paternity is to some extent the transmission of a substance common to all members of a clan, the sharing of one wife does not usually affect the offspring of the people concerned.

Brothers-in-law usually get on well when they live in close proximity. This may be to do with a conscious effort on their part to preserve each other's goodwill for political purposes. A man will be friendly with his wife's brother and his sister's husband but behaviourally this does not extend to their parallel cousins. The result is that there is an inner affinal group who are friendly but beyond this hostility lurks.

As people marry and grow older the relationships between brothers improve, especially when they have wives. At this point clan solidarity increases in opposition to more distant affines and other cross relatives. Most young men have some conflicts with members of their clan whom they consider to be rivals and frequently cultivate friendships with potential affines. After marriage the links between brothers strengthen as they defend the interests of their clan in the political arena of the village and they are no longer rivals for the same women.

The wambet as an alliance arranging unit distinguishes kin from affines. However, as with relationship terminology, there are behaviuoral and attitudinal traits that separate potential and suppressed affines, who are treated as a sort of kin, from actual affines who are treated with more reserve. A child's wambet lives and eats together and in practice is distinguished from the wambet of his potential affines. As a person grows up, some of his potential affines become actual affines by marriage to him or to his siblings. This can continue until such time when almost a whole community can be divided into kin and affine. At this point, personal affections increasingly suppress affinity, particularly with the drawing together of wambet ties while arranging the alliances of children.

Marriage exchange is a form of reciprocity which is perpetuated in social time and space. (Broadly speaking, the classification presented in Århem (1981:149) is useful as a rough guideline.) Generalised reciprocity in terms of marriage takes place between people who are already related as allies. A return need not be made immediately and, in the case of marriage, an exchange can take place over several generations. Balanced reciprocity usually necessitates a more immediate return and occurs between people who are more distant. Negative reciprocity is, in marital terms, stealing or eloping, which involves no necessary return.

Marriage exchanges can be symmetric where the same pair of wambet exchange spouses. Usually this is impossible because of imbalance between the larger number of men than women in the community. Indeed, in 1991 I heard it argued that sister exchange limits fair competition among young men for wives. In spite of the terminological implications, there is no guarantee that sister exchange is necessarily desirable, as will become apparent in Volume 2 (c.f. Needham 1971:20). Where sister exchange (a term used by Arakmbut men) is not possible there are several ways of delaying the return. ZD and FZD marriage are both present among the Arakmbut and are variations of symmetric exchange carried over two genealogical levels (see Needham 1962:109–111, and Rivière 1966).[8]

8. There are several inter-genealogical level marriages in San José. The gender imbalance may account for the fact that there are six cases, as opposed to only three in Puerto Luz where the balance of women to men is more equal. All the marriages are with a classificatory sister's daughter and not a real sister's

It may be tempting to equate marital exchange with balanced reciprocity and ZD or FZD marriage, which is completed over several genealogical levels, with generalised reciprocity. To say this would be to confuse generation with genealogical level. The Arakmbut could, in practice, arrange a ZD marriage as balanced reciprocity if a wambet agrees that a man's BD can marry his WB. Similarly a FZD exchange could be completed 'in one go', even though two genealogical levels are involved, if an agreement enables a man's elder brother's daughter to marry the son of his wife's elder brother. For this reason, types of reciprocity and genealogical categories of marriage partners are independent variables.[9] However, delayed exchanges certainly do take place, although the Arakmbut observe wryly that when the next generation is ready to continue the promised alliance, partners do not always comply with the agreement as so much time has passed. The excessive numbers of men seeking wives is undoubtedly a major factor threatening the smooth running of the marital exchange system.

Every time a man marries the daughter of a mang who is not of his father's onyu he may be preventing a symmetric exchange from taking place. The advantage of men living uxorilocally and carrying out bride services is that it ensures, among other factors, that some reciprocation for the wife is secured. It is quite possible in practice that over a period of time any Arakmbut community can be shown to have some asymmetric exchanges and even 'marrying in a circle' within its boundaries.

It may also be tempting to equate the 'one-way flow' of women in asymmetric exchange with negative reciprocity. However, a group only has to attract a woman in return for one lost to achieve a *de facto* symmetric exchange arising from cumulative negative reciprocity. Thus for the Arakmbut, in practice, neither symmetric nor asymmetric exchanges can be related to any one type of reciprocity.

The Arakmbut see all marriages, *de post facto*, as symmetric exchanges, because the terminological prescriptive structure is auto-

---

daughter, which avoids any complicated reorganisation of how the terminology should be applied after marriage. On the whole, the ages of the spouses in inter-genealogical unions are much the same as in those within the same level (c.f. Rivière 1969:158).

9. This is not always the case in Amazonia. According to C. Hugh-Jones the Barasana make a clear differentiation between FZC and MBC. In her analysis (1979:85) she compares patrilateral unions, which involve a delayed exchange with matrilateral unions which constitute a one-way flow of women. The Arakmbut do not contrast symmetric and asymmetric exchanges in this way.

matically imposed as the new kin terms are uttered at the moment of marriage. Bride service is a part of the reciprocal exchange relationships surrounding marital arrangements and is a fundamental aspect of marriage negotiations. In certain circumstances it can be avoided, as is discussed in Volume 2. The in-laws benefit from the hunting and gold work of the son-in-law who is in return recognised as husband of the daughter. The resulting exchange effectively means that only when there is no negotiation over the union will the marriage not appear to be symmetric in some sense. Even when a couple may have eloped, once a negotiation establishes an agreement between the families the marriage will appear symmetric. Thus a symmetric union in Arakmbut terms is any union between two consenting groups in which there is some reciprocation. In practice we should therefore see the male notion of 'sister exchange in which women move in and out of the clan' as complementing a female perspective where the man 'moves in and then out' of the household during bride service.

Marriages that follow the symmetric ideal either initiate or continue a series of exchanges. The Arakmbut consider the majority of their marriages to be 'serial'.[10] They demonstrate the continuity of exchanges by describing them in terms of alliances between clans within the same communities (identified in terms of maloca groups) which have married each other over several generations. Physically the alliance constitutes an arrangement between two households consisting of different clans and wambet that are embedded within ties crossing the whole community and beyond. There is little need for genealogical explanations. This independence from genealogy enables some correlation to be made between series of marriage exchanges and the types of reciprocity mentioned earlier. Marriages outside a series of alliances constitute negative reciprocity; those which initiate a series are more balanced and those which continue series already started are more generalised.

Asymmetric exchanges that are part of negotiated arrangements are transformed into symmetric exchanges by the relationship terminology and activities such as bride service. These idealised symmetric exchanges are arranged in series of alliances by means of a subtle inter-relationship between clan and wambet, encapsulated

10. Henley (1982:109) – following Kaplan (1975) – defines the principle of 'serial affinity' as a person marrying someone from a conjugal family to which their own conjugal family is already connected by earlier marriages. In the Arakmbut case we have to substitute 'onyu in the same community' for conjugal family. Henley discusses two forms of serial affinity – replication and reciprocation. These correspond to asymmetric and symmetric exchanges respectively.

within the household through the physical buildings of the house and kitchen and embedded within the community through the all-embracing connections of the relationship terminology.

It is now possible to link the various points made in this chapter to see how the onyu and wambet work together in San José. The village consists of a conglomeration of households throughout which are spread the distinctions of onyu and wambet, providing the parameters for marriage exchanges expressed by the relationship terminology. Each person's identity is bound up with his or her clan, the application of the relationship terminology, and the development of the wambet.

Marriage is the moment when the gender relationship is distinct but close. Exchange between spouses not only involves social ties between households and clans, but is also part of a cosmological exchange between forest and river, as noted in chapter two. Furthermore the emphasis on social principles – age for men and residence for women adds another dimension to the exchange which takes place at marriage. The relationship between the onyu and the wambet becomes relevant here. When talking to men, the onyu is emphasised more than the wambet, whereas the information I gathered on the wambet came primarily from women. This reinforces the lineal/age connection with men and the alliance/residence connection with women. Marriage is the moment when women become incorporated into a household which belongs to another onyu while men become incorporated through uxorilocal residence into another wambet. In this way, prior to neolocal residence, both principles undergo a form of exchange.

In daily life the marriage exchange is repeated through production activities. A man develops relationships with the spirit world through knowledge which is usually passed down through the clan line. His success reflects on the prestige of his clan as a whole. When a woman arranges the meat for distribution, she shares it not only with the clan relatives of her husband, but also with her own kin. This establishes a bond between a broad set of people who will form the wambet of her children. In this way, as production activities reflect the complementarity between male and female, they also reflect the clan/wambet complementarity expressed through the marriage relationship. The exceptions to this provide evidence of internal shifts which take place from time to time within the community, and these are dealt with in more detail in Volume 2.

Marriage provides the means to see how the relationship terminology of the Arakmbut is applied. Although the exogamic rule means that it is not possible to tell prohibited from prescribed relatives by referring to the clan of a person, it is, on the other hand, possible to tell this from the clan of that person's parents. People prohibited in marriage are those whose parents share the same sex and clan. Thus the clan operates with terminological categories of classification.

There is some evidence for this in discussing relationships with different people in Arakmbut society. Children up to puberty knew correctly everyone's clan membership in the community but not the correct relationship term, and when unsure they tried to work it out by reference to clan membership. The onyu and the wambet thus work together in applying the terminology and putting its possibilities into action. In both cases, however, it is marriage which acts as a catalyst for creating and suppressing affinity while defining clan membership through exogamy, all of which takes place within the overarching framework of the relationship terminology.

Table 4.3 Comparison of attributes of onyu and wambet

Onyu clan group	Wambet alliance category
Male perspective	Female perspective
Based on corporeality	Based on proximity
Lineality tempered by relationship terminology	Cognatic ties tempered by relationship terminology
Distinguishes father's and mother's relatives but the exogamic rule does not always distinguish prescribed and prohibited relatives.	Distinguishes between prescribed and prohibited relatives but does not distinguish between mother's and father's onyu.
By comparing the onyu of people's parents it is possible to make sufficient distinctions to apply the relationship terminology to specific people.	The wambet does not make enough distinctions to aid any specific application of the relationship terminology but acts as a relative-based alliance arranging unit.
Any marriage is an alliance between two onyu. Every member of the spouse's wambet sees every member of the partner's onyu as actual affines.	Marriages are de post facto alliances between wambet who see each other as actual affines.

Arakmbut social organisation consists of the superimposition of structural principles. In daily life, the classificatory terminology, the onyu and the wambet all co-exist. Marriage is important in articulating the differences between these aspects of social organisation while, drawing them together into a coherent and flexible system. All marriages take place between clans but they are arranged by the wambet, with particular influence from the mother. Women's knowledge of clan membership, the history of malocas, and the relationship terminology throughout Arakmbut communities, provides them with influence in marriage negotiations.

After marriage, members of the spouse's clan who were originally potential affines become actual affines. Therefore, although the wambet arranges a marriage, the repercussions of the alliance involve the whole onyu. San José is made up of what appears to be alliances between onyu, arranged by the wambet of the spouses which in their turn create the wambet of the offspring.

Every marriage is the passing of a woman from one patriline to another, but it is also the passing of a man from one household to another. We noted in the chapter on gender that Arakmbut marriage was an example of complementarity because elements from the forest and river were traditionally exchanged. The most obvious case of complementarity in marriage is the ideal of symmetric sister exchange when two clans become affinally related by swapping 'sisters' or where the patrilineal separation of the women is balanced by a residential separation of the man.

However, an ideal symmetric complementarity becomes asymmetric when the different perspectives on age and residence come to the fore. If the patrilineal clan is emphasised, marriage stresses the asymmetric aspects of the clan in which women cycle through the male corporeal line. This is more likely to take place if a man does not move uxorilocally to his bride's house and can have repercussions throughout the community (see Volume 2). However the relationship terminology contains a fundamentally symmetric idea of exchange, and whatever the situation in the community between households, inconsistencies are ironed out by the application of the terms.

In practice, asymmetric relationships do not go away if behaviour belies the relationship terminological application, wherein arises the possibility of exploitative unequal relationships. In this way, a complementarity between women and men can easily be transformed into one in which women lose their position in the household. This occurs if a husband makes too heavy demands on his wife over food production, cooking, or child-bearing and her relations are not nearby to support her. On the other hand, when sons-in-law carry out their bride service, an asymmetric aspect of alliance can easily shift into a dyadic relationship of exploitation if the in-laws assert their control over the newcomer by taking the products of his hunting or gold work and converting this into prestige for the father-in-law. On the whole, a son-in-law will bide his time because after a few years he has the right to move with his wife into a new house where he can establish himself independently. Fights and conflicts within the community can arise when the ideal orders of complementarity, epitomised in myths such as Wanamey, encounter the contingencies of the Arakmbut socio-cultural world.

This section of the book, following the myth of Wanamey, has looked at Arakmbut social organisation as a series of principles superimposed onto each other, contributing to a complicated pattern of life which is constantly reforming its shape according to the historical conditions in each community. Underlying all of the principles is the gender relationship in which the household and community provide poles of articulation and orientation for male/female relations, emphasising age and residence or onyu and wambet as aspects of status according to the context. Furthermore, the asymmetrical feature of the clan is balanced to some extent by the constantly changing wambet alliance category which, through the spatial and relationship categories, is forged into a system. However the instability between these layers produces a constant dynamic which is further analysed in Volume 2.

Having looked at the social organisation of an Arakmbut community, we should review the ways in which the Arakmbut conceptualise the relationship between the recalcitrant aspects of daily life and a structured framework from the perspective of their cultural ties to the invisible world.

PART II

That which can be and is not is said to exist in potency, while that which already is, is said to exist in act.

– Thomas Aquinas, *De Principiis Naturae*

Drawing: Tomás Arique

She was laughing with the rubber tree Awiruk

PREFACE

Nature and Potentiality

The concept of nature has a broad and overwhelming history. From Thales of Miletus to Lévi-Strauss, nature has been a fundamental source of speculation and explanation. The Arakmbut clearly speculate about the natural world, but within their own framework. To illustrate how this arises we can look at three different non-Arakmbut views of nature.

The early pre-Socratic philosophy was centred around understanding nature – *phusis*. In his study of Greek philosophy, Barnes (1987:19–20), distinguishes two senses of the term: natural objects which grow (animate objects) and a principle of growth within each natural phenomenon. This notion was made into a fundamental principle of physics by Aristotle (Russell 1946:227–8).

A more static view of nature emerged in the eighteenth century, following discoveries in the natural sciences (Hampson 1987:101), when Rousseau, Locke, Hobbes, Montesquieu, and others all used nature as a classificatory concept to aid an understanding of the 'state of society'. This contrast has been taken up consistently by anthropologists since Lévi-Strauss (1962) in varying contexts contrasting nature with culture or, as in Seeger (1977), with society.

A third, more dynamic, view of nature arose in the eighteenth and nineteenth centuries in New England, U.S.A., and the Lake District, England, which looked at nature from a transcendental angle. Rather than seeing nature as opposed to human society, transcendentalists, such as Emerson and Thoreau, thought that nature (material objects) parallelled a higher spiritual realm and was a 'symbol of the spirit'. The soul of human beings gave them the potential to transcend the material conditions of life and, through the imagination, to penetrate spiritual truths (Nash 1967: 86).

In order to see the notion of nature among the Arakmbut, we have to pick our way between meanings. Whereas the Arakmbut might share the notion of an animating principle within phenomena with the Greeks, they would not see this as a strict prerogative either of nature or of growth.

The more static enlightenment contrast between culture/society and nature could make some sense to an Arakmbut through the contrast between the inside world of an Arakmbut village and gardens and the outside world of the river, forest, the spirits, and white people. However, to use the single term 'nature' to cover these categories in contrast to human beings is problematic because those phenomena which appear to be outside (natural species, humans, whites, and spirits) are clearly distinguished by the Arakmbut and not included under one term.

The term 'nature' also had a unitary ring for the transcendentalists. When Emerson claimed: 'Herein is especially apprehended the unity of Nature, – the unity in variety, – which meets us everywhere' (1982:59), he drew together a multiplicity of elements. The transcendental aspect of the soul with a spiritual world connected with natural phenomena is relevant to the Arakmbut, but to unify this as nature would be too deistic for people who have no creator spirit or ultimate Godhead.

In this way there is no 'balance' between society and nature for the Arakmbut. We may be able to contrast human and non-human domains, but to make the non-human domain an 'opposite' to the human would be to ignore the qualitative differences.

The Arakmbut universe consists of clearly marked domains which are interspersed with human settlements. There is no unified conception of 'nature' which draws all these things together. On the contrary it is this very lack of closure which opens the Arakmbut to all sorts of external benefits and dangers. The boundary between the community and the outside world is not fixed and uncrossable, nor is it between two equally balanced domains. What we seem to have is a series of central points (Arakmbut communities) and differentiated spectra of forces and powers which populate the periphery of their world.

Nature is not an irrelevant concept for the Arakmbut when we look at notions of life, contrasts between humans and outside, and transcendence. The problem lies more with the unification of nature and the balance between the inner human and outer non-human worlds. This section looks through myth at the relationship between the Arakmbut and some of these outside worlds – the world of the forest, river, and invisible spirits.

Preface

The distinction between the worlds of invisible spirit and visible matter is more fundamental for the Arakmbut than that between any notions of society, culture, or nature. However, before looking into the relationship between these dimensions, we should look at the existence of spirit. Commonsense empiricists will not accept the existence of the spirit world in reality. I think there are several reasons why we should suspend our disbelief in these worlds.

Soul-matter is tangible but can only be perceived in states of heightened consciousness, known as dreaming *(wayorok)*. The Arakmbut consider that dreams take place in a real invisible world which exists prior to the dream. People can enter into each other's dreams and communicate while asleep. I myself have experienced such vivid dreams when in the rainforest and have encountered phenomena which are most easily explained by the presence of spirits.

The Arakmbut explain their spirit world intellectually as well as experientially. The invisible world provides life to the visible world which would otherwise consist of dead matter. I was once shown a dead animal and told that the difference between the corpse and life was the soul. Whether this is called 'animism' or not is neither here nor there. The difference between life and death is the relationship of the invisible to the visible.

The criteria which we use to defend our notions of reality as opposed to those of the Arakmbut can be answered by them. Not all need agree, but the Arakmbut are convinced of the existence and reality of their spirit world. The term 'belief' here is, as we shall see later, less an intellectual phenomenon than a state of the soul itself.

Spirits animate inanimate bodies, inform people in dreams, and, if someone transgresses acceptable behaviour they respond with appropriate sanctions, usually in the form of sickness. The spirit world guards the potential for production, and ensures the reproduction of Arakmbut social and cultural life through time. Trying to ascertain how to grasp the spirit world is not easy.

Reichel-Dolmatoff (1971:218–9) discusses the animating principle of the Desana cosmos in terms of energy. This would be perfectly appropriate for the Arakmbut, considering that the animating and quantifiable nature of soul-matter and would account for the invisible operating on the visible world. However, the Arakmbut spirits themselves receive form from the visible world. The body *(waso)* and soul *(nokiren)* operate on each other. One provides the 'form', the other 'energy' (an example of an Arakmbut version of the relationship between process and structure). Therefore in order to grasp the nature of the spirit world we have to look at a two-way relationship.

The waso for the Arakmbut is both shape and matter. There can be no matter without shape. Indeed, as we saw earlier, shape components are an important aspect of the Harakmbut language. Waso thus consists of form. The soul is something else.

Aristotle dealt with these questions in his Metaphysics. He saw the world as divided between matter and form. Form gives unity and purpose to an object in the same way that a soul provides form to a body. Things increase in actuality by acquiring form; matter without form is only a potentiality (Russell op.cit.:188). For Aristotle, form and shape are part of the soul, whereas for the Arakmbut they are part of the body.

Aquinas takes these arguments further. The world consists of a multiplicity of substances (visible matter), each of which contains two principles (Copleston 1959:86). Substantial form, like Aristotle's form, determines what a body will be or do. The *materia prima*, on the other hand, constitutes the potential within the body for change.

Whereas for the Arakmbut form and shape are part of visible matter, the invisible world animates that form and itself receives form from the visible world. For Aristotle and Aquinas the one-way transformation of potentiality into actuality leads to a hierarchical system, whereas the Arakmbut have a more egalitarian reciprocal relationship where form and shape pass to the invisible world and life or energy passes to the visible world.

Potentiality is significant among the Arakmbut in several senses. Linguistically, Harakmbut contains a considerable number of particles of conditionality, possibility, and probability (Helberg 1989). Furthermore, power comes from the invisible world and so potentiality in that context should be seen in the sense of potency. The spirit world contains knowledge of what is possible in the visible world, and gaining this harnesses its energetic, animating power – encasing process with form.

The spirit is consequently an animating potentiality which, when meeting shape and form, constitutes a living being. The effect is a dual causality operating between the visible and invisible worlds. This inter-relationship is a dynamic creativity which constitutes the ontology of Arakmbut existence.

The manner in which the Arakmbut communicate with the invisible world takes the form of stories, songs, dreams, rituals, and chants. The framework through which this communication takes place is a connection between a person's soul-matter (nokiren), based in the body, and the spirits. The substance inside human beings and in the spirit world is the same. This invisible energy is tied to the body by one's name (wandik).

The myth of Marinke, which begins this section, draws attention to the important relationship between spirits and animals. Whereas in chapter two we saw how spirits come into the dreams of hunters to inform them of the whereabouts of animals, myths take the listener into a world of homology where animals are used to think about invisible spirits by means of the distinctions between species. In a parallel way, animal imitation is used in ritual to communicate with the spirit world, indicated in the myth by episodes in which human beings dress up and imitate birds in order to enter the invisible domain and tap its powers. In the invisible world humans, spirits and animals are mixed up and so myth and ritual provide the social contexts for communication with the visible world by taking advantage of this capacity to transform between different orders. The details of how this is done is covered in Volume 2, chapters two – four.

In the first section of this book we juxtaposed the myth of creation, Wanamey, with Arakmbut social existence, commenting on the social relativity of sex, age, residence, clan affiliation, and terminology. We encountered a tension between complementarity and an asymmetry which takes place over time and which threatens to transform balance into chaos. Wanamey established the contrast between chaos and order and posited the boundaries of acceptability. This section uses the second great Arakmbut myth, Marinke, to illustrate how myths draw the Arakmbut people into a relationship between their cultural identity and the natural and spirit worlds. The questions which it raises challenge the consequences of each person acting according to his or her self-interest rather than in the interest of the Arakmbut as a whole.

⊲ Chapter 5 ⊳

DEFEAT OF DEATH

The Story of Marinke

Wakuru wa'a – the 'first word' – first section

(1) It was the time when seeds appear on rubber trees. A woman and her husband had just married. She said: 'Let us go and gather seed from the *shiringa* rubber tree.'

They went. And the man climbed the tree to pick fruit. The man was up in the tree. 'Catch this', he said. He threw down the fruit. 'Crush it to see if it is ripe'.

The woman did not want to crush it. She was laughing because the fruit had a face and had stuck out its tongue. She was laughing with the tree. She said: 'Awiruk is laughing with me.'

'Crush the fruit', said the husband. He took another and threw it to her. She did not crush it. Three times he threw a fruit but she did not crush it. She was still laughing with the rubber tree Awiruk. The husband came down furious with his wife. When the man reached the ground he went to hit her but she leapt up into the tree like a frog with her legs wrapped around the trunk and her head hanging down below her feet. The man began to climb up but just as he reached her she leapt to another tree.

He was furious but had no bow and arrow so he went down and returned home to get his bow and arrow. He ran home to get arrows to shoot her. He was gone a short while and returned to the tree but the woman had transformed into a huge honeycomb in which lived large bees *(asinku)*. The man fired an arrow at it but did not kill her.

Then he said: 'I am going home.' He reached the rest of the community alone. The people asked him, 'Where is your wife?' He answered, 'She has been changed into asinku and I shot at her.'

'What can we do?' said the people.

When the husband left, the woman came down from the tree pregnant. She was a woman again and the tree was a man called Awiruk. They went into the forest. There passed a long period of time during which the community heard that the woman had gone to another community and was pregnant.

(2) Then there was a message. It came from a pottery flute sounding in the morning. They could hear it from afar. The people in the husband's community could hear it. There was going to be a fiesta. A great fiesta with dancing, drinking, and food.

'What are we going to do?' said the people. 'Shall we go or not?' Everyone was happy that the time for a fiesta had come. There was also thunder announcing it. 'Let us go', said the people.

At that time all the animals spoke – even the birds. They had all brought the red dye achiote (mantoro) to make a love potion to attract women. Each man in the community had to paint himself in the form of an animal and with red legs. Each person's painting was slightly different. The community were all birds which have red in their colouring: paron and *wadntoropopo*, for example. They all went to the fiesta.

The jaguars were felling trees to make their gardens. As the bird people went to the fiesta, they made a trail and passed the jaguars felling. They saw an old woman who was a jaguar. In the path was an old woman. She said nothing and they passed on. They saw the old woman but she said nothing. The bird people arrived at the place of the fiesta. It was in the house of the rubber tree man Awiruk.

The men prepared their love potion, painted themselves with achiote, and dressed in their feathers. They entered the maloca and arrived in the traditional manner. There was dancing in a circle. One of the dancers was the man Awiruk who had taken the woman when she was gathering the fruit. She too was dancing.

The people saw her. She was pregnant by the man Awiruk. Thus they danced in a circle. The rest of the people were sitting in lines at the side. The woman danced in the centre. The men put out their feet and raised them in order to trip the woman and make her come to them. This was to make the love potion work. All failed except one man. 'I want to try', he said. Then he tripped her up. The woman left the dance and sat with the man who had tripped her. She recognised him by his paint as being from her original community. 'Brother, brother!' she said.

The man Awiruk did not realise that the visitors were going to take his woman away from him. The man Awiruk was the father of Marinke. Awiruk continued to dance without realising that they were going to take away his woman. All the night she remained with her relatives. They said to her, 'We are going back to our house.' She said: 'I will go back with you to our community.' But they said that the woman could not pass the house of the jaguars who were felling trees for they were few in number to protect her. The jaguars were many and she was pregnant. Jaguars always smelt out pregnant women. For this reason she could not go with them.

It dawned and they said to the woman, 'Stay here because you must not go near the house of the jaguars. When you have given birth we want to come for you. After that you can return.' The woman cried because they had left her. She spent two days crying, then she decided to go after them.

Wanopo wa'a. The 'centre word' – middle section.

(3) She set out. She was near the house of the jaguars. She reached the house of the jaguars. And old jaguar said to her, 'Where are you going, grandchild?'

'I am going to my house, nothing more', said the woman. The jaguar had no teeth so he licked his lips and said: 'Let the young jaguars accompany you to your people for protection.' She said: 'I can go alone.' The old jaguar said: 'I have no teeth left to eat you, but I can still smell.' The woman went on terrified.

The young jaguars came onto the path, having finished their work and were ready to eat. The old jaguar told them about the woman. She began to run so that the jaguars might not catch her. Even though she was pregnant she ran. She saw a hummingbird which meant that jaguars were near. She almost reached the river where she would be safe. But the young jaguars arrived there first. They killed her and stripped her body of flesh. They threw away what they thought was her stomach but it was not her stomach. It was Marinke.

They threw the bag with the baby in it into the river. The fish began to eat the bag. The carp-like boquichicos took care of it by hiding it near the river bank. The sabalos and pacos wanted to eat it. The boquichicos took care of the bag. As they did so they kept coming to the surface and so the sun burnt their heads which is why boquichicos always look as if they have burnt heads. Two weeks passed.

(4) There came a man to the river who wanted to spear boquichicos. The man saw the white bag with the child in it. He went to spear the boquichicos but they took away the bag. He fled in terror. 'What can it be?' he thought. He fled to the community. He reached the house. He said to an old woman, 'Grandmother, I have seen a white bag and I do not know what it is. What do you think?'

'I am sure that the jaguars have killed your sister', she replied. Soon the whole community knew about the white bag. 'Come on', they said, and all went to look.

There in the river was the white bag protected by the boquichicos. 'There's the bag' said the man who had seen it first. The old woman waded into the river to pull out the bag with her bark skirt but the boquichicos would not let her. She wanted to take out the bag but could not. The boquichicos disappeared under the water with the bag and reappeared at the other side of the river.

All the rest of the people grew tired of trying to get the bag and left. The old woman was left alone on the sand. They say that she slept there alone. The old grandmother dreamt that the fish came and said to her, 'If you make a basket (*kusogn*) and bring it then you can have him'. The old woman awoke and ran to her village to make the basket from *inkimbi* vine. She made the kusogn.

On the following day the old woman returned to the river. She bought the kusogn with her. The old woman threw herself into the river with the basket. At first the boquichicos did not want to hand over the baby. She had to try three times. She tried for the last time because the fish did not want to hand over the baby in the white bag. Then she went downstream with the basket and the boquichicos handed the white bag over to her. She pulled the baby to the bank in the basket. She opened the white bag and the baby began to cry. When he cried she ran to find something for him to eat. The child cried '*mi'in*' – 'suck'.

'Take this fruit', said the grandmother. But the child did not want it. All sorts of fruit were brought but the child did not want any of them. He wanted the fruit of the Awiruk tree. A squirrel brought the fruit for Marinke. He ate the fruit and grew a little more. He could now walk and talk. From being a baby (sinon) he became a child (isipo). The little boy stopped crying once he had the fruit. The old woman cried because her daughter had been killed by the jaguars. Everyone returned to the community along with the child. Many years went by.

Aiya Wa'a The 'whole word' – final section

(5) One day his grandmother said: 'Marinke, let's go to the chacras'. When they were in the chacra there came a great storm. The old woman tried to look after Marinke by carrying him on her back. As they walked the boy saw a guayava fruit tree. He grasped a branch as he passed and clung onto it. The grandmother carried on unaware that the boy was in the tree. He spent all night in the tree, very wet.

At the same time, all the night Marinke began to grow. The old woman cried all night because the child was lost. It rained all night. When it dawned rain was still falling. Then it stopped. The grandmother went to look for her grandchild. When she was on the path she saw a man. Her grandchild had been transformed into a young man. 'Who are you?' she said. 'It's me, grandmother. Let us go back to the house. I am hungry.' His grandmother did not realise that it was really him. She went straight past him and he went back to the village on his own. The grandmother went on to the chacra but could not find him. All she could see were the footprints of a person coming down from the guayava tree.

Then she realised. 'It's him', she cried, and ran back to the village. The boy reached the house and waited for his grandmother. He was a youth (wambo). In this way Marinke became a young man. The grandmother arrived and said: 'It is really you – left in the tree'. She cooked for her grandson.

(6) Then Marinke wanted to find out who had killed his mother. Marinke wanted to kill many different types of animals and plants because he thought that they had killed his mother. Snakes too he wanted to kill. Every time his grandmother said he was wrong. The grandson was angry because she would not tell him who had killed his mother. Then he said: 'Grandmother, they say that my mother was eaten by jaguars.' It is the truth, grandson', she replied. 'The jaguars ate your mother.' The old woman told the story of how he had been thrown into the river by the jaguars. She told him everything. 'What should I do?' asked Marinke. 'What do you think?' 'I do not know', said the old woman.

(7) Then Marinke said: 'Where will I find the seed of the peach palm?' 'Ask your grandfathers', said his grandmother. 'They know where there are seeds of the peach palm tree. Tomorrow you can go and find them.' Next day came and Marinke said: 'I am going'. All night he had been thinking of where he could find the seeds. Two

aulora parrots, *saro* and *okwe,* who like eating peach palm, went with him. They all went off and reached a place where many peach palms grew and where there would be many seeds. They approached the place with stealth.

The owner of the seeds was sorting them out to dry them in the sun. The owner was Marinke's grandfather. He took much care of his seeds to ensure that the flies could not eat them. Marinke said to the parrots, 'Keep some coca leaves in your mouths and hide some of the seeds with it. Meanwhile I will distract the owner'.

Then Marinke went into the house of the owner. The owner followed Marinke into the house. 'I come to visit you, grandfather', said Marinke. The grandfather answered, 'I always live here. Why do you never normally come to visit me?' The old man received him with friendship and invited Marinke to partake of cooked peach palm fruit. They were enormous fruits. Marinke ate with his grandfather.

Then the aulora parrots began to fight over the peach palm. These parrots always fight over the seeds and make the noise 'yayaya'. When he heard the noise, the owner of the seeds realised what was going on. He realised that the birds were eating his seeds. The old man said: 'Who is it? Where are you? Watch you don't harm my seeds.' He went out to where the parrots were. He then pressed the mouth of one of the okwe with his hand. He put his hand over the mouth of the okwe and squeezed. This is why the okwe has a pointed beak. Out came the peach palm seeds. Then he said to the saro parrot, 'Are you robbing me of my seeds too?'

'No, grandfather', the bird replied, 'I have only coca leaves in my mouth'. Inside the coca the bird had hidden the seeds. 'I have only my wad of coca, look.' And the bird took out the coca and split it into two, saying, 'I have nothing, grandfather'. Then the old man went into the house.

Marinke said to his grandfather: 'I must go, grandfather.' The old man gave him plenty of peach palm fruit all cooked ready to take to his own house. Then the parrot said, and they heard, 'Let's take the seeds now.' The owner of the seeds rushed out and almost killed the bird. He grabbed it by its tail feathers which came out. For that reason the saro has no tail feathers to this day. But it escaped carrying the seeds of the peach palm away crying, 'mboktuwa, mboktuwa, let's carry off what we have robbed.' The owner of the seeds cursed and said: 'You have come to rob me of my peach palm seeds.' First the two parrots went and waited for Marinke.

Afterwards Marinke came and the birds were waiting for him where they had arranged. Marinke arrived and asked them what all the noise at the house had been about. 'He took a seed which I had stolen out of my mouth', said one of the birds. There in the path they sat down for a while and ate the cooked peach palm fruit which the old man had given to Marinke. After eating they said: 'Let's go home.'

They reached the house of Marinke and the people of the community asked them if they had been given any of the peach palm seed. Marinke said: 'He only gave us one.' And the parrots said: 'He would not let us take the other. He only gave us one but we have two. He was not going to give it to us but we hid it in a wad of coca split into two halves.' Thus Marinke and the parrots told their story to the community.

(8) 'Here is the seed. Come on, come on – sow it', they said. They sowed the seeds and the following day two leaves appeared. One was speckled and the other green. Three days passed and the peach palm was tall – so quickly did it grow.

Once more Marinke went to look at the peach palm. But the tree had been cut short by a rabbit (*wero*) which had eaten the spine. Marinke returned late to see his tree cut short. He said to his grandmother, 'The peach palm is cut short.'

Marinke went to look for spines to put on the trunk of the tree but he could not find them. Then Marinke's grandmother provided him with a fence for the tree made out of her pubic hair. This eventually became the spines on the tree. It grew dark. Marinke went to sleep. In the middle of the night he got up and went to see his tree. The tree had already grown leaves. Again Marinke returned happy. Then Marinke arose a third time. The peach palm had fruit. Marinke got up a fourth time and the tree was full of fruit. Marinke was very happy.

Marinke arose again to see his peach palm and it was fully mature. It dawned and the tree was completely grown. It had grown in one night. On one side the fruit was red and on the other it was yellow. The fruit was of different colours. In the morning Marinke cut down the tree. Before he cut down the tree he asked advice of his grandmother. 'Where shall I cut it?'

'Cut it this side' she replied. Then they cut down the tree and all the fruit scattered. The yellow fruit went upriver (*kutayon*) and the red fruit downriver (*toyudn*). Then they gathered fruit for the community. Marinke told the people to cook the peach palm fruit. They cooked and ate the fruit until they could eat no more.

(9) Marinke carved up the trunk of the tree in order to make a *topedn* club for killing the jaguars. Marinke made pieces from the trunk. He

took one and said to his grandmother. 'To whom can I give this to make me a club?'

'Give it to your grandfather' she said.

Then Marinke went to where another of his grandfathers lived. He was received and the old man made him a thin club. The grandfather handed over the club and Marinke wanted to split a large stone. The club broke. He took another piece of the peach palm trunk and again said to his grandmother, 'Who will make me a club out of this piece?'

The grandmother said: 'Give it to the ant *kaka'pi.*'

Then Marinke went to where the ant lived and the ant received him and made a thin club. Again Marinke tried to break the stone but the club broke. He could not split the stone.

Then Marinke said: 'I will take another piece of peach palm'. He asked his grandmother, 'Who will make this into a club?'

'Your other grandfather, the ant *tagnpi.*'

So Marinke went to ask him if he would make the club. The large ant tagnpi made the club and Marinke tried to split the stone. Twice he had tried it and this was the third time. It broke the club but not the stone.

The fourth time Marinke asked the termites *pakshiri* who made the club but this one broke too. Marinke asked his grandmother again who would make a strong club. She told him to give it to the blue bird *wanues.* Marinke asked him and he made one. The cry of this bird, 'wues wues', is the sound of its knife carving the topedn for Marinke.

The club was so strong that it broke the stone in two. Marinke was very pleased to have split the stone and said: 'With this club I will kill the jaguars.'

(10) Marinke said to his grandmother, 'Who knows the path to the jaguars?'

She said: 'A little bird called *wadnpirinana* knows the path.' But really the little bird did not know the path. It only said that it knew so that it could eat Marinke's peach palm fruit. The bird sang 'I know the path.' but the bird did not know.

Marinke asked the bird to take him to the path of the jaguars and they went. 'This way', said the bird and they walked for a distance. Marinke said: 'Where is the path?' The bird answered, 'It is here; I seem to have lost the way.' They looked for the path for ages, then Marinke said 'Let's rest a little and eat some peach palm fruit.' They ate.

Then Marinke said, 'Let's continue with the journey. Where is the path?'

'It is just near here', said the bird. It flew on a little to see if the path was there. Marinke waited. When the bird came back Marinke was angry. He picked up his club and hit the bird, leaving it half lame so that to this day it hops around. He wounded the bird and returned to the house.

He reached his maloca and the people said to him, 'Did you find it?' Marinke replied, 'No', and said that he had lost it and had hit the little bird.

A new day dawned and Marinke said to his grandmother, 'Who can I ask?'

And the grandmother said: 'Speak to the bee, *endopo*.' This bee flies around shit. He went and asked. The bee knew and they went to the house of the jaguars. Marinke went with some birds too. They found the path where the jaguars walked. Then the birds returned. Marinke did not return but stayed with two of the birds. Then Marinke said to the birds, 'I will enter the house of the jaguars on my own.' When he reached the house Marinke became small.

(11) In the house there was only an old grandmother jaguar because all the others were out cutting trees. The old female jaguar said to him, 'You are not he who wants to harm us, I hope.' But Marinke had already transformed himself into a child and he said: 'What can I do, grandmother jaguar, for I am little and they are big.'

Then the child Marinke grew tall again and attacked the old jaguar woman with his club. He grabbed her foot and bound it, hanging her upside down over the fire. She screamed loudly. Then Marinke brought firewood and made a hearth and smoke to suffocate her.

Then Marinke returned to where the birds were waiting at the entrance to the maloca of the jaguars. Then the jaguars came back from their work one by one. Marinke had hidden himself behind the entrance in order to surprise them and kill the jaguars as they passed through to find out what was happening to the old jaguar woman. He killed almost all the jaguars who passed. He killed them with his club.

Then there came the last jaguar who was half mad. This jaguar carried all the axes. Marinke had killed all the other jaguars. 'Grandfather jaguar', said Marinke, 'all your companions have passed me here, will you not pass me too?' But the old jaguar did not do so. He remained on the path holding one of the axes to defend himself and hooked them over his neck.

Marinke wanted to kill the jaguar. He ran out to where the jaguar was standing, but dropping the axes, the jaguar escaped, hiding himself in the burrow of an armadillo.

Then Marinke said: 'Let us smoke the jaguar in the hole so that it will die.' He set fire to the entrance where the jaguar was hiding. It burned but the jaguar transformed himself into a *wawapu* (a bee) and escaped. Marinke looked everywhere but he could not find the jaguar. So Marinke returned to his village, sad because he had not killed all the jaguars. He returned to his maloca.

(12) On the following day there were jaguar prints on the ground. With the one which had escaped many had appeared. Many jaguars still lived. The wawapu and the wero rabbit had mated.

The people said: 'What can we do?'

'We must hide somewhere' they said.

'Where shall we hide? What shall we convert ourselves into?'

'Into a tree.'

'No. They will cut us down.'

'Under the ground.'

'No. they will stamp on us.'

'Among the rocks by the river.'

'No. Impossible.'

'In the river.'

'No. They could take us out and beat us up.'

'What shall we do then?'

There was a boy in the maloca. He was sick and infirm. His name was Noa'yebe. He was lying on his bed sick and all the people were in the maloca. They had not seen him. Then the boy spoke. 'We must go to the sky', he said.

The people were so happy that they applauded. But they clambered on top of each other to reach the sky and trampled the boy who became converted into tobacco (*paimba*). They decided to reach the sky by climbing various trees. The sky then descended until it was close to the ground. They all climbed onto the sky. Marinke and everyone else went up.

But the grandmother of Marinke was very old and could not climb up.

Marinke then said: 'Take this axe and cut firewood. Put one piece on top of another and climb up.' He threw the axe down, but the grandmother missed it. She did not catch it. It fell on her face and hit her. She was then converted into a curassow (*budn*). The red beak of the budn comes from the blood drawn by the axe and its truncated shape comes from where the axe hit her nose. And Marinke became Yuperak (thunder). He cries out when he thinks jaguars are near him. His grandmother is the curassow. She always calls to warn him.

Marinke said: 'I will always use the topedn in the sky and you must warn me when it will rain.' That is why the curassow always cries before a storm.[1]

Ireyo (1980) with details of species identification in 1992.

The myth of Marinke follows a similar pattern to that of Wanamey as both stories are divided into three sections. However whereas the myth of origin is an account of the major characteristics of Arakmbut social life and the initial ordering of the world, Marinke tells of man's growth and his changing relationship with both the human and non-human world. In Wanamey the centre of the world is a vast tree which saves human beings from a cataclysm and presents the conditions for the origin of order out of chaos. The metaphors used for this transformation are both sexual and culinary. Marinke is the child of a tree. The story is not about creation but the persistence of order over time, especially in relation to a recalcitrant world. The sexual and culinary metaphors take a secondary place to the metaphor of growth, which is expressed mainly in plant and animal imagery. In addition, the myth of Marinke uses different animal species to illustrate interconnections not only between the human and non-human world but also between the visible and the invisible 'other' world which is the domain of spirits.

There are two episodes in the first section (wakuru wa'a). The first tells of the seduction and elopement of a married woman from a community and the second tells how members of her community find her and plan her return.

The story begins with a married couple gathering fruit from a rubber tree. According to Califano (1978b:11), this is a custom among newly-wed Harakmbut couples. There is no mention of it in San José and it is probably found more among the Wachipaeri. The

---

1. Califano 1978b collected several versions of Marinke. There are two Arakmbut versions. The one from Shintuya is so similar to the San José version produced here that it is apparent that Arakmbut myths are learnt in terms of episodes which follow the same order. The Wachipaeri and Sapiteri myths of Atunto tell a similar story to the first section of Marinke. They both also include episodes linking death and incest and the story of the two suns mentioned in chapter two.

   Marinke shares several episodes further afield in Peru. The Asháninka culture hero Avieri is similar to Awiruk and Atunto. Avieri's grandson Kiri has several similarities to Marinke and eventually becomes transformed into a peach palm tree. The Matsigenka (Ferrero 1966:389) have a parallel set of myths for Yabieri. The jaguar episode appears among the Amuesha (Wise 1958; Santos-Granero 1991) among the Piro (Alvarez, R. 1960:13–24) and the Cashinahua (D'Ans 1975:45ff). The ascent to the sky episode has similarities to the sky rope story among the Asháninka (Weiss 1969) and the Ese'eja (Aza 1930).

couple live in a community which contains many of the wife's relatives. The man who finds her at the fiesta in the second episode is addressed as 'brother', and the old woman who plays an important part later in the story is her mother. It is possible to deduce from this that the married couple who go gathering come from the same community or from two closely related communities and that the union is more endogamous than that with the rubber tree man Awiruk.

While gathering the fruit the woman is seduced by the tree. She disobeys her husband and laughs along with the tongue sticking out from the fruit. Laughter is a mark of intimacy when it takes place with a member of the opposite sex. The couple then change places. The husband descends to chastise his wife as she ascends the tree. At this point there is a transformation which separates the woman from her husband and literally joins her to the tree. The woman becomes a bees' nest, thereby changing from the human form of her husband to the natural form of her lover. The elopement is not simply from husband to lover but also from human to non-human.

The lovers resume human forms and go into the forest. The woman is taken from her community and her family and so endogamy is replaced by exogamy. She is now pregnant by the tree Awiruk. The story does not make it clear whether the child she carries is actually Marinke, but we do learn later on that Awiruk is Marinke's father.

The myth now moves to the fiesta held in the village of Awiruk. According to the people of San José this place is just like any other forest settlement. The sound of the 'flute' calling people to a fiesta was the original 'bush telegraph' of the Arakmbut. The community hear the call and prepare for the party. At the same time thunder announces the fiesta. The thunder and the flute show the constant dream-like transformative element in the myth between human and non-human.

It becomes apparent that the community of the woman are birds. The men all paint themselves with achiote on their legs and bodies. All the versions of the myth say that the species of birds which have red in their colouring are those species represented by the woman's group. The achiote acts as a love potion attracting any woman who is tripped up by a red leg. The men also put on their feathers. These are the decorations traditionally used in the e'mbaipak ceremony when a youth becomes a man. Several of the versions digress at this point to give an account of the origin of the e'mbaipak ceremony and the correct costume to be worn at the fiesta which consists of feathers from birds associated with the woman's community (Califano 1978b:27–8).

On the way to the fiesta the people pass the jaguars felling trees to make their gardens. Jaguars are considered to be toto. Toto are harmful spirits who live mainly in the forest. Their usual occupation is cutting down trees with their metal axes. Whenever a tree mysteriously crashes down in the forest, the Arakmbut say that it is toto at work. The jaguars are not the only form of toto, but for the purposes of this story they fulfil this role.

The account of the fiesta tells of the traditional welcome and dancing in a circle. The dancing was always an opportunity for men and women to come together formally and to become acquainted. In the story this is achieved by tripping the woman while she is dancing. The man who trips her succeeds in attracting her to his side at the periphery of the dance floor. They recognise each other as brother and sister. The woman and her brother talk. She wants to return to her original community and they want her to come, but they fear for her safety while passing the house of the jaguars. She is pregnant with Awiruk's son and if she approaches the abode of the jaguars her smell will attract them and they could kill her.

The men imitating the initiation rites of e'mbaipak are able to make the return journey to their community. They travel from one community to another and back through the forest. Later in this chapter and in the next we will see that from puberty onwards an Arakmbut man's life consists of perfecting this return journey. The woman, on the other hand, wants to return with the men but she is pregnant. This condition prevents her from passing through the forest safely. Pregnancy, we will see later, is a woman's 'initiation' into adulthood – she does it through the river.

Table 5.1 Main relationships in the first part of Marinke

Inside (Human)	Outside (Non-human)
Woman's first marriage	Woman's second marriage
Relatively endogamous union	Exogamous union with forest world – seduction takes the form of bee's nest attached to tree and birth in river.
Men of the woman's community originally described as human.	Visit to Awiruk's village for the fiesta. Men from woman's community appear as birds when entering the forest domain.
In the e'mbaipak rite of passage the wambo leave 'society' for the duration of the ceremony and return to it later as men.	For the e'mbaipak ceremony men dress in bird feather costumes. By imitating birds they leave society and attract women who are from outside.

The wanopo wa'a section of Marinke consists of two episodes. One tells the death of Marinke's mother at the hands of the jaguars and the other of the birth of Marinke himself. The gender distinction which was important in the first section is now seen from the perspective of forest and river.

Disobeying her brothers, Marinke's mother follows the path back through the forest to her community. On the way she meets the jaguars who track her down and eat her. The jaguars live in the forest. Marinke's mother knows that she is liable to be attacked and rushes to the river where she will be safe from them. The distinction here is between forest (ndumba), where the jaguars are and where it is dangerous, and river (wawe), where the jaguars cannot go and where it is safe for her.[2] Unfortunately for Marinke's mother, she cannot reach the river in time and is caught.

The Arakmbut refer to this incident to warn pregnant women of the dangers of walking alone in the forest. The presence of a hummingbird is a sure sign of the proximity of a jaguar, and when anyone sees this bird in the forest they take great care and often return home. Jaguars are dangerous. They are manifestations of harmful toto spirits and their presence is likely to result in death.

Although Marinke's mother is killed, the jaguars think that her uterus is only her stomach and throw it into the river. Some say the child was kept in a rubber bag. (His father was a rubber tree.) The child in the 'rubber bag' womb is looked after by the carp-like fish called boquichicos. The boquichicos are beneficial creatures who save Marinke's life. They are reluctant to hand the baby over to anyone but eventually Marinke's grandmother receives it. The fish come to her in a dream and tell her to make a kusogn. Among the Arakmbut, beneficial spirits bring advice to people skilled in dreaming. They are thought of as having originated in the river and are known as waweri/ndakyorokeri. A sign of their presence is the imprint of a kusogn on the ground. It is on their advice that Marinke was taken from the river in a such a bag.

The boquichicos are beneficial and appear in the story as creatures of the river. These contrast with the toto spirits which are harmful and appear in the story as creatures of the forest. Similarly there is a contrast between Marinke's grandmother and the old jaguar,

2. Jaguars are creatures usually thought to like water. Yet they are creatures of the forest *par excellence* for the Arakmbut. Arakmbut hunters told me how they could remember in the past seeing jaguars sunning themselves by the rivers in the Wandakwe river. For the purposes of organising their world, zoological phenomena need not necessarily entirely correlate with cultural features.

because the term for grandmother (*mama*) is a word for caiman (a river creature), whereas the term for grandfather (*pane*) is one of the names for jaguar (*apane*). The old jaguar in the story is connected with the forest and is harmful to the pregnant woman – not hurting her directly but acting as an intermediary, telling the young jaguars where to find her. The old woman, on the other hand, is beneficial to Marinke and is an intermediary for boquichicos. Although not a cayman herself, she is in contact with the river spirits.

This information can be put together as follows:

Table 5.2 Forest/river parallels in Marinke

Forest	River
Harmful spirits	Beneficial spirits
Manifest as jaguars	Manifest as boquichicos
Cause death	Enable birth
Old man as intermediary	Old woman as intermediary

The story now changes perspective: from telling of death it turns to Marinke's formation in the river. His period with the boquichicos is a pregnancy without human intervention. He passes through the river in the same way as he would pass through his mother's womb. The foetus is formed by being nurtured in the water. This 'cooking' in cold water parallels the fermentation noted in chapter two.

When Marinke is taken from the river, the only food he will accept is that from the rubber tree – the tree identified with his father Awiruk. As a result of eating this fruit Marinke has the first of his sudden spurts of growth. This shows that food is a direct cause of growth for the Arakmbut but, even more importantly, it emphasises the continuation of the line of paternity. Marinke ingests fruit related to his father and grows quickly. In this way the myth expresses the role of the father in Marinke's growth at the expense of his mother, who is not even necessary for his growth in the womb. Furthermore the womb itself is, according to some additional comments from the Arakmbut, considered to be made from the substance of the father (Awiruk).

There appears to be an attempt to deny women their function of childbearing in the myth, showing them to be far less important than men in the formation of a child. The result is to reinforce the view that all humans are reformations of their father while a woman merely supplies the receptacle through which this can take place. Conception, pregnancy and birth are expressed in the myth as a passage from the forest to the river and back.

The fifth episode tells of Marinke's growth from an isipo to a wambo. He goes with his grandmother to the chacras as an isipo would do. Overnight and during the storm he grows. This is a different means of growth from that mentioned in the previous section, in which he ate the fruit associated with his father.

There are two Arakmbut means of growing, and Marinke makes use of both of them. The main method is through eating, whereby the substance of the food enters the body and soul of the consumer. The other method is used for increasing the growth rate of small boys. They are taken to the river early in the morning to bathe when the water is cool and forces them to take deep breaths. This develops the torso and causes the body as a whole to grow faster.[3]

The Arakmbut say that without eating meat they would die. Meat is the most important food which mankind ingests. It would appear from this and from the evidence of the myth that the two means of growth emphasise the development of different parts of the human being. The wetting method consists of external means of improving body size, whereas ingesting food, particularly meat, increases not only the body but also the soul.

When Marinke descends from the tree he is older. As a wambo (youth) he shows a growing sense of responsibility to his kin. Responsibility is defined by concern and emotional involvement with the lives and fates of others. All affections are states of a developed soul and so Marinke's desire to avenge the death of his mother is another sign of his growth. The subsequent four episodes describe the gradual passage from wambo to wambokerek (adult male) as Marinke learns how to obtain the correct weapons for hunting the jaguars and how to find his way in the forest.

The seventh episode tells of Marinke's visit to the owner of the peach palm seeds. Although Marinke enters his mother's community after his birth, his passage to adulthood is not immediate. It is only when an Arakmbut man is fully grown that he is a fully independent responsible social being with body and soul intact. Marinke's growth parallels the distance he travels from the community. The visit to the owner of the peach palm seeds in the seventh episode is a trip outside of the community in which Marinke is living with his grandmother. He is accompanied by two aulora parrots, which indicates that he is entering the forest world. However, this journey,

3. Califano (1978b:17), sees the growth of Marinke as analogous to the growth of plants. When small children go to the river in the early morning to help them grow, maybe this relates to plant growth too. This also fits with the wet to dry growth period noted in chapter three.

though further than his trip to the chacra, is not as far as his later expedition into the forest to find the jaguars when he does not even know the way.

The object of the visit is to steal the seeds of the peach palm. This is not unlike the stealing of fire by the woodpecker in Wanamey. In both cases the thieves are birds. The owner is distracted while the fire or seeds are stolen and the culprits are almost caught. In the same way that fire is indispensable for the cooking of food and other commodities, so the peach palm seed is essential for Marinke to make his club and reach full manhood. The peach palm holds the secret of a man's growth to maturity.

There are other indications of the change from youth to manhood. One of the parrots carries in its beak coca to hide the seeds of the peach palm. Coca can only be chewed by an adult (wambokerek). It gives strength and stamina to enable him to fight, dance, and sing all night when there is a fiesta. Placing the seeds inside a wad of coca emphasises the strength *(tainda)* of the peach palm wood and which coca gives to a man. There is another parallel between coca and the peach palm seeds. Both are prepared by drying in the sun. We have seen in the second chapter that this is the most extreme 'dry' form of cooking which is performed by men, in contrast to the extreme 'wetness' of fermentation performed by women. These dry cooked commodities are highly significant as signs of Arakmbut manhood.

The owner of the seeds is an old man. Once again in the myth an old person is an intermediary in the course of the action. This man is not dangerous like the jaguar grandfather; in fact, he is presented as being benign and friendly. His role is closer to that of the grandmother in that he is beneficial, albeit unwillingly. He provides access to man's growth because the clubs made of peach palm wood can only by used by wambokerek.

On the way back to the community, Marinke and the parrots stop to eat the peach palm fruits. The ingestion of the tree's fruit is another factor contributing to the gradual growth of Marinke to maturity. From this point onwards there is a parallel between the cultivation of the tree, the fashioning of its wood, and the emergence of Marinke as a wambokerek.

The growth of the peach palm relates in several ways to the growth of Marinke described earlier in the story. The seed is sown and grows well for three days, but then it is cut short by a rabbit. The disruption of the growth of the peach palm parallels the disruption of Marinke's growth in his mother's womb by the jaguars. The connection between the rabbit and the jaguars is compounded when we learn that the rabbit helps the old jaguar to reproduce later in the story.

Marinke puts the pubic hair of his grandmother (*wawepui*) around the trunk of the tree (which is why peach palms are covered in spines) and it grows overnight, in the same way that Marinke himself did in the storm. Marinke and the tree have reached the same level of development. From now on in the story they are related by a contiguity so that the weapon is culturally fashioned from the trunk of the tree as Marinke is socially fashioned into a man capable of using it to kill the jaguars.

Episode nine tells of Marinke's attempts to have a club made from the peach palm. Various ants who are probably associated with the tree try to smash the weapons. Eventually a bird succeeds in making a club capable of breaking stone. Peach palm is important for the Harakmbut. Many of the weapons associated with manhood come from this tough wood. Bows, arrowheads, and clubs are all made with peach palm. Moreover, traditionally, when a wambo became a wambokerek, the youth's lower lip was pierced and a spine of peach palm wood *(hopi)* was inserted.

When Marinke is satisfied with his club he is an adult (wambokerek) and is capable of hunting animals. He goes to kill the jaguars in episode ten and begins to learn some 'forest sense' by being able to discriminate between his guides. The little bird deceives him while the bee does not. The difference could be to do with the behaviour of these creatures. Whereas the bird wadnpirinana appears to fly in a haphazard manner, the bee is a more organised insect with a more apparent sense of direction. There is another reason why the bee is seen as a helpful creature. Marinke's mother appears in the first section of the story as a bees' nest, and so it is appropriate that Marinke should receive help from the bee.

Marinke's journey into the forest to kill the jaguars is similar to that of his kinsmen in the first section of the myth. In both cases the trip through the forest is linked with elements from the e'mbaipak ceremony, when a youth becomes a full man. In the first section the connections were of the feathers used in the fiesta, whereas in the final section the trip itself is the expression of Marinke's arrival at manhood with the peach palm club. When he avenges his mother's death by the jaguars, Marinke reaches his full maturity.

Marinke's life is not only a gradual growth to adulthood which enables him to deal as a person with the domains of the river and forest, it also charts a shift in the relationship between the domains themselves. The beginnings of Marinke's life are spent in the river with the support of the boquichicos. At manhood his body and soul are sufficiently strong to be able to face the dangers of the forest, and in particular the jaguars who are toto. Over the period of his life Marinke replaces a beneficial relationship with river spirits with a hostile relationship with forest spirits. The animals in the myth provide a means of conceptualising not only the power of spirits external to human beings, but also the state of the spirit within people. Animals are pointers or markers to the invisible spirit world.

The first jaguar Marinke kills is the old grandmother. By killing her he is able to wait safely at the entrance to the maloca and club the rest on their way home. Whereas Marinke's grandmother helps him at his birth, the jaguar grandmother unwillingly helps Marinke to mark the end of his youth and the beginning of manhood. The only other time the old grandmother jaguar appears in the story is in the first section when the men from Marinke's mother's community go to Awiruk's fiesta. We have seen that this description matches that of the e'mbaipak ceremony marking the entry into manhood of a youth. It is therefore possible to see the grandmother jaguar as a sign of 'birth' into manhood.

Marinke's grandfathers are channels for the transference of the power of growth from the animal world to human society. They are outside human life but, unlike the jaguars, can be controlled. The jaguar grandfather on the other hand is an example of uncontrolled growth. Through transformation he can reproduce as a rabbit. This ties in with the fact that he is the first jaguar to encounter Marinke's pregnant mother. He is the enemy of human pregnancy because he reproduces in a haphazard manner.

It is now possible to put together the respective parts played by the old people in the myth of Marinke to show how they demonstrate a progression from controlled/safe/proximate to uncontrolled/dangerous/distant and the different roles they play through Marinke's life.

In each case an old person supervises a transitory point in Marinke's life, from birth to the moment when he expects to die and flees to the sky. As he grows older he has to deal with an increasingly dangerous environment in the deep forest. Each old person is also an intermediary character, never doing anything unless by trickery or through contact with the spirit world.

The final episode of the myth of Marinke tells of the flight from the jaguars up to the sky. While seeking the means of ascending there, a boy is transformed into tobacco. This plant is cultivated by Arakmbut men to keep away harmful spirits and increase strength and stamina. Tobacco is the main curing plant of the Arakmbut and prevents the symptoms of death (illness and weakness). The appearance of tobacco coincides with the flight of Marinke and his community from the jaguar.

Table 5.3 The Old People in Marinke

Marinke's Grandmother: Represented as a woman throughout the myth until the final ascent to the sky. She helps Marinke in his 'birth' and with her pubic hair to make the spines of the peach palm.

Marinke's Grandfathers: These come from close communities. They help Marinke, but not always willingly. With their help he passes the final stage of growth from wambo to wambokerek.

Jaguar Grandmother: Dangerous and different but not feared as a killer by Marinke. Her death is Marinke's attainment of manhood. She is trapped in a maloca and so is less 'forest-like' than the jaguar grandfather.

Jaguar Grandfather: He is the most dangerous of the old people. Although mad and without teeth, he represents uncontrolled growth and death in the forest. The flight of Marinke to the sky is to avoid death from this grandfather and his rapidly produced offspring.

The sky is an otiose domain for the Arakmbut. No humans can fly and shamans, even if they can, do not need to as the spirits they contact live in the forest or river. The birds can live in the sky but they are also thought to be the domesticated animals of the spirits and adhere either to the forest or to the river. The sky and the *kurudneri* spirits who live there become important in certain times of crisis which we will look at in chapter ten. Marinke's flight to the sky removes him from the main domains where people go after life. He has thus removed himself from death and life.[4]

The myth of Marinke looks at the consequences of disrupting four major areas of Arakmbut socio-cultural life and connects them with cultural images from initiation rituals.

Marriage

Marinke's mother is married to someone close to her community as she is living with her own relations. This relative endogamy is broken

---

4. The notion of Utopia is important among many Peruvian peoples and an understanding of this might throw more light on Messianic cults (Bodley 1972; Ossio 1973: XXXII; and Regan 1983).

by the elopement with Awiruk to his community. The exchange breaks down because there is no reciprocation: a woman is taken away and no one is given to the community in return. An elopement is a temptation for the Arakmbut because one can build up a stock of women without the need to give any away. A husband of such a union can never be sure that his wife will not try to run off with someone else or back to her community (as is the case with Marinke's mother) or whether she herself might not encounter harmful people or spirits when so far from home. The message of the myth is that, however tempting it may be to elope with a woman, it is dangerous.

Procreation

In the myth there is an attempt to deny women their control over reproduction. Even though Marinke's mother is killed, the boquichicos are just as capable of looking after a foetus which is held within a womb made of a father's substance. However the story cannot totally deny women their role. The fish belong to the domain associated mainly with women. Thus it is the female aspect of the natural world which takes over the nurture of Marinke's mother's pregnancy.

Later in the myth, the old jaguar (who is from the forest) creates multiple offspring without the problem of marriage and its obligations. The story presents this as being very dangerous, only possible with the power of a harmful toto spirit. This form of procreation results in the threat of death to Marinke and his community. Men may wish the patriline to have total freedom to reproduce itself without the obligations to women and their family, but the consequences of this would be very dangerous. Although it may be tempting for an Arakmbut to deny the importance of marriage practices or to resent the power of women in conceiving children, the outcome of changing these would be fatal.

Overkill

When Marinke changes from a child (isipo) to a youth (wambo) he goes to the chacra. From wambo to wambokerek (adult) he goes increasingly further into the forest. He obtains some of the power which resides in the forest world and enables things to grow, he gains control over it, and brings it back to the community to enable social growth to take place.

Men, through increasing contact with the outside world during their youth learn to cope with its dangers by becoming more self-reliant. The visits of a man to and from the outside world are not single events. They constitute the continual interaction between community life and the non-human world, stretching ever further from the village. In the myth, Marinke tries to destroy all the jaguars, but because they are manifestations of toto and prohibited animals they can return to harm him in spirit form.

The reproduction of the jaguars by the old grandfather can be seen in this light. Spirits never die, they only reform. Thus Marinke's attempt to kill all the jaguars unleashes too much uncontrolled death in the animal world, which always has a dangerous effect on the hunter. In everyday life, the Arakmbut have a strong desire to kill the maximum number of animals they can in order to prove their proficiency in the chase, but the myth shows that an excess of killing or the killing of prohibited species breaks up the controlled exchange cycles between humans and the spirit world, causing illness and perhaps death.

Death

Although there are selfish temptations for people to avoid the disadvantages of marriage, procreation, and restraint in hunting, the initial attraction is quickly dissipated on account of the result -sickness and death. The fatal result in each case is caused by a conjunction between normally disparate elements. Women who elope or who are stolen force a conjunction between inside and outside which has involved no intermediary negotiation. To deny a woman the function of producing children is to take what is usually inside the womb and produce it outside. To overkill animals is to encounter powers of the spirit world which, being uncontrolled, could enter society and wreak havoc.

Marinke, in the final part of the myth, offers a way out of this morality. Rather than excessive conjunction between disparate elements sealing the fate of anyone who transgresses the system, he arranges for an avoidance of death itself. By fleeing to the sky, he and his community perform an act of extreme disjunction from the world, removing themselves from the distinction of river/forest and human/spirit. This nirvana in the clouds is otiose and inaccessible. Marinke never dies for he is separate from the world. By implication, he enters a paradise; by removing the possibility of his death, he renders safe all the desirable contravention of the expected behaviour mentioned above. It is the desire of all Arakmbut to be immortal, and Marinke achieves this by opting out of the life/death cycle. Unfortunately he is an exception. As long as Marinke's paradise remains inaccessible, the fear of death should prevent people from being tempted to act too selfishly. Marinke thus appears as a 'morality tale', justifying why people should do what they may not necessarily like.

The myths of Wanamey and Marinke have two opposing messages which present two possibilities to the Arakmbut. The creation myth tells of the advantages of destruction and the formation of a new order, whereas Marinke tells of the advantages of keeping things as they are. It remains to look further into the relationship between the visible and invisible through life and beyond.

cl Chapter 6 �

KEEPING BODY AND
SOUL TOGETHER

The Arakmbut word closest in meaning to human being is 'Arakmbut'. Apart from political contexts, in which it means 'member
of our people' or 'our people' as opposed to other groups, its reference to the human being is in contrast to creatures or objects which
lack the particular configurations of body, soul, and name which constitute a human and humans living together. Embedded within its
meaning is our notion of 'society'. The word Arakmbut does not
always coincide with the English definition of human. In certain cases
it can refer to a large animal with a nokiren (soul in human form). The
definition of what is human or not is contextual and based on poly-
thetic criteria. These criteria are under review in this chapter.

There are several perspectives from which we can perceive the
notion of human being for the Arakmbut. There is the person
(*nognchinda Arakmbut* -one person) who is an amalgamation of body,
soul, and name, while there is the self (*ndo*) which is the conscious
being. This distinction was made by Mauss in his essay on the
notion of person (Mauss 1985). Furthermore, the Arakmbut have a
category *oro*, which means 'we', referring to people who largely
share the same view as a person. 'We' of course varies according to
the circumstances and the criteria used for social identity discussed
in Part I. In terms of human being as a species, the term most relevant is 'Arakmbut'.

All humans have basic attributes which relate to each other in the
same way, constituting a definition of the species Arakmbut. Except
in certain contexts when the soul of a specific person is the object of
reference, the terms for these attributes have the prefix *wa-* before

the stem. Every person has a body (waso), a soul (wanokiren) and a name (wandik). At the same time, the relationship between these three elements of a person are the clearest account of how the visible and invisible worlds interact.

Waso: Body

The body is divided into those parts which are wet *(sayyudn)* and those which are dry *(wa'ai)*. The anatomy of the body is not a functioning system but a visible casing which operates only when animated by the potent presence within it of the wanokiren (soul). In the same way the dry parts of the body act as a casing for the wet parts.

The primary framework of the body is the bones *(wahai)*. The word for bone is similar to that for dry, although the pronunciation is slightly different. Around the bones are the muscles or flesh which are called *waen.* Other dry parts of the body are the head, arm, chest, upper and lower leg, and foot. One organ seems to be classified with wa'ai parts of the body; the heart *(wanore)*; *wano* means centre. The principal internal organs, such as the liver, kidney, lungs, stomach, and intestines, are the wet parts of the body.

The kidneys, lungs, and brain do not have as important a significance as the other organs. They are often referred to simply as *wasiwa* (fat). This is perhaps because they have less to do with the digestive process which is the main purpose of the wet parts of the body. Food and drink go to the stomach *(wandapo)* and emerge from the region of the intestines *(wamin)* as urine and faeces. The liver *(wame')* is the organ which enables the conversion to take place. When meat is prepared for cooking, men normally cut up the dry parts of the carcass and women the wet internal organs.

Emissions from the upper orifices such as the mouth or nose are more socially acceptable than those from below. Breath is a sign of life and, like smoke, contains either beneficial or harmful elements which it receives from contact with the soul. Sputum and blowing are common means of relieving pain from a superficial cut or bruise. Neither vomiting nor coughing is considered pleasant, but they are not dangerous.

The lower orifices have two ambiguous emissions which are distinguished in terms of gender, namely semen *(wandawe)* and menstrual blood *(mimi)*. The way in which semen turns into a foetus is parallel to the way in which fermentation takes place, linking the womb with the container where masato or chicha is fermented.

Blood should normally remain within the body and is considered impure and possibly harmful if it passes outside. The Arakmbut do not practise blood-letting and in fact try to keep blood away from the house as it attracts spirits. Blood is not soul-matter but is in contact with the soul, from which it gets its potency. At the time of a menstruation (*mbedn e'pok* – 'to pass red'), a woman uses an old piece of cloth which she discretely washes in the river. Apart from a prohibition on sexual intercourse, she can carry on life as usual. Her blood is impure but she is not. Menstrual blood is thus treated as urine and faeces and associated with the wetter and lower parts of the body.[1]

The classification of the body contains the associations which have been encountered in several cultural contexts among the Arakmbut: Upper/Lower; Drier/Wetter; Male/Female (see Table 6.1).

Table 6.1 Relationships between various bodily emissions

Substances	Male/Dry	Female/Wet	Excreta
Upper	Breath	Sputum	Vomit
Lower	Semen	Menstrual Blood	Urine/Faeces

These relationships within the human body are diacritical distinctions but they do not constitute a complementarity as defined in this work because they are not expressions of a dynamic principle of interaction.

Wanokiren – Soul

The soul can be called either wanokiren or, when specifying a particular person, nokiren.[2] It means 'that central aspect of someone which is permanent'. 'Central' in this case means all-pervading. The presence of the nokiren within a body is an indicator of life (*e'e* – to be). A nokiren is invisible except in the state of *wayorok* (dream, vision or hallucination), when it is possible to see its invisible form or image.

Everything which has life or is at all animate has some 'soul-matter' within it, but it does not necessarily constitute a nokiren. Small

1. The Arakmbut do not consider menstrual blood to be any more dangerous than blood in any other context. There is a similar attitude among the Siriono (Holmberg 1969:171).
2. The three souls mentioned by Barriales and Torralba (1970:64) following Alvarez (1957/7) are *huamajere, huanokiren,* and *jiriendei.* Arakmbut told me that the first was a class of spirits or dispersed soul (wamawere) and the last is a term given by some Harakmbut peoples for the abode of toto.

creatures, trees, and plants have life, but this is not the same as the nokiren of larger animals, such as peccary or tapir, and humans. These larger creatures have something more than simply animation; they have an awareness and are independent of their immediate environment. The nearest thing I can find to express this is our notion of 'self-consciousness'. Whereas for us existing, living, and self-consciousness are qualitatively different, for the Arakmbut the difference is primarily a direct result of the quantitative allocation of soul-matter. As the nokiren is invisible, the only way of discerning how much is present in any one creature is by its size. Thus the waso (body) is a sign of what the nokiren (soul) within it is like.

It was mentioned in the Preface to Part II that the invisible spirit world is the realm of potentiality. The notion of potency is particularly applicable here, as used in the quotation from Aquinas. It expresses not only the idea of potentiality but also that of power. As we shall see, power for the Arakmbut comes from soul-matter.

A human nokiren constitutes a soul with two attributes. One is concentrated and the other dispersed. It is the same nokiren but some aspects are joined and others spread throughout the body. The concentrated part is located at the base of the spine, called the *wanopo*. This word is translated by the Summer Institute of Linguistics as 'seat of affections' (Hart 1963:2). The Arakmbut conceptualise all emotions, moods, and affective responses as conditions of this concentrated aspect of the nokiren.

The dispersed part of the nokiren is connected with thought. I have heard the Arakmbut refer to this as *wamawere*, but the term refers to a breeze or light which a soul sends ahead of it when travelling. The Harakmbut word for 'to think' is *e'nopwe*. Literally translated this could mean 'not the *nopo*', thereby referring to the dispersed part of the nokiren. Thought is thus conceived as fragmented and ephemeral. Thought and emotion are not different in kind but in quantity or degree of intensity. It could be said that for the Arakmbut feelings are intense thoughts and thoughts less intense feelings. They are different aspects of the same phenomenon, namely the nokiren itself.

The soul-like form of the nokiren is the image in which it appears in the dream-state of wayorok, and this is usually the shape of the human body in which it resides. The nokiren receives its image from the visible world with which it has the most significant contiguous relationship. At the same time the nokiren affects any object with which it makes contact. The Arakmbut describe this as being like an 'infection' which spreads. As the nokiren exists in closest proximity to the waso, the human body is most 'infected'. In its most extreme form, this proximity results in the animation of the body. However, the influence of the nokiren does not stop there. Anything to which the body itself has frequent proximity also has the presence of the nokiren passed on to it. For this reason, the possessions of all people are infected by contact with the soul-matter of their nokiren.

The nokiren receives its image from the visible world and at the same time filters through the visible world connecting disparate objects with affective bonds ranging from total animation of a body to the identification of someone with their possessions. Different states of consciousness are explained by the Arakmbut as the changing relations between the bodily waso and the soul-matter of the nokiren. When someone is awake and fully conscious, his or her nokiren is inside his waso and there is a relationship of contiguity. When that person is asleep or has a dream or hallucination, the waso and nokiren are still related contiguously but with the latter outside the former. When someone dies their nokiren and waso become separated and there is no relationship between the two.

The Arakmbut have formed their ideas about the soul from two sources. The first is through its effects. The moving body, the relation of objects to a possessor, and consciousness are all effects of an invisible cause – the nokiren. The other source is that of the warayok (dreams), which take place on a level of experience different from that of being awake. It is the invisible world that the dreamer perceives, a world where the spirit nokiren takes over the role of perception which would normally be the physical aspects of the waso – such as seeing, hearing, smelling, taste, and touch. The image of the nokiren follows the shape and other characteristics of those things with which it has the most contact in life. There is thus a two-way relationship between the waso and nokiren, the former giving the latter its image and form, the latter giving the former life, consciousness and presence. This is the relationship between body and soul.

We can rephrase this by saying that thought and emotions are properties of the nokiren but they are actions upon, and reactions to, information received by the senses, which are properties of the waso. The waso is thus mediator between the human being and the outside world in a waking state while the nokiren mediates with the outside invisible world in a sleeping state.

Both the waso and the nokiren have diacritical divisions such as upper/lower, dry/wet, and concentrated/dispersed, but it is the body/soul distinction between waso and nokiren themselves which provides the most important and the most dynamic contact in a person's make-up. The waso is visible and tangible, the nokiren invisible and intangible. However, each contains aspects of the other. For example, the waso in action is itself a manifestation of the presence of the nokiren, while the nokiren is conceptualised in terms of the waso. The net effect is a complementarity consisting of a dynamic interaction between the visible and invisible parts of the human being. This interaction constitutes the conversion of potentiality into actuality by animation of the waso, which provides the nokiren with its form.

Wandik – Name

A wandik is not the same as a wa'a, which is a word used as a means of communication; it is a label of identification which denotes an essential individuality to an object, whether human or otherwise. On their own, the waso and the nokiren give the impression of the human being divided into two mutually exclusive physical and spiritual parts. One of the most important functions of the wandik is to unify these.

Collecting information on names was one of the more difficult aspects of fieldwork in San José. People were reluctant to disclose their Arakmbut names to outsiders, preferring to use the Spanish names given to them by missionaries. These Spanish names are basically labels of identification and have no relation to the nokiren or the waso. Traditional names, on the other hand, do relate to the nokiren and waso. There are several types of name, two of which, informal nicknames and adult names, have been discussed in chapter four. It is possible for people to share names, but this does not give two people the same identity. The reason for this is that there is another name which is a unique and personal matter. This name is not given at any time in life but becomes associated with a person gradually. It is not just a label but a part of the person's whole being.

These names are not exactly secret but they are rarely, if ever, uttered. They are tied up with the welfare of the possessor and only a few close kin and special friends use them or admit to knowing what these wandik actually are. When I asked the Arakmbut why they were so reluctant to disclose their names they said that it was because if someone wished to inflict harm on a person he could do so with a knowledge of his or her wandik. Similarly if a spirit overhears someone's name being uttered it can come and attack. Once it was remarked to me that people who were not Arakmbut never seemed to be attacked by spirits. After a discussion, there was agreement that this was because the spirits did not know the names of such strangers.

A person is referred to by the 'safe' labelling first names (informal or Spanish) when alive, but after death even these should not be uttered. This is because the spirit of the dead person, on hearing the name, will unify and return to the community to inflict harm on the people. In this way the misuse of a wandik can either entice a spirit back to the community or call the nokiren out of someone's body and cause harm.

In cases where someone is harmed by means of the wandik it has the effect of attacking the nokiren (soul) while it is in the waso (body) or else of separating one from the other. In both cases the relationship between the nokiren and the waso is severely disrupted and, at worst, ruptured. This is not to say that there is a pure 'balanced' relationship between the waso and the nokiren which is tied together by the wandik, but that the wandik is an essential expression of the parameters within which they operate in life.

In the same way that the senses are associated with the waso while thought and emotion are associated with the nokiren, there is a faculty connected to the wandik. This faculty is memory. This comes from the verb *e'ndikka,* which means to name. The particle *mba'* occurs in words where a large quantity of something is being done (e.g. *e'ka* = to do, *e'mba'a* = to work). The letter *'t'* within a word means 'next to'. We can thus get a rough idea that *e'mbatandikka* means literally 'imitate' or 'to name things with others a lot' – a phrase which could be glossed as 'classify'.

The concept of memory also centres around the word *e'nopwe* (to know). Memory (*e'anopwe* – 'articulation of thought') is the naming of various images in relation to other images and is thus the way in which classifications are arranged in order to make sense of the world. The wandik functions as the boundary marker within which the nokiren and waso shift while retaining the identity of a person. Running parallel to this is memory, which effectively connects thought and affection to information received from the visible world by the senses.

The three aspects of the human body relate together in the same way as the three groups of faculties. The senses and the waso function in the visible world whereas the affections, thought, and nokiren are the 'senses' of the invisible world. The wandik and the faculty of memory are signs of the individuation and the unity of personhood and are expressions of the essential complementarity between the visible and invisible worlds.

Throughout life there are changes in the relationship and the nature of the waso, nokiren, and wandik. These changes are attributable to growth (e'kerek) and the way each person at times in his or her life grows out of the identity and position once held. For the rest of this chapter we will be discussing the development of bodies, souls, and names over a person's lifetime.

The fundamental source of body and soul-matter is in the corporeality of the patriline. Semen contains a mixture of the physical substance of the waso and a soul substance which is not yet the nokiren. Conception occurs when sufficient semen has been deposited in a woman's womb. Intercourse is an activity centred on the lower, wetter regions of the body, and women have to be very careful after intercourse that spirits associated with the river do not enter the vagina during sleep and mix with the semen to form a boa-like creature. Should this happen the pregnancy will be slow, often taking well over a year, and the resulting foetus will eventually wriggle away from the mother into the nearest river.[3]

Bogn dakwe (bad lip) means pregnancy. The vagina is seen in a similar way to the fermentation vessel traditionally used in brewing – wawing bogn (water lip). In both cases the maize or chewed yuca and the semen are placed in a container and are left to ferment. There is a connection between the two uses of the term *bogn* which the Arakmbut themselves do not articulate. The important part of both processes is that the liquids are left to 'cook' on their own. During pregnancy, in fact, sexual intercourse is prohibited and nothing should enter the vagina so that the foetus can form on its own.[4] A woman knows she is pregnant when her nipples become sensitive and when her hands become hot and sticky. During pregnancy a woman will continue with all her work in the chacras, but the mother is subject to certain food restrictions. For example, there is a prohibition on eating monkeys with prehensile tails because their spirit could cause the umbilical cord to be caught up in the foetus.

At birth, the main threat to the mother and child comes from the spirits associated with the river. A mother will always give birth

3. It is interesting to note that the boa produces its offspring as a formed snake and not in eggs as most other snakes. This may be why the Arakmbut consider the boa to have human characteristics.
4. There are several examples of connections between sexual intercourse and cooking in Amazonia. Among the Waiwai the heat inside the mother cooks the semen (Morton 1979: chapter four) while among the Apinayé (Da Matta 1979: 101) blood is transformed into semen in the heat of coitus. The Arakmbut do not refer to heat, but the fermentation analogy appears more appropriate. The prohibition of sexual intercourse during pregnancy may be seen as a parallel to the period when chicha or masato is left in order to ferment. The prohibition thus has three causes: fear of contamination from menstrual blood, allowing the embryo to 'cook' on its own, and the fear of producing clones.

away from the house. The blood attracts river spirits, and if the birth took place at home they would know where the mother and child live and could return to harm them and possibly kill them. Usually the birth takes place in the chacra during the day, but if labour comes on at night, any space away from the house will do. Before delivery a mother should not drink anything. By drying herself out she will keep away any harmful river spirits. The old woman who helps deliver the child is called *mama* and, as has been noted before, shares this term with the caiman which is an animal associated with the river.

A woman gives birth in a crouched position. As in the myth of Marinke, growth from now on is upwards. The baby is born outside the house but is brought back to the settlement when the placenta has been disposed of. The river spirits may follow the mother and child home if the wet placenta is not discarded outside the settlement. The passage from outside to inside the community is the first step in a process of growth which lasts through youth into adulthood.

The Arakmbut say that a child does not really have a clearly defined waso or nokiren of its own until it is born. For a year or two after birth the child is not fully independent, relying on its mother for milk and still being physically and spiritually an emanation of the father without any individuality or personality of its own. For this reason the parents of the child must undergo certain dietary and behavioral restrictions.

The meat which a mother eats passes the characteristics of the hunted species into her milk and onto her child. She must therefore avoid caiman, armadillo, certain birds, and some monkeys, all of which have characteristics which, entering the child, could cause illness or death. The father has to be careful, too, in case when hunting these prohibited species, he attracts spirits associated with the animals to come to the house and harm the family. In addition to this, the parents should not have intercourse for the period while a child is not fully independent and still drinking its mother's milk. This prohibition may be to keep away spirits but, as was noted in chapter four, the reason is likely to be to prevent the creation of people too similar to each other. However, this prohibition is breaking down. Furthermore, in 1991 the first case of twins was reported in San José, which initially caused much concern for the parents, but they have quickly adapted to the new members of their family.

When the child becomes an individual, separate from both father and mother, it is weaned from the breast, has its hair cut, and knows its 'child's' name. This name is often paralleled with a species of animal or natural object, with a change of vowel or consonant to make the association by implication rather than explicitly. The parents have probably called the child by a personal name for a while but they do spread it around the rest of the community.

Children are assumed to have an aptitude for contact with the spirit world because their nokiren is not so firmly tied to the waso, and in dreams they wander about more freely than their elders. One might think that this proclivity to allow the nokiren to wander would be dangerous. However, the Arakmbut say that spirits of the forest which harm adults do not attack children, who have to fear the spirits of the river.

The first major change a child has to encounter is at puberty. A girl never has any initiation rite at this time. She carries on working at her mother's side until marriage. Her change of status from a girl to a full woman comes with pregnancy. To give birth to children is a rite of passage which enables a young woman (*muneyo*) to become a full adult *(wetone)*.

A boy, in the period before the move to the mission of Shintuya in 1956, underwent two rites; that of *e'ohtokoy* (nose-piercing) and *e'mbogntokoy* (lip-piercing).[5] The second rite meant that the waso and nokiren of the man were now fully tied together. He was recognised as a proficient hunter and was eligible for marriage, in particular sexual relations, without getting thin and weak. A full man is completely socialised and a part of society. His greatest fear is no longer from the spirits of the river but from those of the forest with which he comes into contact during his regular hunting expeditions. At the end of the second rite a man would traditionally receive a new formal wandik which was the name of an adult, although nowadays at this time a man is called by his Spanish name. With a new name, the person has the means of keeping body and soul together.

The story of Marinke is particularly important here because the fiesta described in the first part is the prototype of the Arakmbut initiation ceremonies. At the ceremonies men traditionally dressed in costumes of birds' feathers which represented man's entry into the forest. Between the two rites, the experience of the young man in

5. Initiation is found among several other Peruvian peoples. The Amuesha (Wise 1958), the Asháninka (Weiss 1969), and the Shipibo (Morin 1973:122ff) all have or have had female initiation involving isolation. The Matsigenka and Piro, in addition, had a male initiation consisting of a brief seclusion at puberty followed by a fiesta (Alvarez, R. 1962, 1970:41 & Gerhard Baer pers. comm.). No other people appears to have similar male initiation rights to the Arakmbut.

entering the forest increased until he could travel a long way through the bush without fear of his nokiren being snatched from his waso by a harmful spirit. Furthermore the spine inserted into the youth was mythologically formed by the pubic hair of the grandmother.

The piercing of the nose and lip with the spine connects with imagery involved in both sexual relations and pregnancy. The penetration of the lip by 'female pubic hair' is in contrast to the penetration of a woman by a male penis. The mouth piercing takes place in an upper part of the body, as opposed to the planting of the semen in a woman which takes place between lower parts of the body and is wet. While an old man oversees the welfare of a youth approaching adulthood, an old woman takes care of a girl through childbirth. Whereas several years separate nose and lip piercing, a woman has her period of gestation during pregnancy. The man's initiation is complete at lip-piercing, the woman is at child birth. In both cases a 'piercing' is followed by a period of continence during which strength is built up.

In the past, initiation was the moment of adulthood when people could begin the preparation of ritual foods. We noted above a parallel between fermentation, which took place in a vessel known as a *wawing bogn*, and pregnancy, which is known as *bogndakwe*. The maize or yuca was chewed by the woman and spat out and left to ferment. Tobacco was originally taken through the nose by blowing and coca was chewed and left to 'ferment in the mouth'. Both tobacco and coca provided strength. These activities involved some object being put in a lip- or mouth-shaped container which then 'cooks'. The analogies between pregnancy and fermentation is paralleled by the analogy between nose-piercing and tobacco sniffing and between lip-piercing and coca chewing.

This shows that the Arakmbut conceive of growth to adulthood for both male and female as an extreme form of transformation involving dry/male and wet/female elements respectively. The initial piercing involves penetration of the opposite sex by male or female elements and then a period of gestation. The man incorporates female power; the woman, male power. At the end of her pregnancy the female gives birth to a child. The male, on the other hand, does not give birth to anything immediately but his strength has been built up so that he can now produce semen without danger to himself (for as we will see, ejaculation is a form of death and as such can be dangerous if not accomplished in the correct conditions).

The following table compares different patterns of growth for an Arakmbut male and female:

Table 6.2 Connections between rites of passage and ritual foods.

Female Initiation	Male Initiation
Sexual relations	Nose- and lip-piercing
Conception by penis wet semen accumulating in the womb	Spines (mythical female pubic hair) dried and put into nose and then lower lip
Semen left in womb where it transforms	Spines left in nose and lip to give strength
Lower parts of the body	Upper parts of the body
Leads to female adulthood	Leads to male adulthood
Old woman intermediary	Old man intermediary
Analogous to:	
Fermentation	Taking tobacco through the nose and chewing coca
Prepared by spitting	Prepared by drying tobacco and coca, and burning lime.
Ferments in wawing bogn	'Ferments' in mouth (bogn)
Female activity	Male activity
Chicha or masato: major wet ritual drinks	Coca and tobacco: major dry ritual foods

The principle of growth by means of a juxtaposition of elements followed by a gestation can be also seen in the myth of Wanamey. The initial piercing of the woman by the bird with the seed of Wanamey resulted in a 'long night' when all was quiet and the new day when the Arakmbut were reborn. This juxtaposition followed by a period of growth is a framework which relates to production methods on a daily basis and not just for ritual foods. Initiation provides the prerequisites for men and women to pass on their strength to their offspring through the production of food. Men and women achieve their full potential of adulthood when they are at the height of their potency and their soul and body are more firmly bound together than at any other time of life. This is the time when they can prepare and consume ritual foods and take responsibility for a family.

The formation of the person is thus a process. The moment of adulthood is the point at which reproduction of life can take place. After the period of initiation a man can have sexual relations with a woman without becoming weak and sick. In the past, the initiation provided that strength, although now, other factors such as good food suffice. Furthermore, an adult man and woman have a responsibility to provide their children with the means to grow. In order to understand Arakmbut notions of human development it is important to gain some insight into the way a child, which is an emanation of its father, can grow into an adult and on into old age. The basis of a person may be the accumulated semen of the father, but somehow the waso and nokiren must develop further.

The Arakmbut say that before any strenuous activity such as gold work, they always make sure that there is plenty of meat available to give them strength. Crops such as yuca and plantains are also important as accompaniments to meat. Although they have no substance in them to help with the growth of the waso and nokiren as does meat, they must always be at hand to ensure that the digestion is not affected by too much pure meat.

For men, most of their strength is used up in the production, distribution, and consumption of meat (although gold work is increasingly taking over as the most time-consuming task among Arakmbut men). Hunting ability is a prerequisite for marriage. When a young couple decide that they want to be married the girl accepts the meat from her prospective husband and cooks it (chindoi). This is a sign that she is prepared to have sexual relations with him. The presentation of meat is thus the precondition for married life (however this is not an exchange of meat for sexual favours).

There are two aspects to hunting, each of which demands a different quality from the hunter. The ability to catch an animal involves being a skilful tracker and a keen shot with an arrow. On the other hand, it is impossible to hunt anything without knowledge of the whereabouts of the animals or the numbers which can be killed. A hunter receives information about a prospective hunt in a dream (wayorok) from the spirit world in the form of a sexually charged relationship (these aspects were described in chapter two). If he is lucky his contact with the spirit has been beneficial, he finds plenty, and on the following day the hunter pierces the animal and kills it for food.

Hunting and sexual relations act as images that link man and woman in the visible world to contacts with the invisible world. Without the power of the women from the invisible world, a man cannot hunt. The power of women is therefore essential for an adult man's ability to provide semen (from the insertion of 'grandmother's pubic hair' at initiation) and meat to a woman (from dreaming with the beneficial female spirits). The woman converts semen into a child and converts meat into food, providing strength and sustenance for the family.

Meanwhile a woman is responsible for the chacras. Even though men do the initial clearing and help with planting and weeding from time to time, the women of the household are held to blame if the crops do not grow well. They are responsible for the nurturing of the plants in the ground. We can see planting and the gestation of crops through the wet season as another dimension to the production of food. Women nurture crops after planting and they grow accordingly.

When food is brought into the house, the women are responsible for the cooking. We have discussed in chapter two the difference between male and female cooking methods. Men roast or smoke food more than women who boil, steam, and fry. The more usual female forms of cooking are moderate forms of fermentation which are analogous to pregnancy.

The transformation of meat and vegetables into food provides sustenance for the household. Growth through life takes place through various means. The prime element is the accumulation of body-substance and soul-matter by means of eating food – especially meat. Food is converted into the waso and nokiren of the eater through ingestion into the internal organs, which act as a receptacle of transformation.[6]

Digestion consists of two aspects. There is first of all the ingestion of socially prepared food by the upper part of the body and then its disposal as waste from the lower orifices. The strength-giving properties of the food remain and are converted by the stomach and the liver, which lie at the centre of the body. The consumption and digestion of food is a process that moves from dry/upper parts of the body to the wet/lower areas.[7]

This survey of Arakmbut production shows that male and female adulthood is the prerequisite for providing a household with food and sustenance. The principles behind both sexual relations and pregnancy on the one hand and the old male initiation ceremonies on the other are reflected at all levels of production and consumption. In fact, these parallels constitute the reproductive power of Arakmbut existence. The spiritual strength which comes from adult-

6. Meat with any blood in it is too dangerous to eat and for this reason the Arakmbut avoid roasting lest any blood remain. Blood therefore signifies the presence of too much soul-matter. I have been told on one occasion that although blood is not the nokiren, both substances can be found throughout the whole body and so the invisible could well travel through the visible.

7. Another Arakmbut practice which takes place when growth does not take place too quickly is to bathe in the river in the morning. When a *suli* worm goes into a paca it grows, as does the *nadapa*. A small child who goes into water when young will also expand and grow. Mothers send their small children down to soak in the water early in the morning to expand like the *suli* worm – a feature similar to the growth of Marinke in the rainstorm.

hood when the waso and nokiren are tied together provides the means of growth for the household, as the woman provides children and the man provides strength from meat. We cannot say that this pattern 'determines' production but that it is the way in which production reproduces itself over time.

In recent years, changes have taken place in Arakmbut social and cultural life which have altered this pattern. Male initiation rites have not taken place since the 1960s and the ritual foods are not prepared in the same manner as they once were. During a discussion on this question, I was told that initiation provided strength for men to have sexual relations. The changes in diet as a result of contact with the outside world have provided more strength to young men and the initiation rites are perhaps not so necessary nowadays.

With regard to the ritual foods and drinks, tobacco is now smoked and coca is rarely seen in the communities. Ayahuasca seems to be the most used 'ritual food' nowadays, although it was not used in the past. Similarly beer has replaced wawing as the social drink for fiestas. The power of the non-Arakmbut world seems to be used more than the old spirit world for providing strength for adults. Possibly for the increase in gold work, a non-indigenous activity, the Arakmbut have moved to other non-indigenous sources of 'ritual food'.

This discussion sees adulthood as the basic requirement for the continuation of Arakmbut life. The result is a series of relationships which have been transformed over time but which retain a similar pattern:

Figure 6.1 Arakmbut production and reproduction

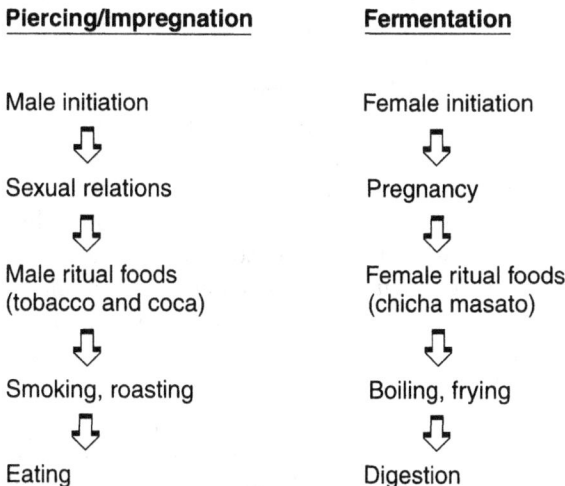

Piercing/Impregnation	**Fermentation**
Male initiation	Female initiation
⇩	⇩
Sexual relations	Pregnancy
⇩	⇩
Male ritual foods (tobacco and coca)	Female ritual foods (chicha masato)
⇩	⇩
Smoking, roasting	Boiling, frying
⇩	⇩
Eating	Digestion

Each of these activities depends on the previous elements as a prerequisite for its continuing through time. In this way production and reproduction are inseparable. We cannot say that the categorisation is somehow prior to the activities, but that the two are interdependent. The only changes which have taken place since contact have been the demise of the male initiation ceremony and the use of ritual foods. This does not significantly change the overall pattern of the production and reproduction framework, although much of the explicit meaning encapsulated in that ritual is disappearing. A contemporary table would look as follows:

Table 6.3 Contemporary Production and Reproduction

Piercing/Impregnation	Fermentation
Male adulthood	Female adulthood
Sexual relations	Pregnancy
Killing animals	Growing plants
Smoking, roasting	Boiling, frying
Eating	Digestion

The last thirty years has not seen any fundamental change in the conceptualisation of Arakmbut production and reproduction. The disappearance of the ceremonies and ritual use of coca and chicha have led to an internalisation of physical manifestations of the cultural aspects of production and reproduction. There has been, however, a shift in the focus of power. The invisible spirit world can now be effectively contacted through ayahuasca and not simply coca and tobacco. Furthermore, strength for sexual prowess is thought to come through the new foods introduced by outsiders, such as beans and rice. The age-grades are increasingly marked by education level or military service, which also demonstrates alternative means of cumulative formation of adulthood utilising knowledge from the world of white people (for more on this see chapter nine).

However, it is important to understand that production and reproduction practices among the Arakmbut cannot be separated from the formation of the person. Adulthood is the central moment from which the continuation of social and cultural life takes place, not only in terms of the continuity of the clan line through marriage, but in terms of the physical capacity to produce and nurture other members of the household.

Life for the Arakmbut begins with pregnancy and birth. The child is associated with wetness and the river. He or she gradually grows through eating meat and learns to participate in the production activities. With age the waso and nokiren become more tightly bound, enabling a person to cope with the dangers of the outside world without being harmed. For a man, travel through the forest for hunting is of more significance than for a woman who is always closer to the river. A man undergoes a 'dry pregnancy' to reach adulthood, in which he increases his strength sufficiently to undertake the hazards of hunting in the forest. Life is a path from inside to outside the community and from helping in production activities as children to adulthood, when it is possible to organise them for oneself and one's family.

However, life is not a continuous path of growth. After the heights of adulthood comes the decline of old age. Here a person gradually returns to the more 'childlike' side of life. An old man and woman have fewer sexual relations, he hunts and she cooks less frequently – they thus depend on their children or other relations in the descending generations. Food prohibitions do not apply to old people, who not only don't do anything dangerous, but are not considered to have long to live anyway. However, old people are not useless and are often revered for their spiritual knowledge, which in many cases they cannot use because of their lack of physical and spiritual power.

Old people have 'one foot in the grave', and so they become increasingly less important members of the community. The interesting question is why people grow old. One reason clearly lies in sexual intercourse. Whenever a man reaches orgasm a part of him dies and so he loses much of his force and energy with time. However this does not answer the question entirely because it does not account for why women grow old, or bachelors who never marry. There are other reasons involved beyond the nemesis of orgasm.

There is a point in life when the amount of food which a person takes into his body does not compensate for the amount of stress he or she undergoes. This is not a question of the expenditure of energy, but the constant pressures on the soul-matter of the nokiren loosening its strong ties with the physical waso. For a man this loosening comes through contact with the beautiful spirit women when hunting. Life alliances gradually build up between men and spirits of certain species. As they grow older, the nokiren become more and more attracted to an afterlife with these spirit women who live under the river. A woman is attracted to the species to which her husband is connected because she cooks and eats the meat of animals connected to her in-laws and her own family. Whereas the body eventually deteriorates, the nokiren does not. The Arakmbut often say that the spirit of a dead person appears as he or she appeared when a full adult. Old age is a phenomenon which affects the body but not the soul.

From this we can ascertain that hunting and eating meat not only provide growth for the body and soul, but also gradually associate the nokiren more and more with the species of the animals which are consumed. There is an exchange here between the soul, which goes to the spirit world upon death, and the meat of dead animals, which provide growth and life. The fact that the death of an old person is a normal 'good' death, and that the nokiren from a 'good' death goes initially to the river, indicates that the passage from adulthood to old age is, for the Arakmbut, a return to the situation early in life. A child has a nokiren and waso which are weakly tied together and has most of its contacts with the spirits of the river. Exactly the same holds for the elderly, with the exception that, whereas spirits of the river are dangerous to children, they are objects of attraction to older people.

The passage from birth to death is only part of a larger process involving both human beings and the non-human world. Death is the boundary of life from the point of orgasm at its inception to the point when the nokiren leaves the waso at the end. We must now turn to look at death and its causes, sickness and misdemeanour, in more detail, in order to see the transition from the visible to the invisible world.

c₂ Chapter 7 ₂○

SICKNESS AND DEATH

The previous chapter looked at the notion of growth (e'kerek) among the Arakmbut from birth to death. With the steady decline of powers at old age, the soul (nokiren) becomes attracted to the spirits in the world Seronwe under the river and eventually dies, by passing to the other world.

However, life is not always like this. Only a minority of people manage to live into their old age. At all times human beings are threatened by dangers from the spirit world which have to be countered. The complication is that the means to combat the dangers of the spirit world come from that same invisible dimension.

We have seen that babies and young children are considered to be under threat from the river spirits – waweri. On fishing expeditions or on river trips, children are regularly painted with red achiote in order to keep the waweri away. Yet a common way for a small child to gain strength is to go down to the river early in the morning and submerge him or herself in the water. The river thus provides the means of growth for a child while at the same time containing a major danger.

Threats from the spirit world reflect the association with the different domains. Children and old people fear the waweri while adults have also to beware of dangerous forest spirits – ndumberi. As people grow older, they enter into threatening relationships with spirits through the two most problematic activities which adults practise – sexual relations and food production.

Sexual relations are fraught with dangers. We have seen that intercourse with relatives who are too close or too distant can lead to sickness. Arakmbut stories even tell of people who had relations within the clan and died as a result. Other tales describe men who made love to strange women in the forest. One vivid story tells of a woman who turned out to be an animal spirit; as a result, the Arakmbut lover's penis festered and rotted away until he died.

The e'ohtokoy (nose-piercing) and e'mbogntokoy (lip-piercing) ceremonies were extremely important to ensure that a man could carry out sexual relations without becoming ill. The dangers of having sexual relations too early in life lead to a drastic weakness of the body.

There is a very popular story among the Arakmbut of San José which tells of this problem. It is interesting because it illustrates the impatience of a boy to become a man and the mortal danger to which he was exposed when he overstretched his abilities. The story is considered so powerful that a married man should not tell it to his children but seek an old unmarried man who will not be affected by its message.

The Story of Chipomeme (Sipomeme)

Chipomeme danced alone. As he danced he sang 'kaing kaing ka!' Chipomeme was happy. His father scolded him because Chipomeme was forbidden to dance, nor could he use a *tayagnpi* (stick for crushing coca lime used only by adult men). Chipomeme was forbidden because he was a wambo not a wambokerek.

The old men were in the forest collecting wood for the *tayagn* and *parakupo* ashes to mix with the coca leaves. Chipomeme was happy. He went to cut the tayagn wood too. But his father's brother (wachio) saw him. 'Why are you cutting tayagn? You are too young.' Chipomeme was angry and threw the tayagn over the cliff.

Chipomeme was furious and stormed off into the forest with his younger brother and made a lean-to (*kuchiakpo*) to wait for partridges. Many birds came to the hide. Quickly he killed many of them. He collected many. They hunted.

Suddenly Chipomeme heard the sound of the low flute whistle announcing a fiesta. His brother had not heard it. Then Chipomeme and his brother rapidly gathered their things and returned from the hunt. The brother went a long way by the path but Chipomeme took a short cut through the forest to get home faster.

Then Chipomeme prepared for the dance. He had ready his tayagnpi, his feather head dress and his *to'mbi* snail shell rattle under his arm. He rushed through the forest to the maloca which was holding the fiesta. He arrived singing 'kaing kaing ka, tero tero ta, kaing

kaing ka!' He sat with his fellow visitors outside the maloca waiting for
the welcome. He sat away from his father. But the other Arakmbut
criticised him. He should have been sitting with his father, not apart.

The sun went down and the villagers were invited to enter the
maloca. At the entrance to the maloca the host greeted them with his
tayagnpi and everyone said '*ijchagi*' (I arrive). There were no other
wambo, only Chipomeme. He greeted Chipomeme also.

Chipomeme wanted a woman (*wanjinji*) whom he wanted to marry.
She was called Muyoni. He wanted the girl very much. Chipomeme
persuaded her to come out of the maloca to eat apik (sugarcane). Then
they went in to dance in the maloca. All through the night until the
dawn there was a dance in a circle. Chipomeme went outside from
time to time and had sexual relations with the girl. Then they began to
dance and those seated began to sing.

And Chipomeme sang 'kaing kaing ka!' and he drank chicha.
Then they went out onto the patio and dawn came.

They finished the chicha. Chipomeme, after the sexual relations,
was weak. Then they all returned to their house. Chipomeme and
his father returned to their house.

One day his wachio invited Chipomeme to come hunting.
Chipomeme told his uncle that he loved Muyoni and had had sexual
relations with her. The wachio was very angry with Chipomeme and
hit him. Chipomeme from that moment became very thin. He was
too weak to go to the next fiesta. He knew that he would die because
he had had sexual relations with the girl when he was too young.

The story of Chipomeme refers to the prime qualities associated
with manhood among the Arakmbut, such as hunting and finding a
wife. The ceremony in which he participated was the e'mbaipak, or
male initiation. But he was not old enough. The Arakmbut explained that one of the main purposes of the traditional ceremonies
was to ensure that young men received the spiritual strength to
enable them to have sexual relations without becoming thin and
sickly like Chipomeme.

The other dangerous area apart from sexual relations is the production of food. The Arakmbut are particularly strict in controlling
hunting. There are several episodes in myths, for example, which tell
of hunters who, provided with wonderful opportunities for shooting
animals, take advantage of their good fortune and overkill.

A hunter who kills too much can either incur the wrath of the
invisible world or forge too close a relationship with the spirits,
which is equally dangerous. This can effect a whole household.

When I caught a fish, for example, I was told to refrain from fishing for at least three days. The problem was that the river spirits (waweri) had provided me with fish because they liked me. Should I fish too much, one of the young spirit women would call me down to the underworld. Furthermore, I may not have caught the fish because the spirits liked me. Maybe they wanted the company of my family and I would be an instrument for their designs unless I was extremely careful when fishing.

Hunting and fishing are not the only dangers in food production and consumption – eating can be also. If too much meat from an animal is consumed at one time, the animal can cause not only illness but death. Overeating is not the only danger from meat consumption. Prohibitions also exist on species at certain points during the life cycle, as was noted at pregnancy over monkeys with prehensile tails. Cold fish and cold peach palm are dangerous at all times.

The dangers of overindulgence are similar to those put forward in the myth of Marinke in chapter five as constituting those desires of life that a person has to control in order to avoid encountering threats from the spirit world. In these cases, the myths act as 'morality tales' warning Arakmbut to live healthily.

A myth illustrates these dangers of hunting and the spirit world:

The Story of Iari (White-lipped Peccary)

A man was a *wayorokeri* (shaman-dreamer) in *iari*. He said that the iari were going to come to his people one day. 'The iari will offer us peach palm *(ho)*.' The spirits of the iari consider peach palm to be iari too.

The wayorokeri had a brother who was not a dreamer. The wayorokeri who was an expert in iari, said one day: 'I am going to the iari but with my body. Others have gone to the iari in spirit but I will go with all my body.' His brother did not believe him.

Two days went by and the wayorokeri began to change. His penis began to cleave to his belly and his skin left his nails. He said to his brother: 'My lover is going to come and offer you chindoi (gift offered at a time of marriage to in-laws). You must receive the gift, not in an open hand, but with two fingers. The woman is a iari. Don't be afraid when all the iari come.'

After the wayorokeri had spoken, hundreds of iari came around the house. One iari, the wayorokeri's lover, had something wrapped in a leaf packet. She came like a huge animal and offered it to him in two fingers. But the man put out his whole hand to receive it. All the iari fled. The wayorokeri followed the iari to beg their forgiveness. The iari calmed down. They agreed to come again.

'Why did you do this?' the wayorokeri asked his brother. 'I have arranged with my iari lover and she will come again to offer the packet.' She came again. This time the man received the packet with his two fingers and the iari were very pleased. They stayed in his house. It was getting dark.

The wayorokeri brother asked. 'Do you need some meat?'

'Yes', he replied.

'Then kill a few iari. Before sleeping the iari will take out their hearts and hang them on a vine. To kill them you must prick them with a spine.'

The thin iari slept towards the outside of the house and the big ones towards the centre. So the man went into the middle of the house to kill them. They were asleep with their hearts hanging above them. The man then pricked all the hearts with spines.

The wayorokeri was angry when all the iari were killed. 'Why have you done this? How can you do this? My skin is thick, my penis is against my belly. I am turning into a iari myself. There is only one thing that I can do.' The brother was told to go and cut down peach palm (singpa or ho) and cut it into pieces. These pieces of singpa he would convert into iari. The brother brought the wood.

When it dawned, the wayorokeri called the iari but they did not arise. He complained to his brother, 'These pieces are not big enough.' So the brother returned to the forest and brought heavy pieces of singpa. He laid them down ready to be converted into iari. The wayorokeri called out: 'Iari! Iari! Iari! Get up!' Nothing.

So the brother cut even larger pieces of singpa. When they had been placed on the ground, the wayorokeri called: 'Iari! Iari! Iari! Get up!' The second time he called, the singpa were converted into iari. 'Ho Ho Ho!', they said, and went off into the forest.

The wayorokeri also become converted into iari. He went and never returned to his brother because he was still angry. No one knows if he is dead or alive but from his own flesh he converted into iari.

This story combines the hunting themes of overkill and the costs of becoming too closely involved with the spirits of an animal species. The brother commits the offence of overkill when he has the opportunity to take advantage of the peccary around him. On the other hand, the shaman is so close to the spirits that he has a iari lover and eventually becomes one himself and disappears from the human social world. The story thus indicates the two dangers of overkill and over-affection for the spirit world that take the perpetrators away from human social life.

Sickness and death do not only come about through the fault of the victim. There are other causes which can affect a person by chance. Sorcerers are people who feel hatred and want to harm a victim. The principles behind sorcery are identical to those of animals seeking revenge. The sorcerer uses the power of hostile toto spirits to make the attack. The most dangerous sorcerer in Arakmbut society is the *wa'itamankaeri*. He usually comes from another community or Taka from some other people such as the Matsigenka or the Ese'eja. *Wa'i* means footprint in Harakmbut and these sorcerers use footprints to work their magic with ayahuasca or some form of incantation. However, any part of the person will do, such as nail parings, hair, or bits of personal property.

Sorcerers are particularly feared by the Arakmbut because there is little hope of curing the victim. When the sorcerer is unknown, accusations are hard to make but everyone has their theories. Sorcery is a state of the nokiren when the concentrated aspect becomes so enraged that it manifests hatred (*ochinosik* – black centre).

There was an example of this type of sorcery in San José involving a young man who left the community for a while to go on military service. He was stationed at a post called Iberia where there were Taka. He was found to have tuberculosis by the army doctors and was in hospital for several months. Even though he recovered, the disease recurred when we were in San José. In spite of the fact that we alleviated the disease for the time being with the appropriate drugs, the people of the village were quite convinced that the tuberculosis had originated from Taka sorcery and was the work of a wa'itamankaeri. We were told that the drugs that we had administrated would only cure him temporarily and that the illness would return again.

Another type of sorcerer is the *chindignwakeri* or *chindignwamankeri*. The term for this sorcerer contains the particle *ndik*, which means name and refers to the fact that he causes illnesses by uttering the name of the intended victim in addition to taking ayahuasca or casting spells. The chindignwakeri usually comes from the same people as the victim, because only someone in close contact can know a person's name. By uttering the name of the victim, the sorcerer lures the nokiren out of the waso so that it does not know the way to return and becomes easy prey for the toto. As the sorcerer comes from within the same Arakmbut community as the victim, it is sometimes possible to cure the resulting illness, as the sorcerer can be found and forced to save the patient.

A third type of sorcery concerns women who become associated with toto and kill others in the community. Califano (1978a) provides an account of his own and others' experiences of the female *chiwembet.* This tells of how young Arakmbut women could harm others by collaborating with a toad *(chiwemui),* noted earlier as a toto. Such women would obtain some part or property of the victim and bury it in a packet of leaves. The closer to the victim the packet was buried, the stronger the sorcery. The toad lived near the girl, who would have regular meetings with it so that the power of the toto could enter her. On the whole this account by Califano was reluctantly accepted in San José. Their reluctance stemmed from an embarrassment to admit that female sorcery ever took place because of the traditional punishment inflicted on the young sorcerer – strangulation and drowning.[1]

People can become ill or die through accidental encounters with spirits in the forest. There are small snakes which are almost invisible which can bite a person so that he or she does not know it. Other dangers in the forest include passing breezes and plants which can brush against a leg causing illness or even death.

When people are ill they say that they are dakwe (feeling bad). Illness can take the form of fevers, diarrhoea, pain, nausea and vomiting, coughing or colds. There are countless different illnesses described by the Arakmbut, but they are usually arrangements of clusters of these symptoms affecting the wet or dry parts of the body.

For the Arakmbut, the presence of an illness becomes apparent gradually. If someone begins to feel unwell without extenuating circumstances such as the expectation of falling ill, then the person will battle on with normal life. But when the Arakmbut decide that they are ill, they take to bed and accept any medicines available in the hope that it will provide a cure.[2] The illness is not yet a social matter.

If the person does not get better in a few days, concern will mount among their relatives. The transition from a personal problem to a social one is gradual too. The patient begins to receive visits from relatives, old men begin to do some traditional curing, and bit by bit the illnesses becomes a concern of the whole village.

An illness becomes a social threat when there is a possibility of death. There is general concern because the patient and the com-

1. Young girls, the most defenceless members of the community, were prime targets for sorcery among the Asháninka (Weiss, 1969) and were dealt with in the same way as Arakmbut girls.
2. There are not many dietary restrictions for a minor illness. With diarrhoea the case is different because sufferers are expected to avoid all liquids in order to dry out their bodies. This 'killer cure' often leads to intense dehydration.

munity are both under attack from the invisible spirit world. On the whole the Arakmbut are a resilient people and put up with much discomfort without complaint. When an illness looks as if it could be fatal, the threshold of their resilience breaks down and they lose their desire to live.

Curing

Curing among the Arakmbut involves many different techniques. Those whose abilities become recognised by the community and beyond are referred to by the following terms:

The *wayorokeri* is a shamanic dreamer who has the ability to use his visionary and dreaming techniques to diagnose illnesses. He knows from messages received in his dreams the most beneficial actions to take in troubled times. The information comes from the *ndakyorokeri* or *ndakmbayorokeri* spirits (good dream people). Throughout his life the wayorokeri builds up a special relationship with some of these spirits, who tell him where and when it is best to hunt or fish. They warn him of future events and, most importantly, they help him in the diagnosis of curing.

The *wamanoka'eri* is a curer who treats the illness through the use of chants *(chindign)*. His methods are to look at the symptoms of the sickness and relate them to animal behaviour or other factors. If his diagnoses are correct then he will use the appropriate chindign, assuming that he knows it. A wamanoka'eri can often ascertain the social or cultural transgressions which were the conditions and causes of the illness, and so he is someone of knowledge and vision.

All men and women can dream and cure to some extent, but only those who regularly succeed in presenting correct diagnoses are recognised as shamans. The most powerful shaman (such as the one who died in San José in 1980) are recognised as both wayorokeri (dreamers) and wamanoka'eri (curers). Curing consists of diagnosing the cause of an illness. The proof that the correct cause has been discovered is the successful recovery of the patient. As was noted in the preface to this part, causality is bound up with relationships between the visible and invisible worlds.

In everyday life, visible causes lead to visible effects. Illnesses with visible or material causes are those which affect the waso (body) of a person rather than the nokiren (soul); examples of these are cuts and bruises, colds, headaches, minor stomach problems, or coughs. They are caused by small accidents, overwork, or exposure to excessive sun or rain. None of these illnesses can cause death on their own and should go away with a minimum of curing.

Invisible causes take several forms. Some manifestations of the harmful spirit toto have a concentration of soul-matter as an intrinsic and permanent quality. Others only become concentrated when they are angered and demand different curing methods. Illnesses caused by permanent toto such as Taka nokiren (souls of dead non-Arakmbut indigenous peoples), sorcerers from other communities, or attacks by jaguars and poisonous snakes are extremely difficult to cure. A shaman confronts such adversaries with the help of his spirit allies. He calls upon these beneficial spirits in his dreams and visions to aid him by fighting the toto. These different types of spirit are engaged in a perennial struggle for power, usually over the nokiren of human beings. The beneficial spirits will teach a shaman songs for curing illnesses caused by some animals, but illnesses caused by certain snakes or jaguars are impossible to cure. The spirits can also give reports as to the whereabouts of the toto. If a nokiren has been captured and taken by the toto, the shaman will to call it back again with chants and songs.

Dangerous animals such as jaguars, snakes, or alligators attack the physical body of people but penetrate the soul at the same time. Others, such as bats and toads, 'infect' people if placed in proximity to possessions (as in the case of bats hiding in the house or the toads used in female sorcery), or if they draw blood, as in the case of vampire bats. Eagles, owls, and vultures do not attack people directly but can infect the soul if someone eats meat which has been killed or scavenged by them. Curing such illnesses as these is not easy and a shaman must make good use of his spirit allies.

If the hostile spirit is normally dispersed but has temporarily become a harmful toto out of anger, a shaman will stand a better chance of curing the illness as he knows the animal spirits more intimately. The spirit usually attacks in the guise of animals, fish, or birds and this guise is the clue to the diagnosis. Every sick person shows symptoms which relate metaphorically to the particular species used by the spirit for the attack. The technique of curing is to identify the animal, imitate the species, pacify or frighten away the spirit, and make it leave the patient alone. After that the spirit should return to its dispersed form.

When someone falls ill the wayorokeri shaman dreams, and his interpretation will aid the diagnosis. The dream should provide a clue as to the nature of illness and to what extent it constitutes a threat to the community. The message may be that the illness has been caused by a species which the shaman is unable to cure, in which case someone else in the community will have to see if they can do better.

It is important for a shaman to demonstrate that his diagnosis is the correct one and that his method of curing has been the means for the patient's recovery. The community as a whole wants an explanation for the social threat from the spirit world, and only the shaman with the most acceptable version of what has happened will gain credit for the cure. A cure is thus only efficacious when it has been accepted as such by the members of the village.

The messages received by the shaman from the beneficial ndakyorokeri spirits in his dream are used in conjunction with the observations of physical symptoms and their relationship to natural species. The encyclopedic knowledge necessary for achieving a cure is only learned after much experience and is proof of the efficacy of the shaman's technique. Of all the species the most common symptoms come from game animals. This is because a shaman can best cure illnesses caused by spirits which he knows, and the ndakyorokeri are exclusively associated with game animals. The following are some of the major species and their accompanying symptoms. Smaller animals such as squirrels are not included as they are not large enough to have much effect on anyone.

White-lipped peccary: loose jaw, chatter of teeth, headache, and high temperature.
Collared peccary: severe stomach pains as the spirit stamps on your abdomen.
Tapir: swollen feet, eye problems, fever.
Armadillo: cough and bronchial disorders; very dangerous for children.
Capybara: wounds which will not heal, skin irritation.
Agouti: pains in the back and central part of the body.
Paca: severe body pains.
Opossum: bad eyes and body sores.

Monkeys can also cause illness. The spider and howler monkeys give fever and the sick person feels shivery and cold. The hands and feet of the monkey are considered to be loose and shaky. One of the main characteristics of monkey illnesses is this twitching of the hands and feet.

Several species of birds can produce symptoms in people. The oriole makes children restless and sleepless, while turkey buzzards give pains in the body and sores. The curassow symptoms are a headache, sharp pains, and skin problems. There are other species which are dangerous, such as the toucan and the partridge, but I was unable to discover their distinctive symptoms. The features of the illnesses all relate in some way to the characteristics of the species. For example, the curassow has a beak which curves at the tip, and the sharp pains are said to be like an invisible curassow squeezing the affected part of the body.

The other group of edible creatures which cause symptoms are the fish. All fish give colic. The sick person looks as if he has gills on his face as it all puffs up. Sometimes there is a fever but this is not necessary. Gastric problems are one of the main complaints. If a person eats too much cold fish it will give him diarrhoea. Someone sick from the fish will have a pallid colour and will also be prone to vomiting.

A sick person is attacked in his invisible nokiren by the spirit, but the symptoms are manifest physically in the waso. All the symptoms can be divided into two groups – wet and dry disorders. We have seen in the previous chapter that the waso is similarly divided into wet and dry aspects. Animals, birds, and fish are either manifestations of forest spirits (ndumberi) or manifestations of river spirits (waweri). These distinctions fit together because river spirits are causes of disorders of the wet parts of the waso and forest spirits of disorders of the dry parts.

The wet symptoms from the river spirits affect the intestines, liver, kidney, and digestive organs and the result is diarrhoea and vomiting. Dry symptoms from forest spirits are those concerning bones, muscles, heart, limbs, and head. An illness usually involves more than one species, and a shaman may have to unravel the various symptomatic threads in order to ascertain the principal causes.

The greatest threat for people comes from those spirits with which they have the most contact at various points during their lives. We have seen that at the 'wetter' parts of their lives (i.e. childhood and old age) people are closer to river spirits and so illnesses are more likely to come from that quarter. Women are associated more with the river than the forest and so they have to take special care in case of attack by the waweri, particularly during pregnancy. Adult men, on the other hand, are 'drier' and relate more to creatures and spirits of the forest and it is from them that threats of illnesses initially appear.

There is another group of illnesses which attack the body rather than the soul. These appeared with the first missionaries and are called 'diseases of God' because the priests' Christian God produced them. Such illnesses are caused by contact with Amiko (whites) and can only be cured by scientific medicine. God created the ailments so that people would go to the missions for medicine.[3] If the medicines have no effect then the illness is not a disease of God but one of the Arakmbut toto spirits. There is no way of disputing this argument because in all Arakmbut ideas of illness and curing, the diagnosis is part of the treatment. If the treatment does not work, it is the diagnosis which is wrong.

In San José we provided medicines but were told that although they would work for 'physical' illnesses and the diseases of God, they could not cure an 'Arakmbut' ailment caused by the spirits. Medicines may possibly alleviate a problem, but if the illness needs shamanic curing it will not respond to other treatment on a permanent basis. If no such means of curing works, then the toto are responsible.

Illness is a personal problem when it physically affects the waso. A spirit illness of the nokiren is a social matter because the 'presence' of infected soul-matter can easily be passed on to others, spreading the spirit attack through the community. The attack becomes intensified if a death occurs, because the spirits of the dead enter the community looking for nokiren to take away.

The diagnosis of an illness consists of connecting two visible events – namely the illness of the victim and some action done by or to that person in the past. The events may have no necessary link, but a shaman makes sense of the problem by interposing a connecting invisible factor – the spirit world. The shaman has to diagnose from the symptoms of the patient whether the illness was caused by sorcery, the transgression of socially accepted behaviour (such as the preparation and consumption of food, or sexual relations with prohibited categories of relative), or whether the cause was an accidental encounter with a toto.

The process of diagnosing an illness is complete if the person survives. The shaman chants his chindign over the patient and if the diagnosis is correct, the sick person will recover. However, when a person dies the process of diagnosis continues. The major question after a death is the reason for its occurrence. There is rarely a single reason and as with establishing diagnoses for sicknesses, theories are

3. Arakmbut notions of God are not clear. In spite of Barriales and Torralba's description of a supreme being, or 'Mapakaro', among the Harakmbut (1970:58), the Arakmbut claim no knowledge of its existence. Some say that God exists and others that it is only the erroneous ideas of missionaries that spread such beliefs. The Arakmbut have difficulty believing in a being which cannot be seen in dreams or visions. Most Arakmbut say that God may possibly exist for outsiders but is not much use to them.

highly politicised according to the situation in the community. The principal fear at the time of a death is one of contagion. Death is 'catching', and if people do not behave in certain preventative ways they will follow the deceased into the other world.

Death

Death (*e'mbuey*) is explained by its causes. The cause is an invisible reason attributed to some spirit or spirits. The nature of death alters according to the type of spirit involved. Death at different times of life presupposes different spirits as the cause. A child is usually considered to have been killed by a concentration of river spirits appearing as a toto. Women are more associated with the river than are men, and when a woman dies the cause is often thought to be the spirit of her dead child which is trying to call her to the river before her time. The fate for these women and children is to be taken to a stream or pool deep in the forest, where they live as harmful spirit toto. A man is almost always attracted by the spirits of the species he has been hunting. Old people, on the other hand, are expected to die and their demise is taken as part of the order of things; they go to Seronwe under the river and those who had close relations with particular species disperse from there into the creatures with which they had the most contact when alive.

What connects all of these examples is that, for the Arakmbut, death marks the transition from life, when the nokiren is mainly within the waso, to the time after death when the nokiren becomes independent, retaining only the image of the waso. Such a dramatic change in the constitution of a person means that the boundary between these states is likely to be regarded as an area fraught with danger.

A 'good' death is expected and comes to the old. When they die there is not much lamentation. The rite of the funeral takes place swiftly. The body is wrapped in pona wood and carried to the cemetery where it is quickly interred. The old people in the community have little property and so there is little to be destroyed. Little thought and deliberation is given to the cause of death because it is expected in the order of things.[4]

4. Barriales and Torralba (1970:62) tell of a traditional practice in which an old person was left to die away from the settlement. In San José no one was ever abandoned against their will according to our knowledge, but once when an old man thought he was going to die he took himself off to the outskirts of the community and sat peacefully by the path. We were told that he had gone there to die so that

The cause of a 'bad' death is a concentrated toto, which either punishes the person for transgressing the socially accepted norms of the society or else has been called by a sorcerer to harm someone he hates. Occasionally toto can attack someone by accident, for example when they brush against a harmful leaf in the forest or are bitten by a snake. The dead person's nokiren is taken to the forest and becomes a part of toto.

In order to ascertain which toto has killed the person there are various methods of diagnosis.

1) A wayorokeri may dream of the offending spirit.
2) The person may have a dream or vision on his death bed.
3) A practitioner of ayahuasca may induce a vision.
4) Balsa ashes are put on the grave.

This last method is used frequently by the Arakmbut in San José, especially if there have been no dreams or visions. When the person dies a fire of balsa wood is made at the head of the grave. This is left for a day or more while the village evacuates to the beach. While they are away the spirits come as usual for their celebration of the death and walk over the ashes of the fire. On the return of the villagers, the ashes are scrutinised for prints. The footprints of forest animals indicate that they were responsible for the death, whereas a damp mark or the imprint of a string bag points to the actions of waweri river spirits. A human footprint shows that sorcery was the cause.

Therefore, if the death is 'bad', the toto will take all or part of the dead person's nokiren into the forest where it will wander as a harmful spirit. If, on the other hand, the death is 'good', the spirits of the dead *(wambetoeri)* will take the nokiren to Seronwe from where it will disperse into various river creatures and some forest animals too.

If an adult person dies a 'bad' death, the whole community enters into the mourning. The remaining spouse cries '*ndoedn opewadn!*', which is the formal relationship term. The house and personal property of the dead person are destroyed, sometimes including chickens and dogs. Even chacras are sometimes destroyed. The body is placed in a pona strip and carried to the cemetery where the people follow, the women wailing and the men silently weeping. After a normal death only the close family are involved in the funeral rites. If an

---

he would not contaminate the house with his death. The old man eventually returned to the house later that day because he felt hungry and thought death could wait after all.

important person such as a shaman dies, the scale of participation is large. Everyone goes to the cemetery. The practices surrounding the burial are done with more deliberation and caution than those following other deaths, when the body is buried as quickly as possible without any ceremony and with only a few present.

Every death is different. According to the context and the person who dies, so do the customs and explanations change. For example, if the dead person has a family, the rest of the villagers would be less likely to destroy the chicken hut or kill the chickens as the survivors would need them. If there is no family at all the chacras would be destroyed. In the case of someone needing the gardens they might be spared.

As with sickness, depending on the cause of death, dietary prohibitions relating to the species involved have to be kept. An old widow would not have to adhere to the strict dietary prohibitions which a young mother with children would have to do.

After a 'bad' death, chaos reigns over the period of the funeral and the wake. Spirits come into the community which normally remained outside, the river rises, and sorcery is rampant. The intensity of social relations is extreme and the village cannot stand the strain. The community separates for a period and if serious problems arise, then the family concerned will leave. After an important death, such as a powerful shaman, the community will move away for as long as two months. For an ordinary death people will move away for two or three days. In cases of small children or old people the community probably would not evacuate.

The reunification of the community marks the beginning of the 'new epoch', when a more moderate balance is restored to the community. This parallels the myth of Wanamey. When someone is ill or approaches death there is an initial excessive contiguity between the visible and the invisible world. On death this conjunction becomes a disjunction by abandoning the village for a while. The eventual restoration of 'balance' corresponds to the re-establishment of order. These correlate with three main sections of Wanamey: excessive conjunction, excessive disjunction, and finally order.

The curing of illness and the explanation of a death follow a pattern of explanations which recur regularly among the Arakmbut. The first reason for an illness or death always seems to be that of sorcery. The initial reaction is to blame an enemy, usually outside of the community. The second reason puts the blame on the sick person or a member of the household for having transgressed the social conventions surrounding the hunting and preparation of meat. However, there are several interpretations as to which species were responsible and who is going to have to curtail their hunting practices. The differences in explanation take on a political tinge which can often split the community into factions.

In order to heal the division a third type of explanation emerges which satisfies everyone. This explains the illness as a result of an unavoidable accident. Accidental attacks by harmful toto involve neither the machinations of a sorcerer nor the transgressions of anyone in the community.

These three explanations cover the three possible causes – murder (sorcery), carelessness (the person's misdemeanour), and accident (toto). Although the process follows through these explanations, at any point in the future they can recur. Thus sorcery may be abandoned as an explanation in 1980, but it may re-emerge during another illness or death in 1990. In this way, diagnoses and explanations reflect the political climate of a community and its external relations.

We must now clarify the concept of death for the Arakmbut. The word e'mbuey which can be translated as 'to die' is used in several contexts by the Arakmbut:-

1) When someone faints, the Arakmbut say *o'mbuey* (he dies). The waso has no life. Temporarily the nokiren has not only left the waso but, unlike dreaming, it has severed all connections with it.

2) In the circumstance of a traumatic or epileptic fit, the Arakmbut say *e'mbuey'e* which means 'to die repeatedly'. The ill person is in a trance and trembles. The nokiren is continually entering and leaving the waso. These traumas take place in times of extreme stress when everything seems to be going wrong for someone and there seems to be no immediate escape (Bob Tripp pers. com. and Califano 1976).

3) The subject of sexuality has several links with death. In the myth of Wanamey (and in Marinke in the Wachipaeri and Sapiteri versions), the origin of death was an incestuous sexual relationship. At the point of orgasm a man will often say *ij'mbueyone* which means 'I'm dead' or 'I'm dying'. The explanation for this can be found in the feeling of excitation when the nokiren seems to leave the waso. The semen which leaves the man contains both aspects of his waso and nokiren, which constitutes a form of death.

4) Finally there is the use of the word e'mbuey in the context of what we would term death. Here the nokiren leaves the waso but this time it is on a permanent basis. Some say that the

nokiren departs with the breath through the mouth, but even so, the Arakmbut use various means to check that someone is dead. They place a mirror over the mouth to see if there is breath as well as feeling the pulse and heartbeat.

The philosophy of e'mbuey is a description of the moment of ecstasy, terror, illness, or death, when the relationship between the waso and nokiren breaks. At the point when the physical waso and spiritual nokiren part company, the body becomes lifeless. The name (wandik) can no longer be mentioned for it will call together the nokiren 'as if' the waso were still there. As we have seen, a nokiren which is concentrated is a dangerous spirit. Death is the time when the visible world of life and growth makes way for the invisible spirit world.

Arakmbut life is framed by the concept of e'mbuey. It begins with the 'death' of orgasm, when the embryo separates from its father, and ends with the final separation of the waso and nokiren. There is a third context in life where death regularly occurs, and that is in hunting, in which an animal is killed and its meat is transferred to humans in cooking and eating. These three contexts are three nodal points in the life/death cycle through which soul-matter passes.

The three examples of death for the Arakmbut are as follows:-

1) The 'death' of orgasm – soul-matter in semen passes from man to woman.
2) The death of an animal – flesh passes from animal to human.
3) The death of a human – soul-matter in a person passes to the invisible world, including animals.

When someone dies, the soul-matter goes to the invisible world of the spirits where it becomes a spirit. The human body decomposes and does not continue in the life/death cycle. We can thus say that in essence it is only the soul-matter or nokiren which completes the process, transferring from life to death while animal flesh comes from death to life, constituting a form of exchange.

The more a nokiren grows, the more firmly it becomes tied to a body. However, the more a nokiren becomes tied to the invisible world, the more likely it is to leave the body, whether in dreams or in death. The non-human world is the principal means of describing the invisible world for the Arakmbut. Spirits are freer and can change their form easily while their shape expresses the power of the soul-matter.

In this chapter we have looked at death as a transition between life in this world, in which the nokiren is mainly within the body, and life in the invisible 'other world', in which the nokiren only appears to have the image of a body. We also have noted in this chapter that there is usually a complementary relationship between the visible and invisible worlds when all is in health. After a 'good death', this complementarity is preserved and the soul goes to Seronwe and can sometimes be further dispersed into animal species. However a bad death is an example of the asymmetry between the visible and invisible worlds where chaos can enter. Toto are all-powerful and can take someone's soul away when they are adults and strong. This demonstrates the inequality which can arise when people are killed by an encounter with a hostile spirit.

Furthermore, we have looked at the crises which threaten the Arakmbut from the invisible world and how death is the transfer of the nokiren from the visible world to the invisible world of the spirits. We should now look in more detail at the spirit world and conclude the passage of soul-substance from life and after death.

C∂ Chapter 8 ℘

BEING INVISIBLE

The Spirits

The existence of spirits for the Arakmbut is a fact and not a matter for speculation. When in a normal conscious waking state you cannot see a spirit, but at night you can hear and sometimes feel them. The main attribute of a spirit is that it is invisible *(chawaywendik)*, whereas worldly objects are visible *(chawayndik)*. This is the basic Arakmbut distinction between 'this world' and the 'other world'.[1]

It is possible to see a spirit when not in a normal conscious state. This is the state of wayorok (dream, vision, hallucination). Dreams, visions, and hallucinations are not passive frames of mind which pick up random messages sent by the spirit world. Each involves skills and techniques which can only be learned over time.

There is a two-way relationship between a spirit of the 'invisible world' of the wayorok and the material 'visible world' of the everyday. We have described the nokiren as 'soul-matter' which is tied to the body when alive. After death the nokiren leaves the body (waso) and joins the world of the invisible as a free spirit.

A free spirit has two principal manifestations. The most common image of a spirit in a dream is that of a human. The spirit is shaped in the form of a waso. In some cases this is the waso it had when alive which was a mould for the nokiren. In other cases the human

---

1. Among some peoples (c.f. Harner 1972, on the Shuar), the 'other world' is the real world, in contrast to the visible world which is an illusion. This is not the case among the Arakmbut, for whom both visible and invisible are equally real. Brown (1985) and Descola (1989) both question Harner's approach.

form can have certain animal characteristics or may even look like a warrior from pre-contact days called Taka.

The form of the spirits comes from the visible world. They can appear as human or animal, and can enter the bodies of both. An image of the visible world is thus projected onto the free nokiren. This is, however, only one of the ways in which a spirit can manifest itself to Arakmbut. The 'soul-matter' is sufficiently free to enter the waso of live creatures and to take on their material guise. We have seen that everything that lives is animated by the same soul-matter as that which animates the waso and which in sufficient quantity becomes the nokiren.

After life the nokiren of shamans and good hunters can disperse and enter the bodies of those creatures with which they had the most intimate relationship during their lifetime as humans. The entry of the nokiren into an animal is not a simple reincarnation. The animal spirit is in no way recognised as a person. The person 'goes to the species' rather than any particular member of the species. Thus the Arakmbut can say that part of the shaman who died went to the peccary, but no one would ever think of saying that 'that peccary over there' was the shaman. The individual nokiren becomes dispersed into each of the members of the species, constituting part of the life-giving factor of that animal. When a wayorokeri shaman dies, the animals with which he has contact come crying to where the dead man lies.

Most spirits are divided into forest and river, the ndumberi living in the forest and the waweri in the river. The otiose sky spirits kurudneri will be discussed in chapter ten, which concerns their rare manifestations. Whether spirits appear as humans or in the guise of animal species, they are still far more associated with the non-human world outside of the community, although, as we shall see, some are more different than others.

A spirit is free to form and reform as an animal or human according to the conception of the dreamer or visionary. He will see a spirit either as an invisible human spirit (perhaps with animal characteristics) or as a visible animal species which contains an invisible spirit (perhaps with human characteristics). Animal species are a measure of the efficacy of a spirit, and according to its position in the general classification of animals a dreamer can ascertain its power and significance. The crux of the technique of a wayorokeri is to be able to relate the species he meets in the forest to the images he dreams about. He looks at human and animal behaviour to see what light one can throw on the other.

This is another example of the two-way relationship whereby the visible world projects form onto an invisible world from which it receives the life potency of animation, as was noted above in the case of the same complementary dynamic interaction between the nokiren and waso. There are many categories of spirit in the Arakmbut universe but they relate to three areas of classification:[2]

a) spirit powers: concentrated (toto) or dispersed (ndakyorokeri)
b) spirit of domains: forest (ndumberi), river (waweri), or sky (kurudneri)
c) spirit controllers: otiose *(wachipai)* or immanent *(apoining/ chongpai)*

This form of classification can be reduced for the purposes of this chapter. The spirits of the river and forest have been dealt with earlier. They are essentially any of the other types of spirit which happen to live in those domains. The otiose wachipai are rarely encountered. They are 'controllers' of specific species and warn people in times of dire necessity. In order, therefore, to look at the spirit world as it relates to Arakmbut life on a daily basis, we should concentrate on toto and its different manifestations, the ndakyorokeri and the apoining/chongpai.

1) Toto – Harmful Spirits

As with all categories of spirits, toto range from those which are very easy to distinguish to those which are similar to other types of spirit and can only be identified with the help of a wayorokeri. Toto can take the form of human beings, animals, or plants.

When asked for a description of toto, the Arakmbut provided two opposite versions of what constituted a frightening image. Older people said that toto were tall, white – almost luminescent in the dark and very thin. Younger people who had more direct contact with the missions

2. The Arakmbut in San José did not recognise the names of some spirits mentioned in the literature. Fejos (1941:236) describes some Sapiteri spirits. Beneficial ones were *ukateh* and harmful ones *kitaveh* and *yoneneh.* Alvarez (1946:11) also mentions two harmful spirits called Huairikuat and Asiira. Barriales and Torralba (1970) mention other harmful spirits Toto-Shin and Oteri (p.54) and various other beings such as a supreme creator Mapakaro (p.58). These spirits were thought by the Arakmbut to be from downriver ('Toyeri').

gave descriptions which tally with ideas of demons. Toto were short, fat, hairy, and black, with horns on their heads and with long fingernails.

Toto come at night. One can hear them making whistling noises. They come up to the walls of the hut and look through, then they fire invisible arrows into a person while he or she sleeps. Sometimes they can take the form of a wind or breeze blowing through the hut, causing illness or even death. Alternately they can come up to the door and knock. A resident who answers and sees toto will die.

Toto in this rather gruesome transformation of the human form are based to a large extent on Arakmbut ideas of hostile Taka. They are thought of as spirits equivalent to the old enemies who used to attack malocas in dawn raids to kill the men and capture or steal the women. Some of the older people still call toto by the name 'Taka nokiren' meaning souls of dead Taka. When a Taka dies, his nokiren is not dispersed among various animal species but remains in a concentrated form. What this means is that the nokiren of the dead person is united as if it were bounded by a waso even though after death the body decomposes. The power of such concentrated soul-matter is deadly.

Another factor connecting Taka with toto is the name of their forest abode. It is called either Totoyo or Takayo and is reputed to be a lake which people enter to find themselves in the underworld of the forest. This place is a parallel to Seronwe under the river, but whereas Seronwe is the destination for a nokiren after a 'good' death, Totoyo is the fate for a nokiren after a 'bad' death and is highly undesirable.

The nokiren of dead Arakmbut may not be as dangerous as the Taka toto, but they are certainly feared. There are two ways in which an Arakmbut dead person can become toto. The first is when a person dies as a result of contact with toto and is taken to Totoyo. There he or she becomes toto and returns to the village to attack other Arakmbut and take them to the forest lair too.

Another way in which an Arakmbut person can become toto is if someone mentions the personal name (wandik) of someone who has died. As the wandik is the unifying factor of a human being when alive, if it is uttered after death it has the ability to call the dispersed parts of the nokiren together. This concentration is toto, which the dead person becomes for a while. However, this is not necessarily a permanent state of affairs. Someone can be proclaimed toto one day and be declared safe the next. Such shifts in interpretation are all aspects of the technique of understanding the 'other world'.

However, all dead Arakmbut have a moment when they cause fear to the living, whether they live in Totoyo or Seronwe. A dying person usually sees his or her dead relatives around the bed beckoning their nokiren onto the afterlife. These feared spirits are called wambetoeri and are the Arakmbut equivalent of Taka nokiren.

There are two ways in which toto relate to natural species such as animals, birds, or fish. The most obvious toto in this context are animals which are very dangerous and physically harmful to someone who encounters them. Such dangerous animals are mainly poisonous snakes and jaguars. They attack humans indiscriminately and take the nokiren off to Totoyo. Snakes and jaguars are the most dangerous manifestations of toto. In the myth of Marinke the jaguars attack and kill his mother, behaving like traditional Arakmbut enemies. In fact the behaviour of the jaguars in the story corresponds with both Taka and toto, showing the three categories to be parallel.

Poisonous snakes are considered to be toto who come from afar to seek victims from the community. Snakes are also the arrows of the armadillo who uses them to attack its enemies. The armadillo itself is not toto unless someone has overkilled members of the species, in which case it will appear as a snake and attack the hunter (probably because snakes live in armadillo holes). Some birds are toto such as owls, eagles, and vultures. Bats and toads are also toto. While the small caiman is not toto, the large alligator is considered to be very dangerous indeed, inhabiting deep ox-bow lakes from which it emerges to kill unwary fishermen. The alligator is associated with the depths of the forest, as opposed to the caiman, which is a river species.

No creature which is toto can be eaten by the Arakmbut. A hunter will not normally seek such species.[3] The reason for this is that the animals concerned are either carnivorous and eat the flesh of other creatures without any intermediary preparation such as cooking, or else are unclean in their eating habits.

There are circumstances when toto can appear in the guise of species which are not usually dangerous, such as animals, birds, and fish which can usually be hunted and eaten by humans. If a hunter overkills a particular species, the spirits associated with that species will attack the man in order to wreak vengeance. In the case of large animals such as peccaries or tapir, the toto use the nokiren of the creature as an intermediary for the attack, transforming what was a beneficial spirit into a concentration of harmful soul-matter.

Most creatures are not large enough to have a nokiren and so the toto work in a slightly different way. If a small animal, such as a mon-

---

3. A similar avoidance of carnivores is found among the neighbouring Amahuaca (Carneiro 1964).

key or armadillo, has been overkilled, the dispersed spirits, which are usually beneficial, unite and become concentrated and attack the hunter. The Arakmbut say that in these cases the spirits of the species 'become' toto.

Creatures which are toto all of the time cannot be eaten because of the danger from the invisible world. Similarly, game animals responsible for an illness have to be avoided until long after a cure has been found. At certain points in the life cycle, particular species have to be avoided for fear of attack. In all these cases, the flesh of the animal can pass characteristics of the species onto the patient.

We can say, broadly speaking, that creatures which are always toto are carnivores while game animals are mainly herbivorous. But there are exceptions – the toad is not particularly carnivorous and the peccary is known to eat meat if it finds any. The distinction is therefore part of a broader division into creatures which consume pure things and those which do not. A clear example among the Arakmbut is their reluctance to domesticate pigs for eating. They say that pigs are scavengers who eat only rubbish and if people eat pig's flesh they will ingest the rubbish too. (However, this aversion is weakening with the growing taste for fried pork.) Nevertheless, the danger from toto through animal species is not simply a threat to the hunter but also to the consumers of the meat.

In certain circumstances toto appear in plant form, although they are not so powerful.[4] Deep in virgin forest there are meant to be leaves which, if touched by a hunter, could cause him illness or even death. Certain vegetables can be dangerous if eaten without care. For example, I have seen people avoid eating peach palm on the same plate as meat because this is thought to give you indigestion. (Peach palm fruit is a substitute meat and mixing two types of meat or fish can be harmful.)

Toto are predominantly male and have their main abode in the forest. However the classification is not rigid. A man may be attacked as

4. This is in contrast to the Asháninka, who attribute immense significance to the power of plants (Chevalier 1982). The Shipibo, who are a Panoan-speaking people like the Amahuaca, have spirits called *yoshin*, who primarily inhabit plants. Among the Asháninka and Shipibo, plants are important for curing. Of all the eastern and southeastern Peruvian peoples, the Asháninka and Shipibo have the most emphasised female puberty rites, which are connected to the growth of plants. We have seen that among the Arakmbut, male initiation is a prerequisite for being a good hunter and so it is possible to make a tentative correlation between the importance of female initiation and the significance of plants in lowland Peru as opposed to the presence of male initiation and an exclusive preoccupation with animals and their relationships with humans.

a result of killing too many fish or other river animals. In this case toto take the form or image of an anaconda. Therefore, although toto are spirits who live mainly in the forest, they can appear in the domain of the river in certain circumstances.

In the same way that toto can appear in the river, it is also possible for them occasionally to be associated with women. One occurs in a myth which tells of a newly married man who goes fishing with his wife. She does not know how to prepare the fish for cooking and eats it raw. She denies him sexual access and he kills her, whereupon she is transformed into a forest bird who calls other toto to attack him. He is saved by the timely arrival of day, which causes the spirits to disperse.

Human beings can become toto when alive if their nokiren becomes sufficiently concentrated with hatred and envy. The two types of male sorcerer parallel the difference between Taka and Arakmbut noted above. The wa'itamankeri usually comes from another people, while the chindignwakeri/chindignwamankeri) carry out their nefarious ends from within the community. Accusations of sorcery in young women were particularly prevalent around moments of intense social crisis among the Arakmbut, particularly during the initial period of contact.

All the examples of toto given here fall into two groups based on form and distance. The most dangerous toto live far away from the community and there is little or no chance of curing the illnesses they cause. These creatures, spirits, or people are intrinsically toto and never change. On the other hand, some spirits which are usually harmless can become toto if they bear a grudge against a person. Illnesses caused by these toto are generally cured if diagnosed in time. The main reasons or occasions for such attacks are contraventions of socially acceptable behaviour such as overkill, poor cooking, overeating, breaking food prohibitions, or sexual restrictions during points in the life cycle.

The major manifestations of toto, Table 8.1, follows. Those toto in the left column are rarely encountered and are very dangerous. Contact with them will often lead to death. Those in the right hand column are closer to social life and the experience of mankind and so the illnesses and problems which they cause can often be cured. The problem is that whereas the toto from further away are clearly recognisable, those nearer to everyday life are difficult to distinguish from normal people, animals, or plants. The skills and techniques of a shaman are the only way in which toto can be distinguished from beneficial spirits.

Table 8.1 Manifestations of Toto

	Toto as a permanent and intrinsic quality of a spirit. Distant from mankind.	Toto as more transient qualities which appear only in certain circumstances in people close or within a community.
Nokiren after death	Taka as well as the Amiko who are highlanders and colonists.	Arakmbut nokiren which have been captured by the toto. Wambetoeri who come to collect the souls of the dead Arakmbut.
Forest species	Creatures which are dangerous to man or which eat impure food such as raw flesh or excreta.	Game animals which have overkilled, undercooked or over-eaten.Also consumed at a prohibited time in the life cycle.
Sorcery	Wa'itamankaeri. Shaman from another community, usually native people, who practise sorcery.	Chindignokeri – a shaman or political leader connected to the community who uses the spirit world for his own ends.
Plants	Toto leaf encountered in virgin forest.	Eating vegetables at the wrong time (peach palm with meat).
Women	Female toto who lure men into marriage and try to kill them.	Chiwembet sorcerer from within the community.

2) Ndakyorokeri – 'those who make good dreams'

Ndakyorokeri are the opposite of toto. They are usually described as those nokiren of Arakmbut who have died a 'good' death and are more favourably disposed to them. After a normal death the dead relatives of the deceased come together and lead the terrified nokiren to Seronwe. From there the nokiren of skilled hunters and shamans disperse to the various species of animals, birds, and fish with which they had the most contact in dreams when alive.

The dispersed state of the nokiren is called wamawere which appears as a light or as a breeze. It enters animals and takes on the form of that animal such as *mokaswere* (collared peccary) or *kemewere* (tapir).

It is not always beneficial, although it is not as harmful as the toto. The wamawere seems to have a capricious element which can cause harm but is feared more as a 'ghost' than as a really harmful spirit.

The beneficial dispersed spirits, the ndakyorokeri, originate in Seronwe and so they are essentially waweri river spirits, in the same way that the toto who live in Totoyo are essentially ndumberi forest spirits. As toto can appear in the river, so can the ndakyorokeri enter the forest. However, most Arakmbut call all dispersed spirits wamawere and if they come to help a person in their dream they are ndakyorokeri whether of the river or the forest.

The ndakyorokeri are beneficial to people and their dispersed nature is effectively a channelling of soul-matter into controlled areas. There are at least five different ways in which a ndakyorokeri can be perceived, and these conform with the classifications of the different types of toto.

Apart from being the dispersed nokiren of dead Arakmbut, ndakyorokeri appear as species which can be hunted. A hunter can succeed in making a good catch through contact with the ndakyoro-keri spirits, who advise him where the most lucrative area is and how much game he can bag without causing any harm to himself or his family. It is the ndakyorokeri spirits who can transform themselves into wamawere or toto as described in the right hand column of the table above, when their advice and warnings have not been heeded.

There are plants associated with the ndakyorokeri. The most apparent are tobacco and coca which the shamans use to frighten away the toto. In fact, the shamans themselves are the human instruments of contact with the ndakyorokeri. The previous descriptions of the toto included accounts of the sorcerers who specialise in contact with harmful spirits and use them or are used by them to inflict illness or death on their victims. It is the shaman (both as the wayorok-eri dream specialist and the wamanoka'eri curer) who has the greatest contact with the ndakyorokeri. The knowledge of the ndak-yorokeri passed on to a shaman in his dreams can inform him of the whereabouts and characteristics of toto who are harming the community and suggest ways of counteracting the threat.

There is one manifestation of the ndakyorokeri which is so distinctive that it overrides all the others as a defining characteristic. The ndakyorokeri appear as very beautiful young women. These are the women who appear to hunters in dreams before a hunting expedition and with whom they have sexual relations. When a man dies and his nokiren goes to Seronwe he marries a female ndak-yorokeri who is presumably one of these beautiful women. It is interesting to note that creatures which a man can eat also have spirits with which he can marry after death, whereas toto whose creatures are inedible do not appear to provide women for the dead. Toto women are highly undesirable; they are anti-social, cook horrible food, are frighteningly unattractive, and dangerous should they have sexual relations with a man.

There are several species of birds which are advisors or which provide warnings to the Arakmbut. If the bird *pikwan* says 'kiss kiss' there will be a good hunt, but if it says 'pikwan' the hunt will be poor. Another bird (the *sipen*) also has various calls warning of bad luck. If it says 'sipen sipen' there will be a bad hunt, and if it sings 'ke'yo ke'yo' (Harakmbut for 'watch out') then you will have god luck. If it says 'sho sho' you must prepare yourself for a disaster.

So far, this account of the Arakmbut spirit world has distinguished permanent toto, which are always concentrated spirits, from the dispersed ndakyorokeri. If an Arakmbut maltreats a species associated with the ndakyorokeri these usually beneficial spirits can become concentrated and toto. In a similar way, under certain circumstances a concentrated spirit can change from a toto into a more beneficial form. It is to such concentrated yet potentially beneficial spirits that we now turn.

3) Apoining/chongpai – the Anaconda

After we had been in San José for a while we began to realise that we were referred to as apoining by the Arakmbut. As time went on it became noticeable that we were not the only recipients of the word. All people who were not Arakmbut and who lived in the community were called apoining. What it means is 'safe Taka' or 'safe Amiko', that is, anyone who would normally be considered to be as potentially dangerous but has been accepted into the community as a friend. Although potentially harmful, they can be beneficial.

The term is used so that powerful people cannot hear that they are being talked about. It is therefore appropriate that apoining refers to those people with dangerous characteristics who can in certain circumstances can be beneficial to human beings if precautions are taken in dealing with them. In these contexts the toto which are usually considered to be inhabitants of the forest enter the domain of the river, and their power is somewhat ameliorated. The quintessential apoining is the anaconda. A comparison of the different names for anaconda illustrate how the apoining relates to other types of spirit.

The anaconda is not a toto in the sense of a permanently harmful spirit. However when the river creatures have been overkilled, over-eaten or undercooked, the waweri become toto. They are called waweri toto (river spirit toto) and are conceptualised as an angry anaconda. In this context the anaconda is called waweri. When the anaconda is not angry it is apoining. It is a regulator of human behaviour on the river. For example, if anyone bathes on their own after dark they should be very careful lest they be carried off. Any noise or laughter while washing can lead to the same fate. This ambivalence towards the anaconda is symptomatic of Arakmbut behaviour to any foreigners living in the community.

Within the last fifteen years ayahuasca has been introduced into San José. The ayahuasca vine is seen as a manifestation of the ana-conda and when it is drunk the snake appears. In this invisible guise the image of the anaconda is called *chongpai,* while apoining is the polite 'reference' term used for chongpai (the same word is used for the vine and the snake). During the drinking sessions the boa chong-pai can take the human form of medical doctors who come with stethoscopes to diagnose illnesses.

Ayahuasca sessions are led by 'shamans' but these are men with different skills from those of the traditional practitioners. These are called *ayahuasceros* or 'practitioners'. The techniques of an ayahuascero are more easily learned than those of a traditional shaman, and although to all intents and purposes he is a shaman, he is viewed by some with a certain amount of suspicion because he could possibly use his skills to further his own political ends rather than those of the whole community. This suspicion is centred, unsur-prisingly, among the traditional shamans who feel their position threatened by the introduction of new techniques for contacting the spirit world.[5]

Women can take ayahuasca but their participation in the cere-monies is not frequent. The most significant female aspect of the ses-sions is the appearance of the beautiful women who are called on by the chongpai to give their advice on the problem under examination.

Table 8.2 summarises the information presented on the toto, ndakyorokeri, and chongpai. There are parallels in social distance and behaviour between the spirit world and several other areas of Arakmbut classification. In each case there are overlapping and

5. Santos-Granero (1991:118) finds a similar distinction between shamans and ayahuasceros among the Amuesha. The ayahuascero has more negative conno-tations there than among the Arakmbut.

opaque regions where one spirit can be interpreted as another according to the shaman and according to the context.

Table 8.2 Main aspects of Arakmbut spirit classification

Toto	Wamawere/Toto	Ndakyorokeri	Apoining/Chongpai
		Characteristics	
Intrinsically harmful - concentrated	Capricious when dispersed but toto when concentrated	Beneficial and dispersed	Benign but concentrated
		Animal Aspect	
Carniverous or impure creatures	Overhunted/ game animals	Ordinary game animals	Anaconda
		Specialist Element	
External sorcerer	Internal sorcerer	Shaman	Ayahuascero
		Female Element	
Female toto	Female sorcerer	Attractive female spirits	Female partici-pation
		Plant	
Toto plants	Plants wrongly cooked	Coca/tobacco	Ayahuasca
		Human Spirit	
Nokiren of Taka/Amiko	Dangerous Arakmbut nokiren (Wambetoeri)	Nokiren of dead Arakmbut - more beneficial	Doctors

Classification of spirits slices through the visible and invisible worlds, covering humans, animals, and plants. The basic elements of every individual human being (body, soul both concentrated and dispersed, and name) correspond to the classification of the invisible world. The Arakmbut person parallels the spirit world and is the vehicle of communication between the invisible and the social, trans-forming the potential inherent in soul-matter into actuality.

Within the framework of Table 8.2 there is room for different emphases when interpreting specific events. The various perspec-tives are most clearly marked in the interpretations of different peo-ple. The Yaromba told me that when someone died the whole nokiren went to Seronwe, where it would be dispersed to creatures of the forest or of the river as ndumberi or waweri. If death was bad, parts or all of the nokiren would go to the toto which had captured the victim. The Idnsikambo, on the other hand, said that the nokiren was made up of dispersed and concentrated parts. The dispersed parts went to the river and then to the dispersed spirits of the river and forest. The concentrated aspect always went to the forest. where it would be captured by toto.

The differences between these versions are not really significant except for the fact that the Idnsikambo (who in 1980 had more hunters associated with dispersed spirits living in the forest than the Yaromba) claimed that some part of the nokiren goes to the forest after every death and not necessarily every part goes to the river. The Yaromba (who were a clan more associated with the river) said, on the other hand, that unless the death is abnormal all the nokiren go to Seronwe, from where the dispersal takes place. Thus the Yaromba have a slight bias towards the river while the Idnsikambo attach more importance to the forest. The difference stems from the dreams and philosophical speculations of members of each clan and the extent to which the rest of the community shares those views. This is dealt with in much more detail in Volume 2.

In San José this transformation appears to be slight, but it shows us that if there are differences of emphasis within a community there will probably be larger ones between communities. For example, the land boa is not particularly venerated by the Arakmbut of San José. For them it is toto of the forest like the jaguar. The people of Puerto Luz who are Kipodneri Arakmbut seem to pay more attention to the land boa (*ka'epu*) than to the anaconda (Thomas Moore pers. comm.). At the same time they do not consider the jaguar to be quite as dangerous as do the people of San José. In fact, evidence from the mythology of Puerto Luz and the local attitude to jaguars may point to that animal being their apoining.

The implication here is that the people of San José are more river-oriented and see forest spirits as more dangerous, whereas those of Puerto Luz see dangers in the river not apparent to people in San José. This almost certainly derives from the philosophical ideas and spiritual relations of the main shaman of San José, who was in close contact with the spirits of the river. Thus ideas in this book are to a large extent those of the shaman in San José, whose opinions and philosophy was widely accepted by most of the community. People frequently couched their explanations of the invisible world and spirit matters with the phrase, 'the old man says that ...'. His life and death provide the thread running through Volume 2.

The consequence of this is that the relativity among men and women in spirit interpretation covers clan allegiance, age, and personal experience. Detailed commentaries on Arakmbut cosmology will thus vary from person to person and even more so from one community to another.

When we move away from the Arakmbut and look at other Harakmbut groups we find that in some writings the situation is reversed. The Wachipaeri and the Sapiteri consider that beneficial spirits live in the forest in a place called Xiliawandei or Jiriendei and that the most dangerous toto come from the river (Califano, 1978a). In this way the worst fears of the Arakmbut in San José are fulfilled because the traditional enemies of each group really do have closer ties with those spirits which they consider to be the most dangerous.

Spirits are defined by the Arakmbut in terms of whether they are harmful or beneficial. This is the basis of their ethical system. It is possible to call toto 'bad spirits' and ndakyorokeri 'good spirits', but we have to be clear what is meant by these terms. Spirits are defined by what they can do to someone; thus what is beneficial is good and what is harmful is bad. The judgement is made according to the event. Goodness and badness do not reside in the spirits, for toto are not all equally bad nor ndakyorokeri equally good. These qualities depend on their relationship with human beings, which is essentially ambiguous.

The nokiren substance of which all spirits consist is not in itself moral. The morality arises from the concentration or dispersion of the nokiren, and as such is a matter of power. Too much power is dangerous. A man who transgresses the socially accepted parameters of behaviour has unpleasant encounters with powerful toto. On the other hand, a skilled wayorokeri who has developed contacts with dispersed ndakyorokeri is likely to gain benefit for himself or on behalf of the community as a whole. The relationship between man and spirit is a connection between human behaviour and power – potency.

There is an important aesthetic aspect to the spirit world which is isomorphic with the ethical aspect. The more harmful a toto is, the more horrendous its appearance. Whether we look at the traditional version of toto as white, thin, and tall, or the more recent notion of short, fat, and black toto, in both cases we see an extreme in Arakmbut perceptions of ugliness. Harmful spirits are ugly.

Spirits which are beneficial, such as the ndakyorokeri, are described as beautiful women. Women may not accept this definition of spirits in terms of ugliness versus eroticism. Their ideas are not easy to report with accuracy because they more often quote men's dreams and visions than talk of their own. In several myths and dreams I have heard references to potentially desirable men. They are not described physically but in terms of their hunting ability and invariably turn out to be toto in disguise. The reason for this is that an eligible man is a threat to the community; he is a possible woman stealer and could even attract wives away from their husbands. Thus an attractive man is depicted by the Arakmbut as a toto in disguise. The 'male aesthetic' which sees handsome men as harmful has a public preponderance in

Arakmbut culture, although this could be connected with what is appropriate to tell an outsider (see Volume 2 for more on this).

Apart from ugliness and beauty, there is another aspect to the differentiation between toto and ndakyorokeri. This is familiarity. The ndakyorokeri are all dispersed nokiren of Arakmbut and so they would appear as wamawere – familiar people to a dreamer. (Indeed, I have heard some people refer to ndakyorokeri as wamawere.) However, it does seem that wamawere are not always beneficial as the ndakyorokeri and have a capricious element to their behaviour. Toto, on the other hand, are either Taka and unknown or appear on death as the wambetoeri, dead ancestors who want their relatives to come with them to the other world. In between come the apoining who, although of an unfamiliar ilk, are known and recognised by the ayahuascero and those participating in the session.

After a good death, the nokiren of an Arakmbut man goes to Seronwe where it lives in conditions not dissimilar to those of the visible world. Even though the nokiren will disperse to other species, its home or base is seen as a house with chacras, domesticated animals and, above all, a wife. Whether these are the actual nokiren of Arakmbut women or, more likely, an idealised image of what those women should look like, remains uncertain.

Such a union of nokiren completes a reciprocation between male and female spirits. Throughout life, the nokiren of Arakmbut men build up a relationship, often sexual, with beautiful spirits which come to visit them in their dreams. After death the men go to the under-river world of these female spirits and live with them. The distinction here is between a 'virilocality' during life, when the spirit women come to the men, and an 'uxorilocality' after death, when the nokiren of the men go to the underworld and their spirit wives.

When women die they go to Seronwe and join the other women there, waiting for a man to come whom they can marry. There are several ways in which life in Seronwe is the reverse of ordinary social life. Female spirits have access to animals (i.e. are able to visit hunters in dreams and tell them where certain species are) and the men have 'their' chacras and domesticated animals. When a man dies, he marries a spirit woman on arrival at the underworld. There appear to be considerably more women in Seronwe than men, and so the imbalance of women to men in Arakmbut social life is replaced by an imbalance of men to women. There are other factors which indicate that women have considerable importance in the invisible world. There is no doubt that, although the invisible world is associated with the forest and river domains, the river is the underworld for those who have had a 'good death', and this is the domain with which women are more associated.

When considering the sequence of events in the life and afterlife of men and women, we can distinguish a series of reversals. In the visible world, sexual relations take place after marriage and lead to conception and pregnancy. In the invisible world the order of events is turned around. The 'dry' social initiation through which Arakmbut men traditionally passed opens the possibility of sexual relations with the female spirits. The frequency of such relations enables the man to kill animals. After his death he goes to the underworld, where he marries a spirit.

Figure 8.1 Parallels between visible and invisible worlds at certain points in the life and death cycle

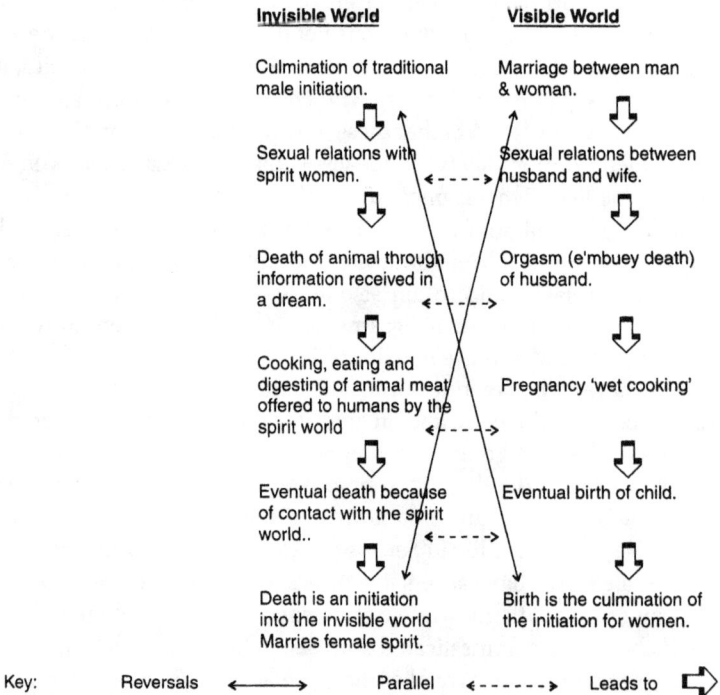

Invisible World	Visible World
Culmination of traditional male initiation.	Marriage between man & woman.
Sexual relations with spirit women.	Sexual relations between husband and wife.
Death of animal through information received in a dream.	Orgasm (e'mbuey death) of husband.
Cooking, eating and digesting of animal meat offered to humans by the spirit world	Pregnancy 'wet cooking'
Eventual death because of contact with the spirit world..	Eventual birth of child.
Death is an initiation into the invisible world Marries female spirit.	Birth is the culmination of the initiation for women.

Key: Reversals ⟵⟶   Parallel ⟵----➤   Leads to ⇨

If a person has a bad death, the reciprocal relations between the visible and invisible worlds break down. Toto capture human nokiren and use them to inflict harm on mankind. They take the nokiren off to Totoyo/Takayo and offer nothing in return. The relationship between the Arakmbut nokiren and the toto is one of negative reciprocity. The Arakmbut say that the toto and ndakyorokeri are always fighting. This is just as the Arakmbut traditionally fought with the Taka in the past. The toto steal Arakmbut souls in the same way that Taka steal women. Toto capture the nokiren of both men and women, but the Arakmbut admit that in everyday life men run much greater risks of death than women because of their contacts with the spirit world when hunting. This is the inverse of the invisible world, where raids are for women rather than for men.

The nokiren consists of soul-matter which cannot be destroyed. Flesh, on the other hand, can perish. Whereas the nokiren can form and reform, transferring from human to animal and back again, flesh cannot continue in this way. People may transform animal flesh by means of cooking and eating it, but it does not return to the animal kingdom after death in the same way as the nokiren. There is a process linking life and death in a continuous interchange or transfer of soul-matter and flesh.

We saw in chapter six that the waso and nokiren of an individual grow through life by means of eating hunted meat. When producing offspring, part of a man dies in orgasm and passes on to the next generation; however the bulk of a person's waso perishes and the nokiren lives on in the invisible world. The aspect of the nokiren which disperses into animal species re-pays the social world by helping the beneficial spirits advise hunters to so that the animal can be caught and its flesh eaten. The result is a dynamic cycling movement of soul-matter through the clan line. After initiation, the spirit world provides a man with the strength to reproduce the clan line and hunt meat; in return, after physical death, the rest of the soul-matter returns to the underworld.[6]

The process of cycling soul-matter through the human being parallels the cycling of women through the clan. Similarly, the 'short cycle' of semen through the woman in pregnancy which enables the clan line to continue has a parallel in the frequent movements by adult men to and from the animal world to hunt meat for the growth of the household. Both men and women have their responsibilities for the perpetuation of society, and these cannot be fulfilled without reaching adulthood.

6. The Ese'eja have a notion of eschatology which parallels that of the Arakmbut. After death people go to the great river of the Dead, where they live on the banks as collared peccary. When they wish to visit their loved ones, the spirits change into white-lipped peccary. In fact, all animals are the manifestations of dead Ese'eja (Zeleny, 1976:136).

However, at the same time, the invisible spirit world contains an uxorilocal residence through which men pass, as in marriage. This provides the basis for the female 'wambet' perspective of social organisation. In this way the relationship between the visible and invisible worlds parallels those of Arakmbut social organisation.

A 'good death' means that the transferring of soul-matter from living to dead takes the form of a complementarity between the visible and invisible world. Bad deaths come from overkilling, sorcery, and capture by a toto. They are all ways in which dangerous spirits can turn the asymmetry between concentrated and dispersed soul-matter into unequal relationships harming human beings and bringing them unexpected sickness and death.

This parallels the relationship we noted in the previous section when the asymmetrical features of the relationship between male and female or old and young can turn into an exploitative relationship. The myth of Marinke which we analysed earlier demonstrates how sexual and hunting activities can open a person to the greatest spiritual dangers. The now non-existent Arakmbut ritual ceremonies were designed to provide the strength necessary to stand up to the spirit world and reproduce Arakmbut socio-cultural life. The next part of this book looks at a new danger in Arakmbut life, against which rituals can provide no protection. At this point Arakmbut history and myth confront each other as never before.

PART III

For it *is*, always *is*, however much we may say It was. Thus speaks the myth, which is only the garment of the mystery.

    –Thomas Mann, *Joseph and His Brothers.*

Aiwe swam the river through dangerous river creatures

Drawing: Juan Carlos Arique

PREFACE

History and Creativity

The history of indigenous peoples is difficult to ascertain. Often the written sources are vague, unclear, or established by colonial oppressors full of prejudice and venom against other peoples; however, a fundamental source, the oral history of indigenous peoples, is too often treated as a sub-species of cultural exotica without any relation to reality.

Anthropologists have several approaches to history. Lévi-Strauss (1974:245ff.) views history as a category of reason which functions like mythology to explain the world and the human condition. Sahlins (1985), in his analysis of the Hawaiian past, argues in a similar vein that history is organised by structures of significance. In contrast, Eric Wolf (1982:3 & 23) says that history 'is a manifold totality of interconnected processes' in which 'both the people who claim history as their own and the people to whom history has been denied emerge as participants in the same historical trajectory'. Jonathan Friedman (1986:36) puts this in an anthropological framework: 'Anthropology must thus be historic ... the very definition of social practice is temporal, because structures of human existence are structures of reproduction, i.e. structures of social processes over time.' This question – whether or not history is reducible to myth – is critical in looking at the data presented in this third part of the book.

Until now, this volume has followed Arakmbut mythology to look into their socio-cultural world, yet hardly a word has yet been mentioned about their present day situation and their history. Ethnographers in the Amazon have recently embarked on some significant indigenous historical work (Chaumeil 1981; Hill 1988; and Whitehead 1988 & 1993). However, apart from these examples, the history of the Amazon contains few references to indigenous peoples' views of their history and these are frequently superficial, consisting mainly of lists of contacts and speculative population movements.

The short genealogical memory of many Amazonian peoples such as the Arakmbut is another factor which makes historical work difficult. The introduction sketched some of the events which have taken place in the Madre de Dios since Inca times, but unless they are juxtaposed with Arakmbut oral history they are but names and dates. The Arakmbut, on the basis of this outside information, appear as a 'people without history'. Because a people cannot remember their genealogical relatives above three or four levels, however, does not mean that they are 'without society'; similarly, because their perspective of history is not the same as that of outsiders, they should not be seen as a people without history.

Carr (1973:30) sees history as a dialogue with the past. This includes human activity, which takes place in a social context, and its interpretation, which is made within a cultural context. The blending of these aspects of history constitutes its creativity, and for the Arakmbut, the socio-cultural descriptions of the previous two parts of this volume comprise the contexts within which history is made and interpreted. These contexts are sufficiently open to embrace a wide range of activities, but there are limits as to what is acceptable both in terms of behaviour and interpretation. As we have seen with the Arakmbut, these boundaries are patrolled by the spirit world.

For the Arakmbut, history moves in different directions; on the one hand activities are interpreted through stories and myths, while the oral performances of the interpretations are themselves historical actions. This juxtaposition of event and interpretation is part of the creative process where the significance of historical events becomes converted into timeless mythological features; meanwhile, timeless mythological accounts are reintegrated into history through performance.

However, history is not only a phenomenon produced internally by the Arakmbut. To separate their own view of history from their position in the broader events of the region is to divide them from the outside world and from any consequences of events which take place outside of their lives. The Arakmbut, like peoples from throughout the Amazon region, have been in constant contact with their neighbours and have developed rich accounts of their relationships with outsiders, particularly non-indigenous colonists. These sometimes take the form of myths and sometimes of stories or tales derived from personal experience. These are often parallel but completely distinct from the history of outsiders which either omits indigenous peoples entirely or places them in an insignificant position. Thus not only is there a distinction between action and interpretation within history but between the extent to which different peoples control their history.

This section of the book looks at Arakmbut life within a temporal framework and tries to blend the creation of history through action with the creation of history through mythological interpretation. However, such work encounters two significant problems. By viewing the Arakmbut through historical time-sequences which necessarily have to include the colonial context of the Madre de Dios, they can easily be explained away and dissolved into a developmentalist structure of progress, covering pre-contact, contact, and post-contact periods. This outside view of history 'colonises' indigenous perspectives and reduces them to effects of historical causes. On the other hand, another tendency is to concentrate on Arakmbut oral history as myth, thereby removing it from history altogether. Both approaches associate history with the colonial perspective and mythology with the Arakmbut perspective, then try to reduce one to the other.

The Arakmbut draw no firm line between history and myth; both are termed *'embachapak'* – storytelling. History and myth co-exist and encroach on each other as the Arakmbut act on and interpret their position in the world. This encroachment is important because it blends the creation of mythical continuity with the discontinuity of historical action. The contingencies of history are discontinuous without a timeless framework within which events can be reproduced. Myths provide the most potent and powerful imagery for doing this.

Eliade (1974:34) argues that 'an object or an act becomes real only in so far as it imitates or repeats an archetype', and explains that these exemplars have arisen in the past from the mythologisation of history. He contrasts 'historical man' (modern man), who consciously and voluntarily creates history, with the man of the traditional civilizations, who 'had a negative attitude toward history' (ibid.:141). Whereas Eliade's book looks at the process whereby history can become myth (something illustrated in this section of the book), he sees this process as a denial of history, rather than, as I do, a part of the historical phenomenon itself.

Myth (*wambachapak*) is a story set in a timeless period *(in illo tempore),* yet it shares features with history. Both consist of a dialogue with another world (the spirit world and the past respectively), reflecting contemporary experience in the light of activities. Action operates in two directions. When a myth is performed, a historical act brings the timeless past into contemporary relevance. Meanwhile, daily activities not only create a history which will have effects in the future but are permeated with mythological connotations. For example, dealings with white people are tempered through the warnings embedded in the myth of Aiwe and the Papas which we will look at below.

Myth endows history with a powerful position in the collective memory by providing it with a timeless framework of meaning which itself is constantly changed by reinterpretation according to historical circumstances. In this sense, history and myth are part of the creative processes connecting the visible and invisible worlds which act on and give meaning to life. Culture is thus a creative dynamic which is constantly shifting (Wagner, 1981). Borofsky (1987:145) sees this as a practical way to make life meaningful:

'Traditional knowledge must continually adjust to changing circumstances, must continually adapt, so as not to die out (or become buried away in some archive). What is at stake is a pragmatic rather than correspondent sense of truth – meaningfulness to the living rather than precise accuracy to the past.'

In this way, myth becomes history through performance while history becomes myth through interpretation. However, the discussion hitherto gives the impression that history and myth are distinct entities. The Arakmbut experience shows that myth and history often slide into each other according to the context. For example, stories about the indigenous non-Arakmbut called Taka range from historical accounts which tell of living and dead persons at identifiable times and places to timeless mythological stories which connect to other myths and resonate with fundamental statements about Arakmbut identity. The relationship between myth and history is not 'either/or' but 'both/and'. The more mythological a story becomes, the more heavily the meaning weighs on the Arakmbut.

For the Arakmbut, a myth provides a framework for interpretation which offers an alternative to the developmentalist notions of non-indigenous history. Myths can, in certain circumstances, resonate so strongly that they are able to capture the dynamism of critical moments in history and help the Arakmbut to explain traumatic events. In this section we will see how the myth of Wanamey embraces moments of great significance in Arakmbut history. This is not reducing history to myth, but using myth positively to understand history.

One of the difficulties a writer on indigenous questions encounters is how to become coeval with history, which means looking at the current questions facing the Arakmbut. Ethnographies on the Amazon have a tendency to present indigenous peoples in different ways, equally sympathetic but looking at them from distinct perspectives. Some, such as Crocker (1985) and Campbell (1989), describe clearly and movingly the dangers which threaten the people with whom they lived. They show that with the movement of history they will never be the same again and could very well be destroyed. Campbell describes the decimation of one group (ibid.:26) and Crocker the self-destructive urge of another (op.cit.:359). In contrast, authors such as Seymour Smith (1988), Gow (1988), and McCallum (1990), state clearly that the people with whom they have lived are part of a historical process which involves irreversible change. The Shiwar, Piro, or Cashinawa need not be destroyed for ever and can change without losing their authenticity or their identity, although they will become different after protracted contact with the national society. The peoples with whom these anthropologists lived are struggling for their rights to land and self-determination, and as a result are still creating their own history.

This distinction is as much a difference of emphasis which can be seen among indigenous peoples all over the world, as in the different theoretical positions of the authors themselves. It is also reflected among organisations and people who support indigenous rights. Some portray indigenous peoples as overwhelmed and suffering a long and slow genocide, while others see them as fighters struggling for their rights to self-determination (Gray 1987a:24).

The Arakmbut demonstrate both of these in the form of 'resignation' and 'resistance' – sometimes simultaneously (Gray: 1986:99). At times the people are convinced that their days are numbered. The women talk, as did the Bororo to Crocker (op.cit:329), of not having more children. They are convinced that they will be wiped out in the next wave of colonisation and that there is nothing that they can do to ensure survival. Almost at the same moment the Arakmbut will, in the face of a direct invasion of their lands or a killing, paint themselves, put on their feathers, and attack the invaders. They not only use the methods of their ancestors but also travel to the nearest town and file formal complaints to the authorities, making presentations on the radio and television with considerable political sophistication.

We cannot categorise a single Arakmbut attitude to colonisation. They express different feelings and emotions at the same time. The contrast between resignation and resistance is important, however, for what it says about history. Expressing resignation, the Arakmbut say: 'Let the history of the Amiko outsiders take its course. We are powerless and must let the world do what it will.' However, at other times the Arakmbut face the threats and prepare to forge a new world for themselves, taking Arakmbut history into their hands. In the former case, outsiders' history becomes so powerful that it overwhelms the mythical legitimation of Arakmbut history and reduces that history into an unreal mythology. However, Arakmbut myth is not unreal. It protects Arakmbut history from the ravages of a colonial ideology by providing inspiration, solidarity, and a sense of place through continuity with a timeless period which only the Arakmbut can control. For this reason, during periods of resistance, the Arakmbut regularly refer to their mythology for inspiration.

It is not possible to reduce history to myth or vice versa. The two worlds penetrate each other and give each other strength. The invisible world can advise on resistance and initiate historical change. Through a creative process, the visible world may carry out these messages which in their turn become transferred into stories and gradually begin to take on mythological features. Some of these features reinforce resignation and some resistance. A process emerges whereby history and myth define each other, articulated through the interaction between the visible and invisible worlds. The complementarity between Arakmbut myth and history works well, but when invaded from outside, the asymmetry of non-indigenous colonisation quickly becomes exploitation and could possibly lead to the final destruction of the Arakmbut.

In order to defeat these colonising threats, the Arakmbut have to assert and determine their lives for themselves. This means an internal affirmation of resistance against resignation, combined with an external fight against colonisation, a topic discussed in Volume 3. Whereas at times when threats from outside are fewer, the creativity within Arakmbut society consists of shifts and changes within the existing framework, once these threats become overwhelming the Arakmbut have to choose whether to 'go under' or to strike out and determine their future in their own way.

Chapter 9

AIWE AND THE PAPA

Wakuru Wa'a: First Section

(1) One day various Arakmbut went to pick brazil nuts. Two Arakmbut climbed up the tree, leaving the rest down below to catch the cases as they were thrown down. While they were throwing down the nuts, up crept some Papa.

Half the Arakmbut were picking the nuts; the other half were in their village.

The Papa attacked and killed all the Arakmbut down below the tree. They sliced up their meat for cooking and, grinding their bones down, they prepared for a good meal. They swapped the meat. One said that he only had child meat and wanted something bigger. Others who had one human wanted more meat. They had their feast.

The Papa noticed that there were still two people at the top of the tree. They decided to send someone up. One Papa strapped his stick to his back and slowly climbed up the tree to the two Arakmbut. They could see him getting closer and closer. At last, when he was almost at the top, one of the Arakmbut, who was a wayorokeri of *okmbu* monkeys, got brazil nut cases and threw them hard at the Papa, who let go of the tree. With a cry he fell to the ground, dead. The other Papa smashed in his body to feast on his blood.

The sun set and the Papa made a camp with guards over the night to keep an eye on the Arakmbut. However, to avoid revenge of the other Papa, the two Arakmbut turned themselves into okmbu monkeys and swung from tree to tree until they were away from the Papa and could return to their village.

(2) The Papa went up to eat brazil nuts again. They were cannibals who had the ability of second sight. They climbed up the tree leaving their arrows and guns below. One Papa guarded the weapons and collected the brazil nuts as they were thrown down. An

Arakmbut came across them when going through the forest. He picked up the gun of the Papa but it weighed a lot. He shot the Papa on the ground dead. The other Papa saw what was happening. They remained quiet in the tree and followed him home.

(3) The Papa then attacked the settlement. They killed all of the people except for one mother who escaped, leaving her child wrapped up in a *kusipe* (cradle). The Papa took the child and brought him up. He was called Aiwe, 'the one who was taken', and lived with them. The Papa took Aiwe to their houses. Aiwe grew into a youth. The Papa said: 'When he is older we will eat him. Let us look after him well until he is fat.'

Wano wa'a: Middle Section

(4) 'Let's go, Aiwe', said the Papa. They went on a long path. From there they went to attack the pygmies (Oromaneya). They were very small – like children, but really adults. There was a man and his wife. The Papa said: 'We must kill them. Let the couple pass without being killed so that they can breed more, and next year we will eat them.'

The Papa killed almost all the Oromaneya except for two persons. The Papa found the house of the pygmies and chopped them to pieces with machetes. They were small. There the Papa killed the pygmies. They made sorcery on the Oromaneya so that they would grow rapidly and have children.

(5) Later Papa sent Aiwe to spy on more pygmies to find out how they were growing and how they could kill them. The Oromaneya build their houses of woven feathers. 'How can I kill my countrymen?' thought Aiwe. And he went to spy and met a woman.

She was the female pygmy and gave advice to Aiwe. She thought that Aiwe wanted to kill her. The woman shouted to Aiwe, 'Do not kill me Aiwe, I am from your people'. So he did not kill her. The woman warned him: 'They also want to eat you when you are older and fatter.' She advised him very much.

The woman said: 'Take also these sweet potatoes.' He told her everything and sat down for a while. The woman advised him very much. Aiwe said farewell to the woman and she fled, no one knows where. Aiwe returned to the house with the sweet potatoes.

The Papa said to Aiwe, 'Is that you, Aiwe? Did you see her?'

'No, no, Papa, I have just brought some sweet potato, nothing else.'

Then the Papa realised and said: 'The woman has given you sweet potatoes. She has warned you, I believe', he said to Aiwe, using his special hidden powers of observation.

'No, Papa, yes, I met her and just killed her.'

'I know you did not kill her. Why did you bring sweet potatoes?'

So Aiwe answered back: 'Really, Papa, there was nothing. The woman went to the forest. She escaped.' Aiwe admitted all. The Papa forgave Aiwe and sent him to kill parrots for food. 'Scarlet macaws are down on the pebble beach where they are wandering like chickens', said the Papa. Aiwe killed the parrots but kept them for himself. The following day he continued on the road with the Papa who were hungry and looking for food.

(6) They arrived and met a tribe called Soweri – monkeys. The Soweri were marksmen. The Papa did not attack the Soweri because they were few and the Soweri had a large company. 'We cannot beat them', said the *wairi* (chief) of the Papa. 'They use their bows on the side like catapults and never miss their mark.'

(7) One Soweri had gone to hunt. Meanwhile the Papa decided to attack and killed all the Soweri in the house. They ate the food and were dividing the legs and smoking the Soweri flesh. The Papa began to realise how many Soweri there had been and how many people they had overcome in the house.

They counted the dead and the number of beds. But there was one space more in the house, which meant that one person was missing. The Soweri who had gone hunting was not there.

Then the Papa realised that one body was missing. Then the wairi (leader) Papa said to Aiwe: 'Wash me the offal of that Soweri.'

'No', Aiwe said to him. 'No, Papa, see to it yourself, I do not want to.' The Papa went to the stream to wash the innards and intestines. He was seated.

Then the Soweri returned from the hunt and spied the wairi Papa cleaning the offal. He crept up slowly and saw him and gave a harsh whistle in a folded leaf. The Papa looked at the Soweri with fear. The Soweri shot an arrow into his eye. 'Ooooooo!' shouted the Papa. The other Papa heard his voice. 'What happened?' asked the family 'What has happened to the Papa?'

Everyone came. The Papa had an arrow stuck in his eye. 'Look at the arrow in his eye', they said. The Soweri escaped as the Papa were in a circle around the wounded chief. Then the Papa followed the Soweri, who leapt down from a cliff. On seeing him leap from the cliff, the Papa did likewise and took him prisoner. 'Why have you killed the Papa?' they asked the Soweri.

In their house they painted a bulls-eye of achiote clearly on a box. One of the Papa said to the Soweri 'Let us see your firing. Shoot the painted eye. Show us how you are such a good marksman.' The Soweri shot an arrow in the eye which they had painted. Before he first shot it they ordered him to shoot his arrow above. Then they ordered the prisoner to shoot the bull and he shot the painted eye. Twice he shot the bulls-eye.

Then they tied up the Soweri in a chest with liana. The chief of the Papa made the female Papa boil water. When the Soweri was tied to a stake they stripped the flesh from his body with very sharp machetes while he was still alive. His arms and legs they cut and put into their pot. His head and all his body they put into the pot and in a while they ate his body medium rare. The Papa belched when they had taken the human flesh. Bones remained. They broke the bones into pieces, put them into the pot, and ate them.

(8) Then the Papa continued their trip and the blind Papa went with them. The new chief of the Papa said, 'Let us continue our journey.'

And they continued. On the road they met Aimere, the large bat. 'What shall we do with this creature?', they said, 'because he will not let people pass by.' Aimere was going to eat the Papa. The Papa then went round in a circle because they could not pass.

(9) They continued and met another monster which stood in the road. It was the only road. They could not avoid passing the creature. The monster lived by cutting off heads. 'How shall we pass?' said the Papa.

'Let us make head dresses (*tangka*) out of pona wood', suggested one. They made huge head dresses and the monster, as they passed, cut off the head dresses but left the heads. In this way they reached their camp for the night.

Aiya Wa'a – Third Section

(10) Then the Papa who had been pierced in the eye said to Aiwe: 'I am going to die. When they come for my body, hide above the hearth. I will tickle you a few moments before I die to give you warning. When you are safe above the hearth you must shout to the Papa. I am going to make a box so that you can keep my bones

when I die. When I die ask for my finger bones so that you can make chicha (wawing) mixing the bones. Keep it in a pit and then it will be sweet. But do not drink too much of it or you will die.'

Thus the blind Papa advised Aiwe: 'You must leave when I am dead, because if you remain here they will eat you. You will want to go. You must go with this box and two axes', he said. 'You will go quickly lest anyone sees you because I am going to die.' The following day the Papa died.

When his companions were told that he had died they soon came out of their houses shouting, 'Papa has died.' They ate his cooked blood. Aiwe mentioned his bones – two finger bones – which they handed over to Aiwe so that he could look after them in his box. With these bones and two axes he was going to escape.

(11) The Papa all went to a village. So Aiwe fell ill on the way. Aiwe could not walk because he had a fever. The Papa wanted to carry Aiwe but Aiwe said, 'I will go tomorrow.' So Aiwe fell ill on the road. They told him to stay with a woman of the Papa. They spent the night together. The old Papa chief had previously warned Aiwe that he must avoid sexual contact with the woman or else the Papa would kill him and eat him. She wanted Aiwe to give his sexual favours to her so that they could eat Aiwe the next day. But she had a chastity belt on so that if Aiwe had sexual relations the Papa could find out.

The Papa returned the next day. They asked the woman if she had sexual relations. 'No' said the woman. They looked at the chastity belt. So Aiwe was well in the morning and carried on to the village where he and the Papa lived.

(12) The Papa took Aiwe to the river to swim. The Papa asked Aiwe if he knew how to swim. Aiwe said, 'No, I do not.' They made him try to swim and Aiwe lied and said that he did not know how to swim. 'I will try for fun', said Aiwe. 'Aiwe is drowning, catch him!' said the Papa. Each time they took him to the river he made out that he did not know how to swim. But it was a lie.

(13) Then Aiwe tried to go out one night but the door made a noise as it opened. The Papa said, 'Take care about escaping.'

'No Papa, I am forgetful. Where am I going to go? I live here. Really I do.'

'Why are you wet? You do want to escape!' said the Papa.

Aiwe said: 'No Papa, I left to urinate.' Aiwe tried to go but the bones of the Papa who had died and the axes also made loud noises in the box. They made a noise to warn Aiwe that one of the Papa was awake. Then Aiwe thought that he would not take both the axes and the Papa's bones to his village. The Papa slept in rows and heard the rattles when he had both the bones and axes.

Two days later, Aiwe also wanted to leave and one night he tried to escape and could not because the bones rattled. Then Aiwe thought 'Tonight I am going'. He took up the box at the middle of the night and crept past some of the Papa. One Papa was eating chili early in the morning – at four o'clock. Aiwe leapt to the other side of the cliff – four metres high he leapt.

Then he at last swam to an island and hid his face. Then he heard: 'Aiwe has escaped, where, where?' With a light they looked where he had gone: 'Perhaps he swam...But he cannot swim'. But Aiwe was on the island. Aiwe heard the Papa on the banks of the river shouting: 'Aiwe has escaped.' One young Papa said, 'I am going to swim to see if he is there.' He reached the island. He saw Aiwe. 'Aiwe, Aiwe,' he said. 'You have escaped. I will not kill you. Take this axe to help you.'

(14) Aiwe spent the night on the island. Just after dawn he continued with the bones and the axes. He swam the river through anacondas and sikidnmbi, dangerous river creatures. He continued his voyage along the path which the old Papa chief had told him. He reached a grove of chapaha trees (yaro). He slept there, and on the same road a jaguar passed.

Aiwe spent all night there until the following day. On the following day he took up two axes which he found on the road. But the Papa had advised him that he would not return home with three axes and told him to take two axes and the box which he had made before dying. Then Aiwe, who had three axes, threw away an axe only leaving two axes and continued along the path, the long path.

(15) In the evening he met an old woman crying at what had happened some years past. Before Aiwe had arrived, the people had dreamt that the Papa were going to come and eat them, but it was not Papa, only Aiwe. But the people had fled and his mother had appeared alone. As soon as she saw her son's arrival she immediately died. Aiwe had white hair on his shoulders.

The Arakmbut came later and were very happy to see him with the box of the Papa. They celebrated with a big fiesta because Aiwe had arrived. The chicha (wawing) was mixed with the ground finger bones of the Papa to sweeten it. The Papa said that he should not make either wawing on successive days or drink too much of it. If he did he would die.

But Aiwe forgot and made it every day. He forgot and died because he did not carry out the Papa's words. He died because he forgot. That is how they celebrated the fiesta.

—Ireyo, San José, 1980.

When talking of the myth of Aiwe and Papa the Arakmbut pointed out that the story was very long and it was impossible to tell it at one sitting. The above version was given at several sittings and broadly follows the most detailed version given by San José's story-teller, Ireyo. Some further details emerged in discussion about the myth, including some descriptive and explanatory stories, and these have been included.

The myth reveals the same three-part structure noted with Wanamey and Marinke. The first part tells of the attack on the Arakmbut and the capture of Aiwe. This is followed by Aiwe's growing realisation of the danger that remaining with the Papa holds for him. The final part describes Aiwe's escape, his return to his mother, and their deaths.[1]

The story of Aiwe and the Papa contains three sets of characters: the Papa, the forest peoples, and Aiwe, the Arakmbut.

1) The Papa

Much of the discussion I had with the Arakmbut centred on the identity of the Papa. There were two approaches to the description. One was mythological and drew interpretations from parallel stories about the Papa or supplementary information as to their clothes and appearance. The other related the description of the Papa to historical accounts of outsiders in the Madre de Dios.

A supplementary myth of the Papa describes them as follows:

One day three Arakmbut – father, son and one other, went to the house of a Papa. They went spying and through the hut saw his place

---

1. The accounts of portions of the myth I received in San José as supplements to Ireyo's version differed slightly. The first part was missing in Ireyo's text, and I was given two separate accounts of how the first part should be. Episode 1 is the version which Ireyo usually tells, but episodes 2 and 3 were also considered correct. In Part 2, one version had two attacks, one on the Soweri and the others on the pygmies, while another links them together by having the Soweri and pygmy inter-marry. The difference, in my view, is of minimal significance for the meaning of the myth, which is about Arakmbut relations with outsiders.

full of arms – loads of machetes, guns, rifles, and pistols all around the house. After a bit the Papa got up and went out to clean the patio. He hung machetes all over his body from his neck, arms, and legs and carried a rifle and pistol. To clean the patio he had to put down his guns and when he had got a little way from them the Arakmbut father fired his arrow which wounded the Papa. Before he stirred, the Arakmbut took all his machetes and guns and ran home.

After a while they did this all over again with the same results – spying on the Papa, waiting until he came out into the patio, shooting him, and stealing the machetes. Finally, they returned a third time spying and waiting out by the patio. They shot the Papa and wanted one more machete. As the boy grabbed one hanging from the Papa's neck, the Papa snatched up a pistol and shot him dead.

The Papa are described by the Arakmbut in general conversation as dressed in white, with broad-brimmed hats, white jackets, trousers, and boots. Their weapons weigh a lot, but they rely on their guns mainly to defend themselves. They are dangerous cannibals.

In November, 1985, a group of Arakmbut, Sapiteri, and one Sowereri (an Harakmbut people who have been almost entirely wiped out apart from one man) sat with me and discussed the Papa myth. Several Arakmbut commented that the Papa did not sound like other indigenous forest peoples. I pointed out that they sounded as if they were dressed in the style of nineteenth century caucheros – rubber colonists. The company immediately became interested. A Sapiteri claimed that his father had seen caucheros who were dressed like Papa. Others described slave raids by caucheros during the childhoods of their parents, and said that the Papa were definitely these people.

On other occasions a myth similar to Papa and Aiwe was mentioned by the Arakmbut but with different protagonists. According to Robert Tripp (pers. comm.), the people of Puerto Luz tell a story of an Inca king whom the people in San José call 'Papa'. A boy and girl were taken away by the Inca and stories tell of their escapes from his power. In the end they fire an arrow into his head and he tells them to go away, come back, and then eat him. After this they escape. In San José a woman mentioned that Aiwe was an Arakmbut boy who is captured by the Incas. These Incas raise children to eat them and have many machetes and axes.

In Boca Inambari, I raised the subject of the Papa and was told of a group of people with metal hats who rode on tapirs. They came down from the headwaters of the upper Madre de Dios. The description here fits well into accounts of Spaniards in the time of the conquest who occasionally penetrated the Madre de Dios in search of gold, coca, and other wealth.

In the myth transcribed above, the Papa take the form of nineteenth century caucheros, but they have also been reported as Spaniards and as Incas. Aiwe and the Papa is a myth which talks of the relationship between the Arakmbut and colonising outsiders. In each case the outsiders are more powerful because of their weapons, they are cannibals, and they attack all forest peoples.

2) The Oromaneya pygmies and the Soweri

The Soweri are people, described as 'monkeys'. We have seen in the other Arakmbut myths that humans and animals easily transform into each other. They are 'good shots', and one manages to wound a Papa with an arrow. We also know that the Papa are afraid of Soweri in large numbers. The pygmies are described as 'small'. They are forest people like the Soweri and Arakmbut. In one version of the myth, the pygmies and the Soweri marry. The pygmies are not reknowned as hunters, but in the story take a 'female' position as adviser to Aiwe.

The Soweri and Oromaneya fulfil similar functions in the story. They provide Aiwe with the means (a wounded Papa) and the knowledge (that Aiwe will be eaten) to make Aiwe's escape from the Papa possible. However the wounded Papa alone enables Aiwe to escape.

The Arakmbut appear little in the story. However, we find that they are people related to both the Soweri and Oromaneya. During the first episode we are introduced to the Papa and Arakmbut. When attacked, the Arakmbut transform into monkeys to escape. Soweri are also monkeys, but of a different species. Later in the myth, Aiwe refuses to wash the intestines of the Soweri and will not kill the Oromaneya woman because she is from his people. (We know that she is not Arakmbut, so this presumably means being related as forest people.)

The relationship between the Arakmbut, Soweri, and Oromaneya appears to be that between different indigenous forest peoples oppressed by the powerful outside force of the Papa. Their co-operation enables Aiwe to escape and return to his village. The Papa treat the three groups similarly, in that they are all fair game to be eaten. The terms 'monkey' and 'pygmy' might also refer to the racist categorisation of indigenous forest peoples repeatedly made by outsiders over the years and which can be read in many historical accounts. However, this was not stated by the Arakmbut.

3) Aiwe and the Arakmbut

Aiwe is an Arakmbut 'orphan', left by his fleeing mother and captured by the Papa. He helps them by spying on other forest peoples (such as the pygmies) and doing menial tasks in their camp. Throughout the story Aiwe never entirely loses his identity as an Arakmbut. Although he left his people as a baby, he recognises himself as linked to the Soweri and pygmies in opposition to the Papa. The story of Aiwe is thus a passage from life as an Arakmbut into the village of the Papa. His escape only becomes possible through the mediation of the Soweri and Pygmies. The Soweri blinds the Papa while the Pygmy woman warns Aiwe of his fate.

On his return to his community, Aiwe brings the bones of the dead Papa which the Arakmbut drink as chicha. This provides them with certain powers. Aiwe is warned not to take too much but, unable to control his desire for more of the brew, he dies.

Unlike the other myths we have looked at, the Aiwe story does not deal much with animal species. The only non-carnivorous animals of the forest mentioned in the story are the monkeys, which are seen as transmutable to and from humans.

In line with the other myths we have discussed, the Papa might be expected to relate to some carnivorous species of animal, such as the jaguar or anaconda. However, we see that the Papa themselves are afraid of the giant bat and head-cutting monster which hover over the road. Jaguars and anacondas are introduced to make Aiwe's escape more exciting, but, in fact, they are less of a threat than the Papa; otherwise, Aiwe would have returned to the Papa rather than face the dangers of the forest and river.

The three-part structure of Aiwe and the Papa covers three related topics over two dimensions. On one level we have the story of Aiwe being taken by the Papa in his cradle (kusipe), his growing up with the Papa, his learning of their intentions, and his final escape to his own death in his village. At the same time there is a thematic movement within the myth. The first part looks at the Papa and the Arakmbut fighting over brazil nuts, while in the second part there is a detailed description of Papa cannibalism. In the final part Aiwe returns to the Arakmbut with some of the power of the Papa, which he misuses.

The narrative of the Myth – Aiwe's Story

Aiwe's story is typical of that of many Arakmbut children during the rubber boom. His village was attacked by the henchmen of rubber barons who kill all the men, women, and children they do not want and take captive women and children whom they can use. Aiwe is taken as a baby in a kusipe, which is a balsa wood board on which the baby lies strapped in with banana leaves and with its head covered by a woven cane shade.

An interesting feature of Aiwe's growth is that the myth assumes that his Arakmbut identity remains constant even though he was taken by the Papa as a baby. At the same time, Aiwe has an identity acceptable to the Papa. He works with them and helps them on some of their raids. He fulfils the role of the 'muchachos', who were orphans brought up to do the dirty work of the rubber bosses such as guarding prisoners or carrying out raids for labour (Taussig 1986). However, Aiwe does not follow the Papa's orders. On two occasions he refuses – when he is asked to prepare human flesh for cooking and when he is expected to kill his fellow countrymen.

These two refusals are bound up with his realisation of his fate if he remains with the Papa. The first case is direct. Aiwe refuses to kill the Oromaneya woman, which leads her to warn him about the Papa's intentions of eating him. The second refusal comes later, when Aiwe will not wash human flesh. For this reason, the Papa goes to the stream and is shot in the eye by the Soweri. It is this Papa who helps Aiwe escape.

The relations can be seen as follows:

Table 9.1 Refusals in the Aiwe myth

First refusal	Second refusal
Aiwe will not kill humans	Aiwe won't prepare human meat
Oromaneya saved from Papa	Soweri wounds Papa
Female Oromaneya hunted	Male Soweri hunter
Advises Aiwe to escape	Provides means of escape

These two refusal episodes each consist of a parallel cluster of features and consequences. They draw contrasts between different aspects of the narrative. Preparing meat is distinguished from killing the victim; the successful male Soweri hunter is contrasted with the female hunted Oromaneya. Aiwe's growing awareness comes from understanding the means to achieve his escape (alliance with the wounded Papa) and the knowledge of his likely fate (alliance with his 'fellow countrywoman').

The final part of the myth shows Aiwe putting this knowledge into use. In the first two episodes the circumstances surrounding the two refusals come to fruition. The dying Papa offers to help Aiwe escape and warns him of his fate. At the same time, the Papa try to compromise Aiwe with a woman so that they can kill and eat him. Aiwe prepares his escape by making out that he cannot swim. The bones of the dead Papa do not rattle when the time is ripe and Aiwe escapes by swimming across the river avoiding dangerous river and forest creatures.

The final episode of Aiwe tells of his mother's death, and eventually his own. She dies from the shock of seeing him, but he dies because he does not adhere to the command of the Papa not to drink too much of his ground bone chicha. On the note of Aiwe learning how to escape the Papa but failing to control the power he has, the myth stops.

Themes within the Myth

There are several themes which comment on the relationship between forest peoples, particularly Arakmbut, and Papa (white people). Each part of the myth takes up a different aspect and analyses it.

An important theme is the competition for resources of the forest. The first part of the myth consists of two stories, each looking at the same set of relationships from opposite angles. On separate occasions, both were given as the beginning of the myth, so neither has precedence over the other. The elements are as follows:

Table 9.2 Comparison of the first two episodes in the Aiwe myth

Episode One	Episode Two
Arakmbut pick brazil nuts	Papa pick brazil nuts
Two Arakmbut climb tree	Papa climb tree
Rest of Arakmbut stay below	One Papa stays below
Papa attack and kill Arakmbut	Arakmbut kills the Papa
Papa tries to catch two Arakmbut	Papa follow Arakmbut home
The Arakmbut kill the Papa	Papa kill the Arakmbut
Arakmbut flee, becoming monkeys	Mother flees and Aiwe caught

These two episodes contrast so strongly that they are almost mirror images of each other, except that the Papa defeat the Arakmbut in both cases. The cannibalistic attribute of the Papa is made clear in both episodes, but the fight centres around the brazil nuts.

Brazil nuts occupy an interesting position in the context of Arakmbut/outside relationships. Whereas the Arakmbut have used rubber and wash gold, these have never been a part of their subsistence economy. Brazil nuts, however, are an important part of the natural resources of the Arakmbut. They are also a major cash crop in the Madre de Dios. The myth discusses fighting in and around a brazil nut tree which is being harvested by both the Arakmbut and the Papa. The connection between the two stories is the competition between the peoples over forest resources.

Conflict between the Arakmbut and outsiders in the past has taken place over forest resources and labour relationships. During the rubber boom, indigenous lands were plundered of their crops while their people were taken into slavery or killed. During the rubber boom the Arakmbut were the only Harakmbut peoples who had no direct contact with the outsiders. Rather, they came into conflict with forest peoples dislocated from the main Madre de Dios (Eori) river, who were forced into the headwaters as they fled slavery or death. The resulting wars will be dealt with in the next chapter.

This myth, however, does deal with events typical of the turn of the century. The descriptions are a blending of a myth which has been linked to the Incas and Spaniards with second-hand descriptions of white colonists moving into the Madre de Dios and causing destruction. Whereas the first part of the myth looks at resource conflict, the second looks at exploitation of people. As we have noted in the previous chapter on the spirit world, the ethical aspects of the Papas' right to take Arakmbut resources or labour by force is not a case discussed in the myth. The power of the Papa is the problem.

Throughout the second part of the myth, Aiwe is kept and fattened so that he can be eaten. He is a sort of domesticated animal of the Papa. This would fit with the transformability of his people into monkeys. Logic might wonder why the Papa would want to fatten Aiwe when there seem to be so many other people around to eat. The answer lies in the domestication of Aiwe and the cannibalism of the Papa.

I would suggest that slavery for the Arakmbut is seen as a form of animal domestication. White people are known for fattening up cattle, sheep, and pigs which, traditionally, the Arakmbut did not do because it 'tamed' the spirit of the animal and made the consumption of the meat less effective for growth.

The labour which Aiwe does for the Papa is actually less important than the fact that he will provide them with food. Indeed, both times in the myth when Aiwe is asked to perform some task he refuses. The reason for this provides the Arakmbut view of white exploitation methods. They kill and enslave to eat people; any labour benefits are incidental. We have to find the heart of the meaning of the Papa myth, then, in cannibalism.

We have seen in previous chapters that growth for an Arakmbut arises from incorporating strength from the flesh of dead animals into the body through eating. The cooking of the meat enables the more powerful and dangerous elements to disappear in the smoke and the rest joins the nokiren and gives strength. When a cannibal Papa eats human flesh the effect is doubly horrifying:

1) The cannibal eats meat from humans who are themselves carnivorous. This makes the flesh extremely potent, to the extent that it is dangerously concentrated.
2) The cannibal Papa who eat human flesh do not cook the meat properly. In the story the meat is described as being 'medium rare'. This means that they do not consume only flesh, but also nokiren, the emotions and knowledge. We have seen earlier that thought and feelings are different states of the nokiren. When the Papa eat human flesh they are consuming knowledge, understanding, and power and incorporating culture into their souls.

The Papa do not just travel around eating up human bodies, they ingest souls – what we might term culture. The myth contains several quite grisly passages of the Soweri being sliced to death with sharp machetes but, what is worse, they ate his flesh half-raw – which in an Arakmbut context is really horrible. This description of the killing takes place after the Papa have proven how adept the Soweri is at shooting. The story places contiguously the demonstration of the Soweri's skill with eating him while still alive with minimal cooking.

The first two parts of the myth demonstrate the Papa's power in taking forest resources from the Arakmbut and stealing their people. However, their greatest threat is their cannibalism, which steals other peoples' skills and knowledge and incorporates it into their own power. All through the history of the rainforest, this form of cannibalism has taken place as indigenous peoples are used for their knowledge and their technical skills. The effect is to increase the power of the white Papa at the expense of the forest peoples.

The third part of the myth is a presentation of a way to escape from the power of the Papa. This is the more didactic part of the myth, which warns people not only of the dangers but of the potentially useful powers of the Papa. The main principle of the story is that to avoid the worst excesses of white people it is necessary to 'ingest' some of their ways – in moderation.[2]

Aiwe finds that the Papa who was wounded by the Soweri is prepared to help him. This Papa, who is wounded, is different from other Papa because he provides support and a warning for Aiwe. The indication is that white people sometimes do help Arakmbut, but they are out of the ordinary. We noted a similar concept with the term 'apoining' in the chapter on the spirit world.

Aiwe is given the bones of the dead Papa which tell him of the optimum moment for escape. He is also told to take two axes with him. We are not told if they are metal or not, but they are definitely something special. Aiwe avoids death at the hands of the Papa by refusing to have sexual relations with a Papa woman.

Aiwe escapes by tricking the Papa over his ability to swim. The final two episodes of the myth show Aiwe's return and what he does with the axes and bones. Aiwe finds two axes on the road and is tempted to take three with him until he remembers the Papa's words and leaves one behind.

When Aiwe returns home, he is told to grind up the bones of the Papa into wawing (traditional Arakmbut chicha which would normally be made of maize). The Arakmbut all drink it. However, Aiwe forgets the Papa's warning not to make chicha on successive days. This causes Aiwe's death.

The axes and the bones are, respectively, technical tools and Papa cultural knowledge. Not only was Aiwe able to escape by means of these, but he was able to return to his community and use them. Whereas he controls his use of tools, he is unable to control the use of the bone sweetener in the chicha and dies.

The following distinctions therefore emerge:

Table 9.3 Axes and Bones in the Aiwe myth

Axes	Bones
Papa technology	Papa strength and culture
Papa says take only two	Papa says not to drink too much
Aiwe leaves third	Aiwe forgets and dies

The message of this third part of the myth is carefully to control contact with white people. Sexual relations are undesirable and too

---

2. In his book on notions of cannibalism among the Arawete people of Brazil, Viveiros de Castro (1992) demonstrates how power can be gained by incorporating an enemy into one's being.

much incorporation of white elements into Arakmbut people will lead to death. Only controlled utilisation of tools such as the axes and a moderate use of outside culture will be of any benefit in the escape from the Papa.

The myth of Aiwe is thus a twofold story. It shows the Arakmbut how to escape from the white people by using knowledge of their technology and culture. At the same time the myth warns the Arakmbut that too much integration will lead to their death. The Papa are more dangerous than carnivorous animals, associated as we saw earlier with harmful manifestations of toto. The myth is about power rather than the ethics of Arakmbut people's prior rights to their resources or lives, which as we shall see in subsequent chapters, emerges through the history of their contact with the national society.

Looking at the myth of Papa in relation to the other two major Arakmbut stories, Wanamey and Marinke, a pattern emerges. The Arakmbut mentioned several times that these three myths are the basis of their culture. 'When you understand these myths you will understand us.' However, while it will never be possible for us to understand these myths completely, the themes which they discuss provide considerable material and insight for drawing together different aspects of Arakmbut cosmology.

Wanamey is about the origin of the world and Arakmbut social life. The fire, cooking, clans, the relationship terminology, all that makes people human, are transformed into existence in that myth. Marinke is about the human condition in relation to the world of animals, and plants, and how they relate to ensure growth, cycling, and stability. The myth of the Papa is quite different. Whereas Wanamey and Marinke end on more or less positive resolutions, Aiwe and Papa is very negative. Aiwe and his mother die, after all. The myth of Papa opens up the possibility of the destruction of the Arakmbut nation as a whole.

For this reason it makes no sense to see Arakmbut socio-cultural life only in terms of the first two myths, as they give a false impression of balance and order. Indeed, these are conditions of life which the Arakmbut would like to have. Unfortunately, the world is not like this. In contrast to the closed structured world of Wanamey, where order emerges from chaos, or that of Marinke, in which it is possible to escape chaos by hiding in a different realm in the sky, Aiwe provides no ultimate escape from the Papa. He still dies even after escaping captivity.

This myth demonstrates that the Arakmbut do not live in a closed system, but a system which is constantly under threat. The ordered pattern of the universe is in fact open to threats which are even more dangerous than harmful spirits. The white people (Papa) present the possibility of annihilation. The myth therefore opens a third dimension onto the other myths, which places them in a completely new perspective.

There is a further difference between the myths of Aiwe, Marinke, and Wanamey. Aiwe and the Papa is a myth which is not told so frequently as the other two. Whereas Wanamey and Marinke have several extant versions stretching back to the 1930s, apart from a brief reference to Papa in the work of Califano, there has been nothing published on Aiwe.[3]

There are two explanations for this:

1) The Arakmbut have associated the Papa with 'white people' and have refrained from telling the story for fear of offence or even fear of the white people themselves. The Arakmbut do consider some white people to be cannibals. Several people remarked that they had seen white visitors to the community licking their lips while looking at children.
2) The importance of Aiwe and the Papa as a story comes into prominence only when the community is at risk from outsiders, which has been the case in San José since the 1980 gold rush. This would imply that the myths reflect the current experience of the community, as well as providing some guidelines for dealing with the problems.

The myth of Aiwe and the Papa differs markedly in its versions. The stories vary considerably, more than those of Wanamey and Marinke. Among the Arakmbut, the Papa have been juxtaposed with Incas and Spaniards while the stories themselves differ in detail. Furthermore, in San José the myth itself was told in a more piecemeal fashion than either Wanamey or Marinke. If we look at the three myths in sequence we can see that the different versions are more varied with each myth. Wanamey changes less than Marinke which changes less than the Papa. I would suggest that this reflects that features of the story can easily be changed in relation to developments in the non-mythical world.

3. Califano (1977:190) makes several references to the Papa. He says that iron (*siro*) was given to the Arakmbut by an Amiko called 'Pappa' who came up river on a mule. The Arakmbut shot the mule in the eye and it fell, killing Pappa. Pappa controls the source of metal.

The myths which we have looked at in this book are reflections of Arakmbut experience. We have seen that Marinke and Wanamey have changed when certain aspects become irrelevant. Marinke lost its 'ritual' passages with the decline in ritual activity among the Arakmbut, meanwhile, Papa appears to take even more frequent shifts according to the tellers or the community.

The conclusion from this is that mythology among the Arakmbut is not only a description of life as it should be and a mechanism for reproducing the cosmological world. The myth is itself a reflection of human experience and as such its meaning lies in the relevance of its message to life as it is experienced by Arakmbut. The myth is therefore producing a world for the Arakmbut which only takes on meaning when the listeners recognise its message.

The storyteller at the beginning of this book leads the audience through a myth they know well. Their comments, songs, sound effects, and jokes all contribute to this process. In this way, I would suggest that myths among the Arakmbut are fulfilling some of the functions of ritual, which catches and controls the raw experience of life and provides it with meaning. Meaning emerges by juxtaposing the myth or the rite with practical experience.

As in the previous two parts of this book, the myth introducing the themes is not only of interest in what its internal relations tell us about Arakmbut views of their world, but it also reflects out into other areas of the socio-cultural system. In this case, the myth of Aiwe draws us into Arakmbut history. The main task of the next three chapters is to link the three main invasions of Arakmbut territory over the last hundred years and look at the Arakmbut interpretation of what took place.

The next chapter will look at the rubber boom and its consequences for the Arakmbut in the headwaters of the Karene and Ishiriwe rivers. Following that we will look at the missionary advance on Arakmbut culture, its effects, and Arakmbut reactions. Finally we will look at the most recent threat to the Arakmbut, the gold rush. In each case, we can see how the Arakmbut have responded to these threats and how they reflect episodes in the myth of Aiwe.

◁ *Chapter 10* ▷

THE GREAT WAR

The Rubber Boom

In June, 1894, Carlos Fermin Fitzcarrald, the richest and most powerful rubber baron in the central lowlands of Peru, returned to the
headwaters of the Ucayali river. The previous year, a group of Piro
had told him of a way to link the Ucayali to the Madre de Dios
rivers via the Manu. The significance of this entry was enormous.
Until then, rubber produced in the Madre de Dios and Bolivia was
transported to Brazil by a hazardous route down the cataract-ridden
Madeira-Mamore rivers. Goods in the area cost 75 percent more in
the Madre de Dios as transport was so difficult.

Accompanied by a thousand indigenous slaves and a hundred
labourers Fitzcarrald forged a twelve kilometre trail between the
Ucayali and Madre de Dios rivers (Rummenhöller: 1985:22).[1] It
took him three months to complete the passage. His steamboat was
dismantled and reassembled on the Manu river, from where he
moved down the Madre de Dios to Carmen in Bolivia. This feat
marked the beginning of the genocidal destruction of the Harakmbut, who until this period had managed to avoid the worst excesses
of outside infiltration.[2]

1. Understanding of the Arakmbut past has been enriched by the work of Klaus
    Rummenhöller and Lizzie Wahl, who in their works of 1984 and 1987 respec-
    tively, have provided the most succinct accounts of indigenous history in the
    Madre de Dios.
2. The Harakmbut had been in contact with outside peoples for centuries before
    the rubber boom but the consequences were not severe. Earlier in this work, we
    have encountered the influence of Inca cultural attributes such as metal axes,

Europeans had been aware of the existence of rubber in the Amazon since the eighteenth century, but it was not until the work of Macintosh and Goodyear a hundred years later that its potential become realised (Gray 1990: 2 ff). Between 1827 and 1887 the value of rubber exported from South America rose from £1,000 to £6,591 annually. Initially tapping took place near Belém in Brazil, but by the 1850s tappers were entering the Xingu and Tapajos, and during the 1870s they were in the Madeira, Purús, and Yurua rivers. The boom proper, however, took off in 1894 with the demand for pneumatic tyres for bicycles.

Fitzcarrald had built up his position in central Peru by trading on the Ucayali river from Iquitos. The system by which the rubber boom functioned was the *aviador* or *habilitación* chain of debts. The system operates according to a pyramid or 'dendritic' structure, consisting of a long chain of debtors and creditors. The big merchant

---

coca, growing maize, and fermenting chicha in Arakmbut mythology. Inca outposts in the highland region bordering on the Madre de Dios enabled trade and contact between highlands and lowlands in pre-Colombian times when gold, coca, peppers, and maize were exchanged for feathers, cotton, palm, and medicinal plants.

The Incas did not usually travel further than the headwaters of navigation when they made their annual incursions to the lowlands during their slack work cycle in July to September (Lyon cited in Wahl, 1987:66). They were therefore inclined to trade for gifts, which they could refer to as tribute. Throughout this period, however, the Harakmbut maintained their political autonomy, a fact which the Arakmbut are still proud of today.

The Incas produced coca from Qosnipata in the headwaters of the Madre de Dios and some gold from Carabaya in the headwaters of the Inambari and Tambopata rivers. The colonists of European descent first approached Harakmbut territory after 1534, when Pedro Anzures entered the Madre de Dios, and a few years later, when mining was stepped up in the Carabaya region. The colonial economy shifted trade relations and a capitalistic 'boom and bust' enclave system took over which remains to this day.

According to Lyon (mss) and Fuentes (1982:8), there was a boom in coca production of Qosnipata from the 1520s to 1575. Wahl (op.cit.:75) estimates that 1.5 million pounds of coca were taken from the area annually in the latter part of this period. Apparently this affected the Wachipaeri enough to make them move away. Meanwhile, a gold rush in the Carabaya region during the same period brought over three thousand workers into the area until the 1570s, when Potosi became the main mining centre of the Spanish colonies.

The coca haciendas continued in the Marcapata, Tono, Paucartambo, and Qosnipata valleys, but went into a steady decline in competition with coca reaching Cusco from Bolivia. In spite of references to settlers being attacked by 'Tuyuneris, Wachipaeris, and Sirineris' in the seventeenth century, it is thought that the coca production declined for economic rather than political reasons. Even after the decline at the beginning of the republic period there were as many as three hundred farms in the Paucartambo and Qosnipata valleys.

houses of Belém, Manaus, or Iquitos would provide supplies and credit for intermediaries through goods, unobtainable by any other means. The debtors would repay with rubber. Thus goods would flow up the rivers and rubber return. In an economy where there was little cash available, this system could operate. However, the creditors usually took advantage of their power and prevented the debtors from paying their dues. As a result, debt-bondage became endemic throughout the Amazon.

By controlling transport, particularly steam vessels, entrepreneurial rubber barons were able to control vast areas through debtors. Fitzcarrald built up his empire between 1880 and 1893, by which time he became the richest and most powerful 'cauchero' (rubber baron) in the whole Ucayali region (Rummenhöller op cit:22). It was on the crest of this wave that Fitzcarrald moved into the Madre de Dios along the isthmus which now bears his name.

'By the time Fitzcarrald arrived in the Madre de Dios,' writes Wahl, 'not only had Bolivian and Brazilian rubber tappers been long at work along the Madre de Dios river and many of its affluents, but several indigenous groups in these areas had already been eliminated' (Wahl op.cit:194). Fitzcarrald was, however, able to take advantage of the route over the isthmus to offer considerably lower prices for goods in the habilitación chain than already existed in the region. All goods until then had to be brought from Belém down the Amazon, Madeira, and Beni, including a 230 km land route between Porto Velho and the Madeira.

The two main rivals to Fitzcarrald in the Madre de Dios were Nicolás Suárez and Vaca Diaz. Both were disturbed by the power Fitzcarrald had to take over the economy of the Madre de Dios. Suárez offered Fitzcarrald 500,000 bolivianos for use of the isthmus and suggested dividing the Madre de Dios between them. In 1896 the two barons formed a joint company 'Sociedad Suárez-Fitzcarrald'. Vaca Diaz did not have the capital to deal with the new situation and travelled to Europe to raise money. He succeeded, formed the 'Orton (Bolivia) Rubber Co. Ltd.' and tried to do a separate deal with Fitzcarrald in 1897. On 9 July, Vaca Diaz and Fitzcarrald met on board his steamboat. As they crossed the rapids of the Upper Ucayali, the boat sank, drowning Suárez' two rivals.

Suárez, a Bolivian, was now master of the Peruvian Madre de Dios. The Peruvian state decided to try to 'integrate' the area and formed a scientific commission 'Junta de Vias Fluviales', in 1901. The members spent several years studying the navigation potential of the area looking for ways to make the most of the rubber resources. Meanwhile the Peruvian government, concerned at the unclear boundary between Peru and Bolivia, decided to encourage development in the Madre de Dios. In 1902, in return for a massive concession for rubber exploitation, the Inca Mining Co. (Philadelphia) agreed to construct a 130 km trail linking the Juliaca-Cusco railway line to the Tambopata river which took three years to complete. Also in 1902 a boundary between Peru and Bolivia was fixed and Suárez withdrew.

Suárez' position on the Tahuamanu was taken over by the Spaniard Máximo Rodríguez. However, the two rubber barons fought each other for the next ten years or more. Rodríguez gained control of the area between the Madre de Dios, Piedras, Acre, and the Bolivian boundary. Carlos Scharf held control on the other side of the Piedras and in Manu another Spaniard, Bernardino Perdíz, had extensive lands.

The Peruvian government sought to establish its claims to the border territory by issuing concessions, primarily on the Piedras, Inambari and Tambopata rivers. According to Fuentes (op cit. 1982:14), 905,000 hectares were given in concessions out of a total 1,935,974 hectares of land in the Madre de Dios during the rubber boom. Three main companies, the Tambopata Rubber Syndicate, Inca Mining Co. and Inca Rubber Co., controlled 74 percent of the conceded lands, which were centred around the Inambari and Tambopata rivers.

In this way, between 1905 and 1910 when the price of rubber was at its highest, most of the Madre de Dios was under the control of international companies or rubber barons.

Effects of the Rubber Boom on the Harakmbut

The incursion of rubber exploiters passed without opposition from the Harakmbut in the 1890s, even when Fitzcarrald first entered the Madre de Dios in 1894. By the following year, however, the Toyeri, who were the first group he encountered, realised that posts were being established in the Manu and at strategic points down the Madre de Dios river. Furthermore Fitzcarrald and his men were looking for rubber workers among the indigenous population to work in Manu and Tahuamanu. The Toyeri refused.

A report was delivered at this time to Fitzcarrald that one of his rubber posts had been attacked on the Manu. He responded with vicious determination. Toyeri settlements gathered to defend themselves at the enormous cliff now known as El Mirador Grande, where a mass killing of hundreds of indigenous warriors took place on the banks of the Madre de Dios river. Although estimates of two thousand dead and the river running with blood may be hyperbolic (Reyna 1942), the use of machine guns caused death on a scale never witnessed in the Peruvian Amazon before. From this time onwards the resistance against the caucheros became more sporadic and a war of attrition ensued. Fitzcarrald was now in control of the main course of the Madre de Dios.

The descendants of Toyeri today tell of their raids on caucheros sleeping on the banks of the river in a vain attempt to stop the attacks on their people. The attacks on villages for native labour, known as *correrias*, took place all down the Madre de Dios river against the Toyeri and along the Inambari and the Tambopata river against the Arasaeri.

In 1907 the Junta de Vias Fluviales censured the government for the killings of the Harakmbut because killings were detrimental to the rubber trade in the Madre de Dios and created a shortage of labour. During this period the attention of the caucheros concentrated on the Inambari and Tambopata rivers.[3]

On the Inambari (and among the Ese'eja on the Tambopata), the foreign companies which had been given concessions by the Peruvian government attacked the Arasaeri, poisoning and capturing them for labour. Anti-Slavery International has in its archives at Rhodes House, Oxford, several letters and dispositions accusing the companies on the Inambari of persecuting the Indians. At this time Bolivians were still penetrating Peruvian territory for slaves. The Arasaeri and Toyeri were reduced by 95 percent during the period 1894 and 1914 (Wahl, op.cit. 197). The three causes were murder, enslavement, and disease accompanying the penetration of colonists.[4]

3. During the first years of the twentieth century the Isthmus of Fitzcarrald no longer served its purpose and the mule trail going from the Cusco-Puno railway to the Tambopata river opened for a few years under the auspices of the rubber companies working in the region. In 1907 the Rev. H. Allen Jacob Job travelled down the trail, providing a detailed diary and atmospheric account of the journey and the people in the area. Through the kindness of his daughter, Mrs. Hope Hewisham, I have been able to read these fascinating documents, which emphasise most clearly the horrors of the rubber boom in the Madre de Dios.

4. In the same way that correrias in the Madre de Dios transferred large numbers of Arasaeri and Toyeri to Bolivia, the rubber boom was responsible for bringing indigenous people from other parts of Peru into the Madre de Dios. Fitzcarrald started the practice of bringing indigenous labourers from the northern parts of Peru to work rubber, particularly the Huitoto who were subsequently to suffer so much at the hands of the Casa Arana (Gray 1990). Máximo Rodríguez brought a considerable number of indigenous people into the Madre de Dios, not just as individuals but as families. The result is that there are now in the

Many of the Toyeri and Arasaeri fled from the affluents of the Madre de Dios and Inambari. They sought refuge in a place where white people could not find them and where there was no rubber. The effect was to force those people living on the main rivers Madre de Dios and Inambari up into the headwaters. In the headwaters were the Arakmbut. The Arakmbut say quite explicitly that this movement of native people was the cause of the 'Great War' or 'World War' of their people. They explain this in two ways. Outsiders are known by the Arakmbut as 'Taka'. Although the word usually refers to non-Arakmbut people, it can also refer to native people who are not considered Harakmbut either because they are very different or because they are hostile to the Arakmbut.

The Taka are those who came up from the main rivers at the turn of the century and fought with the Arakmbut for several decades. The Taka would raid in the middle of the night or just before dawn by ambushing their victims. They were expert archers.

The Arakmbut say that they came either as live people wanting to take their resources or else as dead Taka Toto who had been killed by the whites and were seeking other souls. People began to die of mysterious diseases such as influenza, yellow fever, or tuberculosis. These illnesses were largely due to the souls of dead Taka, killed by white people.

Thus, whether living or dead, the indigenous people attacked by the caucheros penetrated Arakmbut territory. The Arakmbut do not label the Taka as being exclusively from any particular group. They mentioned to me three origins of the Taka:

1) People who lived on the Karene (Colorado) and Ishiriwe. These were mainly Sapiteri, although they took the names from the rivers on which they lived. They were displaced by the Toyeri on the Eori (Madre de Dios) and were forced up into the headwaters where the Arakmbut lived.
2) People up in the Shintuya area of the Madre de Dios were both Sapiteri and Sowereri. They were forced across the headwaters of the affluents of the Madre de Dios to the Ishiriwe.
3) People from the Araza river, which is an affluent of the Inambari, and those living between there and the Karene (Arasaeri, Pukirieri, Kisambaeri).

Madre de Dios communities of Asháninka, Shipibo-Conibo from the Ucayali and Santarosinos from the Río Napo of Ecuador (Rummenhöller 1984:98). In 1912 Delboy calculated that there were two thousand imported Indians in the Madre de Dios.

The homeland of the Arakmbut was therefore the first place that fleeing Harakmbut people tried to seek refuge during the rubber boom. The shortage of resources, according to the Arakmbut, led to an unprecedented period of fighting between the different Harakmbut groups. This is not to say that the Harakmbut had not fought before. There is simply no evidence one way or another. Oral history first takes over from myth from the time of the parents of Arakmbut who are old now. This stretches history back for about a hundred years.

The Arakmbut in the Wandakwe and Kipodnwe

Traditionally the Arakmbut lived in communal houses called *haktone*. These were situated on the banks of rivers in a clearing. A maloca measured on average 30 x 40 x 6 metres; it was oval in shape, with a roof of leaves that came right down to the mud floor. The two entrances, one at either end of the house, opened onto a central area used for dancing and drinking parties.

The entire community would live in one house, although if there were too many people in the one building, or if any male outsiders were staying there for an extended period, a number of scattered lean-to huts would spring up around the main maloca. Inside the house, on the two longer walls, there were partitions making small open rooms called *wamba*. These contained beds and a hearth where a family would eat and sleep.

Each maloca was a residential community which took its name from some object in the environs. The Arakmbut were divided into two groups: the Wandakweri, which had seven maloca groups, and the Kipodneri, which had five. Each house had its chacra which was communally cultivated in a circular fashion making full use of the diversity of crops. The plan of the maloca and the chacra parallel the communal life style of the Arakmbut.

Arakmbut malocas were not isolated from each other. We know from talking to old people who remember the pre-mission days that fiestas would frequently take place, encouraging contact and the exchange of information, songs, and stories. The Arakmbut today have a wide repertoire of songs, many of which they say were passed on to them from the Toyeri or Sapiteri.

Arakmbut peoples based their contacts on contiguity between malocas but information could spread throughout the area. We know, for example, that Harakmbut peoples were in close contact with other groups on their borders. The Arasaeri with the Ese'eja, the Toyeri with the Amahuaca and the Wachipaeri with the Matsigenka (Gray, 1987b:307; Lyon 1984; Adolfo Torralba and Thomas Moore pers.comm.).[5] Apart from songs there was inter-marriage, mythical episodes, shamanic skills, and economic exchange.

Figure 10.1 Arakmbut malocas and chacras prior to contact

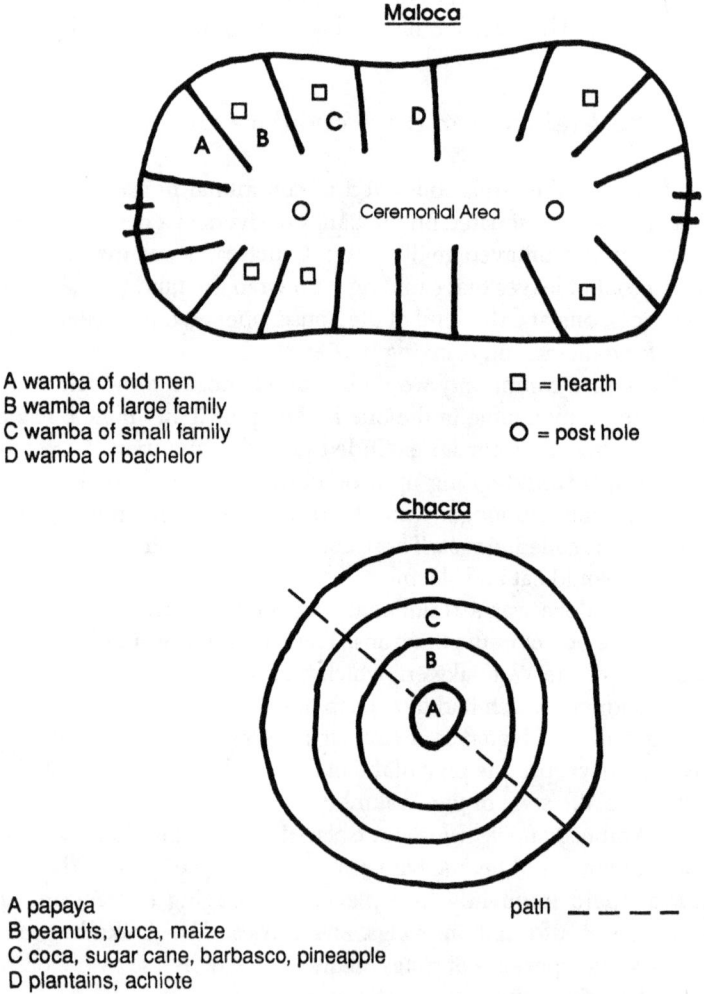

Maloca

A wamba of old men
B wamba of large family
C wamba of small family
D wamba of bachelor

□ = hearth

O = post hole

Chacra

A papaya
B peanuts, yuca, maize
C coca, sugar cane, barbasco, pineapple
D plantains, achiote

path _ _ _ _

5. Perhaps the most interesting example of this cultural contact was recorded by Padre Aza in 1927. Among the Matsigenka, he heard an Arasaeri song. There is no direct contact between the Matsigenka and Arasaeri, so it would have to have travelled via the Wachipaeri.

Arakmbut memory of the pre-mission period is dominated by the Taka. What should be emphasised here is that Arakmbut oral history operates according to its own logic, but that logic blends very smoothly with the non-Arakmbut accounts of the incursions of white rubber tappers into the Madre de Dios and Inambari rivers at the turn of the century. We should now look more closely at the Arakmbut perception of the Taka and how this relates to the shift from myth to oral history.

The distinction between myth and oral history is not clearly marked, as the following stories demonstrate. The period of the 'Great War' with the Taka contains stories which are both 'mythological' and 'historical', and others which are neither. The following three examples demonstrate this point.

1) Mythological stories about the Taka

There are several 'mythological' stories about Taka. By mythological I refer to elements which either involve transformations between the human and animal world or stories which directly reflect mythological themes. The story reproduced below is interesting because it parallels the story of Aiwe and Papas, but in this case it is the Taka who capture the Arakmbut boy:

It is said that a man and his son left the village and came across a tree whose fruit was eaten by many birds. Then the father said to his son: 'I am going to make a hide up in the tree to wait for birds'. And the son went to collect branches and liana to tie firm the hide. Then the boy went to grab one more branch from the river bank and saw the Taka. They were coming and so the boy ran and said to his father: 'Father, I see the Taka'.

The old man did not listen because his death was approaching. The boy called again: 'Father come down!'

The old man said: 'Ahh! What is happening? Ahh! What is it?'.

The boy replied: 'The Taka are coming!'

The old man continued to cry: 'Ahhh!'.

Then the Taka were there – about twenty metres away. The boy said: 'The Taka are coming – I am going!'.

So the boy escaped and hid behind the tree trunk. The Taka then saw the man who was up in the tree and shot him with an arrow, killing him. One Taka moved back and came close to the boy without realising that he was behind the tree. The Taka wanted to kill his father but the other Taka had already killed him.

The boy noticed the Taka coming back past the tree where he was hidden so he killed the Taka by shooting an arrow at him. 'Ahhh!' said the Taka.

'What has happened?' asked the other Taka.

'I am dying', said the shot Taka.

The boy, after avenging his father, escaped, but the Taka saw him, and running after him, captured the boy. 'Shall we kill him or leave him an orphan?' one said.

The other Taka said: 'Let us take him to our village'.

The boy was taken prisoner by the Taka. He lived his youth there. In the evenings he would walk looking for a way to escape. On the paths were big cliffs where the Taka put their rubbish. The Taka noticed this and one day said: 'Don't go by the cliffs, it is very dangerous to go there in the evening.' Thus the Taka spoke to the boy.

Every evening the boy would take walks by the cliffs to seek escape and make his revenge. The Taka said to him: 'What are you doing in the evenings?'

The youth answered: 'I am hunting *torogn'* (opossum). One evening he secured his arrows and went on his way. That night the Taka had a feast and one Taka told how he had killed the boy's father. The boy remembered his father and decided to carry out his revenge. On the same night the Taka danced and sang around the man who had killed the boy's father. The boy did not participate but took up his arrows and killed his father's killer. He escaped. The Taka was left dead. The youth ran to the cliff where he had made his escape route. An old Taka saw him escaping and said: 'Young man, do not kill the man you see.' The youth took no notice of him. He carried on running through the forest at night and reached his village. He told his story to his people. The Taka followed him but did not find him.

The mythological element of this story parallels several other myths we have looked at concerning the fate of Arakmbut children. The two stories which this resembles are Wainaron (chapter two) and Aiwe (chapter nine). This story resembles Wainaron in the beginning. In both stories, a father and his son go hunting and the father climbs a tree. In Wainaron, the father is killed by the giant bird, while in the other myth the Taka kill the father. In both cases, the boy travels through the forest, to the lair of the Master of the Forest and the Taka respectively.

In contrast, Aiwe and the Papa tells of the child being captured by the Papas, leaving his mother alive but childless. The period of the orphan with the Taka resembles Aiwe's time with the Papa in that he is kept against his will, whereas the orphan in the Wainaron myth is told to return to his community. As in the myth of Aiwe, the boy secretly plans to escape but by finding a path down the cliffs rather than swimming. However, there is a difference between the Taka and the Papas. Taka are not cannibals and although they keep the orphan, they do not intend to fatten him up for eating.

These contrasting features can be seen as follows:

Table 10.1 Contrasting features of Wainaron, Taka, and Papa.

Wainaron	Taka	Papa
Boy with father	Boy with father	Boy with mother
Father killed	Father killed	Mother escapes
by Bird	by Taka	from Papas
Boy held voluntarily	Boy held against will	Boy held against will
Animals are man-eating	Taka not cannibals	Papa cannibals
Old man protects boy from bird and toad	Old Taka does not alert the others	Old Papa helps Aiwe escape
Boy commits error	Boy makes plan	Boy makes plan
Boy sent home	Boy escapes	Boy escapes

These three myths share several elements but they make various contrasts. These contrasts, I suggest, reflect distinctions which would seem obvious to the Arakmbut but which we need to spell out in order to demonstrate the difference between forest creatures, the Taka, and the Papa.

We have already noted that the Papa are not spirits or transformed animals of the forest. However, they are strange as humans because they have 'second sight' and are cannibals. The Taka, on the other hand, are human. They live in the forest and kill Arakmbut in living and dead forms. Indeed their dead souls are spirits of the forest. Throughout the stories of the Taka neither the Arakmbut nor the Taka consistently win. The two are thus more or less evenly matched. The Taka, like the Arakmbut, are thus bodily similar to the Papas but in their souls closer to the animals.

2) General Taka stories

Most of the stories about the Taka are told for an evening's entertainment, and although they are not necessarily mythological, there are familiar patterns to the tales which could, however, just as easily be based on the memory of events which actually took place. The following is an example of a story which does not necessarily relate to any other myth or involve any transformation of people, animals, or other outside creatures:

A group of Arakmbut went on a two day hunt and, on returning, saw many footprints. The prints passed downriver. Returning, the Arakmbut rubbed out the prints of the Taka. They had left the children in the house that was full of the women and old people. The Arakmbut said: 'Let us go and look for the Taka and attack them, because all our children must be dead.' They saw a narrow canyon, like the Kiraswe (a stream near San José), where it was impossible to climb up on either side. There was a path but on both sides the banks were high. So the Arakmbut waited opposite. They waited for half an hour. They were ready, and the women had hidden themselves too. Then the Arakmbut waited until the whole line of Taka passed before attacking them from behind. The Arakmbut began to shoot the Taka. The Taka were confused because their footprints had been rubbed out. 'Is this mine?' They could not see the Arakmbut in waiting. The Arakmbut fired from behind – 'tatata!' They killed all the Taka but one. They say that one managed to leave the blood-filled stream of the Taka. He escaped by hiding in the river as if he were dead. He lay underwater – well hidden. Then he ran. All the other Taka were dead. The Arakmbut continued to their house, crying. When they arrived all the children were hung up dead. The women and old people had spears in their guts. The Arakmbut mourned.

This particularly grisly story demonstrates clearly the fact that the Taka and the Arakmbut fight as equals and they both kill each other in a power struggle. The Taka do not exploit the Arakmbut as do the white people. Arakmbut and the Taka fighting tactics are similar, involving much use of footprints and ambushes.

3) Oral history about the Taka

The oral history stories about the Taka are similar to the general stories in that they have no mythological element involved. However, they are fixed in time by reference to specific people, known to those still living. Although it is unusual for Arakmbut to utter the names of dead people, they have done so in these cases:

An Arakmbut man, Keme, went to the beach to fish. He went to look for fish and the Taka were there. The Taka were waiting for him behind a trunk on the beach to kill him. The Arakmbut man was fishing. The Taka killed an Arakmbut man. They shot him with an arrow and left him dead. The dead person whom the Taka had killed was Keme. They went back downriver. Many Arakmbut went onto the beach. There were many of them: Imopwe (Miguel's father), Risanewa (dead now), Iowa (Morimo's father), Kayani (dead), and Iapwa (father of Kendiwe in Shintuya). They saw it. The Taka had come to the Arakmbut's chacras and had taken and stolen maize for their house. They had come again when the maize was ripe. They came in the night to kill the Arakmbut when they were sleeping but killed Keme in the morning.

This story describes an event which took place around the time of the childhood of people still alive today. Morimo and Miguel are still alive, both aged over sixty. Although this story was not told by them, it lists a group of people living in the headwaters of the Ishiriwe river about seventy years ago or more. The early morning ambush on the fisherman and the night raid on the Arakmbut chacras to steal maize are features of Taka armed strategy.

The Taka in Myth and Ritual

The following myth was told in 1985 and is interesting because it demonstrates a different sort of mythological story than the one mentioned above. In the first place, the Taka Chief is presented as some sort of Goliath, a giant of a man who frightens the Arakmbut no less when he is dead than when he is alive. This larger-than-life man is balanced by the Arakmbut Chief, Makawi, who manages to convert himself into a jaguar, becoming invincible and shooting the Taka Chief in the chin.

The point of interest in this myth is that it relates directly to an Arakmbut ritual and caused me to reanalyse all the material which emerged in the Marinke chapter. The myth explains the only account of jaguar conversion encountered in Arakmbut society, which I was told had actually occurred several times:

The Arakmbut went to fish. 'Let's go fishing for catfish. Let's go to the beach now', they said. They did not use barbasco. The river Wandakwe was clear. They went to the mouth of the Mamawetapo stream which joins the Wandakwe.

Two young boys (wambo) went ahead. There were no fish in the palisade. 'Better to look in a pool. There we will catch them,' said the boys. They did not want to stay with all the other Arakmbut. The boys went one bend upstream and began to fish with arrows.

Suddenly one saw the footprint of a Taka fresh in the wet sand. It was a tremendous print. He could hear the enemies in the caña brava. So to trick them he called to his companion: 'Come, my arrow has broken!' He beckoned the other boy not to say anything. He came and looked at the huge Taka print. 'Look what a tremendous foot print is made by water and stone.'

Then they began to make preparations to cook and sleep to trick the enemy, to escape them. The Taka were still hidden nearby so the boys spoke in a loud voice so that the Taka would hear. 'Let us go a little downriver to collect firewood and then return,' said the boys. They then began to chop firewood and work their way slowly downriver. When they reached the Arakmbut they threw down their firewood and ran to warn the people. The Arakmbut were afraid and all fled towards their house.

The Arakmbut Makawi was an *ohpu* war leader. He had set off to a *kuchiakpo* hunting hut, taking a rotten tapir carcass as a bait to shoot gallinazo (type of vulture) for their wing feathers. He wanted the gallinazo feathers to make arrows. When the boys arrived with the news of Taka, they told Makewi's daughters, who ran to find him. 'Father, father, Taka are coming!'

Makewi responded 'What have the Taka brought? I want a machete!' Then Makewi said 'Take my arrow and return to the house. I am going to kill the Taka. Go ahead and wait for me there.' Then the daughters went ahead. Behind them he came, roaring in the voice of a jaguar. Makawi had converted himself into a jaguar. He was happy because he was going to kill Taka. 'I am not going to die', he said, 'because many years ago I dreamt of a hummingbird. I killed a hummingbird and it made me dream that I would kill Taka.'

Makawi reached the maloca and turned back into a person. He began to leap around the patio with his son's arrow. All the arrows were ready. They sent the women and children to hide. The men then made leaf hides (*ekmbika/echunkmbika*) so that they could wait for the Taka without being detected.

And so all the Arakmbut set out with the Chief in front. They went to a high cliff overlooking the river so that they could see far away. The Arakmbut hid behind their hides and waited. They saw someone coming onto the beach from the bank. It was an enormous Taka Chief who stood there with giant legs. He was standing on the other side of the river. They saw that he was going slowly, looking at the footprints of the Arakmbut. Behind him the Arakmbut thought they saw a curassow chick. But it was not, it was the feather of an arrow. The branch seemed to have many arrows. They looked through into the branches. They saw numerous Taka, both men and women. The Taka had waited and come, following the Chief by the river, who had left the point of an arrow to indicate where he was going to go.

The Taka began to come down from the forest to the river bank. There were many of them. They then began to talk, ready for the attack. They crossed the river to the port. They reached the beach. They stood in a group at the bottom of a log bridge leading up to the Arakmbut maloca. The Taka chief Wambognsik made a singing speech (*chiwa*) about standing up to the Arakmbut. 'The Arakmbut will not kill me. I will win.' They all sang and the Taka women wept, singing: 'We will die for our people.' In a tremendous voice the Taka Chief called them and told them not to talk. Everyone fell silent. They moved out of sight. Some Arakmbut thought that they had gone. The Arakmbut almost began to speak but suddenly Wambognsik appeared again with his arrow at the ready.

According to the hummingbird dream, Makawi had been told that the Taka must not see him. Wambognsik did not see him. Makewi placed his screen in front of him as he was leading the party up the log and put an arrow into his bow. Boom! The arrow hit Wambognsik and passed through his ribs from one side to the other. He fell. Blood poured forth from Wambognsik's wound onto the ground. Wambognsik began to die and called a warning to the others that the Arakmbut were shooting from above. 'Ahh, ow, the best of the Arakmbut has killed me!'

The Taka behind began to shout, the Taka women shouted: 'They are attacking us!' Several Taka were killed by Makawi. Then Taka arrows fell like rain; they made a noise like rain. There were few Arakmbut and many Taka.

'Let's go' said Makewi. 'Let's go!' One Arakmbut ran, afraid at the falling arrows which followed them like wasps. 'Let's go!' shouted Makewi. But another Arakmbut misheard him and he thought he should stay and follow from behind. As he moved he was shot in the mouth. Another Arakmbut returned to see what had happened and was also killed.

The Arakmbut then went to the women who were hiding by the beach and said: 'Let's go into the forest because we don't want to go to the house. The Taka are going to the house. You must escape.' The Arakmbut spent two days waiting in the chacra. Meanwhile two groups of Taka went into the forest to cut off the Arakmbut. However, the two groups surprised each other and several Taka were killed by their own people. The Taka, meanwhile, went to the Arakmbut maloca with Wambognsik. They had their arrows ready to kill the Arakmbut when they returned.

On the third day the Arakmbut returned to see what had happened. They saw fresh ashes in the house and footprints. They were not really sure if Wambognsik had died. They followed the footprints and found a tree which had been dug up. When they dug into the hole, they found the body of Wambognsik in a seated position. The body had dried up. Then they went to look more closely. First they looked at his face, then fled. Then they returned and looked at his penis which was bright red. Then they fled again. Then one Arakmbut man said, 'I will take it,' and they helped him drag the body to the beach where it was eaten by the gallinazos.

This story mentions a particular person, Makawi, and his ability to transform into a jaguar. This story encompasses the mythological and historical stories about the Taka we have noted above. It relates both to transformation and to a historical person.

In 1981, Padre Torralba mentioned to me that the Arakmbut had a ritual which involved a blue/green bird falling from the sky. He had thought it paralleled the episode in the Bible following the baptism of Jesus by John the Baptist when the dove appeared. On trying to follow this up I initially got nowhere, but after talking about the Taka in detail during the 1985 visit it emerged that the blue bird is one part of a ritual called *mbakoykoy* which has been obsolete for many years.

This ceremony took place long ago in the maloca. The Arakmbut would invite people from neighbouring malocas and light fires in a circle around a small boy who they laid on a *tori* wood, like balsa. The people would take a feather to keep the child completely clean, and he would be painted with jaguar spots. Then the people would sing and the sky would come down to earth enveloping people in smoke. The child would sweat considerably and cry with the heat. Its mother, seated next to the child, would also cry. Then the kurudneri sky spirits would come in. Tall, thin, and white, they would give their power to the child, who would then be a strong ohpu. Their sign is the form of the bird mbakoykoy, which appears when the kurudneri do. The kurudneri come with a drink – *haiapa* – which is very bitter. They give it to the child to gain strength. Not only does the child get jaguar spots but he becomes a jaguar when fighting

Taka. If all goes well, the child will be an ohpu and destroy all enemies. The child will be a war leader.

Aika and Mamatone in San José knew of the ceremony and saw it when they were small. Mamatone sang me the song calling the kurudneri down from the sky. They remember that it happened to Makawi. Interestingly enough, this is the name of the hero in the myth who became a jaguar to defeat the Taka. The Arakmbut tried once to perform the ritual before they went to Shintuya but the sky did not come down. This was because someone went out to urinate in the middle of the ceremony.

This ritual introduces several elements which we have not encountered in Arakmbut cosmology before. The ceremony is little known and many of the young people in the village did not know that it even existed. There are several elements which can be seen in the context of the Arakmbut as a whole:

1. The Existence of the Kurudneri Spirits from the Sky

The kurudneri have not been a major feature of the Arakmbut spirit world. Indeed, before 1985 I was completely unaware of their existence. When I asked who they were, they I was told that they lived in the sky and went there with Marinke. They do not come down to earth unless summoned through the correct ritual procedure of mbakoykoy.

The kurudneri are otiose and do not have any part to play in the daily life of the Arakmbut spirit world, which is usually perceived as relating between the river and forest domains. The power they bring down from the sky (kurudn) is only needed when the Arakmbut are in great danger and they need a special strength which goes beyond the river-forest distinction.

2. Dry and Bitter Substances

In our previous discussions of wet and dry we noted the connection between dry preparations and maleness. This occurred in cooking and in the growth rituals for men. The ceremony of mbakoykoy is about the growth of a child but to a greater extent than normal. It also takes place when the child is a young boy. Dryness appears here in the extreme. The child lies on a piece of wood like balsa which gives a fine dry ash. The child is surrounded in the maloca by fires, which not only make the atmosphere claustrophobic but enable the kurudneri to descend in the smoke.

The drink haiapa actually contains the particle '*hai*', which means dry. I do not know what the drink was, except that it was extremely painda (bitter) – like rum. As we know, bitterness keeps away powerful dangerous spirits. The drink presumably protects the child from being harmed by the kurudneri. Furthermore, we have noted in chapter three that dryness is more associated with height. The dry nature of the ritual and the presence of sky spirits continues the correlation.

The child on which the ceremony centred was always a boy and the aim of the ceremony was to make that boy as strong as possible – indeed invincible. The ceremony therefore constitutes a use of dry features taken to an extreme not encountered elsewhere among the Arakmbut.

3. The conversion of the child into the most powerful forest creature – the jaguar.

The child on the balsa wood platform is kept clean with a feather. Not a piece of dirt must mark him. Spots are painted on him to enable him to become a jaguar. The kurudneri enable the conversion to take place. The child will grow into a powerful ohpu war leader who can, if necessary, convert into a jaguar to destroy the enemies of the Arakmbut.

The myth presented above demonstrates the form of conversion. The leader still appeared as a human being but was a jaguar. Some Arakmbut did say that it was possible also for the warrior leader to transform physically into a jaguar, although this does not always seem necessary. The jaguar is the most powerful creature of the forest and, as maleness is more associated with the forest than the river, it would appear reasonable that the Arakmbut warrior leader should become a jaguar.

4. The Connection between the Ritual and Myth

There are several elements which link the ritual of mbakoykoy with myths. We have seen the connection with Wambognsik, but there is also an important connection with Marinke. The kurudneri are considered to be the people of Marinke in the sky. He fled there, away from the jaguars who sought revenge. The connection with jaguars is therefore twofold:

1. Marinke flees to the sky away from jaguars and thus becomes safe from them. He is able to avoid the destructive power of the

jaguar. He and his people, from this perspective, are therefore more powerful than the jaguars who cannot follow.

2. Marinke's people, the kurudneri, descend from the sky and provide the power to enable the child become a human jaguar. There is no evidence to suggest that the kurudneri are jaguar people, only that they are otiose spirits with strange powers.

The Arakmbut regard the hummingbird as a sign of the proximity of a jaguar – sometimes even to the extent of abandoning a forest trip if a hummingbird appears. In the myth of Wambognsik and the Taka, Makawi mentions how he became a jaguar because he dreamt of a hummingbird.

The accounts of the rare ceremony, mbakoykoy, have arisen only in relationship with the Taka. Neither the kurudneri nor the bird appear in any other significant context. The reason for this is that the Arakmbut have only used the ritual successfully in connection with the Taka war which took place before contact with the missionaries.

My discussions with the Arakmbut about the Taka wars were all centred around a world which no longer exists. The stories and descriptions of rites and the associated cosmological features such as the sky spirits and jaguar chiefs, were presented as having taken place before the coming of white people, as a result of the incursions into the territories of those Harakmbut living on the main rivers surrounding Arakmbut territory.

Although the Arakmbut had probably been fighting with Taka for centuries, the rubber boom is the first moment when history and myth begin to relate for the Arakmbut. Events of the rubber boom survive as experiences of the parents and grandparents of adults living today. Known relatives had participated in these fights, could remember the Taka and the war.

The Taka provide an example of the inter-relationship of myth, ritual and history. The Taka wars are historical events. The souls of dead Taka still do exist in the forest. Whereas some Arakmbut myths, which have remained unchanged for twenty years, refer to no specific period, there are examples of myths and rituals placed within a particular historical framework. Most Taka stories are of this type, linked by the Arakmbut to the period around and after the rubber boom, which enables them to stand astride the boundary between history and myth.[6]

6. In Reeve's review of lowland Quichua histories she contrasts mythic time-space and the present to 'beginning times': 'By contrast to beginning times, which incorporates a specific referent to past time and past peoples, mythic time-space

Arakmbut utilise both history and myth in a way which relates the two but does not reduce one to the other. For them, myths reflect current experience, while history is about past experience. Stories can shift between these two perspectives. History constitutes the experience which makes elements of myths relevant or not, while myth constructs a framework for the meaning of history. The myths and stories about the Taka are placed within a historical epoch. They are the first element of that framework which links memory to the present. The end of the 'Taka' period and the rubber boom's consequences come at the point at which the Arakmbut faced extinction.

The diseases spread throughout the Madre de Dios by the rubber workers and subsequent colonists took a few decades to reach the headwaters of the Karene, Ishiriwe, and Mbero. Yellow fever, smallpox, and influenza all took their toll. The Arakmbut were dying in numbers unprecedented in their experience. They assumed initially that these were the souls of Taka who had died from diseases brought by the outsiders or caused by female sorcerers. They gradually learned, however, that these diseases came originally from the white peoples' God, and so it was to the white peoples' God that the Arakmbut turned for their salvation, thereby entering the second phase of their history.

---

refers to an undifferentiated state of the universe, a period before the earth had its present form and before humankind and animals were separate beings' (1988:25). The period of Taka is similar to 'beginning times' but it encompasses both mythological times and specific historical events.

◁ Chapter 11 ▷

CHRISTIAN INVASION

In August 1940, the largest and most expensive Peruvian expedition ever to enter the Madre de Dios reached the headwaters of the Karene. Financed by the Wenner Gren Foundation under the direction of Dr. Paul Fejos, international explorer, the fifty-six members of the expedition were backed up by twenty armed Peruvian soldiers, radios, motor boats, and aircraft for reconnaissance. The intention of the exploration was to make a detailed geological survey of the Karene with the aim of finding and exploiting gold and other resources in the area.

The idea of an expedition originated in 1936 as part of a wild scheme by a Swede, Sven Eriksson, to found a city (El Dorado) at the mouth of the Karene based on an economy of gold, rubber, cacao, tea, and barbasco served by indigenous people tamed by the use of tear gas (Anon. 1936). The then Swedish Consul, a Mr. Karel, had received from the Peruvian government a sizeable gold concession in the hitherto unexplored Karene and he agreed to look into Erikson's scheme for an initial expedition. Wenner Gren (a Foundation with a strong Swedish connection) fitted the bill admirably as a sponsor (Fuentes op.cit:19).

The massive expedition took twenty-six days to reach the mouth of the Karene from Puerto Maldonado. Several air reconnaissance flights had crossed the area noting communal houses between the Karene and the Upper Madre de Dios. On 25 July, 1940, a group of twenty men moved on up the Karene. On 4 August the party made friendly contact with a Sapiteri leader, Paijaja. They handed radio earphones to him and to his astonishment he heard the words '*Paijaja, ndoen Wamambuey*' (Paijaja my brother). The speaker was José Alvarez, the interpreter and guide on the Wenner Gren expedition.

Padre Alvarez first entered the Madre de Dios in April 1917. Throughout the 1920s and 1930s he had worked with Ese'eja and Arasaeri on the Madre de Dios, Tambopata, and Inambari rivers. His experience with Harakmbut peoples and their languages, particularly the Arasaeri, during the 1930s made Bishop Sarasola recommend him for the expedition. His task was to accompany the expedition and look at the potential for missionary work in the Karene and beyond. After this expedition, Padre Alvarez went on to become the leading figure in the proselytisation of the Arakmbut, indeed of all the Harakmbut.

Fejos and his twenty men continued up the Karene and camped on a beach. A group of Arakmbut passing through the area suddenly encountered Fejos and his men on the other side of the river. At this time, the war with the Taka was still at its height. The Arakmbut fired their arrows on the expedition, which responded with gun shots. They disappeared, but after a while returned and resumed firing. The expedition shot at the Arakmbut again. Several turned to run, but one Arakmbut remained, exhorting the others to hold their ground. He was gunned down, shot in the thigh and leg. The Arakmbut retreated, leaving two more of their countrymen shot dead. Fejos ordered an immediate withdrawal (Alvarez 1940a & b; Barriales nd.:51, Secretariado de Misiones Dominicanas nd:65).

The expedition was a failure. Resources in the area seemed unclear and the local indigenous people were still hostile. However the Wenner Gren expedition is significant because it constitutes the encounter of two histories. The search for gold and souls as part of an expedition, known in Peruvian national history, burst into the indigenous history of the great war between the Taka (in this case Sapiteri) who were fighting the Arakmbut. The three dead Arakmbut were the first casualties of contact.

The expedition was also significant in that it signalled the end of the Great War. After returning to base camp at the mouth of the Karene, Padre Alvarez, on hearing of what had taken place, immediately set off for the point where the Wasorokwe joins with the Karene (SMD op cit:52). After saying mass on the beach, he was approached by two Sapiteri who took him to Paijaja. This contact provided the Dominicans with the foothold they needed to continue their missionary work in the future.

Although it was more than ten years before the Arakmbut were under missionary control, the Taka with whom they had been fighting for so long were gradually incorporated into the mission system which had been operating in the Madre de Dios since the beginning of the century.

The Dominicans arrived in Madre de Dios in 1902. Recently seconded from the Philippines, Padre Zubieta made two trips to the Wachipaeri and later to some Ese'eja on the Inambari. Until 1906 they concentrated their efforts on the Wachipaeri. However, after meeting Von Hassel, Chairman of the Junta de Vias Fluviales in 1904, when he visited the Upper Madre de Dios, the priests decided to travel to the Manu.

After several trips to baptise indigenous people, the Mission of San Luis del Manu was opened on 12 October, 1908. In the maelstrom of rubber gathering, the mission nevertheless manifested several of the traits to be seen later throughout the Madre de Dios. San Luis was sponsored by a notorious benefactor, Bernardino Perdíz, the first of a line of unscrupulous supporters of mission work. The mission established a boarding school, run by Padre Aza, which would take the children away from evil influence (Fernández Moro 1952:143).

Over the next few years the priests established contacts around the Inambari and Tambopata. The contours of the relationship between the missionaries and the more powerful production and trading interests in the rubber boom became even more apparent with the construction of San Jacinto, the missionary centre of the Madre de Dios in Puerto Maldonado. The Sociedad Rimac, Inca Rubber Co., Braillard, Bernardino Perdíz, and the even more notorious Máximo Rodríguez all contributed. Indeed, Rodríguez even gave some of his slaves to the mission to help the missionaries learn the indigenous languages (Rummenhöller op cit.:73).

However, the Dominicans were strongly opposed to the horrors perpetuated by the rubber barons. They attempted to get a law passed stopping slavery and Padre Aza went to Lima to voice their criticism. But although the complaints were loud, they were also general. On specific instances they were more muted because many of the perpetrators were supporters of the mission. As happened in the Putumayo case, Peru's President, the authoritarian Leguía, was not interested.

Madre de Dios became a Department during the Presidency of Billinghurst in 1912. Throughout the next decade, San Jacinto was the starting point for missionising the Ese'eja, and proselytisation increased as the rubber boom declined. A mission was opened in the Tahuamanu river in 1921 under Padre Alvarez. In 1930 the mission station of Lago Valencia was established. Meanwhile the end of the rubber boom in Manu led to a mass exodus from the mission of San Luis in 1922. It was moved to Pantiacolla, close to the Wachipaeri.

The aim was to work mainly with the Matsigenka, who did not take to the missionaries. Within four years the Pantiacolla mission closed down and the missionary work was moved to Puerto Maldonado (Fuentes op.cit.:22).

The missions' work with the Ese'eja of the river Tambopata brought the priests into increasing contact with Harakmbut, primarily Toyeri and Arasaeri. During the 1930s there was an invasion of gold seekers into the territory of the Arasaeri on the Araza (Marcapata) river. Padre Alvarez took one trip up the Araza in 1935 and reached the Karene. He stayed only long enough to ascertain that the people there were Harakmbut speakers (Barriales & Torralba op.cit:31).

The central and most dangerous area of the Madre de Dios was still considered to be the Karene (Moro op cit.:287,467–8; Sarasola 1929:31–2). Having ascertained that the people living between the Inambari and Upper Madre de Dios were of the same language family, the priests, using the name 'Mashco' for them, made the Harakmbut the primary objective of missionary work over the next twenty years.

From 1940, Padre Alvarez established friendly relations with the Sapiteri, who in the previous decade had lived near and fought the Wachipaeri because they were unwilling to trade goods such as knives and machetes. Having lost in warfare, their chief Paijaja now hoped to obtain similar goods from the priests. The priests, however, wanted Paijaja to help them reach their ultimate goal, those people farthest into the interior of the area – the Arakmbut.

Between October 1941 and February 1942, José Alvarez and Padre Gerardo Fernández returned to the Karene. Padre Alvarez wanted to enter the headwaters of the Karene and cross to the Upper Madre de Dios but this was impossible because of the Arakmbut. Paijaja then agreed, somewhat reluctantly, to return to his homeland and take the missionaries around via Manu to the Upper Madre de Dios, penetrating the Nahuene river where he contacted the Sapiteri of the area – called Sirineri (Alvarez 1942; Barriales & Torralba 1970: 31ff). The Arakmbut were surrounded and the Dominicans established their presence in the area to prepare for the final strike on the Arakmbut.

The establishment of the Dominican presence in the Madre de Dios demonstrates that the problems they encountered with the Arakmbut were by no means unique. In May 1943, the mission San Miguel de Kaichihue was established on an affluent of the Inambari, consisting of a large farm with yuca and plantains, maize, rice, etc., a small chapel, and buildings for the missionaries (Alvarez 1944).

Over the next three years Arasaeri, Pukirieri, Toyeri, and Sapiteri all came to the mission. San Miguel became the base for all expeditions into the Arakmbut area over the next ten years. Accounts of the mission show that at this time the recently contacted Harakmbut were disappearing fast.

> At the same time, and with much grief, the groups of Mashcos which were all their [the missionaries'] hope were moving away or disappearing: those from the Nahuene were victims of influenza; those from the Sirive killed by enemies, those from Jinnue and Huasorokhue, went over to civilised people of doubtful morality; those of the Pukiri returned to their dominion; the Wachipaeri we have just learnt had been totally exterminated by smallpox (Alvarez, J. 1952:64).

Although the Wachipaeri were not completely decimated, the effects of these smallpox epidemics were disastrous. The Sapiteri from the Nahuene, Ishiriwe, and Wasorokwe were the most seriously affected by disease. They had been the main enemies of the Arakmbut in the war and as a result, during the 1940s, the people who had been fighting with the Arakmbut since the turn of the century and before began to move from their homelands to the mission.

> For almost four years, there was no corner which he (José Alvarez) did not reach, except for the place where no one wished to accompany him, the Arakmbut region. From each trip, he returned to the mission of Kaichihue with a new group of Mashcos (Barriales nd:57).

According to Martín (1946:57), a local Harakmbut leader behaved to the others as if he were head of all the mission, making the Sapiteri 'surrender' to him. The relations between the groups were not good, and illness is a constant feature of the descriptions. In 1947 there were reports of Arakmbut travelling as far as the Kaichihue itself and attacking the mission. This would imply that there had been a massive depopulation throughout the headwaters of the Karene and that the Arakmbut were pursuing their former enemies in the hope of raiding some goods such as knives or machetes. The situation in Kaichihue become so bad that in 1952 the mission was closed. Those from the mission station travelled down the Pukiri where they currently live.

The Dominicans are, to this day, proud of their work in the homelands of the Harakmbut, which some missionaries call a 'conquest' (Rummenhöller op. cit.:82) and others a 'liberation' (Barriales op.cit: 57). The initial 'taming' or controlling of their lives by pacification and reduction into missions was preparation for the main aim of subjugating their souls. The spiritual conquest meant to destroy the existing beliefs to which the Harakmbut were 'enslaved' and to 'liberate' them into the Christian faith. They would then be prepared for the world of progress and integration into the national Peruvian society (Wahl 1987:141).

The Dominican history of contact with the Arakmbut has been written many times, because in those terms, it represented the greatest achievement of missionary activity in Peru. Fresh from a trip to Europe where he had met with General Franco and Pope Pius XII, in August 1950, Padre Alvarez and a group of eight indigenous followers penetrated Arakmbut territory from the river Shintuya. After four days the party met an estimated hundred and fifty Arakmbut on the Ishiriwe.[1] They appeared hostile but not violent and allowed them to leave after promises to return with gifts.

The second trip to the Ishiriwe was prepared for the following year. Several aerial reconnaissance trips were made. In December 1951, the missionaries returned to the Arakmbut. In spite of another apparently hostile reception, Padre Alvarez handed out his gifts. During the night the people sent messages to other Arakmbut to come from the Ishiriwe, Wandakwe, and Kipodnwe. These arrived in great numbers seeking gifts too. By now the Dominican gift supply was exhausted and the hostility and disappointment of the Arakmbut was intense. After three days waiting, the group was given permission to leave by the local leader who sent them two arrows (Alvarez 1952).

Padre Alvarez followed up these visits with trips to the Arakmbut from the upper Karene in November 1952, where he learnt that the reception they had been receiving was not as hostile as they had thought (Alvarez 1953). The problem was that everyone wanted the goods that they brought. From the new mission station at Palotoa, the Dominicans repeated the same work pattern that they had practised at San Miguel de Kaichihue. They went on numerous expeditions to specific rivers, bringing back groups of Arakmbut to settle in the mission, and from 1956 Arakmbut groups arrived from Ishiriwe.

The Arakmbut version of these events are eye-witness accounts from the early 1950s. Old men from the Wandakwe and Kipodnwe rivers still remember their history around the period when the Dominicans came. The Wandakwe information comes from San

1. In spite of Padre Alvarez' writing that he encountered the Arakmbut on the Mberowe (Blanco) river, the Arakmbut themselves explain that he did not know where he was and that they met him on the Ishiriwe.

José and Barranco Chico and the Kipodneri information from Padre
Torralba when he was in Puerto Luz.

Wandakweri

The Wandakweri consisted of seven named groups. Each group had
the term *-eri* added to the stem, while the maloca itself was referred
to by the stem plus the suffix *-ote*. Thus the Pewingboteri lived in the
pewingbote maloca. The Pewingboteri were called Wakutangeri by
the other Arakmbut because they lived nearer to the headwaters of
the Wandakwe. This name has survived. The names, in descending
order of the river, are: Pewingboteri, Atayoteri, Apikmboteri, Yaw-
idnpoteri, Kukamberi, Sakimboteri, and Kipodniritneri.

Kipodneri

The Kipodneri consisted of five named groups: Chitoeri, Kupibem-
poeri, Panketapoeri, Kapiteri, and Endoweteri. It appears that
between 1950 and 1952 the Kipodneri moved to the upper Karene
and eventually united in the Wasorokwe river in the headwaters of
the Karene (Moore nd.). This was before they had made contact
with the Dominicans (excluding the three Kipodneri who were killed
by the Fejos expedition). The Arakmbut knew that white people
existed long before there was permanent contact. They also knew
that outsiders were the source of knives and machetes. The move by
the Kipodneri to the upper Karene in 1952 was probably partly to
obtain these goods.

Several of the older members of San José described the first contact
the Wandakweri Arakmbut made with the Dominican missionaries in
the 1950s. First planes would fly overhead and drop machetes, knives,
and metal pots. The Wandakweri say that they moved in the early
1950s to get closer to the source of the trade goods – in their case they
moved towards the Upper Madre de Dios. The Wandakweri reorgan-
ised their malocas and a new alignment took place. The Pewingboteri
joined with the Yahuidnpoteri and moved from the Opagntapo affluent of the Wandakwe across to the headwaters of the Ishiriwe (the
Mboraiwe) and became known as Wakutangeri.

The Atayoteri, Sakimbiboteri, and some Apikmboteri moved to
the Arognka'wetapo on the Ishiriwe where they built a large maloca

with metal tools. They used aguaje leaves (*kotsimba*) for the first time to make their maloca and became known as Kotsimberis. Close to them another maloca was formed, combining the rest of the Apikmboteri and the Kukamboteri, which was renamed Jintapoeri. A few years later they moved closer to the Upper Madre de Dios to the Shirimawe river.

The final Wandakwe group to move were the Kipodnirtneri who kept their name, moving towards the Madre de Dios and possibly staying for a brief period further over to the Mberowe before they joined the other Harakmbut in the mission of Shintuya (see Map 4).

When the Wandakweri were on the Ishiriwe there came the news that Padre Alvarez (Apaktone) had arrived at the Mbognpetednwetapo and was coming to visit the Kotsimberis and the Jintapoeris. Ireyo tells the story as follows:

The Arrival of Apaktone

On a beach the ancestors of old were making toasted maize. Others had gone to look for catfish (ta'met). Some had gone to bring catfish and the rest stayed. When they were on the beach they met some Taka. The Arakmbut wanted to shoot them with arrows because they were afraid.

'Don't shoot me, brother,' said the Taka. The Arakmbut looked at the Taka and saw that he wore clothes. He said to them, 'Brother!' The Arakmbut looked at his shotgun. The women thought that it was a *weri* digging stick.

The Arakmbut had no clothes and went completely naked. The Padre had promised to give a machete to them. 'I will give you a machete. Have no fear!' he said. The Arakmbut became very happy. 'Have no fear!' he said to them. The Padre laughed. 'Ha! Ha! Ha! Have no fear, children.'

Mbariotakis did not know who the Padre was and said that he was Taka. The Padre gave a big machete to him and Mbariotakis lifted it up and then divided the big machete into pieces to give to each family. Each piece was a small blade with which they could make arrows. He divided it for all the families. The owner of the machete kept the handle. When the other Arakmbut heard that some had received these things, they also went to look for Taka.

On other occasions the Padre also gave machetes and knives and then, little by little, the Arakmbut moved towards Palatoa. They wanted to be on the Ishiriwe and did not want to go to the mission.

Map 4 Movement and Realignment of Arakmbut Malocas

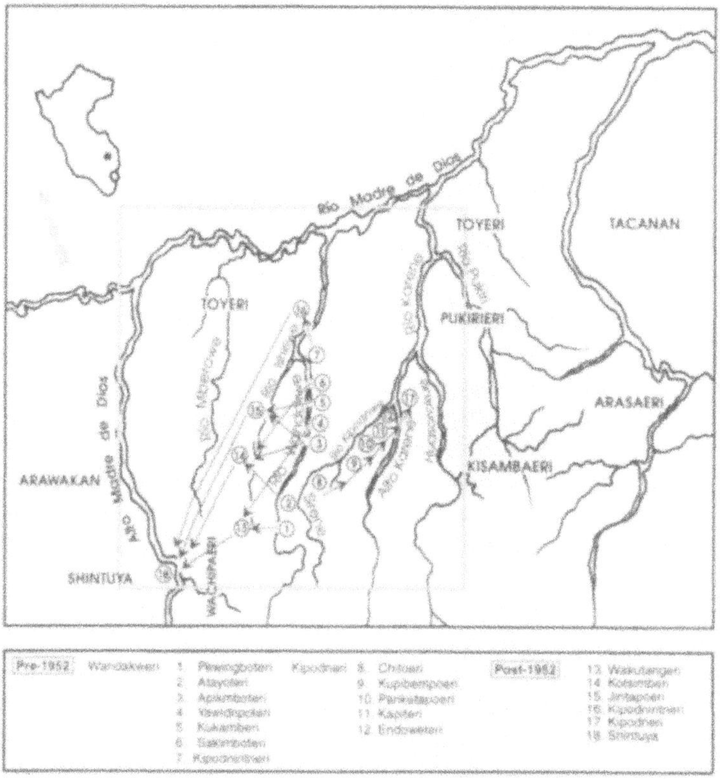

The Padre said to them, 'Let's go to the mission.' In Shintuya the Padre gave clothes, and in exchange the Arakmbut worked in the gardens. Padre Alvarez died and the Arakmbut went to San José. They only went to Shintuya because the Padre was there.

Before, when the first plane flew over the Arakmbut they nearly shot it. They say that the plane was hanging from a high tree. When the plane reached Ishiriwe it dropped machetes, sweets, and cartridges for a shotgun. The Arakmbut did not know cartridges and to fire them they wrapped them in a cloth and smashed them between large stones – boom! And after they threw the remains away.

Not all the Arakmbut were in favour of the Padre. Others said that they must kill him. As he was Taka he might kill Arakmbut. They met and made arrows to kill him. Then they stood on the opposite bank of the river and showed a white stone to the Padre saying that it was cotton so that he would come over quickly and the

Arakmbut could kill him. But the Padre did not come because he was afraid.

Wahl in Shintuya found other descriptions by the Arakmbut of the first contacts. She mentions the importance which western goods had for the Arakmbut but also mentions the illnesses which came at the same time as the goods falling from the sky.

> 'They say that during this same period great numbers of people began to die, thus concluding, whether rightly or not, that the clothing and food cans were the source of these deaths. They thus buried these goods and carefully washed all steel goods before using them' (Wahl op.cit.:256).

The Arakmbut in San José confirm that whereas the desire for metal goods and matches first attracted them to Padre Alvarez and Dominicans, it was sickness and death which led them to leave their homelands for good. Every adult person in San José had some close relative in the ascending generation who died during the 1950s. Yellow fever was particularly prevalent and eye diseases left people blinded overnight. The diseases came from outside and are now thought by the Arakmbut to have been connected to the souls of the thousands of Taka killed during the rubber boom.

The illness could not have been caused by normal forest spirits or they could have been cured. The sickness was the result of 'God's diseases', and consequently could only be cured by God's medicine. During the last years of the 1950s, the Arakmbut steadily made their way to Shintuya in the hope that they might be saved from decimation by the medicine of the Dominicans. Once in Shintuya they were caught – religious conquest and 'liberation' was to be their fate.

In December 1957, a flood destroyed the Palatoa mission which was resettled on the small river of Shintuya nearby. Shintuya was the site of the reduction of the Arakmbut by the Dominicans and remains there to this day. During the same year, the Summer Institute of Linguistics first appeared in the upper Karene and made contact with the Kipodneri who had united in the Wasorokwe river. The missionaries, Raymond Hart and Robert Tripp, returned by seaplane to visit the community of Puerto Alegre. Apart from the time when the Arakmbut from that area spent a short period in Shintuya, Puerto Alegre and, later Puerto Luz, remained largely independent from Dominican influence until 1979. However, all Arakmbut who were originally contacted by Padre Alvarez spent some time in Palatoa and Shintuya, and it is this experience which constitutes the second period in their history after the Great War.

'Reduction' in missionary terms refers to the practice, carried out by the Jesuits in the early Spanish Empire, of bringing together indigenous peoples into a settlement which was run rather as a large community farm under the auspices of the missionaries. The Dominicans in Madre de Dios carried out this model in San Luis del Manu, Palatoa, Kaichihue, Lago Valencia, and the mission to which it was moved in 1948, El Pilar, constructed through the generosity of Máximo Rodríguez, the rubber baron.

The banner used by the missionaries is that of Saint Michael fighting the dragon of savage superstition (Wahl op.cit.:258). The arrival of the Arakmbut in Shintuya has been presented by the missionaries as a triumph for the Saint: 'What pride we have to know that those who were called "fierce Mashcos" live united, forming a community with Priest, Primary School, medical post and a new Church' (SMD nd:74). Shintuya held up to five hundred indigenous people, and the priests carried out a 'civilising' plan for the Arakmbut.

In the early 1960s, Shintuya contained three hundred and fifty Arakmbut and Wachipaeris. For the Arakmbut, who were used to living in groups of from fifty to a hundred people, this was a major change in lifestyle. Most of the maloca groups split up and made their own settlements within the radius of the mission, with those who lived nearer the missionaries being more integrated into the sphere of the mission (Fuentes op.cit:167).

From the missionary perspective, education and production were the main features of 'civilising' and were closely tied to religion. During the first years of schooling, the boys were separated from the girls, and those boys considered bright enough were sent away to Quillabamba School in the Ceja de Selva of Cusco, where they were educated in Spanish and trained in farming methods on the hacienda. Meanwhile the priests tried to organise ways in which the reduction could subsist.

Whether cattle, agricultural goods, or, more recently, lumber, the missionaries have kept a close rein on the marketing of any surplus produced in order that the Arakmbut avoid exploitation by outside middlemen. Shintuya received its land title several years in advance of the independent Arakmbut communities in the name of the mission.

The main problem in Shintuya, however, which the Arakmbut mention frequently, was that they lived in close proximity to so many other people. Padre Torralba (pers.comm.) explains that in the early days in Shintuya it was not clear which people belonged to which group; when Padre Alvarez met groups on the Ishiriwe (although he thought he was on the Mberowe), it was clear that they did not all come from that area. Some could have been on hunting trips, others visiting relatives. Documentation of each person was not very clear, and so the priests did not realise that they frequently transgressed the social system of the Arakmbut.

Relationships between the Wachipaeri and the Arakmbut deteriorated over the first few years together in Shintuya. According to the older members of San José, the Arakmbut initially got on well with the Wachipaeri and joined in their masato fiestas. Before, the Arakmbut did not have masato but had chicha made from maize. Disputes with the Wachipaeri arose over relationships with the priests concerning goods and women.

Wahl (op. cit:268) accounts for this in the shift which took place in the relationship with goods from outside. During the period of contact Padre Alvarez had attracted the Arakmbut to the missions with gifts of highly desirable goods, but once they were in the mission, these became commodities which were available only to those who behaved correctly. The missionaries thus held the power and the economic initiative, which ultimately bred resentment among those who lost out.

The problems over women arose from the shortage of eligible female marriage partners and the priests, unaware of Arakmbut practices, arranged inappropriate marriages and ignored unacceptable liaisons. Sorcery accusations arose, and at least two women were put to death by Arakmbut. Apart from a few marriages with Wachipaeri and Matsigenka, of whom there were a few in the mission, the Arakmbut largely continued to marry within and between their groups.

In Shintuya the Arakmbut lived in their communal house groups. There were four main divisions: Wakutangeri, Kotsimberi, Kipodniridneri, and Jintapoeri. The Wakutangeri were most opposed to the priests and generally discontented. One night in 1969 they escaped from the mission. Over the next three years the Kotsimberi and the Kipodniridneri left. The Jintapoeri remained in Shintuya.

The story of the escape from Shintuya takes the form of a mythical story about the founding of San José del Karene:

The Padres were a problem in Shintuya but the Wachipaeris were to blame. They had killed several people by sorcery. Then people started to die, people became sick and died. Even the dogs were dying. The people decided to go secretly. The night was chosen. An old man had heard of a river called 'Colorado'(Karene) where there were good beaches and lots of animals. The shamanic dreamer 'Psyche' dreamt when they should go.

The night of the escape the people prepared. The whole village area just down from Shintuya was cleared. From every house and every part of the patio, all the rubbish from the kitchens was thrown into the river. This was to prevent sorcery, which takes place by a person getting a part of someone's property – hair is a favourite – and blowing on it. Thus the whole area was cleared and the canoes were filled with all their belongings. As they left they heard the dogs howling; they had been left behind with the chickens, ducks and pigs.

The Arakmbut went downriver all night. The next day they heard a forty horsepower motor. They landed and hid the boats and themselves on the bank of the river. The 40 h.p. passed but was not the Padre so they went back to the river and continued the voyage.

They passed the first river [Mberowe] and asked Psyche: 'Is this the Colorado?'.

'No', he said.

They went on. At the second river [the Ishiriwe], they asked: 'Is this the Colorado?'

'No', he said. The third river he said was the Colorado.

It had taken three days to get there. They started to go up the river. Again they asked twice if this was the Pukiri but he said no. Eventually they found the Pukiri and stopped there. They lived on the beach below the Pukiri for half a year where they had a temporary camp. But the floods made them move up the Pukiri to where Chauchau lives today. They stayed there a half a year but their things were stolen and they asked Psyche where to go.

He dreamed about the place upriver. The waweri told him to go. They went upriver to the *widnba* pebble beach where they made a permanent camp. In the second year there was a big flood which came up to the stilted floor of the huts.

One family moved up the Kiraswe and lived there for a while. One day after fishing there the woman had an attack and her head ached and she could not sleep or even talk. They carried her back to the village where she later died. With this her house was burnt and everything destroyed. Then they all lived in another spot on the beach.

Mariano (colonist) lived the other side but he had few or no chacras. The people needed to go up to Puerto Alegre for seeds to plant their chacras. At this time, one man stole a wife from Puerto Alegre. The Puerto Alegre people stopped at the San José and tried to steal another wife. There was a lot of fighting. They went away and came back later. They used fists with stones in their hands. The fight went on and although Puerto Alegre did not get the women they inflicted enough injuries to win.

That night Psyche asked the waweri why they had not helped him and why his people had suffered defeat. He went to his bed and at that moment a great storm arose upriver. The Puerto Alegre people out on the beach had their encampment washed away. Despite Psyche's victory, the San José people decided to go up to Puerto Alegre. They waited on the opposite side of the river and shouted insults across. Then, to the satisfaction of the people of Puerto Alegre, the San José people went into the forest. The Puerto Alegre people crossed but the San José people returned with sticks and a big fight started again. Eventually it was finished and peace was made.

When the San José people were in the Pueblo Viejo, the good Padre Antonio made it up. He offered them cattle and wood, schools etc. He came up from the Mission of El Pilar near Puerto Maldonado. To get there he stopped overnight at the Tres Islas. At that time there were Taka there and he was bewitched and died. They took his body for burial. This is why San José has nothing now. Antonio would have made it there but he was bewitched.

After a second flood the people moved San José to its present site. This is the history of San José.

The account of the origin of San José del Karene describes a change which comes as dramatically as the period of contact and entering the mission of Shintuya in 1960. The story deals with a break and a re-establishment of relations on Arakmbut terms. The situation in Shintuya shows the Arakmbut in conflict with both the priests and the Wachipaeri. After the escape they fought and eventually made peace with the people of Puerto Alegre, who eventually moved downriver to found Puerto Luz. They also began to re-establish relations with the mission. However the loss of Padre Antonio meant that the community could not rely any more on the charity of outsiders. The story is frequently told and has taken on several points which have spiritual characteristics. Psyche's dream interpretations revolve around the three rivers and three camps the third of which are the rivers Karene and the present site of San José.

The escape from the mission was the corollary of contact and the decision to go to Shintuya. The deaths coupled with hope of a brighter future led them to move and the feeling that they were escaping was undoubtedly justified. When families from Shintuya left, one of the Padres would take the 40 h.p. canoe to pick them up and bring them back. Several of the children of the founders of San José were in Quillabamba at the time of the exodus from Shintuya and it was several years before they were finished in their schools and were able to join their parents on the Karene river.

The flights from Shintuya over the next three years caused some commotion in the Mission (Torralba 1979:83-5). Some missionaries said that the Arakmbut just did not appreciate civilisation, while others understood that they had rejected a mission ideology which was incompatible with their traditional life. The Dominicans tried to heal the rift by making anthropological analyses of the problem and by sending priests up to the villages.[2] In spite of this, the decision to leave the Mission propelled the Arakmbut into a completely new episode of their history.

The Arakmbut who established their village on the banks of the Karene appeared very different to those who had entered the mission ten years previously. A substantial number of changes had taken place in their lifestyle since they had been living with the priests and making contact with the national Peruvian society. The first and most noticeable change was that they no longer lived in malocas. An Arakmbut, telling me of the move from Shintuya, mentioned that when they first reached the Pukiri they made a communal house, but in the end continued to live in family houses which had been encouraged by the missionaries in Shintuya and was the norm among white people and highlanders.

The Arakmbut were returning to the homeland of the Harakmbut and found various colonists and indigenous peoples in the area living in individual family houses. The Sapiteri of the Pukiri, who had come from the Kaichihue mission fifteen years previously, and the Arakmbut of Puerto Alegre, who had only been in Shintuya for a short while, had also abandoned communal houses. The people of San José followed suit.

The communal effect of living in a maloca was preserved to some extent by arranging the houses in a circle, frequently around a football pitch which took the place of the open space in the centre of the house. But there were several other features which the Arakmbut no longer continued after their period in Shintuya. They no longer performed their rites of initiation – the e'ohotokoy and the e'mbaipak festivals. These would normally take place in the central part of the maloca and were fundamental entries into adolescence. In the same way, the dances and songs associated with the rituals were no longer practised and the detailed body painting (Califano: 1982: 102–3), feathered crowns, and percussion instruments which had been part of the ceremonies were rarely, if ever, apparent in San José. The

2. An article by Alain Monnier (1982) analyses some of the explanations the missionaries made of the failure at Shintuya. He discusses the way in which anthropological techniques were used to ascertain whether missionary work could take more account of indigenous culture and institutions. However he sees the ultimate problems as lying in the missionary work itself.

tayagnpi is occasionally seen in the community but it is not used for ceremonial purposes.

When asked why they no longer carry out their rituals, the Arakmbut replied that they stopped in Shintuya because there was no need to perform them. One or two say that they were ridiculed by the priests, and the other indigenous peoples in the mission who did not practice these rites may have been another factor. Robert Tripp (pers. comm.) says that even though the people of Puerto Alegre spent only a few months in Shintuya in 1956, they no longer built malocas or carried out their ceremonies afterwards. It would appear that the significance of the rituals was tied up with the maloca itself because the maloca was a microcosm of the universe (c.f. C. Hugh-Jones 1979:247). In its centre, the rituals and colourful ceremonies of the Arakmbut ensured the growth of boys to adulthood and public contact between people and the spirit world in order to reproduce social and cultural life.

A whole complex of Arakmbut culture disappeared after ten years in the mission at Shintuya, consisting of all visible aspects of their culture connected with ceremonial contact with the spirit world. These made sense primarily in the context of living in a communal house and once that was gone all aspects of the culture connected to that disappeared. However, the Arakmbut held on to the 'invisible' aspects of their culture which they could easily hide. Myths and stories continued to be passed on within households, although there are still examples of public storytelling. Many of the children in the Arakmbut communities are familiar with the general outlines of the main myths and a smattering of stories, although the details remain with those recognised as being good storytellers, such as Ireyo, in San José.

Dreaming and confidence in the spirit world remained as strong as ever among the Arakmbut after the period in Shintuya, and curing practices, contact for hunting, and seeking advice from spirits continued to take place regularly. However, myth telling, dreaming, and curing need not be at all apparent to the casual visitor to the community because the Arakmbut have 'internalised' their cosmology. Discussing the spirit world with outsiders is difficult for the Arakmbut and they are reluctant to talk about their religion to strangers in case the listener does not take them seriously.

Whereas the loss of the maloca affected the ceremonial life of the Arakmbut, it also changed aspects of their social life. The households are now more separate from one another than they were in the past, although there were occasionally some individual houses outside of the maloca. They were built by families who were moving in or out and who had not been integrated into the community as a whole. Now all the houses are separate and the ceremonial rites which bound the community together cannot take place in the open air. The communal chacras have also been replaced on a parallel level by gardens for each household as described in chapter three.

There is a connection between the 'internalisation' of Arakmbut cosmology and the replacement of the malocas with individual households. The maloca was the central point for social and religious community action and when the Arakmbut stopped living in their malocas, outward ceremony stopped and religion became more internalised. During their period in Shintuya the Arakmbut ceremonies were replaced by Christian rituals which took place every Sunday in the church, and when the Arakmbut moved to San José this ceremonial aspect itself disappeared.

Whereas the mission contributed to the destruction of the visible signs of religion, it also caused Arakmbut resentment, which led to an internalisation of indigenous religious life. This had the effect of preserving Arakmbut heritage from pre-mission times, through the period at the mission and into contemporary native communities. While internalising their own religion, the Arakmbut have 'externalised' Christianity, dividing the world clearly into their own religion, which they try to control, and the religion of 'God' which the priests and white people claim to control. Even though 'God's diseases' are cured by 'God's medicine', the Arakmbut consider that their own inner religion is the more powerful (cf. chapter seven).

Another change which took place during the period in the mission has affected contemporary life for the Arakmbut. While in the mission the priests acted as intermediaries in several ways. The first was in relations between the Arakmbut and the Christian God. The moralistic notions of right and wrong or correct and incorrect behaviour were instilled by the missionaries as a part of what they termed the 'civilising' process. Good and evil were bound up with a Christian ethic stemming from one powerful source – God. As with indigenous ethics, power is at issue, but whereas the transgression for the Arakmbut has a direct result based on the invisible causality of the spirit world, in the mission, transgression was determined by the intermediary of God, namely the priest. It was the priest who decided what is and is not appropriate behaviour (Wahl op.cit:273–5 and 283).

The priests did not simply reward appropriate Arakmbut behaviour with the promise of an afterlife; those who conformed to the strictures of the mission were considered worthy of benefitting from the advantages held by the power of the priests, such as western goods or support in their lumber, cattle, or coffee cultivation. In Shintuya, the priests stood, and still stand, as intermediaries in the hierarchy between God and the Arakmbut, channelling benefits through their second intermediary position linking the Arakmbut to outside economic interests. The mission thus supported capitalist ventures, provided credit, and heavily influenced the economic decisions made by the Arakmbut in the mission (Fuentes op.cit.: 190).

The missions tried to train the Arakmbut as small-scale farmers, using cattle, coffee, and more recently lumber work to subsidise their subsistence economy, but constantly kept a paternalistic eye over their activities. The Arakmbut were thus never entirely able to deal with the national capitalist system directly while they lived in Shintuya. In their concern for ensuring that the Arakmbut became proselytised and were not exploited by dealers and traders, the missionaries became intermediaries between the Arakmbut and the outside world of Peruvian society, both spiritually and economically.

By leaving the mission the Arakmbut rejected the mediating role of the priests, both in terms of deciding what was good or evil and the possibility of making money or being exploited by the capitalist system. The mission had furthermore acted as a regulator for marriages and decided over educational matters. The Arakmbut realised that while in the mission they would be neither rich nor poor, good nor evil, educated nor uneducated; they were held in a sedentary world where they were effectively in a limbo between their own internalised inner religious world and the external world of Peru.

The tensions between the Arakmbut groups and with the Wachipaeri arose in a highly concentrated settlement where the ultimate arbitrators were the priests. It was easy for missionaries to exploit these conflicts in order to obtain compliance with their plans for the mission. Conflict thus constantly arose in competition for access to resources such as money, goods, women, grace from God, and education. Whereas the priests were not necessarily hatred, tensions arose from the intricate socio-cultural relationships between the different Arakmbut maloca groups and with the Wachipaeri. The form in which the tensions emerged were accusations of sorcery against other groups, rather than aggression against the priests. However, the accusations were primarily directed at those in whom the missionaries appeared to have the most confidence (Fuentes op. cit.:186).

The period in Shintuya introduced the Arakmbut to the national society with which they had had no contact before the late 1950s. Production of cash crops, money, and trading were all aspects of the external world of which they were increasingly aware. A growing generation of young men was taken from their parents and instructed in Spanish and agricultural methods. All of the Arakmbut were pressurised strongly to convert to Christianity and were taught about the existence of good and evil. In spite of these strategies of conversion, forty years of Christian proselytising seems to have been markedly superficial and has had minimal effect on Arakmbut religion and spirituality (Padre Mixtel Fernández pers. comm.). Furthermore, many Arakmbut say that they appreciate the efforts which missionaries made to bring education and technical knowledge to their people. They consider that, even though the missionaries imposed a new way of life, if they had been left to fend for themselves against the colonists who were beginning to come into the area in the 1950s, the Arakmbut could have shared the fate of the Toyeri.

The escape from Shintuya took place as a result of several factors: the concentration of peoples from different groups in one settlement; the loss of ceremonies and exchange patterns which aid social and cultural harmony; and the internalisation of Arakmbut religion which left a public vacuum, increasingly filled by the priests in their role as spiritual and economic intermediaries with the world outside of the mission. The increase in accusations of sorcery demonstrates that a break down of relations between the Arakmbut peoples in Shintuya was taking place.

When the Arakmbut escaped from Shintuya and gradually made their way to San José del Karene they were asserting their independence from the power of the missionaries and other powerful Harakmbut people, while creating a new social and cultural existence for themselves. The establishment of the native community became a replacement for the maloca and the ceremonies which went with it. Instead of expressing relationships with the outside world on the basis of one Harakmbut group to another, the Arakmbut had to re-create a relationship with an external world which had been cushioned by the priests. The vacuum was filled with the very issues which the missionaries had kept at bay control over economic production, spiritual morality, education, and, above all, the political power of self-determination.

◁ Chapter 12 ▷

THE ARAKMBUT COMMUNITY
AND THE GOLD RUSH

On the night in 1980 when the news arrived in San José del Karene of the death of Anastasio Somoza, ex-dictator of Nicaragua, there was a fiesta. The Arakmbut opened some bottles of beer and celebrated. The reason for this rejoicing was that the community of San José knew that an international company called Central American Services wanted to utilise five thousand hectares of their land, already in the process of titling, for cattle ranches. They also knew that Central American Services was largely financed by money from the Somoza fortune.[1]

By this time the Arakmbut from Shintuya had been ten years in San José del Karene. They were working gold, had their own school, and were about to make contact with the national organisation for indigenous peoples of the Amazon in Peru – AIDESEP (Asociación Interetnica de Desarrollo de la Selva Peruana). The community was self-sufficient and managed itself independently in the face of pressures from outsiders. The Arakmbut had changed considerably since their period in Shintuya, and yet they were still as much Arakmbut as ever.

During the previous twenty years, as the Arakmbut began to relate with the outside world through the mediation of the Dominican missionaries, the exploitation of the resources of the Madre de Dios had increased substantially. After the rubber boom, cattle and agriculture

---

1. For more on this see Moore (1980:457). This article is a very useful summary of oil, gold, and other multinationals working in the Madre de Dios, most of which are still there or have concessions to which they can return.

had been the main economic occupation of colonists in the area. Máximo Rodríguez, the rubber baron, had even built himself a massive business based on these alternatives to rubber until the 1940s. Apart from an interest in gold in the river Araza during the 1930s and 1940s and a rise in rubber production during the Second World War when Japan occupied the Southeast Asia plantations, the expansion of economic interest in the Madre de Dios was limited in comparison to the period of the rubber boom. In the late 1940s, flights to Cusco became more frequent and brazil nuts became a major export crop for the Department. According to Rummenhöller (1985:93), there are twenty-six commercially viable species of wood in the Madre de Dios, and in the 1950s wood production increased throughout the region. The timber economy spread during that decade from Puerto Maldonado to the Manu and the Upper Madre de Dios. The mission of Shintuya linked itself into this economic system and used its direct access to Cusco by road via Paucartambo as an outlet for the timber logged by the Harakmbut.

The opening of the road from Cusco to Puerto Maldonado via Quincemil in 1961 opened up more possibilities for people moving into the Madre de Dios, particularly for trading on the rivers. Throughout the 1960s and 1970s oil companies explored the Madre de Dios, and in 1973 Cities Service and the Andes Petroleum Company explored in Shintuya and Puerto Alegre respectively. The Dominican missionaries in Shintuya and the Summer Institute of Linguistics in Puerto Alegre took the position of accommodating the companies while trying to prevent any harm coming to the communities. An analysis of what took place in Puerto Alegre (Moore 1979) is particularly revealing about the role of the Summer Institute of Linguistics in an Arakmbut community. However, it was the gold rush of the 1970s and 1980s which put Madre de Dios on the economic map of Peru.

When the Arakmbut determined to take their future into their hands and leave the mission in 1969 and after, they had to re-establish themselves on traditional Harakmbut territory. But it was impossible for them to return to the life they had lived before contact because after ten years in the mission they had learnt of the advantages and disadvantages of life outside Arakmbut malocas. At the same time the social and cultural mechanisms which they had used to deal with other Harakmbut became unnecessary because of the vast decrease in population. They consequently had to re-establish a community which inter-related with a different external world – a world made up predominantly of Amikos, or non-indigenous people, who previously had a mythological position in the Arakmbut universe.

The Arakmbut have revived in new ways the lost socio-cultural features from their past such as communal activities, particularly feasts, the defence of their territory from outsiders, and the utilisation of spiritual power and knowledge from invisible sources. At the same time, during the 1970s, the Arakmbut gradually became more immersed in relations with the national and international society. The new conditions in which they lived forced them to seek means to redefine their lives.

This chapter looks at the restructuring of Arakmbut social life in the formation of the community and at how they relate with the external world. The most significant areas which we should look at in order to understand this process are gold and the formation of the 'native community'.

Gold

Gold was mined in the Madre de Dios area from Inca times. There were gold diggers on the trail to Tambopata in 1907 and in the 1930s the Arasaeri faced the consequences of a boom in prices. However, from the early 1970s, the potential for gold work in the Madre de Dios became apparent on a hitherto unprecedented scale. When the Arakmbut first moved to San José they did a small amount of gold washing, but it was not until 1978 that all the Arakmbut com-munities – Puerto Luz (previously Puerto Alegre), Barranco Chico, San José, and Boca Inambari – regularly began to mine.

The gold is found in the rivers mixed with sand and pebbles. It comes from the Andes from where it is washed down annually in the rainy season to be deposited on beaches. Gold deposits, or 'placers', are worked either on the sides of the rivers or inland in the dried up beds of old streams. Inland finds are usually richer but involve dig-ging large quantities of earth while the beaches need less digging but produce less gold and are exposed to the sun and insects. Usually the Arakmbut work inland, particularly in the wet season (October to March) when the beaches are flooded. They will seek out an area and, if it is far from the main village, will construct an encampment where they will live for the few months it will take to mine the area. The workers will return to San José once a week to collect goods from the chacras and swap news.

The method of finding gold deposits is not unlike hunting. Small groups of 'hunters' go into the forest and test the ground or the beaches by sieving sand in the water or prodding with a rod to find old river beds. They return to the village and discuss with their close kin who will work together to mine the area. The clearing of topsoil down to the pebbles can take up to a week. When the pebbles appear, a wooden sieve is constructed and the stones, dug out with pick and shovel, are conveyed in a wheelbarrow up to the sieve where a man stands with buckets of water, or, more common now, a pipe attached to a motor pump. The water washes the pebbles and sand away while sacking under the sieve holds the black sand which contains the gold, which is preserved in buckets and later mixed with mercury, which draws together the gold dust. The mixture is then panned by the riverside and the mercury is burnt off leaving the gold.

The social organisation of gold work varies according to the circumstances. In the early 1980s when motor pumps were scarce, large groups of men would work together around a pump linked by clan ties. Since then, as people began to afford pumps, the groups have become smaller, consisting of siblings or in-laws (particularly sons-in-law and fathers-in-law working together). In San José women, when they do work gold, tend to do it on a small scale with a parallel operation to the men and without motor pumps. In Puerto Luz and Barranco Chico, on the other hand, family clusters of wives and husbands work together on the gold rather in the same way that they do in the chacras. Predicting the organisation of gold work is not possible because each community has created its own means of carrying out tasks. As of 1985, San José's model paralleled hunting while Puerto Luz' was more similar to horticulture. However since both communities are now bringing in their own peons these arrangements may well develop in new directions.

Gold is exchanged at Boca Colorado at the mouth of the Karene river. The Arakmbut use the money to buy the following types of items. The value of the items has changed over the years since they started working gold.

1) Capital expenditure: This consists of motor pumps, outboard motors and equipment for gold mining, shotguns etc. These goods were originally brought by the priests and were jointly owned by several households in the community. Since 1980, however, numbers of these capital goods have increased considerably and are now the property of each extended household.

2) Food: Another change that has taken place since the Arakmbut started working gold is the development of the subsistence econ-

omy. In 1980 goods such as pasta, rice, oil, salt, and sugar were special commodities which could be bought with the money from the gold. However by 1985 the Arakmbut were insistent that without these basic necessities they could not survive.

3) Prestige goods: These goods are mainly the aim of young men and newlyweds establishing their position in the community. They include goods such as radios, tape recorders, and battery gramophone players. Records and tapes of Amazonian music are very popular for dancing.

4) Beer: Alcohol is probably the largest single item of expenditure after the capital goods. In 1980, beer fiestas involving the whole village took place every three weeks or so. In 1985 the drinking parties were smaller and more frequent but fiestas involving most or all of the community did continue to take place about every six weeks or whenever a sizable number of the community were together.[2]

The effect of the gold has been twofold. First of all the gold economy has been grafted onto the subsistence economy of hunting, fishing, gathering and horticulture without establishing a dual economy of subsistence in opposition to gold. The Arakmbut consider themselves to be miners. In 1985 the threats to their gold placers from colonists was a major preoccupation and they were certain that if gold dropped out of their lives, they would not survive (Gray 1986).

The second effect of the gold economy has been highly significant in terms of creating a replacement for the loss of the communal life of the malocas. In the past, fiestas involved not only members of a maloca but visitors from neighbouring houses. Women made the wawing chicha and there would be formal invitations to other malocas. People came and were served by the women who controlled the manufacture and distribution of the chicha. Dancing and singing took place and the fiestas were a prime opportunity to establish relations, complain or fight out differences in formal duels. Nowadays the beer is bought at the Boca Colorado trading post and at a recently established village shop. A person organises the festivities acting as host. Beer is drunk while rum and cherry brandy are distributed in a circle of men. Everyone drinks until they are drunk (e'simbore); the older men sing old songs while

2. For a detailed statistical view of the gold mining profits from San José and Boca Inambari see Rummenhöller (1987). For a more general view of gold mining in the Amazon, with an extremely useful analysis of the social organisation of non-indigenous mining settlements, see Clearly (1989).

the young men dance to Amazon music and eventually pass out or fight over some problem.

The fiestas have the effect of continuing social traditions, on a more informal basis. However, there is one major difference. Women no longer control the supply of beer. As a result, the men are drunk far more often than before; even more important are the effects on the responsibility and position of women in Arakmbut society. Previously, a woman who produced wawing would have to have managed her chacras well, possibly in co-operation with another household, and received the respect and prestige due to the wife of the host. Nowadays, however, the women are not responsible for the fermentation of the beer, and the men produce the money to buy and distribute it. The resulting loss of position for women is perhaps one of the factors behind the increasing inequality between men and women among the Arakmbut. This is discussed in more detail in Volume 2.

For the first time in their history, the people of San José and the other Arakmbut communities are forging a direct relationship with the wider socio-economic formation within Peru. Previously, contact with outsiders had been through intermediaries such as the Taka or the priests, but nowadays the Arakmbut manage their own affairs as a native community. Some of them are Peruvian citizens and they are familiar with many aspects of national life.

The first people with whom the Arakmbut have contact are the other miners in the vicinity of their community and the traders or merchants *(comerciantes)* who ply their goods to the community itself or else have stalls or shops at the bank trading post. Thomas Moore (1985c:180–183) says that the dominant economic sector of the Madre de Dios Department are these traders who on the whole came from the Cusco region over the last thirty years and made their money by importing goods which they sell at double or triple the prices found at the trading posts on the rivers. Some of them have settlements on the Karene and sell some basic commodities to the Arakmbut for high prices and sometimes get them into debt, but there is no evidence of Arakmbut working for these merchants on their lands.

The merchants and others who control transport and capital equipment in the area are often patrons. The patrons are known as *'medianos'* – medium-scale miners, to distinguish them from the large businesses whose owners usually do not live in the Madre de Dios. These medium miners live at sporadic distances down the Karene and up the Pukiri. They are reputed to be dangerous people who treat their workers badly. Several of them have met violent deaths at the hands of their workers. These peons live in awful conditions. They come from Cusco or Puno on contracts of several months and frequently are indebted to stay working for the patron. Documented cases of child labour and human rights abuses in the Madre de Dios have been published by Peruvian and international organisations (CODEH-PA-Sicuani 1983; Whittaker 1985).

It is estimated that most of the forty thousand miners who come down to the Madre de Dios to work gold are peons. The conditions of the semi-slaves has been so bad that they have been known to flee in order to work for native employers. The patrons in the Karene area have an ambivalent relationship with the Arakmbut which is mirrored throughout the Madre de Dios. On the one hand, the Arakmbut try to preserve peaceful relationships and avoid open conflict; on the other, they feel considerable resentment towards the patrons who live in their territories and extract resources from indigenous lands. Rummenhöller (1987:239–249) discusses the importance of ritual kinship (*compadrazgo*) with the local patrons. These relationships frequently enable a patron to grant credit to a villager in return for promised gold or a willingness to acquiesce to their presence on community lands. The consequences of these ties can give rise to internal divisions within the communities when conflicts with local patrons cause loyalties to be divided.

Gold miners who work without peons constitute one of the largest employment sectors in the Madre de Dios. The majority (90 percent) are '*pequeños mineros*' (artisan miners) who work individually or in small groups on the river banks. Although many now work on the Karene, particularly on the lands of Puerto Luz, San José is primarily surrounded by merchant patrons and their peons (currently there are over one thousand invaders on the lands of these communities). The indigenous people of the Madre de Dios who work gold are self-employed gold workers like the artisan miners, but even so they consider themselves to be different. They mine gold when they want to and do not maximise the financial benefits.

The Arakmbut do not work their gold in isolation and many local national, and international factors affect their lives. However, they do not fit blindly into a world economy which dictates the details of their lives. At each level – international, national, and local – other factors enter which prevent any overall determination of community economics from an international level. The effect is a complex pattern of overlapping influences and relations of exploitation which reach the Arakmbut at the local level.

Land and Community

The Arakmbut were affected by the gold rush and swarms of miners moved into the area. The river Pukiri was the main entry point, and concern was exacerbated by the expansion of the exploitation of the Karene. The numbers of peons increased, until by 1991 there were an estimated five hundred patrons, peons, and artisan miners living on San José's lands alone – five times the figure for 1981. This problem has been consistently ignored by the authorities, and the only way in which the Arakmbut have defended their lands has been through the legal concept of community.

Law No. 22175 was passed in 1978 which establishes guaranteed titling for officially recognised and constituted 'native communities'. The titles consist of a topographical survey of the community lands based on the extent of their daily subsistence activities, the potential of the land for pastoral and forest use, and ecologically protected areas such as the margins of rivers. The area defined has to undergo a complicated process of no less than twenty-six procedures, through largely unwilling bureaucrats, before it even reaches the Ministry of Agriculture in Lima. The titles for the Arakmbut communities were secured in 1986 thanks to the work of the community, the native federation FENAMAD, and technical assistance from the local environmental institution, Centro Eori.

With the Arakmbut campaign to obtain territorial rights, the importance of the native community emerged as a major factor of indigenous identity and proof of their connection to the land on which they lived. The Arakmbut, although they originated in the headwaters of the Karene and Ishiriwe, nevertheless consider all the area from the Inambari to the Upper Madre de Dios as the territorial homeland of the Harakmbut people and base their right to live there on hundreds, if not thousands, of years of occupation in the area. Indeed in 1991 FENAMAD and Eori began the process of getting much of this area recognised as a Harakmbut communal reserve. The Arakmbut word for territory and land is *wandari*. They use the term to cover both the idea of territory and the earth as a whole. *Oroedn wandari* means 'our land', 'our territory', or 'our earth', and currently refers to the community titles. The sense of ownership here is a communal one, in which territorial property is defined by social and spiritual relations and activated when sovereignty is infringed (this aspect of territoriality is discussed in Volume 3).

When discussing the concept of native community with the Arakmbut nowadays, it appears very clear that the concept does not simply

refer to the village but includes the territory and its indigenous offi-
cials. The officers of the community operate in conjunction with internal political systems (see Volume 2, chapters six to eight).[3] The village
itself is increasingly becoming a base for the Arakmbut, who spend
much of the year in different parts of their territories working gold. A
family will often hold two houses, the main one in the community and
a smaller but substantial construction at the gold camp. The Arakmbut
say that they move to these outlying areas of their community as a
form of patrol to stop illicit outsiders moving in. If they make full use
of the potential of their land area, people will think twice about invad-
ing their territory. Although this has not resulted in any of the merchant patrons who live on San José's land moving out, it has enabled
the Arakmbut to deter several potential invaders from their lands.

Thus the village itself is socially diffused throughout the Arakmbut's demarcated territory. The fixed area covered by their titles is
what the Arakmbut of San José see as constituting their community.
Their identity as community members comes no longer from the maloca but from their territory. The social space within the maloca for
entertaining friendly outsiders has been transformed too. In the past
there were special ceremonies for entering a different maloca, using
the tayagnpi and performing an oration, and at the end of the fiesta
the agonistic relationships between different communities were fought
out in duelling and drinking. Nowadays drinking takes place outside
in the open area outside their houses and formal fighting has, in many
respects, been overshadowed by football.

On several evenings a week, the Arakmbut play football on the
central patio on which most houses look. If any part of the village has
taken the place of the communal central part of the maloca it is the
football pitch. On Sundays, the Arakmbut sometimes take their boats
and go to play matches with local teams, both white and indigenous,
who sometimes come to San José as well. Thus the parties and the
football matches take place in the central part of the community. These
matches reflect relations with the colonists.[4]

In this way the social characteristics of the maloca have been separated. Its ability to unify the community at a fixed point in the uni-

3. Rosengren's analysis (1987) of the new leadership in a Matsigenka community is
   particularly relevant for its explanation of the lack of esteem for the office of
   President by traditional political leaders.
4. Rummenhöller (1987) says that we should not underestimate the importance of
   football matches in the Arakmbut native communities as a means of establishing
   internal and external relations. The agonistic element of the game is an important means of releasing tension (261–267).

verse has been taken over by the boundaries of the land titles, while its central locus for festivals and entertaining friendly visitors still operates through the football pitch and the patios outside the houses.

The Arakmbut have re-created a social and cultural system based on the communal house by transforming it into a native community. This has also happened to the original maloca groups. Although all Arakmbut recognise their maloca groups of birth, each community has formed itself so that it is coterminous with a new alignment. San José was the first community to be formed after leaving Shintuya in 1969 but it was followed by Barranco Chico and Boca del Inambari in 1971 and 1973. The maloca groups and native communities are:

Shintuya	Shintapoeri
San José	Wakutangeri
Puerto Luz	Kipodneri
Barranco Chico	Kotsimberi
Boca Inambari	Kipodniritneri

The Arakmbut used their maloca names to reorganise themselves during the mission period, drawing the groups together so that they merged with the native communities they were founding. However, this process took over a decade to come to fruition. It was not automatic but was the result of countless decisions taken at the community and household levels. Historically the maloca group has shifted according to context. With each reformulation of maloca groups people can change their loyalty. Even before contact there were plenty of examples of people shifting maloca allegiance if there were problems. The maloca groups shift and die, sometimes being reborn again in another place. However, the stable element in these processes is the clan, which provides both physical and spiritual continuity. In this way, as with women and spirit matter, the residential groups 'pass through' the clan line.

However at the same time it is possible to see this from another perspective. Through constant movements, clans have become distributed throughout maloca groups and communities. This occurs when men and women change maloca or community affiliation at different times in their lives. This movement usually involves marriage or elopement and takes place frequently enough to ensure a spread of clan membership throughout Arakmbut communities. The overall effect is that each community has a core of dominant clans with a selection of smaller groups sharing the same settlement. As was noted in chapter three, the majority of people from different communities are women marrying into the village. For this reason, a perspective which sees clans as dispersed throughout communities rather than concentrated in others constitutes the 'female' point of view, which accounts for why women have such a detailed knowledge of genealogical relationships in all of the other communities.

The effect is a complementary relationship connecting a patrilineal view of clan cores which remain constant as settlements change to a 'female' view where clans are constantly dispersed throughout settlements. This parallels the clan/wambet perspectives noted in the first part of this book and the visible/invisible gender orientations noted in the second part. Provided the two viewpoints operate in harmony, both views are possible. However, should the balance become uneasy, the shift provides us with the means for looking at social change; this is the subject of Volume 2.

These three examples consist of a complementarity between male/female, visible/invisible, and inside/outside which are brought together spatially in the maloca and now in the community. These features present a cycling through the clan, which ensures a controlled continuity for the Arakmbut socio-cultural existence complemented by a dispersion of the clan core throughout the Arakmbut world. It is this interplay of renewal and reproduction which enables the Arakmbut to remain themselves and change over time.

Until now, this section has looked at the changes which have taken place for the Arakmbut over the last forty years in terms of socio-cultural activities. It remains now to look at the interpretations of that history and how it is conceptualised by both indigenous and non-indigenous people.

History

When talking of history among the Arakmbut it is important to grasp the different perspectives which authors have produced. Until now, this part of the book has looked as history in the sense of creating life through praxis and practice. However the other aspect of history is interpretation and 'dialogue with the past'. Outsiders usually see history as a stream of events ready for interpretation and reconstruction. This distinction between event and interpretation establishes a gap between experience and its meaning which history tries to draw together by reconstructing views of events.

Non-indigenous scholars have presented Arakmbut history from several different perspectives. In a previous article (Gray 1987b: pp.

311-316) I have presented these as three alternatives, each divided into two:

1. Colonial Perspectives

'Colonial' refers here to the perspectives of people whose interests were in the resources of the Madre de Dios and who saw indigenous peoples as obstacles to its development. Erikson (Anon 1936) and Reyna (1942) discuss the history of the 'Mashcos' as elements in the 'march of progress', and according to them, if the Arakmbut act to prevent the drive to improve communications and establish colonies, then they have to be dealt with. Erikson's tear-gas and Reyna's uncritical descriptions of Fitzcarrald's killing of the indigenous people of the Madre de Dios demonstrate their lack of regard for the lives of those they saw standing in the way of their progress.

A less extreme colonial position was given to me orally by a gold miner working gold on the Pukiri in 1985. He told me that the Arakmbut were originally from the highlands and spoke a dialect of Quechua. According to this perspective, the Arakmbut should not have any prior rights to the resources of the area. The influx of colonists into the area is no more than the most recent wave of migrations which takes place all the time.

The first colonial view says that the Arakmbut are backward and should be disposed of, while the second says that they have no prior position in the region and should be ignored. Both use historical time as a way of interpreting their own claims to the area. Their ideological position is clearly embedded in their perspective that the Arakmbut are low on the scale of progress and are slow in development.

2. The Missionary Perspective

The earlier missionary writings of Padre José Alvarez juxtapose the terrible threats and devastation suffered by the Harakmbut during the rubber boom and the 'progressive leap' which they needed to leave the state of savagery and enter civilisation (Barriales nd.:4–13, and Alvarez 1941:175). The missionary perspective of development is made clear in Santos' discussion of the Toyeri in 1942 (p. 98): 'It is important to take the Toyeri out of their jungle environment, away from their prejudices and ancestral customs, in order to introduce them, gradually, on the road to civilisation'.

In contrast to this developmentalist perspective, some priests have looked more closely at the perspectives of the Arakmbut themselves. Padre Torralba's article of 1979 discusses why the Arakmbut left Shintuya. He sees Arakmbut history not as a progressive movement to missions but a dialectical shift, initially to missions and then back to communities. Torralba agrees with the other missionary position that the Arakmbut were attracted to the mission because of the threats facing them, but in contrast considers that they are in control of their lives and should choose what sort of lives they should lead.

3. Radical perspectives

These views are similar to those of Torralba but they are secular. A radical view looks at Arakmbut history as a struggle for the recognition of their rights and self-determination under threats from economic interests and ideological pressure from colonists and traditional missionaries.

In 1953, V.J. Guevara made one of the first statements on Harakmbut rights, recommending that they be granted land between the Upper Madre de Dios and the Karene. He considers that the Harakmbut should have full rights as Peruvian citizens, particularly those 'adaptable to civilisation and of good character' (Guevara 1953:109). His position is radical in that it acknowledges Harakmbut rights to land, but his overall aim is integration into the nation state of Peru.

In contrast to this national paternalistic view several recent articles look at Arakmbut history from an international perspective (Rummenhöller 1984; Wahl 1985; Moore 1985a b & c, and Gray 1986). They look at the Arakmbut in relation to economic booms, the role of the missions and the international economy. These authors (including myself) have all emphasised Arakmbut resistance to these forces and their desire for self-determination and control of their own destinies.

These non-indigenous perspectives of Arakmbut history emphasise different elements. The colonial perspective sees history in terms of the development of the resources of the area – the indigenous people do not feature in the accounts except as obstacles to development. The missionaries include the Arakmbut in their accounts and see their deliverance from ungodly ways as their main prosetylising aim. In contrast, the radical perspective sees Arakmbut self-determination and the recognition of rights as a fundamental framework for their history.

Between 1920 and 1960 these three approaches were dominated by the first option in each case (the hard-line colonist, old missionary and paternalist radical), whereas over the last twenty-five years the initiative has moved to the alternative positions of each perspective.

Furthermore, these perspectives overlap. The older missionary perspective is more in line with the colonist's view, while the more recent missionary perspective has more in common with the political activists of the radical persuasion.

The reason for setting out these different perspectives is to show that, whereas the 'facts' of Arakmbut history are generally agreed upon, the interpretations as to what really happened or should happen to them differs markedly. History is thus not some 'reality' which takes place outside of our control. It is something influenced by peoples' actions and further shaped by their interpretation.

When looking at Arakmbut views of their history, from the war with the Taka through the mission period to the establishment of native communities, we can see that there is a marked difference from the perspectives given above. Foremost is the fact that the accounts are from the inside projecting out, rather than from the outside looking in. For the Arakmbut there is a constant interplay between personal experience and myth.

It might be tempting to see this as a gradual 'progression', from the stories about the Taka, which were more mythological, to those based on experience in more recent times. The result would be a transformation from descriptions based on indirect accounts, which are more mythological, to the direct accounts which are more historical. The implication of this position is that the Arakmbut somehow became a historical people during the twentieth century as they were acculturated into the national society – that they somehow 'entered' history. This approach is misleading because it places the Arakmbut as a whole in some form of evolutionary line moving from cold, closed societies to hot open ones. This approach misrepresents both Arakmbut notions of time and their mythology.

The Arakmbut have at least three approaches to the idea of time which we have seen in this book:

1. Natural phenomena as measurements of time

We noted in chapter three that the Arakmbut are aware of alternations between day and night, new moon and full moon and wet and dry seasons. The elements used for measuring time are natural phenomena.

2. Settlement as measurements of time

Every time a maloca moved it was re-established in a new spatial and temporal position. By remembering the maloca names and who lived in them, it is possible for the Arakmbut to construct a relative time scale based on the position of settlements. History is thus measured spatially through the communal house name. The history of San José, by this reckoning, is Wandakwe – Shintuya – Karene, made up of the reforming of seven communal houses to the current four (in the Kipodneri case, five malocas have condensed to one).

3. *Types of people as measurements of time*

There are actually two ways in which outsiders provide relative time differences. The Arakmbut distinguish between Incas, Spaniards and Papas (caucheros) in their myths and their discussion about the myths. In the historical narrative of their contact, the shift is from pre-mission 'Taka' to post-mission 'Amiko' who are *wahaipi* (highlanders), Blancos (Peruvians), Españoles (priests), or Grinkos (non-Peruvians).

The Arakmbut do not see time as a flowing stream taking people with it (see chapter three). Time is rather a series of locations which mark change, where it is the position of elements in the world that measures time and not the flow of time that determines the positions. For the Arakmbut time is not progressive or even moving in any particular direction; e'pok means to pass in the sense of a river passing a settlement, or a person walking past you. If the world travelled with time, nothing would change because time passes by. The rate of change comes from the patterns which it leaves behind.[5]

The experience of time itself need not be any different for those who see themselves moving with time in an irresistible flow and for those who see time passing them. However, the implications for the meaning of history and myth are very different. For those who move with time, history is a part of that time, moving from a beginning to a future, while myth is the means of making sense of this movement. Thus, for those non-indigenous perspectives marked out above, the interpretation and reconstruction formed from history can be seen as a 'myth'. The interpretations are therefore linked to ideological positions which reflect the position of the authors in time.

For those who do not see themselves moving through time or with time, the position is different. History, in the sense of human action and experience, is measured by change. Time is not a movement from beginning to end, but something which changes certain patterns revealed through natural phenomena, settlements, or peo-

---

5. Sarah Skar has pointed out to me that the Quechua say that they 'head into the future backwards'. This would also be the consequence of the Arakmbut spatial view of time.

ple. These are all visible manifestations of the passing of time and either repeat themselves cyclically or fade and die as time passes by.

The invisible world, however, does not die, it only transforms itself. This is the world encapsulated in myth, an invisible world of the spirits which defies time by moving in it, thereby becoming the means of making contact with the past and future. Potentiality is therefore an ability to pass with and over time; transformation, transfiguration, and transmigration are the results. Contact with the spirit world, whether through myth, ritual, singing, or dancing, is a way of capturing the potentiality bound up in time and harnessing it for use in the world of experience. This can be seen in terms of repetitive patterns, as we have seen in chapter three, or in terms of changes which do not repeat themselves.

Arakmbut views of history therefore incorporate two sets of principles:

1) The repetition of patterns as time passes, such as night/day or wet/dry season, are on the one hand similar actions even though they happen at different times. When the Arakmbut moved from one maloca to another they would rebuild their malocas in a different place but with the same structure within a continuity provided by the clan line.

2) Alternately, the change which took place within Arakmbut society after missionary contact was not repetitive, the malocas were not reproduced, and life changed substantially. The way in which we can explain this from an Arakmbut perspective is through a parallel with the myth of Wanamey.

In his article on the Arakmbut and the new missionary situation, Padre Torralba (1979:83) comments that in the 1950s the Arakmbut moved into the Dominican missions in the form of a messianic movement. Later in 1985, he mentioned to me that the mythological way in which the Arakmbut came and left the mission was 'like a repeat of Wanamey'.

When looking at the history of the Arakmbut from the rubber boom to the present day, the parallels become markedly striking. None of the Arakmbut has ever postulated this parallel, neither have they rejected the suggestion; after all the function of Wanamey is not to postulate connections but reflect them.

During the rubber boom, waves of Taka fled from downriver up into the headwaters. They fled from the rubber barons, who, as we have seen in chapter nine, were similar to the Papa in dress and behaviour. The devastation wrought by the rubber boom led eventually to the Arakmbut facing their own flood of danger – the war with the Taka. This directly parallels the flood coming from downriver and facing the Arakmbut with destruction.

During the second period of their history, from the 1940s onwards, the Arakmbut were contacted by missionaries who offered them salvation. They moved towards the headwaters of the Upper Madre de Dios (where some say Wanamey appeared first) to seek refuge from yellow fever in the mission of Shintuya. There they were protected while at the same time unable to create their own society, and as in Wanamey, the mission held the Arakmbut in limbo. They did not have direct contact with the outside world except through missionary 'branches'; Taka and Arakmbut lived together in the tree.

When it was no longer possible to remain in the mission, the Arakmbut escaped and travelled downriver where they founded their new maloca groups in the form of native communities. They reformulated their social and cultural practices and started their lives anew. This newfound independence directly parallels the sequence in Wanamey when the Arakmbut leave the tree and travel downriver in their clan groups to found malocas. The parallel breaks down to some extent when we reflect that in Wanamey there was no tension which forced the Arakmbut to escape; however, the moment of descending the tree was a particularly dangerous moment in the story when most of the Arakmbut left too soon and drowned in the burning mud. Furthermore, the Arakmbut might object that to draw a parallel between Wanamey and the mission would be to paint the missionaries in a more positive light than they deserve. However, it is not so much that the mission is Wanamey, but rather that it had a similar position in history as the tree does in the myth. It held the Arakmbut aloft from the worst excesses of contact with the forces of their destruction. The Arakmbut were ready to leave when its protection no longer become necessary.

The history of the Arakmbut shares the tripartite structure of the myth. To some extent this is a contrivance of the way it has been written, because no Arakmbut has ever told their history as one long narrative, preferring to tell portions here and there. However, the importance of the entry into, and departure from, Shintuya are, without doubt, moments of crisis in Arakmbut history which they emphasise repeatedly. The tripartite structure therefore reflects the way that history is expressed by the Arakmbut when all the different pieces of information are placed together into one framework.

The pattern expounded here has emerged by comparing historical events at the time of the entry of white people into Harakmbut territory and the resulting catastrophe with the mythological cataclysm of Wanamey. But an important objection to this approach is that only three communities left Shintuya between 1969 and 1973. The other two communities had a different history. The historical pattern and its relationship with Wanamey will not necessarily be the same in each community. The pattern shifts between two points, represented by the communities which spent the longest period in Shintuya and those which spent the shortest. The result is three different interpretations of Arakmbut history.

1. Puerto Alegre/Puerto Luz

Missionary contact with the Kipodneri took place in the 1950s. Although these Arakmbut decided to keep away from the mission at Shintuya, they moved there for a brief period of six months, after several died. They were consequently the first native community to leave Shintuya. The Kipodneri have had more contact with the Summer Institute of Linguistics than with the Dominican missionaries, except in recent years when Padre Torralba lived in Puerto Luz.

2. Shintuya

The community of Arakmbut in Shintuya differs from the others in several ways. They did not move from Shintuya with the others and instead of working gold they spend more time working lumber. However, it is possible to see from Aldo Fuentes' study of Shintuya (1984) that several of the processes which have taken place in the other communities have appeared in Shintuya without the physical escape of the Arakmbut from the clutches of the priests. In Shintuya the Arakmbut live further away from the mission than the Wachipaeri and are more distant from the priests.

3. San José del Karene, Barranco Chico and Boca Inambari

The other three Arakmbut communities left Shintuya between 1969 and 1973, although some members moved for a period to the mission of El Pilar near Puerto Maldonado, from where they moved on after a year or so to the established communities. These three communities provide the clearest examples of the principles of the Wanamey myth, but this does not mean that the overall pattern is not similar. The shift from pre-mission independence to post-mission independence is part of a process which has taken different forms.

All five native communities of the Arakmbut have to a greater or lesser extent forged their own new indigenous identity and emerged from a period when they were represented by intermediaries. This has taken place at different speeds and at different times, according to the problems facing them. The founding of the indigenous communities has, in these cases, been acts of self-determination to forge a new world each reflecting the message of Wanamey.

All the three main myths of the Arakmbut, Wanamey, Marinke, and Aiwe, share the tripartite structure whereby a movement takes place from one situation to another via an intermediary stage. In Wanamey this intermediary stage was the period in the tree; for Marinke it was his growth and the realisation who killed his mother; while for Aiwe it was the understanding of the dangers of the Papa. At the end of the myth the world is a different place from the beginning. In this respect myth parallels rituals. In the rites which we have mentioned among the Arakmbut – e'ohot, e'mbaipak, and e'mbakoykoy – the situation at the end of the rite is different from that at the beginning. Similarly, in curing orations, the cure consists of re-establishing the relationship between the body and soul.

Myth and ritual take on the task of harnessing the non-repetitive aspects of life and drawing them into a framework. This stops time and freezes it into stages or sections. Myths or rites are vehicles for this. Thus when a myth is told it makes sense because it reflects and organises experience. In this way the experience of the Arakmbut moving from their independent lives in their malocas where they fought the Taka into another independent life where they fight the Amiko gradually takes on the structure of a myth. History can become a myth which reconstitutes history in the telling; however, they cannot be reduced to each other analytically.

The Arakmbut create and re-create their traditions through myth and history. But traditions are not some ultimate truths set in the past which somehow contrast with 'inauthentic' contemporary existence. On the contrary, tradition is the self-conscious reformulation of custom relating past to present in a mythic-ritual framework. This reformulation is itself an act of history.

CONCLUSION

Myth and Experience

No conclusions exist which can explain away the Arakmbut into neat categorical patterns; on the contrary, anyone viewing them from the marginal perspective adopted here may well encounter other equally viable interpretations. However, the insights written here have emerged from mutual discussion and are not arbitrary. They have been based on information which I have tried to understand and reproduce in a manner appropriate for both an indigenous and non-indigenous readership.

This book constitutes a 'mythological' approach to Arakmbut life. In the first place, the three myths which the Arakmbut consider to be their main philosophical orientation to their world frame its structure: Wanamey tells of the creation of human life, both social and cultural; Marinke looks at human life from birth to death and discusses growth, relationships with non-human species, and contacts with the spirit world; Aiwe and the Papas explains the threats from outsiders who are neither animals nor spirits but are equally dangerous. The Arakmbut who proposed making these three myths the framework for this book saw their triadic mythical structure as an appropriate framework for this text.

The interpretation of the information which is expressed here is an attempt to reproduce Arakmbut activities and practices in a way which goes beyond my personal experience in the field. In one respect this book could appear as the performance of a myth, where certain unchanged aspects of the story take on different shapes and forms according to the context of the telling. As Arakmbut myths use analogies with everyday activities to explain change and process, so this book uses analogies and connections to place events within an encompassing framework

When reading this book, an Arakmbut will most likely respond, 'yes, you could put it like that', meaning that the presentation of the information would be strange and not the way they would portray themselves. For the Arakmbut, myths reflect experience. A further exegesis of this material is unnecessary; they do not need to analyse what is already an analysis. Just as the myth enables them to find meaning in life as it is lived, so most of the descriptions set out in this book explain what for the Arakmbut is 'implicit'.

In each of the three parts of this book, I have tried to break down the distinction between structure and process. Arakmbut life constantly questions this distinction in different ways and three concepts have proved useful for trying to reflect their flexible challenge to rigidity: relativity, potentiality, and creativity.

Perspectival relativity is important because it enables us to glimpse the multi-dimensional features of Arakmbut socio-cultural life. The Arakmbut recognise not only that the world appears differently to humans and non-humans, but also that within human life the world looks differently according to the position a particular person occupies. This will depend not only on the person but which socio-cultural categories they emphasise at any one time. Different perspectives have recurred in several contexts covering both the visible and invisible worlds, and we have found that the process of 'engendering' is fundamental to Arakmbut perspectival relativity.

The use of the term 'relativity' should not be confused with 'cultural relativity', which emphasises that the Arakmbut live lives based on their own distinct principles separate from others. Relativity here is perspectival and refers to the fact that, at any moment, a person's identity undergoes shifts according to contexts which are both internal and external to their socio-cultural formation. The effect is that instead of there being fixed Durkheimian 'social facts' influencing a person's view of the world, it is as if social facts were also social values, relating to people with different intensities according to the situation. Thus to be an Arakmbut or a member of a community will be shared by all members of a village. However according to gender, age, residence, clan, and terminology, a multiplex of possibilities emerges both for appropriate behaviour and for understanding the world (Gray 1984).

Potentiality is a vague term, but it is useful for looking at the invisible world. Trying to grasp the meaning of 'soul-matter' in terms of concepts such as 'energy' goes part of the way to understanding spirit life. However there is an anticipatory aspect of potentiality which combines with a notion of potency. These blend to provide soul-matter with something of a 'structural causality', whereby a cause becomes known through its effects. The relationship between visible form and invisible soul-matter provides an Arakmbut account of the nature of life.

An Arakmbut person's identity is defined through the state of the nokiren, which combines affective and intellectual knowledge according to the concentration or dispersion of soul-matter. Soul-matter is the potential (in the sense of possibility and potency) which comes from the invisible world. These potentials are actualised through contact with the material body. Every moment, act, or thought is thus a creative transference of potential to actual.

Creativity has been used to look at the making of history in action as well as its reproduction through mythical performance. Each Arakmbut person makes use of social and cultural phenomena to create and re-create interpretations of the world which bring to life his or her spirit potentiality and place him or her as a person in the world. Daily life for the Arakmbut is thus the creative materialisation of possibilities which are relative to each person. As these juxtapose within the person, material form becomes animated and socio-cultural organisation takes on life.

These three concepts of relativity, potentiality, and creativity have no direct Arakmbut translation, but they are the dynamic elements which make up a person. Throughout the book the relationship between the waso (body), nokiren (soul) and wandik (name) integrates the three aspects of personhood. In the same way that relativity concerns the position of the body in the world, potentiality concerns the presence of the soul, while creativity is the harmonising of both elements within an embracing name which encapsulates both.

The philosopher A.N. Whitehead (1942:172) uses these three terms in his discussion of the relationship between 'subject' and 'object'. He argues that each occasion of experience is a creative process of becoming which defines the relationship between a subject and object. There are no absolute distinctions between either subject and object or one event and another, as everything is essentially relative. He writes, 'The creativity is the actualization of potentiality, and the process of actualization is an occasion of experiencing' (p.175). The way in which relativity, potentiality, and creativity merge in Whitehead's analysis are markedly similar to the Arakmbut as they creatively harness the potential of the spirit world into the relative actuality of experience.

These three words, combined with my trying to avoid explanatory reductionism, may give the impression that, for the Arakmbut, everything is in flux. Yet on the other hand the myths, socio-economic formations, and cultural frameworks provide an impressive array of order and structured form. The temptation when producing an ethnography is to reduce everything either to process or structure. In this case neither aspect is mutually exclusive. When looking at processes forms appear, and when looking at forms, processes reappear.

The juxtaposition between form and process which we find among the Arakmbut is something which is extremely difficult to grasp unless we take on board the invisible spirit world. The invisible spirit world is about process and the visible world is about form. The reciprocal relationship between these worlds, therefore, is the dynamism of existence. The social, cultural, and spiritual framework enables relativity, potentiality, and creativity to operate together in the mutually producing movement between history and myth.

Complementarity and Asymmetry

A recurring feature throughout this book has been the notion of complementarity and asymmetry and the transformation of this balance into an exploitative inequality. In Part I we considered the repetitive cycles of time such as the days, months, and seasons and saw how they reflected the differences between men and women. At the boundary points between temporal categories, men and women come together in their activities whereas at other times they are apart. In these contexts male and female are equals of each other as they behave in a mirror-image manner, shifting from contiguity to separation and vice versa. Both elements move in formation. Another element of the complementarity between male and female was noted in the relationship terminology and the conceptualisation of marital exchange. At marriage, male and female artifacts are exchanged, demonstrating not only a balance between the married couple, but reflecting the cosmological complementarity between river, forest, sun, and moon.

Gender relations comprise a form of complementarity but, in contrast, another set of relations are asymmetrical and stem from the clan and wambet, respectively. Asymmetry connected with the clan arises from the principle of patrilineality which appears different from a male or a female perspective. The patriline establishes a physical and spiritual continuity between every man stretching back to

Wanamey. Women can trace continuity back through their father but not onto their children because the rule of exogamy makes every woman marry into a different clan. The effect of this is a cycling through time whereby, as the clan loses a sister it should gain a wife.

The wambet can reconcile the potential contradiction between the relationship terminology and the clan by its appearance as a cognatic unit. The wambet joins together the kin and affinal distinction created in the parents' generation and women play a key part in its activities of arranging marriage alliances. In this way the wambet provides an element of gender complementarity which brings the patrilineal clan in line with the symmetric prescriptive exchange of the relationship terminology. Thus, as long as the wambet is clearly present, a complementary balance will take place with the clan. However, most of the time there is no balance. The implications of this for social change are analysed in Volume 2.

The asymmetry of the clan or wambet can appear in the structuralist sense, as used by Da Matta (1982:162); however, they can easily become exploitative, leading to social inequalities, such as when a husband demands too much from his wife or when a father-in-law demands too much from the son-in-law.

In the second part of the book several other examples of complementarity appeared, also connected with gender relations. Initiation is the point at which gender relations are established. Indeed, male and female initiation could be seen as 'engendering' occasions. Women become adults after they have produced children, which involves penetration by a male, pregnancy, and childbirth. In the past, male initiation into adulthood involved two separate ceremonies of nose- and lip-piercing by peach palm spines which were mythologically seen as female pubic hair.

Piercing by an element from the opposite sex followed by a period of transformation not only covers initiation into adulthood, but the practices of producing ritual foods and drink, hunting and cooking, planting and nurturing, as well as eating and digestion. All these activities are framed by a complementary set of activities involving the contiguity of disparate elements in a controlled manner leading to a transformation. This generating pattern recurs mythologically in Wanamey and Marinke as the basis for understanding growth among the Arakmbut.

A complementary relationship exists in the transference of soul-matter from the visible to the invisible worlds in return for meat. At the height of adulthood men and women can control their relationships with the spirit world and utilise this power to support their household through the hunting of meat, the production of food, and cooking. In a healthy household, the complementary sexual division of labour transforms the meat into consumable food and the children can grow. However, should this complementarity break down as a result of over-hunting, under-cooking or uncontrolled sexual activities, the result will be illness and maybe death, as harmful toto spirits always appear when there is a breakdown of relations with the invisible world.

On death, some of the soul-matter, particularly that belonging to powerful wayorokeri and wamanoka'eri, becomes dispersed into animals. In this way the soul-matter in the underworld 'passes' through the female spirits of Seronwe, returning to animals. From there, through the animal controlling spirit, they tell the invisible female spirits where and how many prey can be caught by any one hunter. There is a tendency for some clans to be better at hunting certain species than others, which can lead to over-kill. Should this happen, the nokiren of the hunter and his household become threatened by toto who are eagerly looking for the soul-matter of dead humans to fill their ranks. This gathering of soul-matter by the concentrated toto poses a danger for the Arakmbut and constitutes an inequality of power which threatens the continuity of Arakmbut life.

The spirits who try to prevent this are the beautiful women from the invisible world who explain the limits on killing in a hunting expedition. The uxorilocal female structure of the afterlife under the river in Seronwe parallels the structure of the wambet during life. Both act as foils to the asymmetrical concentrating tendencies in the clan system and operate to disperse threats. Without the compensating, complimentary aspect of female residential and affinal ties, life would be considerably more dangerous.

In the third part, the myth of Aiwe showed how a controlled relationship with non-indigenous peoples can be beneficial to the Arakmbut, but too close relationships or an over-reliance on outside knowledge can lead to death. As with the spirit world, non-indigenous peoples are a permanent threat which could destroy whole communities if the Arakmbut do not keep a certain distance. However, unlike the invisible spirit world, where some form of gender complementarity exists, women have fewer contacts with non-indigenous outsiders than men. The reason for this is explored in the next volume.

At several times throughout their history the Arakmbut have moved their communal houses and villages. Sometimes this has involved reforming old ones, creating new ones or renaming. The continuity of the clan is complemented by movements from one residence site to another, which takes place every few generations. The clan

membership remains constant but the members shift maloca affiliation. In this way the residential groups can be seen as 'passing through'
the clan line. Movement from a settlement arises frequently as a result
of conflict within the community or after a death. These are times
when soul-matter has accumulated or concentrated too much, such as
when political leaders are taking on too much power and emotions are
high. Resettlement is a response to a crisis when the complementarity
or asymmetry between male and female, visible and invisible, or
human and non-human break down into exploitative relations.

The way of avoiding the disintegration of communities is to ensure
a dispersion of hostility. For this reason, in spite of the reluctance of
both men and women to move settlement, there is a gradual dispersion of clans throughout the five Arakmbut communities as a result of
marriage or conflict. The Arakmbut who are most mobile are women,
and it is they who have most of the detailed knowledge about other
communities. The women therefore provide the links which enable
people to find residential alternatives in other communities.

The three examples of continuity of a line broken by elements
passing through that line – women, soul-matter, and settlement
groups – demonstrate that the clan has to be reproduced by means
of the contiguity and separation of marriage exogamy, death, and
resettlement. This has the effect of dispersing people and soul-matter
and preventing a cumulation or concentration of power, whether
through the excessive control of women, the domination of a settlement, or endangering soul-matter by excessive hunting and meat
consumption. The danger lies in the breakdown of complementarity
into its asymmetric components, which can lead to a life based on
exploitative hierarchy, social tensions, and spiritual conflict.

The Arakmbut reproduce themselves by trying to prevent concentrations of power. This makes them aim towards being more egalitarian sociologically and more free-thinking cosmologically, and
attempt to break down tensions building up in a settlement. Whereas
among the Arakmbut we can distinguish symmetry from asymmetry
and continuity from discontinuity, we have to see that complementarity and cyclicity through time are not balances which are eternally
harmonious. Too much complementarity leads to discontinuity and
defencelessness, whereas too much continuity and accumulation of
soul-matter leads to inequality and a breaking up of the society from
within. Arakmbut life varies from peace to war, from order to chaos,
and these result from the relationship between these structural principles. Therefore, to the extent that there is a system, Arakmbut life
is not a balanced pattern but one of imbalance, shifting from sym-

metry and asymmetry to inequality and exploitation. The ultimate aspect of this imbalance is the threat from non-indigenous colonisation which could transform exploitation into annihilation. (These topics are the subjects of Volumes 2 and 3 respectively).

Mystery and Decolonisation

The preface to this book referred to the need to respect mystery and political aspirations as two aspects of the decolonisation of anthropology. At the end of this work, hopefully, these two areas are still intact. Although the discussion of myths and dreams has looked at relationships with the spirit world, there is still no final explanation of the Arakmbut in our grasp.

When the shaman died in San José in December, 1980, the old men predicted that his flock of chickens would transfigure themselves into spirit river birds and it happened. When spirits visited the community after a death we all heard them. When we heard whispers down at a local stream we were told that at last we could hear the spirits talking as everyone else could. How do the Arakmbut shamans cure someone who is, to all intents and purposes, within moments of death? I cannot explain these events. They can be rationalised, of course, but that will not bring us closer to the Arakmbut

The broad brushstrokes which have painted this sketch of the Arakmbut leave many things unanswered, many experiences unaccounted for. Various themes can be drawn together, some hypotheses presented as in this conclusion, but they are more rhetorical questions than definitive answers. The mystery remains unsolved.

Rather than being a closed society untouched by a national society, the Arakmbut were affected by the international economy before they had even seen white people. We cannot assume, however, that placing the Arakmbut in an international and national context means that they have no boundaries to their own society. On the contrary, the Arakmbut are quite clear that they are different from outsiders and they are aware that outsiders, particularly Amiko, can be as dangerous as the most hostile toto, if not more so.

The difference between white people and the spirit world is that, whereas spirits are fundamental for the continuation of Arakmbut life, white people constitute a different domain. Amiko knowledge comes from God or the State and so problems stemming from these sources need different techniques based on education, medicine, and the affirmation of legal rights (see Volume 3).

Whereas toto are concentrations of soul-matter both of Arakmbut and others, white people are of a different order – neither human nor spirit. They constitute, therefore, a different threat. The toto or Taka can cause death and can destroy people, but the Arakmbut can defend themselves by uniting behind a war leader or shaman. White people, on the other hand, have the capacity to destroy the whole social and cultural fabric of Arakmbut life.

Curing problems caused by white people is not a question of trying to readjust the balance of the universe, it is question of using all the forces available to defend themselves. Sometimes the power seems overwhelming and resignation takes control of the people, while at other times their determination to resist is as strong as ever.

At this point the Arakmbut recognise that escaping, as Aiwe did from the Papa using their knowledge, is not sufficient. The Arakmbut face a cataclysm which can only be resolved by seeking salvation through the utilisation of outside forces which may be able to protect them from the worst excesses of the threats. They did this during the movement into the missions in the early 1960s, but they also realised that they had to determine their own future or perish under the control of those from whom they sought salvation. They escaped the mission and recreated their own society as a native community.

The passage from history to myth and the re-enactment of the Wanamey myth demonstrate clearly how the Arakmbut see different intensities of threats to their future. Escape from threats or handling them through contacts with the dream world is fine when the imbalance is about the symmetric complementarity and the asymmetrical cyclicity of the social and cultural world. When that very system is under threat, an almost 'messianic' approach is needed, whereby one epoch is replaced by another.

Wanamey is about that shift and the original act of self-determination, creating social and cultural life through fire and water. Arakmbut history shows that origin myth in practice during the recreation of Arakmbut existence after near-annihilation from the rubber boom, but this does not mean that the Arakmbut have turned history into myth for ever. On the contrary, they re-enact myth in history. They have turned myth into experience.

The performance of a myth should reflect each person's own experience while enacting collective experience. This is a part of the process whereby personal and communal experience relate through shared ideas. The myth is a reflection of experience and experience is a reflection of myth.

Wanamey tells of the descent of the Arakmbut from the tree to assert sovereignty over their lands. When that sovereignty was threatened after the rubber boom, they returned to the pattern of that story to assert their right to control and determine their own lives. Now that the threat comes from white people, this right is gradually becoming expressed consciously as a form of indigenous political self-determination.

The framework of this book has left many questions unanswered. Myths do not draw us either into the intricacies of daily life or the processes whereby social and cultural organisation operate on a personal and collective level. The second book in this trilogy will take up the Arakmbut story from the life and death of San José's shaman, Psyche. By looking at the shamanic and political dimensions of Arakmbut life, it is possible to illustrate what happens when complementarity does not fit with a recalcitrant world. This provides the basis for understanding how large-scale social change arises out of the events of daily life. The final volume looks at the historical emergence of indigenous rights in Arakmbut social and cultural life as they strive against the threats of the outside world. In this way, the presence of the Wanamey myth continues as part of their political struggle.

It has taken the whole of this book to place the Wanamey myth into a context. We have travelled through social, cultural, and spirit worlds and have traced Arakmbut history. We ended where we started, seeing the Arakmbut living their creation myth. Hopefully it will now be possible for the reader to look once again at the Wanamey myth at the beginning of the book and to read it without need of exegesis. Perhaps now it will be possible for the non-Arakmbut reader to make the first tentative, respectful step to the door of Arakmbut life and glimpse through the crack. We can then join them with a nod or murmur in recognition at some of the images in the myth.

ORTHOGRAPHY

The Ministerio de Educación (Republica Peruana) has an Arakmbut orthography which was prepared by Robert Tripp of the Summer Institute of Linguistics. This orthography uses an alphabet which conforms to that of Peruvian Spanish. Heinrich Helberg (1984) has adapted this to accommodate the phonetic alphabet. This orthography largely conforms to Peruvian Spanish, but several Arakmbut students have advised me on the spellings they prefer.

Each Arakmbut community has its own accents, words, and expressions which means that there is no fixed spelling system for the language as a whole. Some of the words written here may well be rewritten in the future, as young Arakmbut find a system which is appropriate for all the communities.

Some Arakmbut vowels can be un-nasalised or nasalised but I have not made this distinction in the text. I have substituted an *'h'* for the Spanish *'j'* or *'x'* and *'w'* for *'hu'* except in quotes from Spanish-speaking authors. Where the 1973 orthography has *'ti',* I have written *'ch'* or *'tch',* depending on how strongly the *'t'* sounds; where it has *'si'* I have written *'sh'*. The 1973 orthography recognises that *'b'* is pronounced *'mb'* by the Arakmbut. However, in some cases the *'m'* is more apparent than in others. I have therefore written *'mb'* where the *'m'* is pronounced and *'b'* where the *'m'* is silent. Similarly the *'d'* in the 1973 orthography appears as *'nd'* at the beginning or *'dn'* at the end of a word. I have written the letters *'n'* and *'d'* as they sound because in some examples the *'n'* is silent. I occasionally heard a *'v'* and a *'j'* sound which are not in the orthography but are used here.

Vowels

a as in 'apple'	(also nasalised)
e as in 'egg'	(also nasalised)
i as in 'into'	
o as in 'pot'	(also nasalised)
u as in 'moon'	

Consonants

b as in 'book' but with varying degrees of semi-nasalisation *(mb)*.

ch as in 'church' but also accasionally with a slight *'t'* as in 'pitch'.

d as in 'dog' but with varying degrees of semi-nasalisation as in 'and'.
At the end of a word, a *'d'* sounds *'dn'*.

g appears with semi-nasalisation (*'ng'* as in tongue') but often at the
end of a word as *'gn'* as in 'gnu'.

h as in 'hat'

k as in 'kite'

m as in 'mouse' also as semi-nasal to *'b'*

n as in 'nature' but also as semi-nasal to *'d'* and *'g'* or after *'d'* and *'g'*
at the end of a word.

p as in 'pig'

r as in 'rainbow'

s as in 'sea'

t as in 'top' but sometimes present before *'ch'* or *'sh'* as in 'pitch'.

w or *hu* as in 'window'

y as in 'yacht'

a stop as in the glottal stop before *'I'*

GLOSSARY

Arakmbut Words Used in Text

A

aiya	whole
akidnet	capybara (*hydrochoerus hydrochaeris*)
akodnyo	lower chacras
amara	a hill from which Amarakaeri take their name (Barriales & Torralba)
amerinkipi	a plant from which Marinke takes his name (Califano)
amiko	highlanders or other colonists
apagn	formal term for F
apane	A Harakmbut word for jaguar (*Panthera onca*) – the Arakmbut also use *petpet*. Also formal term for GF
apik	sugar cane
apoining	anaconda, spirit, or person who is potentially harmful but is beneficial
asign	MZ, capybara
asiira	harmful spirit (J. Alvarez)
asinku	bee's nest
asuk	bark cloth skirt or blanket
awiruk	rubber tree, character in Marinke

B

biign	fish (generic term)
bogn	mouth, lip, entrance

bogn dakwe	pregnant
bogntokoy	lip-piercing
budn	curassow (*Crax carunulata*)

C

chawayndik	visible
chawaywendik	invisible
chign	MB
chimbui	spouse's sibling or sibing's spouse of opposite sex
chindign	curing oration, sorcery
chindignwakeri	sorcerer, usually from within community
chindignwamankeri	sorcerer, usually from within community
'chinditeumankaeri'	[Barriales and Torralba use this word for sorcerer]
chindoi	marriage presentation – meat in particular
chio	same-sex sibling's son
Chipomeme	character in a story who wanted to be an adult
chiumbu	same-sex sibling's daughter
chiwa	song speech
chiwembet	young girl sorcerer
chiwemui	toad used by chiwembet
chongpai	anaconda/ayahuasca
chou chou	song of the sipen bird

D

dakwe	bad, unpleasant
dwayo	grandchild

E

e'	infinitive prefix
e'anopwe	remember
e'chipoa	blow
e'e	to be/ life
egn	brother (man speaking)
ehuimaneri	master of rain (Califano)
e'ka	to do
e'ka biign	to fish with barbasco

e'kerek	to grow
ekmbika/echunkmbika	leaf shield/hiding place
e'machunka	to hunt
e'mba'a	to work or do someting a lot
e'mbachapak	story telling
e'mbaipak	second initiation ceremony
e'mbatandikka	to imitate
embi	creeper
Embieri	name of a clan
e'mbogntokoy	lip-piercing ceremony
e'mbuey	to die (or to have an orgasm)
e'mbuey'e	repeated death or type of fit
e'mbuiyuk	to suck
en	brother-in-law (man speaking)
enchipo	brother-in-law (man speaking)
e'ndikka	to name
endopo	type of bee
e'nopwe	to think
e'ohotokoy	nose-piercing ceremony
e'ok	to vomit
e'pawet	to become erect
e'pok	to pass
-eri	suffix meaning 'people of'
e'sikon	sudden nightfall, to become dark quickly, long night
e'simbore	to be drunk/high
e'toepak	to marry/to join/to be together
e'wet	to hit or have a successful shot
e'widnbe	to dry in the sun

H

hai	dry
haiapa	ritual bitter drink
haiya	bland-tasting
hak	house
haktone	maloca
ho	peach palm *(Guilielma speciosa Mart)*
hopi	splinter inserted in lip at initiation
hotnda	rich, tasty

I

iari/akudnui	white-lipped peccary *(Tayassu pecari)*
iariwere	spirit of white-lipped peccary
Idnsikambo	name of a clan
ijmbueyone	I'm dead, 'I've come' (orgasm)
inang	formal term for M
inkimbi	vine
isipo	child

J

jiriendei	spirit abode in the forest (Barriales and Torralba)

K

-ka-	root of verb 'to do'
ka'epu	land boa
kaing kaing ka	song of Chipomeme
kakapi	ant
kambu	opposite-sex sibling's daughter
kapiro	heron *(Egretta alba)*
katchiapo	why
keme	tapir *(Tapirus terrestris)*
kemewere	spirit of tapir
ke'yo	watch out
kiss kiss	song of the pikwan bird
kitayeh	harmful spirit (Fejos)
konig	like, as
kotsimba	aguaje leaf *(Mauritia flexuosa)*
koya	chapo banana drink
kuchiakpo	hide
kuka	coca *(Erythroxylon coca)*
ku'mbarak	cemetary
kumo	barbasco *(Lonchocarpus sp.)*
kurudn	sky
kurudneri	sky spirit
kusipe	cradle
kusogn	basket
kutayon	upriver

M

mama	old woman, grandmother
mang	FZ
mantoro	achiote red dye *(Bixa orellana)*
Mapakaro	supreme being (Barriales & Torrabla)
Marinke	culture hero of the Arakmbut
Masenawa	name of clan
mba'	particle of quantity
mbakoykoy	ceremony for ohpu
mbedn	red
mbedn e'pok	to menstruate
mbedntoktok	large oriole
mbegnko	woodpecker *(Melanerpes cruentatus)*
menpa nopwewe	chaos
mi'in	to suck
mimi	blood
ming	sister (woman speaking)
miokpo	sun
mokas	collared peccary *(Tayassu tajacu)*
mokaswere	spirits of collared peccary
monka	'causality' – imperative of e'ka – to do
muneyo	young girl
Muyoni	wife of Chipomeme

N

nang	mother
-nda	adjectival suffix
ndaka e'mae	order
ndakyorokeri/ndakmbayorokeri	good dreaming spirits
ndariyokewakewa	Wanamey parrot
ndik	root of e'ndikka – to name
ndo	self, I
ndoedn	my, mine
ndumba	forest
ndumberi	forest spirit
nes nes	song of a particular bird
nognchinda	one
nognchinda Arakmbut	one person

nognda	other, different, opposed
nogn onyu	different clan
nokiren	soul
nopo	centre
nopwe	root of e'nopwe – to know
nowenda	sad, upset, distraught ('centreless')

O

o'chimuyate	it was born
ochinosik	hatred
o'epo	therefore
ohpu	warrior leader
okakihi	Ashaninka equivalent of the wambet
okmbu	night monkey
okwe	parrot
o'mbuey	he dies
o'me	morning, day
onyu	pure, patrilineal clan
opedn	formal term for wife
opewadn	formal term for wife ('she who sits next to me')
o'pogika	it always passes
o'poknda	passing
oro	we, us
oro onyu	our clan
o'sik	night, it is dark
Oteri	harmful spirit (Barriales and Torralba)
oteyo	high chacras
owing	white-crested turkey buzzard

P

pagn	Father, FB
paimba	tobacco
painda	bitter
paipi	fire-stick for kindling
pakshiri	termites
pane	old man, grandfather
parakupo	ashes
paron	turkey hen

Peimpi	mythological person responsible for creating male initiation rites (Califano)
pet pet	jaguar
pikwan	small bird
pisnoe	species of flower
-po	causal suffix
pogn	person of opposite sex in same genealogical level who is not an affine
pugn	moon
pugntone	full moon

S

sapite	hill (Barriales & Torralba)
saro	parrot
Saweron	name of clan
sayyudn	wet
Seki	mythological person responsible for creating male initiation rites (Califano)
Seronwe	world under the river
setnda	sweet, rotten
shuchi shuchi	a bird's song
sikidnmbi	large whale-like fish
singpa	wild peach palm
Singperi	name of clan
sinon	baby who can sit
sipen	name of a bird
sipikutapa	plant eaten in Wanamey
-sipo	diminutive suffix
sisi	raw meat

T

tagnpi	isula ant
tainda	strength
Taka	enemy, non-Harakmbut
Taka nokiren	harmful souls of dead Taka
takapi	type of stinging ant
Takayo	place in the forest where Taka souls and other harmful spirits live

takui	rat/rodent
tamba	chacra
tam'et	catfish
tangka	headress
tayagn	tree bark used for coca lime
tayagnpi	stick for crushing lime when taking coca
terweng	sister-in-law (woman speaking)
toayo	son-in-law
-toe-	root of e'toepak – to marry or join
toku	dragonfly
to'mbi	snail shell rattle once used in rites of initiation
-tone	suffix meaning large or older
tong	young relative
tonko	twine
topakari	Wachipaeri (shaman)
topedn	club
tori	wood like balsa
torogn	opossum
toto	harmful spirit
Toto shin	harmful spirit (Barriales &- Torralba)
Totoyo	place in forest where toto live
toyo	down
toyon/toyudn	downwards/downriver

U

uayokokeri	shaman of the Toyeri (Barriales & Torralba)
ukateh	beneficial spirits (Fejos)

W

wa-	generic prefix
wa'a	word
wa'ai	bone
wachio	FB
wachiosipo	same sex sibling's son
wachipai	master of a species
wachopi	branch
wachiumbu	same sex sibling's daughter

wadnpirinana	little bird
wadntoropopo	red bird
waemba	leaf, hand
waenpogn	potential spouse (Puerto Luz)
wahaipi	highlander
waho	father
wa'i	foot
wai	water
wai bogn	chicha or masato trough
waidn	teeth
waipa	stick
Wairekurat	harmful spirit (Barriales & Torralba)
wairi	respected person
wa'itamankaeri	sorcerer from another community
waiwit	root
waka	brother's son (woman speaking)
wakambu	opposite-sex sibling's daughter
wakpo	eye
wakuru	head, first
wamachinoa	song
wamachunkeri	hunter
wamama	grandmother
wamambuey	same-sex sibling
wamandakeri	curing shaman (Barriales & Torralba)
wamanoka'eri	curandero
wamawere	dispersed nokiren
wamba	room
wambachapak	story, myth
wambayok	dry season
wambet	alliance-arranging cognatic category
wambetoeri	dead Arakmbut spirits
wambign	agouti *(Dasyprocta aguti)*
wambo	new, youth who has passed first age-grade
wambokerek	man, fully grown adult male
wambokererksipo	baby boy
wambokerektone	adult man with large family and experience of the world

wambo o'me	new day after long night in Wanamey
wambo pugn	new moon
wambuey	dead man
wame'	liver
wamey	trunk of a tree
wamin	intestines
wana	fruit from Wanamey, oval fruit
Wanamey	tree of salvation in the creation myth
wandapo	stomach
wandari	territory
wandawe	semen
wandik	name
wanjinji	lover
wano	centre
wanokiren	soul
wanopo	seat of affection
wanore	heart
wanues	type of bird
wapa	penis-shaped object
wapane	old man
wari	leader (Göhring)
wasewe	sister-in-law (woman speaking)
wasi	MZ
wasikon	sudden nightfall
wasipo	child
wasiwa	fat
waso	body
wasu	FZ
watamukidn	testicles
watochi	MB
watoe	spouse
watone	old person
watopakeri	Wachipaeri shaman (Califano)
watowayo	son-in-law DS (woman speaking)
wawa	wasp
wawaka	brother's son (ws)
wawapu	a type of bee
wawe	river
wawepui	pubic hair
wawewe	brother-in-law (ms)

waweri	river spirits
waweri toto	harmful river spirits expressed as an anaconda
wawing	chicha
wawiyok	wet season
wayayo	grandchild
waye	mother
wayeri	person from afar
wayok	year
wayombu	daughter
wayorok	dream
wayorokeri	shaman who dreams
wayut	daughter
wendari	lower ground by river
wenpu	string bag
weri	digging stick
wero	rabbit
wetone	woman
wetonesipo	little girl
widnpo	opposite-sex sibling

X

Xiliahuandei	forest abode of toto (Califano)

Y

yaro	type of setico palm tree
Yaromba	name of a clan
'Yaromberi'	Wachipaeri word for harmful spirits (Califano)
yasion	son
yombedn	baby who cannot yet sit
'yoneneh'	harmful spirit (Fejos)
'yoshi/yoshin'	Panoan spirit
yuperak	thunder

BIBLIOGRAPHY

Aikman, S.H. 1982. Informe preliminar sobre hallazgos arqueológicos del río Karene (río Colorado), Madre de Dios. *Amazonía Peruana* Vol. III, No.6. Lima.

Aikman, S.H. 1994. *Intercultural Education and Harakmbut Identity. A Case Study of the Community of San José in Southeastern Peru.* PhD Thesis, University of London.

Aikman, S.H. nd. The Keme Women. Mss.

Alvarez, J. 1940a. Con la expedición Wenner-Gren al Colorado: Sobre los ríos y las chozas de los mashcos. *Misiones Dominicanas del Perú* 22, 125–33.

Alvarez, J. 1940b. Con la expedición Wenner-Grenn: De Maldonado al Colorado feliz encuentro con los mashcos. *Misiones Dominicanas del Perú* 22, 173–83.

Alvarez, J. 1941. Con un pie en el estribo. *Misiones Dominicanas del Perú* XXIII, 171–6.

Alvarez, J. 1942. Del Colorado al Nauene, por las tribus de los mashcos. *Misiones Dominicanas del Perú* 24 (129), 41–56.

Alvarez, J. 1944. La misión de San Miguel de los maschos en la actualidad. Misiones Dominicanas del Perú 26 (145), 245–56.

Alvarez, J. 1946. Creencias y tradiciones mashcas. *Misiones Dominicanas del Perú* XXVII, 10–15.

Alvarez, J. 1952. San Miguel del Colorado. *Misiones Dominicanas del Perú* 33 (191–2), 62–6.

Alvarez, J. 1953. Al Kipoznue y alto Colorado. *Misiones Dominicanas del Perú* XXXIV, 44–50.

Alvarez, J. 1956/7. Creencias y tradiciones de los mashcos. *Misiones Dominicanas* XXXVII, 117–80, 210–13; XXXVIII, 3–6.

Alvarez, J. 1958a. Los aviadores nacionales en la exploración del Colorado. *Misiones Dominicanas* XXXIX, 15–22.

Alvarez, J. 1958b. Los mashcos en la antiguedad. *Misiones Dominicanas* XXXIX, 103–119.

Alvarez, R. 1957/8. El Folklore Piro. *Misiones Dominicanas* XXXVIII, 88–90; XXXIX, 11–15.

Alvarez, R. 1960. *Los Piros, Hijos de Dioses.* Lima; Santiago Valverde S.A.

Amich, J. 1854. *Compendio Histórico*. Paris: Libería de Rosa y Bourel.

Andino, J. 1906. Cartas sobre la entrada de aquel en los indios Chunchos 1768–9. In *Juicio de Limites entre Perú y Bolivia*. (ed.) V. Maúrtua. Vol. 12, 164–175. Barcelona: Henrich.

Anon, 1936. La pavorosa región de los maschos – su colonización – industria aurífera – misiones. *Misiones Dominicana Peruana* 18 (92), 14–21.

Århem, K. 1981. *Makuna Social Organization. A study in Descent, Alliance and the Formation of Corporate groups in the North-Western Amazon*. Acta Universitatis Upsaliensis. Uppsala Studies in Cultural Anthropology 4. Stockholm: Liber Tryck.

Aurora Perez Jiménez, G. 1981. Anthropology in my View. *IWGIA Newsletter* 28/9, 82–86.

Aza, P. 1927. Folklore de los salvajes Machiguengas. *Misiones Dominicanas del Perú* IX, 237–245.

Aza, P. 1930. La Tribu Huaraya. *Misiones Dominicanas del Perú* XII, 1–12, 50–55.

Aza, P. 1936. *Vocabulario Español-Arasairi*. Lima: Sanmarti & Co.

Baer, G. 1979. Religión y Chamanismo de los Matsigenka. *Amazonía Peruana* Vol. 2, No.4, 101–140.

Banco Minero del Perú. 1981, 1982, 1983. *Boletín Estadistica* Anual Oficina de Planamiento y Estudios Económicos, Departamento de Información Estadisticas.

Barnes, J. 1987. *Early Greek Philosophy*. Penguin Books.

Barriales, J. nd. *Apaktone*. Vitoria: Heraclio Fournier.

Barriales, J. and A. Torralba. 1970. *Los Mashcos*. Lima: Santiago Valverde.

Basso, E.B. 1970. Xingu Carib Kinship Terminology and Marriage: Another View. *Southwestern Journal of Anthropology* Vol. 26 (4), 402–16.

Belaúnde, V.A. 1911. Las expediciones de los Incas a la hoya Amazonica. *Revista Universitária de Lima* Ano VI, Vol. 11, 134–154.

Berreman, G. 1968. Is Anthropology Alive? Social Responsibility in Social Anthropology. *Current Anthropology* Vol 9, No. 5.

Bodley, J. 1972. A Transformative Movement among the Campa of Eastern Peru. *Anthropos* 67, 220–228.

Borofsky, R. 1987. *Making History: Pukapukan and Anthropological Constructions of Knowledge*. Cambridge University Press.

Bovo de Revello, J. 1848. *Brillante Porvenir del Cuzco*. Cuzco: Imprenta Libre.

Bloch, M. 1977. Past and Present in the Present. *Man* Vol. 12. No.2 pp. 278–292.

Brandenstein, C.G. von. 1971. The Phoenix Totemism. *Oceania* 41, 39–49.

Brown, M. 1985. *Tsewa's Gift: Magic and Meaning in an Amazonian Society*. Smithsonian Institution Press.

Butt, A. 1967. The Birth of a Religion. In *Gods and Rituals: Readings in Religious Beliefs and Practices*. (ed.) J. Middleton. pp. 377–435. Sourcebooks in Anthropology, New York: The Natural History Press.

Califano, M. 1976. Muerte, miedo y fascinación de la crises de embüye de los Mashcos de la Amazonía Sudoccidental. *Runa* 13, 125–151.

Califano, M. 1977. La Incorporación de un nuevo elemento cultural entre los Mashcos de la Amazonía Peruana. *Relaciones de la Sociedad Argentina de Antropología* Vol. XI. N.S. Buenos Aires.

Califano, M. 1978a. El complejo de la bruja entre los mashco de la Amazonía sudoccidental (Perú). *Anthropos* 73, 401–433.

Califano, M. 1978b. *Análisis comparativo de un mito mashco.* Entregas de I.T. Instituto Ticlan, Centro de Investigaciónes Regionales Facultad de Filosofía y Letras. Unversidad de Buenos Aires.

Califano, M. 1982. *Etnografía de los Mashcos de la Amazonía Sud Occidental del Perú.* Buenos Aires: FECIE.

Califano, M. & A. Fernandez Distel. 1978a. L'emploi du tabac chez les Mashco du l'Amazonie sud-occidentale du Pérou. *Bulletin de la Société Suisses des Americanistes* No. 42, 5–14.

Califano, M. & A. Fernandez Distel. 1978b. El empleo de la coca entre los mashcos de la Amazonía del Perú. *Årstyck.* Etnografisca Museum Göteborg.

Campbell, A.T. 1989. *To Square with Genesis: Causal Statements and Shamanic ideas in Wayapi.* Edinburgh University Press.

Carneiro, R. 1964. The Amahuaca and the Spirit World. *Ethnology* 3, pp. 6–11.

Carr, E.H. 1961. *What is History?* Pelican Books.

Chaumeil, J-P. 1981. *Historia u Migraciones de los Yagua de finales del siglo XVII hasta nuestras dias.* Lima: CAAAP.

Chaumeil, J-P. 1983. *Voir, Savoir, Pouvoir.* Paris: Éditions de L'École des Hautes Études en Sciences Sociales.

Chevalier, J. 1982. *Civilization and the Stolen Gift: Capital Kin and Cult in Eastern Peru.* University of Toronto Press.

Cleary, D. 1989. *Anatomy of the Amazonian Gold Rush.* Macmillan.

CODEH-PA, 1983. *La Selva y su Ley: Lavadores de Oro.* Sicuani: Comité de Defensa de los Derechos Humanos de las Provincias Altas.

Collier, J., & M. Rosaldo 1981. Politics and gender in simple socieites. In *Sexual Meanings: The Cultural Construction of Gender and Sexuality.* (eds.) S. Ortner & H. Whitehead. Cambridge University Press.

Copleston, R. 1959. *Aquinas.* Pelican Books.

Crocker, J.C. 1985. *Vital Souls: Bororo Cosmology, Natural Symbolism, and Shamanism.* University of Arizona Press.

d'Ans, A-M et al. 1973. *Problemas de clasificación de lenguas no-andinas en el sur-este Peruano.* Centro de Investigación de Lingüística Aplicada. Lima: Unversidad Nacional Mayor de San Marcos.

d'Ans, A-M. 1975. *La Verdadera Biblia de los Cashinahua.* Lima: Talleres de Industrial Gráfica.

Da Matta, R. 1979. The Apinayé Relationship system: Terminology and Ideology. In *Dialectical Societies: The Gê and the Bororo of Central Brazil.* (ed.) D. Maybury-Lewis. pp. 83–127. Havard University Press.

Da Matta, R. 1982. *A Divided World: Apinayé Social Structure.* Harvard University Press.

Delboy, D.E. 1912. Conferencia sobre las regiones del Madre de Dios y Acre. *Boletín de la Sociedad Geográfica de Lima* XXVIII, 301–340.

Deloria, V. 1970. *Custer died for your sins: An Indian Manifesto.* New York: Avon.

Denevan, W. 1976. The Aboriginal Populations of Amazonia. In *The Native Population of the Americas in 1492.* (ed.) W. Denevan. pp.205–234. University of Wisconsin Press.

Descola, P. 1989. *La Selva Culta: Simbolismo y praxis en la ecología de los Achuar.* Quito: Coedición Abya-Yala/MLAL.

Dumont, J-P. 1976. *Under the Rainbow: Nature and Supernature among the Panare Indians.* Austin: University of Texas Press.

Duvoils, P. 1976. La Capacocha: Mecanismo y Función del Sacrificio Humano, su proyeción geométrica, su papel en la política integracionista y en la economía redistribución del Tawantinsuyu. *Alpanchis* Vol. IX, 11–59. Cuzco.

El Comercio. 1985. Noviembre 1. Lima.

Eliade, M. 1974. *Myth of the Eternal Return or Cosmos and History.* London: Routledge and Kegan Paul.

Emerson, R.W. 1982. *Selected Essays.* Penguin.

Fejos, P. 1941. La región del río Colorado. *Boletín de la Sociedad Geográfica de Lima* LVIII, 221–42.

Fernandez Distel, A. 1976. La decoración pintada aplicada a elementos de la tela de corteza entre los indígenas mashco de la amazonía peruana. *Archiv für Völkerkunde* XXX, 5–39. Vienna.

Fernandez Moro, W. 1952. *Cincuenta años en la Selva Amazónica.* Madrid.

Ferrero, A. 1966. *Los Machiguengas: Tribu selvática del sur-oriente peruano.* Puerto Maldonado: Instituto de Estudios Tropicales Pío Aza.

Friedman, J. 1986. Prolegomena to the Adventures of Phallus in Blunderland: An anti-anti-discourse. *Culture and History* 1,31–49.

Fuentes, A. 1982. *Parentesco y Relaciones de Producción en Una comunidad Harakmbut en el Sur-Oriente Peruano.* CAAAP mss.

Garcilaso de las Vegas. 1945. *Comentarios reales de los Incas* (1609). Buenos Aires: Emecé Editores.

Göhring, H. 1877. *Informe al supremo gobierno del Perú sobre la expedición a los valles de Paucartambo en 1873.* Lima: Imprenta del Estado.

Goldman, I. 1963. *The Cubeo Indians of the Northwest Amazon.* Illinois Studies in Anthropology 2. Urbana: The University of Illinois Press.

Gow, P. 1988. *The Social Organisation of the Native Communities of the Bajo Urubamba River, Eastern Peru.* PhD Thesis, London School of Economics.

Gow, P. 1989. The Perverse Child. Desire in a Native Amazonian subsistence economy. *Man* Vol. 24, No.4 pp. 567–583.

Gray, 1984. Los Amarakaeri: Una noción de Estructura Social. *Amazonía Peruana* Vol. V, No. 10, pp.47–64. Lima.

Gray, 1986. And After the Gold Rush? … Human Rights and Self-Development among the Amarakaeri of Southeastern Peru. *IWGIA Document* No. 55. Copenhagen.

Gray, A. 1987a. *The Amerindians of South America.* Minority Rights Group (Report 15). London.

Gray, A. 1987b. Perspectives on Amarakaeri History In *Natives and Neighbours in South America* (eds.) H.Skar & F. Salomon. pp.299–328. Göteborgs Etnografiska Museum.

Gray, A. 1990. The Putumayo Atrocities Revisited. mss.

Guevara, V. J. 1953. La Importancia del Nacionalismo de los Mascos y Machiguengas. *Perú Indígena* IV x/xi.106–110. Lima.

Hampson, N. 1987. *The Enlightenment. An Evaluation of its Assumptions, Attitudes and Values.* Pelican Books.

Harner, M.J. 1972. *The Jívaro. People of the Sacred Waterfalls.* Garden City, N.Y: Doubleday.

Harner, M.J. (ed.) 1973. *Hallucinogens and Shamanism.* New York: Oxford University Press.

Harris, O. 1978. Complementarity and Conflict. An Andean View of Women and Men. In *Sex and Age as Principles of Social Differentiation* (ed.) J.S. La Fontaine. ASA Monograph 17. London: Academic Press.

Hart, R.E. 1963. Semantic components of shape in Amarakaeri grammar. *Anthropological Linguistics* Vol. 5, No. 9, 1–7. Bloomington.

Hart, R.E. & R. Tripp, 1960–63. Un analisis tentativo de los componentes semánticos de los terminos de parentesco. *Ethnographic data.* Información de Campo. No. 27. Rollo 3. Summer Institute of Linguistics. Archives.

Hassel, J.M. von. 1905. Las tribus salvajes de la región amazónica del Perú. *Boletín de la Sociedad Geográfica de Lima* XXVII, 27–75. Also In *Colección de Leyes, Decretos.* (ed.) Larrabure y Correa. 1905 Vol. VII, 637–677. Lima: Imp. La Opinion Nacional.

Helberg Chavez, H. 1984. *Skizze einer Grammatik des Amarakaeri.* Dissertation der Fakultat für Kulturwissenschaften der Eberhard-Karls-Universitet Tübingen.

Helberg Chavez, H. 1989. Análisis funcional del verbo amarakaeri. In *Temas de Linguistica Ameríndia* (eds.) R. Cerron-Palomino and G. Solis Fonseca. CONCYTEC & GTZ, Lima.

Henley, P. 1982. *The Panare. Tradition and Change on the Amazonian Frontier.* Yale University Press.

Holmberg, A.R. 1969. *Nomads of the Long Bow. The Siriono of Eastern Bolivia.* Garden City N.Y: Doubleday. Natural History Press.

Holzmann, G. 1951/6 La tribu mashca. *Misiones Dominicanas del Perú* (during 1956 the publication became *Misiones Dominicanas*) XXXII 2–4, 53–6; XXXIII 51–3, no. 193 no page number; XXXIV 17–19; XXXV 64–66; XXXVI 340–3; XXXVII 97–99. Lima.

Howe, L. 1981. The Social Determination of Knowledge. Maurice Bloch and Balinese Time *Man* NS 16. 220–34.

Hugh-Jones, C, 1979. *From the Milk River. Spatial and Temporal processes in Northwest Amazonia.* Cambridge University Press.

Hugh-Jones, S.P. 1977. Like the leaves on the Forest Floor … ; Space and Time in Barasana Ritual. *Actes du XLIIe Congrés International des Americanistes* Volume II, 205–215. Paris.

Hugh-Jones, S.P. 1979. *The Palm and the Pleiades. Initiation and Cosmology in Northwest Amazonia.* Cambridge University Press.

Hugh-Jones, S.P. 1993. Clear Descent or Ambiguous Houses? A Re-examination of Tukanoan Social Organization. *L'Homme* 126–128. XXXIII, 95–120.

Jackson, J.E. 1977. Bara Zero Generation Terminology and Marriage. *Ethnology* 16, 83–104.

Jackson, J.E. 1983. *The Fish People. Linguistic Exogamy and Tukanoan Identity in Northwest Amazonia.* Cambridge University Press.

Junta de Vias Fluviales 1903/4. *El Istmo de Fitcarrald.* Lima: Publicación de la Junta de Vias Fluviales.

Junta de Vias Fluviales, 1904. *Nuevas exploraciones en la hoya del Madre de Dios.* Lima: Litografía y Tipográfica de Carlos Fabbri.

Junta de Vias Fluviales 1907. *Ultimas exploraciones ordenadas por la Junta de Vias Fluviales a los ríos Ucayali, Madre de Dios, Paucartambo y Urubamba.* Lima. Oficina Topográfica de La Opinión Nacional.

Kaplan, J. Overing. 1975. *The Piaroa, A people of the Orinoco Basin.* Oxford: Clarendon Press.

Kaplan, J. Overing. 1982 The Paths of Sacred Words. Shamanism and the Domestication of the Asocial in Piaroa Society. Paper given at the symposium – *Shamanism in Lowland South American Socieities. A Problem of Definition.* 44th International Congress of Americanists, Manchester, September, 1982.

Kauffmann-Doig, F. 1980 *Manual de Arqueología Peruana.* (7th Edition). Lima: Iberia.

Kensinger, K. 1977. Cashinahua notions of Social Time and Social Space. *Actes du XLIIe Congrés International des Americanistes.* Vol. II, 233–244. Paris.

Kensinger, K. 1984. An Emic Model of Cashinahua Marriage. In *Marriage Practices in Lowland South America.* (ed.) K. Kensinger. Illinois Studies in Anthropology No. 14. University of Illinois Press.

Kirk, G.S. 1974. *Myth. Its Meaning and Functions in Ancient and other Cultures.* Cambridge University Press and University of California Press.

Lambert, C., 1948. *Music Ho!* London. Pelican Books.

Lathrap, D.W. 1970. *The Upper Amazon.* New York: Praeger.

Leach, E.R. 1961. *Rethinking Anthropology.* London: The Athlone Press.

Lévi-Strauss, C. 1962. *Totemism.* London: Merlin Press.

Lévi-Strauss, C. 1970. *The Raw and the Cooked.* London: Cape.

Lévi-Strauss, C. 1973. *From Honey to Ashes.* London: Cape.

Lévi-Strauss, C, 1974. *The Savage Mind.* London: Weidenfeld and Nicolson.

Lévi-Strauss, C. 1978. *The Origin of Table Manners. Introduction to a Science of Mythology 3.* London: Cape.

Lizot, J. 1977. Descendance et Affinité chez les Yanomami. Antimonie et Complementarité. *Actes du XLIIe Congres Internacional des Americanistes* Volume II, 55–70. Paris.

Llosa, E.S. 1906. Las hoyas del Madre de Dios y Madera y La nueva ruta de Urcos, Marcapata y Tahuantisuyo. Conferencia dada en el Cuzco. *Boletín de la Sociedad Geográfica de Lima* XVI, XIX, 260–301.

Loukotka, C. 1968. *Classification of South American Indian Languages.* Latin American Centre Reference Series Vol. 7. U.C.L.A. Los Angeles.

Lyon, P.J. 1967. *Singing as Social Interaction among the Wachipaeri of Eastern Peru.* Unpublished PhD Thesis. University of California.

Lyon, P.J. 1976. Tribal Movement and Linguistic Classification in the Madre de Dios Zone. Typewritten corrected version of the paper published in the XXXIX Congreso Internacional de Americanistas, Lima, *Actas y Memorias,* Vol. 5, 185–207. Lima.

Lyon, 1984. Change in Wachipaeri marriage patterns. In *Marriage Practices in Lowland South America.* (ed.) K. Kensinger. Urbana and Chicago: Illinois Studies in Anthropology 14. University of Illinois Press.

Lyon, P.J. nd. The Attackers or the Attacked? The Invention of Hostile Savages in the Valleys of Paucartambo, Cuzco, Peru. Mss.

Martín, A. 1946. Qué hacen los mashcos? *Misiones Dominicanas del Perú* 27 (153) 54–9.

Maúrtua, V. (ed.) 1906. *Juicio de límites entre el Perú y Bolivia: Prueba presentada al gobierno de la república de Argentina.* 12 vols. Barcelona: Imprenta Henrich y Cía.

Mauss, M. 1985. A Category of the Human Mind; the notion of Person; The notion of Self. In *The Category of the Person: Anthropology, Philosophy, History* (eds.) M. Carrithers, S. Collins and S. Lukes. Cambridge University Press.

Maybury-Lewis, D. 1979. *Dialectical Societies. The Gê and Bororo of Central Brazil.* Cambridge Mass. and London: Harvard University Press.

McCallum, C. 1990. Language, kinship and politics in Amazonia. *Man* Vol. 25 No.3.

McQuown, N.A. 1955. The Indigenous Languages of South American Indians. *American Anthropologist* LVII, 501–570.

Mendoza Marsano, J. 1974. Oro en el Perú, *Minería* 124, 200–204. 8 Congreso Mundial de Minería. Lima.

Ministerio de Educación (República Peruana), 1973 *Mokas (El Sajino).* Cartilla de Lectura No. 5, Amarakaeri. Programma de Educación Bilingue de la Selva (Con la colaboración del Instituto Linguistico de Verano). Yarinacocha, Pucallpa: Centro Amazónico de Lenguas Autoctonas Peruanas Hugo Pesce, Yarinacocha.

Monnier, A. 1982. Evangelisation structurale. *Bulletin de Société Suisse des Américanistes* 46, 31–35 Geneva.

Moore, T.R. 1979. Sil and a New-Found Tribe. The Amarakaeri Experience. *Dialectical Anthropology* 4, 113–125. Amsterdam.

Moore, T.R. 1980. Transnacionales en Madre de Dios. Implicaciones Para Las Comunidades Nativas. *Shipihui* 5 (16), 451–63.

Moore, T.R. 1985a. El Banco Minero y el oro de Madre de Dios. *Bolepra* Año III, No. 8, 20–1.

Moore, T. R. 1985b. Qué pasa en el Banco minero? *Bolepra* Año III, No. 8, p. 21.

Moore, T.R. 1985c. Movimientos populares en Madre de Dios y regionalización. In *Promoción campesina, regionalización y movimientos sociales.* (ed.) M.Remy. pp. 166-192. Centro de Estudios Rurales Andinos Bartolomé de las Casas y DESCO.

Moore, T.R. nd. Resumen de la organisación social y religión Harakmbut. mss.

Morin, F. 1973. *Les Shipibo de L'Ucayali* Thèse de Doctorat de 3ème Cycle presentée a L'École Practique des Hautes Études (6ème Section). Paris.

Morton, J.A. 1979. *Conceptions of Fertility and Mortality among the Waiwai Indians of Southern Guiana*. B.Litt. Thesis. University of Oxford.

Nash, R. 1967. *Wilderness and the American Mind*. Yale University Press.

Needham, R. 1962. *Structure and Sentiment. A test case in Social Anthropology*. University of Chicago Press.

Needham, R. 1971. Remarks on the Analysis of Kinship and Marriage. In *Rethinking Kinship and Marriage*. (ed.) R. Needham ASA Monographs 11. London: Tavistock Publications.

Needham, R. 1984. *Exemplars*. University of California Press.

Nilsson, M.P. 1920. *Primitive Time Reckoning*. Lund: C.W.K Gleerup.

Noble, G.K. 1965. Proto-Arawak and its Descendents. *International Journal of American Linguistics* Vol. 31. No. 3. Pt. II. Publication 38 Indiana University Research Center in Anthropology, Folklore and Linguistics. Bloomington. Indiana University.

Nordenskjöld, E. 1905. Beiträge zur Kenntnis Einiger Indianerstämme des Rio Madre de Dios – gebietes. *Ymer*, 25. e arg. haft 3, 265–312. Stockholm.

Olivera, J.M. 1907. Informe. In *Ultimas exploraciónes ordenadas por la Junta de Vias Fluviales a los ríos Ucayali, Madre de Dios, Paurcartambo y Urubamba* pp. 395–429. Lima: Oficina tipográfica de La Opinión Naciónal.

Ossio, J.M. (ed.) 1973. *Ideología Mesiánica del Mundo Andino*. Lima: Edición de Ignacio Prado Pastor. Gráfica Morson.

Platt, T. 1980. Espejos y Maiz. El Concepto de Yanatin entre los Macha de Bolivia. In *Parentesco y Matrimonio en los Andes*. (eds.) E. Mayer and R. Bolton. pp. 139–183. Lima: Pontificia Universidad Católica del Perú Fondo Editorial (A selection of the articles in this book were published by the American Anthropological Association under the title Kinship and Marriage in the Andes, 1977).

Portillo, P. 1914. Departamento del Madre de Dios, *Boletín de la Sociedad Geográfica de Lima* XXX, 139–87. Lima.

Raimondi, A. 1874–9 *El Perú*, Vol. I–III. Lima: Imprente del Estado.

Ramos, A.R. & B. Albert, 1977. Yanoma descent and affinity. The Sanum/Yanoman contrast. *Actes du LXIIe Congrés International des Americanistes*, Volume II, 71–90. Paris.

Reeve, M-E. 1988. Cauchu Uras. Lowland Quichua histories of the Amazon Rubber Boom. In *Rethinking History and Myth. Indigenous South American Perspectives on the Past* (ed.) J.Hill. University of Illinois Press.

Regan, J. 1983. *Hacía La Tierra Sin Mal. Estudio de la Religión del Pueblo en la Amazonía*. (2 Volumes) Iquitos: CETA.

Reichel-Dolmatoff, G. 1971. *Amazonian Cosmos. The Sexual and Relgious Symbolism of the Tukano Indians*. University of Chicago Press.

Reyna, E. 1942. *Fitzcarrald, el Rey del Caucho*. Lima: P. Barrantes Castro.

Ribeiro, D. & M.R. Wise. 1978. *Los Grupos Etnicos de la Amazonía Peruana Comunidades y Culturas Peruanas* Instituto Linguistico de Verano.

Ricoeur, P. 1978. *The Rule of Metaphor*. London: Routledge and Kegan Paul.

Rivet, P. & C. Loukotka. 1952. Langues de L'Amerique du Sud et des Antilles. In *Les Langues du Monde par un groupe de linguistes sous la direction de A. Meillet et Marcel Cohen*. Nouvelle édition pp. 1099–1160. Société de Linguistique de Paris. Paris: H. Champion, Depositaire.

Rivière, P.G. 1966. A note on Marriage with the Sister's Daughter. *Man* Vol. I, pp 550–556.

Rivière, P.G. 1969 *Marriage among the Trio: A Principle of Social Organisation*. Oxford: Clarendon Press.

Rivière, P.G. 1984. *Individual and Society in Guiana. A Comparative Study of Amerindian Social Organization*. Cambridge University Press.

Roe, P.G. 1982. *The Cosmic Zygote. Cosmology in the Amazon Basin*. Rutgers: State University of New Jersey.

Rosengren, D. 1987. *In the Eyes of the Beholder. Leadership and the Social Construction of Power and Dominance among the Matsigenka of the Peruvian Amazon*. Göteborgs Etnografiska Museum.

Rummenhöller, K. 1984. Ein Beitrag zur historischen Entwickling der Arazairi, einer marginalisierten ethnischen Gruppe im Department Madre de Dios/Peru *CaMak*, 4, 6–8. Berlin.

Rummenhöller, K. 1985. *Vom Kautschukboom zum Goldrausch*. Ila wissenschaftliche Reihe 3. Bonn.

Rummenhöller, K. 1987. *Tieflandindios im Goldrausch. Die Auswirkungen des Goldbooms auf die Harakmbut im Madre de Dios, Peru*. Mundus Reihe Ethnologie, Band 12, Bonn.

Russell, B. 1946. *History of Western Philosophy and its Connection with Political and Social Circumstances from the Earliest Times to the Present Day*. London: George Allen and Unwin.

Russell, J. 1985. *Francis Bacon*. London: Thames and Hudson.

Sahlins, M.D. 1974. *Stone Age Economics*. London: Tavistock Publications.

Sahlins, M.D. 1985. *Islands of History*. University of Chicago Press.

Santos, A. 1942. La Tribu Toyeri del Palma Real Educada en la Misión. *Misiones Dominicanas del Perú* XXIV, 92–98.

Santos-Granero, F. 1991. *The Power of Love. The Moral use of Knowledge amongst the Amuesha of Central Peru*. LSE Monographs on Social Anthropology No. 62. London: The Athlone Press.

Sarasola, Sabas, 1929. La Región de los Maschos. *Misiones Dominicanas del Perú* 11 (50), 31–40.

Secretariado de Misiones Dominicanas. nd. *Hijos de la Selva* Lima: Santiago Valverde.

Seeger, A. 1981. *Nature and Society in Central Brazil. The Suya Indians of the Matto Grosso*. Harvard University Press.

Seymour Smith, C. 1988. *Shiwiar, Identidad y Etnica y Cambio en el Río Corrientes*. Lima: CAAAP & Abya Yala, Ecuador.

Siskind, J. 1973a. Tropical Forest Hunters and the Economy of Sex. In *People and Cultures of native South America* (ed.) D. Gross. pp. 226–240. New York: Doubleday/ The Natural History Press.

Siskind, J. 1973b. *To Hunt in the Morning*. New York: Oxford University Press.

Stocks, A.W. 1981. *Los Nativos Invisibles. Notas sobre la historia y Realidad Actual de los Cocamilla del Río Huallaga, Perú.* Lima: CAAAP.

Strathern, M. 1988. *The Gender of the Gift.* Unversity of California Press.

Taussig, 1986. *Shamanism, Colonialism and the Wild Man. A Study in Terror and Healing.* University of Chicago Press.

Tizón y Bueno R. 1911. *La Hoya Peruana del Madre de Dios.* Lima.

The Observer, 1985, *Gold. The Glamour Returns.* E.F.L. Service, May.

Thomas, D.J. 1978. Pemon Zero Generation Terminology. Social Correlates. In *Working Papers on South American Indians No. 1. Social Correlates of Kin Terminology.* (eds.) K. Kensinger and D.J. Thomas. pp. 62–81. Vermont: Bennington College.

Torralba, A. 1979. Los Harakmbut. Nueva Situación Misionera. *Antisuyo 3* Publicación de los Misiones Dominicanas en la Selva Sur-Oriente del Perú. pp. 83–141. Lima.

Torralba, A. 1981. Sharanahua. *Antisuyo 4,* Publicación de los Misiones Dominicanas en la Selva-Oriente del Perú. pp. 37–84. Lima.

Tripp, R. 1963. Analyzed Texts (Textos analizados). Analises preliminar de las oraciones simples y sus elementos en varios textos. *Información de Campo* No. 25 Rollo 3 b) 203 Summer Institute of Linguistics Archives.

Turner, F. 1986. Reflexivity as Evolution in Thoreau's Walden. In *The Anthropology of Experience.* (eds.) V.W.Turner & E.M.Bruner. University of Illinois Press.

Turner, V. 1969. *The Ritual Process.* Pelican Books.

Tylor, E.B. 1871. *Primitive Culture.* New York.

United Nations 1988. *A Compilation of International Instruments.* New York: UN.

Uriate Lopez, L.M. 1976. Poblaciones Nativas de la Amazonía Peruana. *Amazonía Peruana* Vol. I, No. 1. 9–59. Lima.

Van den Eynde, E. 1972. *Léxicos y Fonología Amarakaeri y Wacipairi (Harakmbet o Mashco).* Documento de Trabajo No. 7 Centro de Investigación de Linguisitica Aplicada. Universidad Nacional Mayor de San Marcos. Lima.

Vickers, W.T. 1978. Meat is Meat. The Siona-Secoya and the Hunting Prowess – Sexual Reward Hypothesis. *Latin Americanist* Vol. 11, No.I, 1–5. Florida.

Viveiros de Castro, E. 1992. *From the Enemy's point of View. Humanity and Divinity in an Amazonian Society.* The University of Chicago Press.

Wagner, R. 1981. *The Invention of Culture.* Chicago.

Wahl, L. 1985. La Federación Nativa del Madre de Dios. Informe de un Congreso. *Amazonía Indígena* Ano 5, No. 9.

Wahl, L. 1987. *Pagans into Christians. The Political Economy of Religious Conversion among the Harakmbut of Lowland Southeastern Peru, 1902–1982.* PhD. Thesis, The City University of New York.

Weiss, G. 1969. *The Cosmology of the Campa Indians of Eastern Peru.* PhD. Thesis, University of Michigan. Ann Arbor.

Whitehead, A.N. 1942. *Adventures of Ideas.* Penguin Books.

Whitehead, N. L. 1988. *Lords of the Tiger Spirit. A History of the Caribs in Colonial Venezuela and Guyana, 1498–1820.* Dordrecht-Holland: Foris Publications.

Whitehead, N.L. 1993. Ethnic Transformation and Historical Discontinuity in Native Amazon and Guyana 1500–1900. *L'Homme* XXXIII 126–128, 285–305. Paris.

Whittaker, A. 1985. Slavery and Gold in Peru. *Anti-Slavery Reporter.* Series VII, Vol.13 No.2. pp.63–70.

Wise, M.R. Animism in the Amuesha Bio-Culutral Configuration, *Información de Campo* 30e Rollo 4, Summer Institute of Linguistics Archives.

Zeleny, M. 1976. *Contribución a la etnografía y clasificación del grupo etnico Huarayo (Ece'je).* Ceskoslovensko. Praha: Univerzita Karlova.

INDEX

www.ingramcontent.com/pod-product-compliance
Lightning Source LLC
Chambersburg PA
CBHW060024030426
42334CB00019B/2168